HUMAN RIGHTS IN THE UK AND THE INFLUENCE OF FOREIGN JURISPRUDENCE

Human Rights in the UK and the Influence of Foreign Jurisprudence represents the first major empirical study of the use of foreign jurisprudence at the UK Supreme Court. This book focuses on the patterns of use and nonuse of rulings from foreign domestic courts in human rights cases before the UK Supreme Court. Results are drawn from quantitative and qualitative research methods, presenting data from the first eight years of Supreme Court activity. The evidence includes interviews with active and former members of the senior judiciary, as well as a focus group with some of the Supreme Court Judicial Assistants. It is argued that foreign jurisprudence is more intimately woven into the fabric of judicial reasoning, and serves a wider range of functions, than the term 'persuasive authority' might imply. Foreign jurisprudence is used mainly as a heuristic device, providing judges with a fresh analytical lens. Foreign jurisprudence is also important when interpreting a common legislative scheme, supporting dialogue between the Supreme Court and supranational courts such as the European Court of Human Rights. The perspectives offered by foreign jurisprudence can also support a stronger conception of domestic human rights. In these ways, this book addresses a broader political question about the source of human rights in the UK.

Volume 22 in the series Hart Studies in Comparative Public Law

Hart Studies in Comparative Public Law

Recent titles in this series:

Australian Constitutional Values
Edited by Rosalind Dixon

The Scope and Intensity of Substantive Review
Traversing Taggart's Rainbow
Edited by Hanna Wilberg and Mark Elliott

Entick v Carrington
250 Years of the Rule of Law
Edited by Adam Tomkins and Paul Scott

Administrative Law and Judicial Deference
Matthew Lewans

Soft Law and Public Authorities
Remedies and Reform
Greg Weeks

Legitimate Expectations in the Common Law World
Edited by Matthew Groves and Greg Weeks

The Dynamics of Exclusionary Constitutionalism
Mazen Masri

Constitutional Courts, Gay Rights and Sexual Orientation Equality
Angioletta Sperti

Principled Reasoning in Human Rights Adjudication
Se-Shauna Wheatle

Human Rights and Judicial Review in Australia and Canada
Janina Boughey

The Foundations and Traditions of Constitutional Amendment
Edited by Richard Albert, Xenophon Contiades and Alkmene Fotiadou

The Federal Idea
Public Law Between Governance and Political Life
Edited by Amnon Lev

Comparative Federalism
Constitutional Arrangements and Case Law
Francesco Palermo and Karl Kössler

Human Rights in the UK and the Influence of Foreign Jurisprudence

Hélène Tyrrell

•HART•
OXFORD • LONDON • NEW YORK • NEW DELHI • SYDNEY

HART PUBLISHING
Bloomsbury Publishing Plc
Kemp House, Chawley Park, Cumnor Hill, Oxford, OX2 9PH, UK

HART PUBLISHING, the Hart/Stag logo, BLOOMSBURY and the Diana logo are trademarks of Bloomsbury Publishing Plc

First published in Great Britain 2018

A catalogue record for this book is available from the British Library.

A catalogue record for this book is available from the Library of Congress.

ISBN: HB: 978-1-50990-494-5
ePDF: 978-1-50990-496-9
ePub: 978-1-50990-495-2

Typeset by Compuscript Ltd, Shannon
Printed and bound in Great Britain by TJ International Ltd, Padstow, Cornwall

To find out more about our authors and books visit www.hartpublishing.co.uk. Here you will find extracts, author information, details of forthcoming events and the option to sign up for our newsletters.

Acknowledgements

This book could not have been written without the support of Professor Kate Malleson and Professor Merris Amos, who supervised the doctoral thesis from which it grew. Special thanks are also due to Professor Alan Paterson and Professor Ian Cram for their invaluable comments, challenges and suggestions, during and after the viva voce. Queen Mary University London provided financial support for the project through a Graduate Teaching Award. The students and staff at that institution influenced this book more than some of them will have realised.

I also thank my colleagues and friends at Newcastle Law School, where I was welcomed into the wider academic community and where I completed the final manuscript. Special mention must be made to the Newcastle Law School librarians, particularly Catherine Dale, Rebecca Knight and Claire Leighton, for whom nothing was ever too difficult. Professor TT Arvind found time to read the draft manuscript and provided useful suggestions. Timothy Sayer helped with the table of cases and pointed out oversights. Tina Martin pointed out some more. I take all responsibly for remaining errors.

I am particularly grateful to Bill Asquith, Linda Staniford, Rosamund Jubber, Jon Lloyd, and the rest of the team at Hart Publishing for believing in the book and for their patience during the final stages. My thanks extend to the anonymous reviewers for taking the time to read and provide invaluable feedback on the draft manuscript. The project would also have been very different without the contributions of those who agreed to be interviewed: 10 Justices of the Supreme Court, one Lady Justice of Appeal and a number of Supreme Court Judicial Assistants. Each of the judges took additional time to write with permissions and comments, proving both the transparency and generosity of the modern judiciary (though none should be assumed to agree with the analysis or the conclusions that I reach).

Finally, I am indebted to Steven, to my friends and to my family for unyielding encouragement and patience in the years leading up to this publication. It is to them that this book is dedicated.

Contents

List of Figures and Tables

Figures

Tables

Table of Cases

United Kingdom

Australia

Canada

Court of Justice of the European Union

European Court of Human Rights

Fiji

France

Israel

New Zealand

The Netherlands

South Africa

United States

1

Introduction

TWO CENTURIES AGO, Friedrich Karl von Savigny wrote of his despair that England, which 'in all other branches of knowledge actively communicating with the rest of the world, should, in jurisprudence alone, have remained divided from the rest of the world, as if by a Chinese wall'.[1] In tune with the relative reluctance to compare, there was, as one great comparative scholar has put it, 'a remarkable dearth of comparative law teachers, books and articles'.[2] In the late twentieth century, the citation of foreign case law in domestic courts grew immeasurably and, in the early 1990s, Lord Bingham wrote his hopeful prognosis that the decade would 'be remembered as the time when England ... ceased to be a legal island, bounded to the north by the Tweed'.[3]

As this book will show, the courts have moved decisively away from this isolation. Foreign jurisprudence is now used extensively by the courts in a range of areas and is deeply integrated into judicial reasoning. The main use of foreign jurisprudence is as a heuristic device: it provides judges with a different analytical lens through which to reflect on their own reasoning about a problem. Judges may also use foreign jurisprudence when interpreting a common legislative scheme and in support of their conclusions. However, foreign jurisprudence is used differently according to the audience to whom reasons are addressed. In human rights cases, for example, foreign jurisprudence can assist the Supreme Court to enter into dialogue with supranational courts such as the European Court of Human Rights. Recourse to foreign jurisprudence can also weave international human rights law into the common law, enabling the Supreme Court to develop the domestic law of human rights that many hoped the Human Rights Act 1998 would foster.

The influence of foreign jurisprudence is reflected in a vast literature on comparative law,[4] including on judicial recourse to comparative law

[1] As quoted in Tom Bingham, 'There is a World Elsewhere: The Changing Perspectives of English Law' (1992) 41 *ICLQ* 513, 514; Tom Bingham, *The Business of Judging: Selected Essays and Speeches* (Oxford University Press, 2000) 88.

[2] Basil Markesinis (ed), *Foreign Law & Comparative Methodology: A Subject and a Thesis* (Hart Publishing, 1997) 2.

[3] Bingham, 'There is a World Elsewhere' (n 1).

[4] See, eg, Konrad Zweigert and Hein Kötz, *An Introduction to Comparative Law*, Tony Weir trans, 3rd edn (Oxford University Press, 1998); Esin Örücü and David Nelken (eds),

in particular. As one Justice of the Supreme Court, Lord Mance, recognised: 'Increasing attention has been paid over recent years to the basis on which judges use foreign authority'.[5] The research in this field also reflects a general interest in judges and judicial reasoning more generally.[6] Most of the published work in the field of judicial comparativism focuses on the legitimacy of using foreign jurisprudence or on the possibility that uses of foreign jurisprudence have provided for a dialogue between courts around the world. All such studies usually make an implicit assumption: that the courts are, in fact, using such sources. Very few, however, seek to set out the reality of the practice, making it difficult to get a real sense of the extent to which the courts are actually using foreign jurisprudence. As one recent publication in the field notes, 'studies have focused extensively on the theoretical aspects of this practice ... while empirical analysis of the frequency and meaning of citations remain generally still rare'.[7] By providing an analysis of foreign jurisprudence in human rights cases before the UK Supreme Court,[8] this study contributes a fresh perspective to the vast literature in the field, describing the use of foreign jurisprudence by domestic courts as a phenomenon that has given rise to a 'migration of constitutional ideas',[9] or similar characterisations on the theme, such as 'judicial internationalisation',[10] 'judicial cosmopolitanism'[11] and 'trans-judicialism'.[12]

Comparative Law: A Handbook (Hart Publishing, 2007); Pierre Legrand and Roderick Munday (eds), *Comparative Legal Studies: Traditions and Transitions* (Cambridge University Press, 2003); John Henry Merryman and David S Clark, *Comparative Law: Western European and Latin American Legal Systems. Cases and Materials* (Bobbs-Merrill, 1978); David Nelken (ed), *Comparing Legal Cultures* (Dartmouth, 1997).

[5] Lord Mance, 'Foreign Laws and Languages' in Andrew Burrows, David Johnston and Reinhard Zimmermann (eds), *Judge and Jurist: Essays in Memory of Lord Rodger of Earlsferry* (Oxford University Press, 2013) 87.

[6] The burgeoning literature on the UK House of Lords and now the UK Supreme Court was recognised by Penny Darbyshire, *Sitting in Judgment: The Working Lives of the Judges* (Hart Publishing, 2011) 362; a helpful review of the most important works is given at 363–68. More recently, see, eg, Alan Paterson, *Final Judgment: The Last Law Lords and the Supreme Court* (Hart Publishing, 2013).

[7] Tania Groppi and Marie-Claire Ponthoreau (eds), *The Use of Foreign Precedents by Constitutional Judges* (Hart Publishing, 2013) 3; See also Elaine Mak, *Judicial Decision-Making in a Globalised World: A Comparative Analysis of the Changing Practices of Western Highest Courts* (Hart Publishing, 2013) 2.

[8] The Supreme Court was established by Part 3 of the Constitutional Reform Act 2005, assuming the judicial functions of the House of Lords as the highest appellate court in the UK (other than for Scottish criminal cases). It started work on 1 October 2009.

[9] Sujit Choudhury, *The Migration of Constitutional Ideas* (Cambridge University Press, 2006).

[10] Cass Sunstein, *A Constitution of Many Minds* (Princeton University Press, 2009); Richard Posner, *How Judges Think* (Harvard University Press, 2008).

[11] John L Murray CJ, 'Judicial Cosmopolitanism' [2008] 2 *Judicial Studies Institute Journal* 1; Posner (n 10).

[12] Anne-Marie Slaughter, 'A Typology of Transjudicial Communication' (1994) 39 *University of Richmond Law Review* 99; Anne-Marie Slaughter, *A New World Order* (Princeton

This non-exhaustive list broadly describes the simple practice of judges from one jurisdiction citing jurisprudence from another jurisdiction.[13] There is also significant and important research concerning the opportunities offered by comparative law in a 'shrinking world',[14] forming part of 'global dialogue' or 'transjudicial dialogue'.[15] As Bell has written, the use of foreign jurisprudence

> is taken to be one of the indicators that legal systems are not self-contained but develop as a result of ideas coming from outside as well as from inside the system. In addition, it is seen as evidence of the increasing globalisation of the law. Such potentially expansive claims from the importance of comparative law as a judicial method of decision-making need to be put in context.[16]

The claim made by many of these works is that judges from different jurisdictions are in conversation with each other as to the interpretation and development of certain legal norms. Markesinis and Fedtke wrote of foreign law's 'overt' influence in Canada, Germany and South Africa, and its 'covert' influence in France and Italy.[17] Much has been written about the comparative approach of the Israeli Supreme Court, which is now well known for its reliance on foreign jurisprudence.[18] The New Zealand courts regularly engage with the jurisprudence of foreign domestic courts. In fact, some have suggested that the willingness to refer to foreign decisions 'is not the exception in New Zealand, but the rule'.[19] Foreign jurisprudence has even found its way into a handful of judgments from the US Supreme Court,

University Press, 2004); Justice L'Hereux-Dube, 'The Importance of Dialogue: Globalisation and the International Impact of the Rehnquist Court' (1998) 34 *Tulsa Law Journal* 15.

[13] See also Mak (n 7); Sam Muller and Sydney Richards (eds), *Highest Courts and Globalisation* (Hague Academic Press, 2010); Antoine Hol et al, 'Special Issue on Highest Courts and Transnational Interaction' (2012) 8(2) *Utrecht Law Review* 1.

[14] Basil Markesinis, *Comparative Law in the Courtroom and in the Classroom* (Hart Publishing, 2003).

[15] Slaughter, 'A Typology' (n 12) 99; Slaughter, *A New World Order* (n 12); David S Law and Wen-Chen Chang, 'The Limits of Global Judicial Dialogue' [2011] *Washington Law Review* 523.

[16] John Bell, 'Comparative Law in the Supreme Court 2010–11' [2012] *Cambridge Journal of International and Comparative Law* 20.

[17] Basil Markesinis and Jörg Fedtke (eds), *Judicial Recourse to Foreign Law: A New Source of Inspiration?* (University College London Press, 2006).

[18] See, eg, Daphne Barak-Erez, 'The International Law of Human Rights and Constitutional Law: A Case Study of an Expanding Dialogue' (2004) 2(4) *International Journal of Constitutional Law* 611.

[19] Jeremy Waldron, *'Partly Laws Common to All Mankind': Foreign Law in American Courts* (Yale University Press, 2012), 18. Waldon cites *Taunoa v Attorney General* [2007] NZSC 70, [2008] 1 NZLR 429 as an example. In determining questions about the application of the New Zealand Bill of Rights Act, the New Zealand Supreme Court cited cases from the US, Canada, South Africa, the UK, the European Court of Human Rights and the UN Human Rights Commission. The number of US cases alone outnumbered the number of New Zealand cases cited.

which is usually given as the paradigmatic example of insularity.[20] The use of foreign jurisprudence in UK domestic courts, however, has been given relatively little attention by researchers in the past. While some studies have addressed the topic in the context of private law,[21] the human rights context has attracted less attention.[22]

Human rights, as a field of enquiry, was chosen for two reasons: first, human rights claims raise some of the most interesting and divisive issues, and are often sensitive and subject to cultural interpretation. Second, there was a strong sense in the literature that judicial comparativism is more prevalent in human rights cases than in other fields,[23] although it is also said that the extent to which judges draw from foreign jurisprudence in human rights cases varies greatly between jurisdictions. This is despite the fact that empirical evidence about the correlation between the citation of foreign jurisprudence and the type of issue is rare. As Bobek has written:

> There are no conclusive empirical studies which have, for instance, qualitatively studied and compared the amount of comparative references made by the same jurisdiction in the various areas of law, thus confirming or rebutting the

[20] *Atkins v Virginia* (2002) 536 US 304; *Grutter v Bollinger* (2003) 539 US 306; *Lawrence v Texas* (2003) 539 US 558; *Roper v Simmons* (2005) 543 US 551. These high-profile decisions on the death sentence, criminalised sodomy and abortion are responsible for much of the literature on recourse to foreign jurisprudence in the context of US constitutional interpretation. See, eg, Sujit Choudhry (ed), *The Migration of Constitutional Ideas* (Cambridge University Press, 2006) 2: 'Advocates of the migration of constitutional ideas, however, appear to have gained the upper hand.' *cf* Gordon A Christenson, 'Using Human Rights Law to Inform Due Process and Equal Protection Analyses' (1983) 52 *Cincinnati Law Review* 3, 5: 'most united states courts ... show less inclination now than at the beginning of the Republic to use sources of foreign and international customary law to aid interpretation, especially in constitutional cases'; Bruce Ackerman, 'The Rise of World Constitutionalise' (1997) 83 *Virginia Law Review* 771, 772: 'The typical American judge would not think of learning from an opinion by the German or French constitutional court'; Basil Markesinis, 'National Self-Sufficiency or Intellectual Arrogance? The Current Attitude of American Courts towards Foreign Law' [2006] *CLJ* 301; Angioletta Sperti, 'United States of America: First Cautious Attempts of Judicial Use of Foreign Precedents in the Supreme Court's Jurisprudence' in Groppi and Ponthoreau (n 7).

[21] See, eg, Richard Fentiman, *Foreign Law in English Courts* (Oxford University Press, 1998); Shaheed Fatima, *Using International Law in Domestic Courts* (Hart Publishing, 2005); Richard Bronaugh, 'Persuasive Precedent' in Laurence Goldstein (ed), *Precedent in Law* (Clarendon Press, 1987) 217; Albert Kiralfy. 'The Persuasive Authority of American Rulings in England' (1948–49) XXIII *Tulane Law Review* 209; Bingham, 'There is a World Elsewhere' (n 1) 513; Keith Stanton, 'Comparative Law in the House of Lords and Supreme Court' (2013) 42 *Common Law World Review* 269; Andrew Burrows, 'The Influence of Comparative Law on the English Law of Obligations' in Andrew Robertson and Michael Tilbury (eds), *The Common Law of Obligations: Divergence and Unity* (Hart Publishing, 2016).

[22] As Groppi and Ponthoreau have pointed out, studies cataloguing the different approaches adopted by constitutional or supreme courts in their use of foreign jurisprudence are relatively rare: Groppi and Ponthoreau (n 7) 3.

[23] See, eg, Groppi and Ponthoreau (n 7) 416: 'The research clearly shows that citations of foreign case law prevail in ... human rights decisions'; Christopher McCrudden, 'A Common Law of Human Rights?: Transnational Judicial Conversations on Constitutional Rights' (2000) 20(4) *OJLS* 499, 527, asking 'is there something specific to human rights that explains the apparently greater use of foreign case law in human rights cases?'

> assumption that the greatest amount of comparative reasoning is indeed carried out in the area of human rights adjudication.[24]

Groppi and Ponthoreau's edited volume made a significant contribution to this question by reference to data gathered from a number of courts from jurisdictions working in the common law and civil law traditions. One of the main conclusions of that volume was that citations of foreign case law are most common in human rights decisions,[25] but this is a finding which has yet to be substantiated in the UK context.

Third, the diet of the top court has been increasingly balanced towards public law and human rights cases.[26] Judges adjudicating on human rights claims often have to consider the jurisprudence of supranational courts. For example, where Convention rights are at issue, UK courts must 'take into account' any relevant jurisprudence of the European Court of Human Rights (also referred to as 'the Strasbourg Court').[27] The influence of the Strasbourg jurisprudence also raises a question as to the approach that would be taken to foreign jurisprudence should a claim fall outside the scope of the Human Rights Act (HRA) 1998. In that case, judicial reasoning may reflect a different balance between foreign (domestic) and supranational jurisprudence. Where no supranational jurisprudence exists, the degree to which foreign jurisprudence is used by (or is useful to) domestic courts may also differ. Thus, human rights cases provide a useful variety of perspectives on the uses of foreign jurisprudence by domestic courts.[28]

'Human rights cases' covers case law that arises from claims under the HRA 1998 (rooted in the European Convention on Human Rights (ECHR)), cases engaging international human rights treaties such as the Refugee Convention or the Convention on the Rights of the Child, and 'common law rights' cases. Categorising cases like this is important for two reasons: first, a common theme in the scholarship on judicial comparativism is that the legitimacy of recourse to foreign sources depends on the context for which it is sought; and, second, different human rights instruments may require judges to engage with different sources. For example, the HRA 1998 requires judges to 'take into account' the Strasbourg

[24] Michael Bobek, *Comparative Reasoning in European Supreme Courts* (Oxford University Press, 2013) 64.

[25] ibid 416.

[26] This was mentioned by a number of the Justices interviewed for this study and is confirmed by another report of similar interviews conducted by Mak in 2009: Elaine Mak, 'Why Do Dutch and UK Judges Cite Foreign Law?' [2011] *CLJ* 420, 432. Paterson also found that 'the type of case which now predominates is radically different ... tax, shipping and criminal law cases have declined, whilst public law and human rights cases have dramatically increased': Paterson (n 6) 17, Table 2.1.

[27] Section 2 HRA 1998.

[28] Other scholars have conducted valuable research on the judicial recourse to comparative law in other areas of law. See, eg, Stanton (n 21) 269, surveying the use of comparative law in tort cases; and Burrows (n 21).

jurisprudence.[29] While the Strasbourg case law itself does not fall into the definition of 'foreign' jurisprudence for the purposes of this study, it would not be surprising if a court were to extend the exercise to take into account the jurisprudence of other Council of Europe jurisdictions (the jurisprudence that the European Court of Human Rights would be likely to consider).[30] Equally, it would not be surprising if such references remained relatively infrequent, given the Strasbourg Court's own approach to surveying the interpretation of the Convention among Member States. The quantitative results indicate that the latter approach prevails.[31]

In cases that engage international human rights treaties, one might expect to see a greater number of references to foreign jurisprudence. The Vienna Convention on the Law of Treaties 1969 (hereinafter 'the Vienna Convention') encourages judicial comparativism in such cases. Article 31 provides the general rules of interpretation, including a direction to take into account 'any subsequent practice in the application of the treaty which establishes the agreement of the parties regarding its interpretation'. Article 32 of the Vienna Convention states that 'supplementary means of interpretation' may be employed in order to 'confirm the meaning resulting from the application of Article 31', or when the interpretative approach under Article 31 either leaves the meaning 'ambiguous or obscure' or 'leads to a result which is manifestly absurd or unreasonable'.[32]

Finally, the continued reference to common law rights has been an interesting feature of recent judicial reasoning at the Supreme Court.[33] In *Osborn*, Lord Reed felt it necessary to point out that human rights 'continue to be protected by our domestic law, interpreted and developed in accordance with the [Human Rights] Act when appropriate'.[34] In *Kennedy*, Lord Toulson again emphasised that the analysis had been 'based on common law principles and not on article 10 [ECHR]', which, in the context of the case, 'add[ed] nothing to the common law'.[35] Paying specific attention to these cases is important because the influence of foreign jurisprudence is likely to

[29] Section 2 of the HRA 1998.

[30] Mak (n 7) 143.

[31] Chapter 5 (see, eg, Figure 5.10).

[32] Vienna Convention on the Law of Treaties 1969. See also Brice Dickson, *Human Rights and the United Kingdom Supreme Court* (Oxford University Press, 2013) 34–35; Shaheed Fatima, *Using International Law in Domestic Courts* (Hart Publishing, 2005) 141.

[33] Mark Elliott considered it possible to identify three strands to this 'common law resurgence': 'common law resilience', 'common law primacy' and 'common law dynamism'. See Mark Elliott, 'Beyond the European Convention: Human Rights and the Common Law' (2015) 68(1) *Current Legal Problems* 85, 92–95. See generally, Dickson (n 32) 20–34; Richard Clayton, 'The Empire Strikes Back' [2015] *PL* 3; Phillip Sales, 'Rights and Fundamental Rights in English Law' [2016] *CLJ* 86; Eirik Bjorg, 'Common Law Rights: Balancing Domestic and International Exigencies' (2016) 75(2) *CLJ* 220.

[34] *Osborn v The Parole Board* [2013] UKSC 61; [2014] AC 1115

[35] *Kennedy v The Charity Commission* [2014] UKSC 20; [2015] AC 455 [133].

be different in character to cases where primacy is accorded to the ECHR. In these cases, it would not be surprising if judges were to continue referring to the jurisprudence of other common law countries. Lord Toulson's approach in the Court of Appeal was illustrative of this point. In *R (Guardian News and Media Ltd)*,[36] he explained:

> I base my decision on the common law principle of open justice. In reaching it I am fortified by the common theme of the judgments in other common law countries to which I have referred. Collectively they are strong persuasive authority. The courts are used to citation of Strasbourg decisions in abundance, but citation of decisions of senior courts in other common law jurisdictions is now less common. I regret the imbalance. The development of the common law did not come to an end on the passing of the Human Rights Act. It is in vigorous health and flourishing in many parts of the world which share a common legal tradition. This case provides a good example of the benefit which can be gained from knowledge of the development of the common law elsewhere.[37]

In tackling these questions, this book addresses a broader political question about the source of human rights in the UK. This question is of heightened importance in the changing legal landscape. The extent to which the courts see human rights as European, as foreign or as a part of the UK common law can provide important lessons ahead of any revision to the human rights regime or any change to the relationship between the UK courts and foreign or supranational courts.

I. STRUCTURE OF THE BOOK

This book provides evidence of the influence of foreign jurisprudence in the UK Supreme Court, as well as the reasons or purposes for which foreign jurisprudence is used. The following research questions are answered: does the Supreme Court consider foreign jurisprudence in human rights cases? How is the jurisprudence used? For what purpose does the Supreme Court use foreign jurisprudence? What effect has the HRA 1998 had on the use of foreign jurisprudence? Questions of this kind have been considered in the context of other jurisdictions,[38] but few researchers have focused on the UK.

The heart of this book is the empirical study. For this reason, Chapter 2 is devoted to an explanation of the research methodology. This decision also reflects the reality that empirical legal research can feel like a lonely business.

[36] *R (Guardian News and Media Ltd) v City of Westminster Magistrates' Court* [2012] EWCA Civ 420; [2012] All ER 551.

[37] ibid 88.

[38] See, eg, Groppi and Ponthoreau (n 7); James Allan, Grant Huscroft and Nessa Lynch, 'The Citation of Overseas Authority in Rights Litigation in New Zealand: How Much Bark? How Much Bite?' (2007) 11 *Otago Law Review* 433.

I felt hugely supported by the warnings and advice given by researchers before me and it felt fair to explain my own choices in similar terms.

One of the main arguments in this book is that foreign jurisprudence can provide a useful perspective in human rights cases. It was therefore necessary to establish that the Supreme Court may legitimately use these sources. It is explained in Chapter 3 that there are no rules governing the judicial use of foreign jurisprudence, whether in human rights cases specifically or other cases more generally. While the HRA 1998 provides that courts must 'take into account' the jurisprudence of the European Court of Human Rights in Strasbourg, the Act is silent on the use of jurisprudence from the domestic courts of other jurisdictions. UK courts are under no duty or obligation to follow the decisions of a foreign domestic court, but neither are these sources prohibited: 'it was always clear that the courts could also consider jurisprudence from other jurisdictions'.[39]

The non-binding status of these sources can give rise to criticisms—often raised in the US debates—that the use of foreign jurisprudence is instrumental and opportunistic.[40] The UK Supreme Court does appear to use foreign jurisprudence in this way, but this is not problematic. Chapter 4 closes with an explanation that the use of foreign jurisprudence per se is not the problem; rather, concern about the legitimacy of the practice usually stems from a perception that courts are liable to use foreign jurisprudence in an unprincipled and unsystematic way. If that is the case, the risk is that foreign jurisprudence may mask judicial creativity or obscure the political judgments that a court might be minded to make. In other words, it is uncertainty about the reasons for using foreign jurisprudence that is likely to attract criticism.[41] The aim in Chapters 5–8 is therefore to identify the way in which foreign jurisprudence is used at the Supreme Court and the purposes that these sources serve.

Chapter 5 sets out the reality of citations of foreign jurisprudence at the Supreme Court by reference to the empirical research. The data is important: 'studies have focused extensively on the theoretical aspects of this practice ... while empirical analysis of the frequency and meaning of citations remain generally still rare'.[42] The data demonstrates that judges are using the jurisprudence of foreign domestic courts and that there are some clear patterns to the use. The main finding is that—because there are no formal rules governing the use of foreign jurisprudence—judges have developed

[39] Helen Fenwick, *Civil Liberties and Human Rights* (Cavendish Publishing, 2007) 192.

[40] See, eg, Richard Posner, 'No Thanks, We Already Have Our Own Laws' *Legal Affairs* (July/August 2004), www.legalaffairs.org/issues/July-August-2004/feature_posner_julaug04.msp; Choudhry (n 20); Yash Ghai, 'Sentinels of Liberty or Sheep in Woolf's Clothing? Judicial Politics and the Hong Kong Bill of Rights' (1997) 60 *MLR* 459.

[41] Elaine Mak concluded that there was a lack of a systematic approach in the use of foreign legal materials at the UK Supreme Court: Mak (n 26) 449.

[42] Groppi and Ponthoreau (n 7).

their own practices. Whether or not foreign jurisprudence is used is dependent on the approach of each individual judge. For example, Lord Collins is known to have been a more enthusiastic user of foreign jurisprudence, particularly from the US. It is not surprising, therefore, that a large proportion of cases contained explicit citations of foreign jurisprudence prior to Lord Collins' retirement in 2011. The change in judgment styles may also have an impact on the use of foreign jurisprudence at the top court. In particular, the data illustrates an increase in single judgments at the Supreme Court, which may reduce the scope for the sort of judicial individualism that might have provided the space for reference to foreign jurisprudence.

Other practical considerations also affect the way that foreign jurisprudence is used at the Supreme Court. The interview evidence confirms that the Court is still highly dependent on counsel's submissions, although some Justices also introduce foreign jurisprudence through their own research. Nevertheless, the most obvious variant is that some Justices simply have a greater interest in foreign jurisprudence than others, which is often a product of personal connections with a particular jurisdiction. However, this book does not support theories of 'transjudicial dialogue' as expressed in much of the literature.[43] While citations of foreign jurisprudence are mostly drawn from a small family of courts, it is not found that the UK Supreme Court considers itself to be part of a global conversation. A more realistic conclusion is that foreign jurisprudence is used as a heuristic device; the Justices use foreign jurisprudence instrumentally and only when it is helpful.

The use of foreign jurisprudence as a heuristic device is the subject of Chapter 6. Some of the classical explanations for the use of foreign jurisprudence fall into this category. A clear example of this is the popular theory that judges would be most likely to use foreign jurisprudence in order to fill 'gaps' in the indigenous case law. However, it is not accepted that the 'gap filling' thesis accurately explains the use of foreign jurisprudence at the UK Supreme Court. Although the Justices might be likely to consider foreign jurisprudence in those situations, filling the 'gap' is not the aim of the exercise; rather, it is argued that some Justices use foreign jurisprudence as an analytical lens to help elucidate the issues or to seek reassurance about a conclusion reached independently of foreign jurisprudence. The purpose served by foreign jurisprudence in these circumstances is either to provide an opportunity for reflection or to form 'part of the process of reaching a more fully theorised ... agreement'.[44]

The only evidence for the 'gap-filling' theory might be the tendency to review foreign jurisprudence in human rights cases where the Strasbourg

[43] See, eg, Slaughter, 'A Typology' (n 12); Slaughter, *A New World Order* (n 12); Groppi and Ponthoreau (n 7).

[44] Christopher McCrudden, 'Judicial Comparativism and Human Rights' in Esin Örücü and David Nelken (eds), *Comparative Law: A Handbook* (Hart Publishing, 2007) 371, 374.

jurisprudence was unhelpful or non-existent. Foreign jurisprudence may nevertheless be used to confirm the Strasbourg position and the UK Supreme Court has shown a willingness to use those sources to that end. This is also affected by the well-reported tendency to elevate clear and constant Strasbourg jurisprudence to a status of binding, rather than persuasive, authority.[45] Chapter 7 explains that this is to do with a drive towards uniformity among the states signatory to the ECHR. The most obvious purpose for using foreign jurisprudence is as a tool to identify a consensus in cases where it is necessary to maintain a uniform interpretation of a common instrument. Thus, where there is clear and constant Strasbourg jurisprudence, the Supreme Court is likely to follow it.

One effect of the HRA 1998 duty to 'take into account' the relevant Strasbourg case law might therefore have been a reduction in the number of references to the jurisprudence of other foreign courts. The logic would be intelligible: the conclusions of foreign courts interpreting similar but distinct instruments would not necessarily ensure compatibility with the ECHR, as the UK courts are bound to do. Thus, even where it would be of interest to the Supreme Court to review the position of the other states signatory to the Convention, it is argued that the Court prefers to accept the results of the supranational (Strasbourg) court's research on the point. Or if other foreign jurisprudence is cited, it would be for different reasons.

The effect of the existence of a supranational court on the use of foreign jurisprudence is made clearer still by a review of the cases where no such court exists. The second half of Chapter 7 provides examples of the Supreme Court's greater willingness to use foreign jurisprudence in such cases. It is explained that the emphasis on maintaining uniformity among contracting states is particularly prevalent when the Court is interpreting an international instrument with no supervisory body. Nevertheless, anxieties remain about the legitimacy of references to foreign jurisprudence, especially if recourse to those sources leads to an interpretation that unduly enlarges the scope of rights or the obligations under the common instrument in question. In part, this risk also explains the Supreme Court's reluctance to make advances on the Strasbourg jurisprudence in questions engaging the ECHR.

[45] See, eg, Roger Masterman, 'Section 2(1) of the Human Rights Act: Binding Domestic Courts to Strasbourg?' [2004] *PL* 725; Elizabeth Wicks, 'Taking Account of Strasbourg? The British Judiciary's Approach to Interpreting Convention Rights' [2005] *European Public Law* 405; Francesca Klug and Helen Wildbore, 'Follow or Lead? The Human Rights Act and the European Court of Human Rights' (2010) 6 *European Human Rights Law Review* 621; Lord Irvine of Lairg, 'A British Interpretation of Convention Rights', Lecture at University College of London's Judicial Institute (London, 14 December 2011), https://www.ucl.ac.uk/drupal/judicial-institute/sites/judicial-institute/files/british_interpretation_of_convention_rights_-_irvine.pdf.

There is, however, some evidence that deference to Strasbourg may be on the decline. The Supreme Court is showing a greater willingness to reject the Strasbourg jurisprudence where it is unhelpful or at odds with the constitutional arrangements in the UK. This is most obvious in cases where the Strasbourg jurisprudence has been thought to be outdated. Implicit in the construction of the ECHR as a 'living instrument' is the presumption that domestic courts may properly conclude that Convention jurisprudence has lost its relevance with age.[46] Other opportunities for divergence are created by the 'margin of appreciation' doctrine or the accuracy, clarity and reasoning of the Strasbourg jurisprudence itself. In such cases, foreign jurisprudence may provide a valuable and underused perspective on the Strasbourg jurisprudence, especially where the relevant case law of that court is unclear, unhelpful or has misunderstood some aspect of domestic law. It is argued in Chapter 8 that foreign jurisprudence can lend confidence to the Supreme Court's reasoning in these cases, ensuring that the Court is not simply a 'Strasbourg surrogate'.[47] Viewed in this way, the jurisprudence of foreign domestic courts is more valuable than has so far been considered. By taking those sources into account, the Justices may begin to take a more theorised approach to human rights cases, working with the Strasbourg Court in human rights cases rather than under it.

It is concluded that the influence of foreign jurisprudence in judicial reasoning is more important than many have recognised. Foreign jurisprudence is far more intimately woven into the fabric of judicial reasoning and serves a wider range of functions than the words 'persuasive' and 'authority' might suggest. This is both legitimate and appropriate. The value of foreign jurisprudence can be quite different in flavour from other persuasive sources. The judgments of foreign domestic courts represent valuable empirical tools or heuristic devices. In human rights cases, the perspectives offered by foreign jurisprudence have the potential to support a stronger conception of domestic human rights. Paradoxically, it may be the jurisprudence of foreign domestic courts that assists the Supreme Court to realise its full potential: to develop the domestic law of human rights which many hoped the HRA 1998 would foster.

II. STYLE

The lack of any single gender-neutral pronoun in the English language has led many writers to forge a sense of equality by using 'they' or 'their' rather

46 *Tyrer v UK* (1978) 2 EHRR 1 [31].

47 *R (Prolife Alliance) v BBC* [2002] EWCA Civ 297; [2002] 2 All ER 756, 771–72; see also Masterman (n 45) 725; Wicks (n 45) 405.

than 'him', 'her', 'his' or 'her'.[48] This approach is not adopted in this book. Instead, the masculine should generally be taken to include the feminine wherever there may be ambiguity about the gender of the subject. The choice of masculine over feminine has been made only on the basis that there was, in the years for which data was gathered, just one female Justice of the Supreme Court. Using the feminine pronoun when talking about judicial practices may therefore give the unintended impression that Baroness Hale is always the subject of the sentence in point. It was felt that a better balance would be achieved by dividing this attention among the male Justices, especially where anonymity was to be preserved.

An inconsistency also lies with the treatment of numbers. In this book, numbers are written both as numerals and words depending on the nature of the passage and analysis. The widely adopted rule about spelling out single-digit whole numbers is therefore occasionally ignored when discussing quantitative data, as in Chapter 5.

[48] Simon Heffer, *Strictly English* (Random House, 2010) xiii.

2

Research Methodology

LESS THAN A decade ago, Poole and Shah described quantitative analysis as 'uncommon within UK legal scholarship'.[1] In fact, Poole and Shah were so stuck for guidance on empirical research methods that they turned to a foreign journal: the *Harvard Law Review*.[2] It is impossible to make the same claim now. Empirical legal research has become an increasingly common feature of the academic landscape.[3] As Bradney has written, quantitative and qualitative empirical research 'provides information of a different character from that which can be obtained through other methods of research'.[4] Empirical research does, however, present certain challenges. The conclusions in this book rely heavily on the empirical data, gathered from analysis of the Supreme Court's judgments as well as the information obtained through interviews with the Justices of the Supreme Court and the Judicial Assistants. It was particularly helpful that other researchers working in these methods have explained their methodological choices explicitly. I have seen fit to do the same.

I. RESEARCH PARAMETERS

The focus of this book is on the influence of jurisprudence from foreign domestic courts (foreign jurisprudence) in human rights cases before the UK Supreme Court. In drawing these parameters, other persuasive sources commonly used in UK courts were excluded from the study. These might include, for example, the judgments of lower courts, obiter dicta, academic

[1] Thomas Poole and Sangeeta Shah, 'The Law Lords and Human Rights' (2011) 74(1) *MLR* 79, 83.

[2] ibid 84.

[3] Although it has not been universally adopted. Mak refrained from quantitative analysis of judgments, preferring to avoid 'any drawbacks related to the quantitative analysis of a small research sample': Elaine Mak, 'Why Do Dutch and UK Judges Cite Foreign Law?' [2011] *CLJ* 420, 422.

[4] Anthony Bradney, 'The Place of Empirical Research in the Law School Curriculum' in Peter Crane and Herbert Kritzer (eds), *The Oxford Handbook of Empirical Legal Research* (Oxford University Press, 2010) 1031, cited in Mandy Burton, 'Doing Empirical Research' in Dawn Watkins and Mandy Burton, *Research Methods in Law* (Routledge, 2013).

literature and the decisions of the Privy Council. Incorporating the UK Supreme Court's use of all persuasive authorities was considered in the early stages of the research design, but could not be pursued for reasons of time and space; such a study would be of great interest, but would be better undertaken as part of a larger project. Some of the findings about the use of foreign jurisprudence in this book may nevertheless contribute to understanding the use of other persuasive sources more generally. In particular, it is plausible that many of the findings reported in Chapters 5 and 6 (how foreign jurisprudence is used and the use of foreign jurisprudence as a heuristic device) would be likely to reflect the approach to persuasive sources more generally. Other findings are felt to be peculiar to the use of foreign jurisprudence. These most obviously include situations where a court is looking to maintain consistency (Chapter 7) by identifying a common understanding or consensus among other jurisdictions or as a way to distance itself from a particular human rights regime (Chapter 8). For these reasons, the research in this book contributes strictly to the specific literature on the judicial use of foreign jurisprudence and comparative law.

A. The Time Period and Object of Study (Target Population)

The empirical research draws from judgments handed down by the UK Supreme Court since the start of its work in October 2009 and up to the end of the eighth judicial year in August 2017.[5] The findings were triangulated with qualitative data from the text of the judgments and interviews with 10 active and former Justices of the Supreme Court as well as one Lady Justice of Appeal.[6] The choice to focus on the Supreme Court was made on the basis that the Justices of the Supreme Court were the most likely to face the complex legal problems that would trigger the use of persuasive authorities such as foreign jurisprudence.[7] Stanton made the same choice on the basis that the Supreme Court's decisions were 'likely to be the most

[5] The Supreme Court was established by Part 3 of the Constitutional Reform Act 2005, assuming the judicial functions of the House of Lords as the highest appellate court in the UK (other than for Scottish criminal cases).

[6] On triangulating research, see, eg, Eugene J Webb et al, *Unobtrusive Measures: Nonreactive Measures in the Social Sciences* (Rand McNally, 1966); Norman K Denzin, *The Research Act in Sociology* (Aldine, 1970); Alan Bryman, *Social Research Methods*, 2nd edn (Oxford University Press, 2004).

[7] Bobek considers there to be two reasons for this: first, on an institutional basis, '[s]upreme jurisdictions have a larger mandate: to look beyond the individual judicial file and case and see the broader picture'; and, second, '[c]omparative analysis is, in terms of time, expertise, and resources, a demanding exercise' and 'it is at the level of supreme jurisdictions where human resources (analytical backup) and also procedural tools (lesser docket, selection of cases) may be available. These allow judges to concentrate on contentious legal issues in greater detail': Michael Bobek, *Comparative Reasoning in European Supreme Courts* (Oxford University Press, 2013), 44–45; Konrad Schiemann, 'The Judge as Comparatist' in Basil Markesinis and

far-reaching in terms of the development of the law and the wider picture'.[8] These parameters also make it possible to answer some of the unknowns identified by other researchers. For example, in her study of foreign precedents used by the South African Constitutional Court, Rautenbach concluded that 'empirical research into the propensity of the UK court to cite South African courts would be needed in order to determine whether the ... relationship between these two countries has led to cross pollination or not'.[9]

A more extensive analysis of the way in which foreign jurisprudence is used in courts at all levels was prevented by the usual limitations of time and resources. The Supreme Court may decide between 50 and 90 cases in any given legal year, while the Court of Appeal may decide as many or more in a single month. Such a large database would have taken the project beyond 'manageable bounds'.[10] This is a shame, for the interview at the Court of Appeal made clear that a study of the influence of foreign jurisprudence below the Supreme Court would be valuable, given the number of cases that are heard but not appealed.[11] The opportunity may arise to expand the research question in future.

B. The Data

There has been an increasing willingness on the part of both scholars and publishers to present data in a digestible format, using charts, graphs or tables. This is a key feature of the data presentation in this book, but it is not an approach that all academics agree upon. Some commentators have expressed doubt that this sort of analysis can provide any meaningful results at all. Bobek explained his own methodological choices from that viewpoint:

> This study is not a study in statistics or the increasingly popular 'quotation metrics', the purpose of which were to generate a set of colourful, but for a real understanding of a phenomenon often quite useless, graphs or tables.[12]

Jorg Fedtke, *Judicial Recourse to Foreign Law: A New Source of Inspiration?* (University College London Press, 2006) 369: 'The lower down the judicial ladder a judge finds himself the greater that pressure is in general.'

[8] Keith Stanton, 'Comparative Law in the House of Lords and Supreme Court' (2013) 42 *Common Law World Review* 269, 272.

[9] Christa Rautenbach, 'South Africa: Teaching an "Old Dog" New Tricks? An Empirical Study of the Use of Foreign Precedents by the South African Constitutional Court (1995–2010)' in Tania Groppi and Marie-Claire Ponthoreau (eds), *The Use of Foreign Precedents by Constitutional Judges* (Hart Publishing, 2013) 200.

[10] Stanton (n 8) 272.

[11] In a letter to the author, Lady Justice Arden noted that the subject of this work is also relevant to courts below the Supreme Court, including, in particular, the Court of Appeal. Letter from Lady Justice Arden to author (17 January 2014).

[12] Bobek (n 7) 74.

I have taken a different view. Compiling data figures is a time-consuming task, but there is more than aesthetic value to the product. It is through these that it is possible to illustrate data patterns or trends, which are especially interesting if one is seeking to set out changes in judicial reasoning or consistencies in practice.[13] Indeed, other recent works have made use of such techniques to good effect, enabling the representation of findings which might not otherwise have been possible to outline fully.[14]

C. The Data Sample

The basic elements of the data collection relied on a reasonably straightforward counting exercise. But even a simple case count involves methodological choices. Of the total 550 reported decisions, 533 were considered to be distinct 'cases' for the purpose of analysing the use of foreign jurisprudence. Cases with different neutral citations but which were essentially parts of the same case (perhaps reporting a judgment on costs or preliminary references to the CJEU separately) were also counted as one. My approach for calculating foreign jurisprudence citations would combine *Willers v Joyce and Another* [2016] UKSC 43; [2016] 3 WLR 477 and [2016] UKSC 44; [2016] 3 WLR 534 as one 'case'. The substantive issue in the appeal had been decided in *Willers v Joyce and Another* [2016] UKSC 43; [2016] 3 WLR 477, but the UK Supreme Court issued a separate judgment reported as [2016] UKSC 44; [2016] 3 WLR 534 to address the narrow issue relating to the status of decisions handed down by the Judicial Committee of the Privy Council (JCPC). In fact, the Supreme Court files both reports under the same case page on its website.[15] Occasionally, the Supreme Court website combines the reports into a single file.[16] Conjoined appeals were also counted as being one 'case'. Appeals are conjoined when dealing with the same questions of law and are usually decided on the same reasoning. It would have skewed the data to record the use of foreign jurisprudence in such instances more than once. This is in harmony with the approach

[13] Lee Epstein and Andrew Martin, *An Introduction to Empirical Legal Research* (Oxford University Press, 2014) 224.

[14] See, eg, Poole and Shah (n 1); Groppi and Ponthoreau (n 9); Alan Paterson, *Final Judgment: The Last Law Lords and the Supreme Court* (Hart Publishing, 2013); Martin Gelter and Mathias Siems, 'Citations to Foreign Courts—Illegitimate and Superfluous or Unavoidable? Evidence from Europe' (2014) 62(1) *American Journal of Comparative Law* 35; James Lee, 'The Judicial Individuality of Lord Sumption (2017) 40(2) *University of New South Wales Law Journal* 862.

[15] UK Supreme Court Website, 'Decided Cases', www.supremecourt.uk/decided-cases/2016.html.

[16] See, eg, *R (on the Application of ClientEarth) v Secretary of State for the Environment, Food and Rural Affairs* [2015] UKSC 28 and [2013] UKSC 25, www.supremecourt.uk/cases/docs/uksc-2012-0179-judgment.pdf.

adopted by Paterson in *Final Judgment*,[17] making it possible to compare findings for the overlapping research period; it was reassuring to find that we had arrived at the same figure (246) for cases decided in 2009–13 (whereas the sum of neutral law reports was 257).

The data was approached a little differently in relation to analysis of judgment types (single judgments, dissenting judgments and concurrences). Since it is possible for judges to dissent on even procedural matters, it felt unfair to calculate these reports as one. This creates a disparity between my results and those presented by Paterson. For example, Paterson reports that there were dissenting judgments in 24 per cent of cases decided by the Supreme Court in 2009–13.[18] By my calculations, dissents could be found in 58 cases decided by the Supreme Court in the same period. Combining appeals and taking the total number of cases decided in 2009–13 as 246 (as described above) would give 24 per cent as the proportion of cases including a dissenting judgment. As a proportion of separately reported cases in 2009–13 (257), the figure comes out at 23 per cent. Given the deviation from Paterson's method on this point, it was helpful to be able to cross-check my coding against other researchers that had conducted analysis on this footing. James Lee, for example, took the 'seventy-five decisions handed down in the 2015–16 court year' as the starting point for his analysis of judgment types (whereas combining the two reports in relation to *Willers v Joyce and Another* would have led to a sum of 74).[19] Lee's findings were identical to my own.

D. Human Rights Cases

A case was categorised as a 'human rights' case where it had one or more of the following attributes: where the words 'human rights' are found in the judgment and are used to substantive effect (that is, as more than a passing reference, comparison or analogy);[20] where human rights legislation or

[17] Paterson (n 14) 14: 'When it comes to calculating the rates at which judges dissent, or write judgment or concurrences the fairer approach appears to be to focus on "cases" rather than "appeals".'

[18] Alan Paterson, 'A Scarcity of Dissents?' *UK Supreme Court Blog* (6 March 2014), www.ukscblog.com/scarcity-dissent.

[19] James Lee, 'The United Kingdom Supreme Court' in Emmanuel Guinchard and Marie-Pierre Granger (eds), *The New EU Judiciary* (Kluwer, 2017) 92.

[20] For example, the judgment in *AB and Others v Ministry of Defence* [2012] UKSC 9; [2013] 1 AC 78 makes one reference to 'human rights' and was therefore captured by the database search. This reference, however, serves merely to note the history of the case and the claimant's knowledge of another case before the Strasbourg Court. It has no direct bearing on the instant case and it would therefore distort the data to categorise the judgment as one concerning 'human rights'; in *Taiwo v Olaigbe* [2016] UKSC 3; [2016] 1 WLR 2653, the Court made brief mention of the approach adopted to the concept of nationality 'in other contexts', including the ECHR.

instruments are cited, again, with substantive effect; where the word 'rights' is discernibly associated with human rights, even if it is not explicitly stated. This goes beyond Paterson's classification criteria in including judgments where the human rights discussion is obiter dicta (discussion that does not go to the principle upon which a case is decided). The result is that the dataset includes cases such as *R (Sturnham) v Parole Board*, in which Lord Mance's review of the position adopted by the European Court of Human Rights served only to support the conclusion that there were no human rights issues to prevent ongoing detention.[21] Given that the aim of the research was to understand the influence of foreign jurisprudence on UK human rights law, it felt important to include any cases that gave rise to substantial human rights discussion. Indeed, obiter dicta can be a very strong persuasive authority.[22] This broad definition of a 'human rights case' risks an amount of overlap with cases that might readily be classified under alternative categories, most obviously including 'criminal law' or 'public law' cases.[23] This overlap is not felt to have a significant bearing on the findings in this study, since the primary aim is to consider the effect of using foreign jurisprudence where there are human rights issues at stake. As such, breaking down the categories further was not felt to be a useful exercise. Nevertheless, the implications of the overlap are that the research findings must be considered to apply strictly to the parameters of this enquiry. If the cases were reorganised into these further categories so as to avoid the overlap, it is entirely possible that the overall data patterns would be slightly different.

Human rights instruments included international human rights conventions, such as the UN Convention on the Rights of the Child, the Convention against Torture and Other Cruel, Inhuman or Degrading Treatment or Punishment, the Convention on the Status of Refugees 1950, and the International Covenant on Civil and Political Rights. Some of these (or some parts of these) have been incorporated into domestic law by primary legislation other than the HRA 1998.[24] Cases engaging the EU Charter

[21] *R (Sturnham) v Parole Board* [2013] UKSC 23; [2013] 2 AC 254.

[22] Explored further below (see ch 3, text following n 37).

[23] In fact, there is a disparity between this approach and that adopted by Alan Paterson. In *Final Judgment,* Paterson works from the same figure for the total number of cases decided in the first four years (246), but divides these into six categories: 'Criminal'; 'Human Rights'; 'Public'; 'Private/Commercial'; 'Family'; and 'Tax'. The result is that just 35 cases are categorised as 'human rights' cases. As Paterson explains in a footnote: 'Any case classification contains room for quibbles. Many cases do contain human rights points, but where they are obiter, I have not classified them as human rights cases. Here I can do no better than quote from Louis Blom-Cooper and Gavin Drewry, *Final Appeal* (Clarendon Press, 1972) 244. "Any subject-classification we construct is essentially arbitrary, and the assignment of marginal cases to particular categories is extremely difficult."' See further Paterson (n 14) 17, Table 2.1 and note 17.

[24] For example, in *R (Adams) v Secretary of State for Justice* [2011] UKSC 18; [2012] 1 AC 48, the Court was concerned with the meaning of the phrase 'miscarriage of justice' in s 133 of the Criminal Justice Act 1988, which was enacted to give effect to Article 14(6) of the International Covenant on Civil and Political Rights 1966.

of Fundamental Rights or other rights derived from EU law were also included.[25]

Recognising that foreign jurisprudence may have greater or lesser influence in relation to the source of the human rights, I also coded cases according to whether they raised issues under the ECHR, another international human rights convention and/or the common law. Some cases were easier to classify than others. The HRA 1998 makes identifying cases engaging Convention rights easy. Cases engaging other international 'human rights' conventions were more difficult, but—given explicit references to these instruments—manageable. Identifying cases that could be described as recognising or engaging common law rights was much harder. As others have noted, there is no catalogue of common law rights,[26] but the courts clearly recognise rights with a foundation in the common law. Indeed, it was on this basis that rights were protected prior to the enactment of the HRA 1998, and in the early days of the Act, the judges appeared to be clear on the continued role for the common law.[27] To some extent, the narrative around repeal of the HRA 1998 made it easier to identify these rights at work: some judges have been explicit about bringing the common law into focus.[28] Common law rights might be taken to include (but are not limited to) the right to open justice,[29] access to the courts,[30] freedom of expression,[31] citizenship,[32] legal professional privilege[33] and equal treatment.[34]

[25] In *Sadovska and Another v Secretary of State for the Home Department (Scotland)* [2017] UKSC 54; [2017] 1 WLR 2926, the Court noted Articles 8 and 12 ECHR, but allowed the appeal on the basis of rights protected in EU law.

[26] Brice Dickson, *Human Rights and the United Kingdom Supreme Court* (Oxford University Press, 2013); Mark Elliott, 'Beyond the European Convention: Human Rights and the Common Law' (2015) 68 *Current Legal Problems* 85; Roger Masterman and Se-shauna Wheatle, 'A Common Law Resurgence in Rights Protection' (2015) 1 *European Human Rights Law Review* 57.

[27] Elliott (n 26) 91; See also Stephen Sedley, *Lions under the Throne* (Cambridge University Press, 2015), 199, claiming that the Law Lords' goal in *R v Secretary of State for the Home Department ex parte Daly* [2001] UKHL 26; [2001] 2 AC 532 had been 'to make clear that, irrespective of the introduction of a statutory system of human rights adjudication ... the common law itself recognised that fundamental rights were entitled to legal protection in domestic law'.

[28] *Kennedy v The Charity Commission* [2014] UKSC 20; [2015] AC 455; *Osborn v The Parole Board* [2013] UKSC 61; [2014] AC 1115.

[29] *Kennedy* (n 28).

[30] *R v Shayler* [2002] UKHL 11; [2003] 1 AC 247.

[31] *R v Secretary of State for the Home Department ex parte Simms* [2000] 2 AC 115.

[32] *Pham v Secretary of State for the Home Department* [2015] UKSC 19; [2015] 1 WLR 1591.

[33] *R v Secretary of State for the Home Department ex parte Daly* [2001] UKHL 26; [2001] 2 AC 532.

[34] *AXA General Insurance Ltd v Lord Advocate* [2011] UKSC 46; [2012] 1 AC 868. Some common law rights are also listed in Lord Cooke of Thorndon, 'The Road Ahead for the Common Law' (2004) 53 *International and Comparative Law Quarterly* 273.

A total of 152 cases were found to meet one or more of these criteria and were thus classified as concerning 'human rights'. To some extent, confidence in the classifications could be confirmed with cross-checks to other surveys. For example, the 2015 and 2016 editions of *The UK Supreme Court Yearbook* include chapters on human rights cases. In the 2015 edition of *The UK Supreme Court Yearbook*, Christopher Sargeant recorded 18 cases raising human rights law in the 2014–15 legal year.[35] This was identical (both in number and in the cases identified) to the result of my analysis in the same year. For the 2015–16 legal year, Jeremy Johnson QC reported that human rights law issues had been raised in 16 cases.[36] There was just one difference between Johnson's count and mine: Johnson included *R (on the Application of O) (by Her Litigation Friend the Official Solicitor) v Secretary of State for the Home Department* [2016] UKSC 19.[37] My reading of *R (O)* let me to classify the case as primarily concerned with administrative questions of procedure and policy. This therefore fell closer into line with cases that might have raised human rights issues, but that did not attract substantive human rights discussion (which were omitted from my 'human rights' cases database).

E. Foreign Jurisprudence

In the context of this study, 'jurisprudence' encompasses case law, legal instruments and relevant *travaux préparatoires*.[38] For that reason, 'foreign jurisprudence' has been preferred over 'foreign law' or 'foreign precedents', unless referring specifically to a clear sub-category (as in the quantitative data analysis). The only exception to this is where other scholars have used the alternative terms in quoted material, in which case the original sense has been retained. This definition is important since different sources of law may be useful for different purposes. As Saunders has hypothesised:

> One possible variation, which should be noted at the outset, is the nature of the foreign source on which a court draws. It may be a conclusion of law or a constitutional or legal norm, whether articulated by a court or otherwise. Equally, however, it may be an argument, a value, a perception, an interpretative approach,

[35] Christopher Sargeant, 'Human Rights Law' (2016) 6 *UK Supreme Court Yearbook* 392.

[36] Jeremy Johnson, 'Human Rights Law' (2016) 7 *UK Supreme Court Yearbook* 459.

[37] *R (on the Application of O) (by Her Litigation Friend the Official Solicitor) v Secretary of State for the Home Department* [2016] UKSC 19; [2016] 1 WLR 1717.

[38] Literally: 'preparatory works', referring to material produced during the drafting of legislation or related instruments; see, eg, *R (Adams) v Secretary of State for Justice* [2011] UKSC 18; [2012] 1 AC 48 [86]–[87], in which Lord Phillips examined the *travaux préparatoires* relating to Article 14(6) of the International Covenant on Civil and Political Rights 1966 in order to ascertain the international meaning of the phrase 'miscarriage of justice' in s 133 of the Criminal Justice Act 1988. Lord Phillips examined the *travaux préparatoires* to ascertain the international meaning of the term.

or merely a happy turn of phrase. The list is intended to be illustrative, rather than exhaustive.[39]

'Foreign' takes its natural meaning and refers to non-domestic matters. A case was considered 'foreign' if it was decided by the court of another country which does not also fall under the jurisdiction of the UK Supreme Court for the purposes of Part 3 of the Constitutional Reform Act 2005. Cases from Wales, Scotland and Northern Ireland were therefore excluded from the definition. While Scots criminal cases fall within the broad definition of 'foreign jurisprudence' (the High Court of Justiciary in Scotland sitting as an appeal court is the final court of appeal for criminal cases), the Supreme Court remains the final court of appeal in civil cases. As such, the Scots jurisprudence is slightly different in character from the case law of other foreign courts and is likely to be more familiar to the UK Supreme Court, where, by convention, care is taken to ensure that at least two of the Justices have experience of the Scottish legal system.[40] A similar approach was taken by Stanton in his study of comparative law in tort cases decided by the House of Lords and the Supreme Court from 1990 to 2013.[41] Stanton's feeling was that Scottish judges in the Supreme Court 'clearly' saw the incorporation of Scottish law into the Court's decision-making as part of their judicial function. Stanton's conclusion was that the inclusion of references to Scottish law would 'distort' the data.[42] Burrows, too, excluded references to Scottish law from his study of the influence of comparative law on the English law of obligations, though he explained that this was 'because of the House of Lords and Supreme Court in being the highest court for both systems'.[43] References to decisions of the Privy Council have also been excluded from the dataset.

Crucially, 'foreign jurisprudence' only encompasses foreign domestic law and does not refer to the jurisprudence of international courts.[44]

[39] Cheryl Saunders, 'Comparative Constitutional Law in the Courts: Is There a Problem?' (2006) 59(1) *Current Legal Problems* 91, 98–99; Cheryl Saunders, 'The Use and Misuse of Comparative Constitutional Law' (2006) 13 *Indiana Journal of Global Legal Studies* 37.

[40] See, eg, Constitutional Affairs Select Committee, *Judicial Appointments and a Supreme Court (Court of Final Appeal)* First Report of Session 2003–04, HC 48-I [43].

[41] Stanton (n 8) 269.

[42] ibid.

[43] Andrew Burrows, 'The Influence of Comparative Law on the English Law of Obligations' in Andrew Robertson and Michael Tilbury (eds), *The Common Law of Obligations: Divergence and Unity* (Hart Publishing, 2016) 23–24.

[44] This is in contrast to the approach taken by some other studies. For example, in her 1990s study of comparative law in British courts, Örücü counted any citation of any non-English jurisprudence, including the jurisprudence on international treaties or conventions: Esin Örücü, 'Comparative Law in British Courts' in Ulrich Drobnig and Sjef van Erp (eds), *The Use of Comparative Law by Courts, 14th International Congress of Comparative Law* (Kluwer, 1999); Mathias Siems, 'Citation Patterns of the German Federal Supreme Court and the Court of Appeal of England and Wales' (2010) 21 *King's Law Journal* 152.

It thereby excludes, for example, the jurisprudence of the European Court of Human Rights in Strasbourg from the quantitative analysis of foreign case citations.[45] Although the Strasbourg jurisprudence is technically 'persuasive' rather than binding, the HRA 1998 places UK courts under a duty to 'take it into account'. This direction gives the Strasbourg jurisprudence a different character from the decisions of foreign domestic courts.

For more obvious reasons, 'foreign jurisprudence' also excludes the decisions of supranational courts which UK courts are bound to follow. During the research period, and at the time of writing, this included decisions of the Court of Justice of the European Union (CJEU) under section 3 of the European Communities Act (ECA) 1972. Questions of EU law were taken to be questions of law, not fact.[46] Further, the Supreme Court (as the domestic court of last resort) was under a duty to ask the CJEU for a preliminary ruling concerning 'the interpretation of the Treaties' and 'the validity and interpretation of acts of the institutions, bodies, offices or agencies of the Union', where a decision on the question was necessary in order to give judgment in the case before it.[47] The 'Practice Direction on the Citation of Authorities' also excluded these sources from its guidance on foreign jurisprudence:

> For the avoidance of doubt, paragraphs 9.1 and 9.2 do not apply to cases decided in either the European Court of Justice or the organs of the European Convention of Human Rights. Because of the status in English law of such authority, as provided by, respectively, section 3 of the European Communities Act 1972 and section 2(1) of the Human Rights Act 1998, such cases are covered by the earlier paragraphs of this Direction.[48]

Bobek drew similar distinctions between 'mandatory', 'voluntary' and 'non-mandatory' uses of foreign legal rules. The former included 'instances in which the national courts are obliged, by virtue of domestic law, to use

[45] Strasbourg jurisprudence remains strictly 'international law' notwithstanding s 2 of the UK HRA 1998, which provides that domestic courts must 'take into account' Strasbourg jurisprudence (so far as it is 'relevant') in cases which engage the ECHR. On the use of Strasbourg jurisprudence in domestic courts, see, eg, Roger Masterman, 'Section 2(1) of the Human Rights Act: Binding Domestic Courts to Strasbourg?' [2004] *PL* 725; Elizabeth Wicks, 'Taking Account of Strasbourg? The British Judiciary's Approach to Interpreting Convention Rights' [2005] *European Public Law* 405; Jonathan Lewis, 'The European Ceiling on Human Rights' [2007] *PL* 720; Jonathan Lewis, '*In Re P and Others*: An Exception to the "No More, Certainly No Less" Rule' [2009] *PL* 43; Francesca Klug and Helen Wildbore, 'Follow or Lead? The Human Rights Act and the European Court of Human Rights' (2010) 6 *European Human Rights Law Review* 621; Helen Fenwick and Roger Masterman, 'The Conservative Project to "Break the Link between British Courts and Strasbourg": Rhetoric or Reality' (2017) 80(6) *MLR* 1111.

[46] Section 3(1) of the European Communities Act 1972; Rupert Cross and JW Harris, *Precedent in English Law* (Clarendon Press, 2004) 184: '[Q]uestions of Community law … differ in this respect from questions of foreign law.'

[47] Article 267 of the Treaty on the Functioning of the European Union.

[48] Section 9.3 of *Practice Direction (Citation of Authorities)* [2001] 1 WLR 1001; [2001] 2 All ER 510.

foreign legal rules in deciding cases'.[49] His conclusion was that the 'status enjoyed by the decisions of either of the European courts (Luxembourg as well as Strasbourg)' meant that they 'belong in the "must" and not a mere "may" category', being treated by UK courts 'essentially as domestic precedents'.[50]

One consequence of the UK's withdrawal from the EU will be to alter the relationship between UK courts and the CJEU. The precise nature of the post-Brexit relationship between UK domestic courts and the CJEU was not clear at the time of writing, when the EU (Withdrawal) Bill was still in the early legislative stages.[51] The most that could be said is that domestic courts are likely to continue drawing from the jurisprudence of the CJEU, as a persuasive if not binding source of authority.[52] One of the clearest conclusions in this book is that the nature of 'persuasive' authority implies a legitimate degree of discretion around the use of such sources. Parliament might create rules to limit, protect or direct judicial discretion (and some judges expressed a clear desire for direction in this particular arena),[53] but *some* degree of discretion is almost certain to remain. The relationship between domestic courts and the European Court of Human Rights in Strasbourg has also been under review in recent years,[54] making it possible that the domestic duty to 'take into account' Strasbourg jurisprudence would be altered. Again, this would not affect the research conducted during 2009–17, but would be likely to have some consequences on the use of jurisprudence from foreign domestic courts.

[49] Bobek (n 7) 21.

[50] ibid 78.

[51] European Union (Withdrawal) Bill, as introduced, www.publications.parliament.uk/pa/bills/lbill/2017-2019/0079/lbill_2017-20190079_en_1.htm.

[52] Lord Reed, 'Comparative Law in the Supreme Court of the United Kingdom', Lecture at the Centre for Private Law, University of Edinburgh (13 October 2017), www.supremecourt.uk/docs/speech-171013.pdf.

[53] Lord Neuberger, 'The Role of Judges in a Post-Referendum World', opening address to the Public Law Project Annual Judicial Review Trends and Forecasts Conference (2 November 2017), www.publiclawproject.org.uk/resources/265/the-role-of-the-judges-in-a-post-referendum-world, from 16:35; Select Committee on the European Union Justice Sub-Committee, corrected oral evidence, 'Brexit: The Jurisdiction of the CJEU', 21 November 2017, http://data.parliament.uk/writtenevidence/committeeevidence.svc/evidencedocument/eu-justice-subcommittee/brexit-the-jurisdiction-of-the-cjeu/oral/74225.html.

[54] The 2015 Conservative Party Manifesto included a commitment to 'break the formal link between British courts and the European Court of Human Rights': Conservative Party Manifesto 2015, 'Strong Leadership, a Clear Economic Plan, a Brighter, More Secure Future', www.conservatives.com/manifesto2015, 62. The 2017 Conservative Party Manifesto diluted this position, but did not rule out changes to the UK's relationship with the ECHR. It stated that a Conservative government 'will not repeal or replace the Human Rights Act while the process of Brexit is underway' and that the UK would 'remain [a] signator[y] to the European Convention on Human Rights for the duration of the next parliament': Conservative and Unionist Party Manifesto 2017, 'Forward, Together: Our Plan for a Strong Britain and a Prosperous Future', www.conservatives.com/manifesto, 37.

For each case and for each Justice, I recorded the number and source of any jurisprudence cited. As databases do not always record references to foreign jurisprudence, a manual reading of the cases was necessary. This task was made easier by the structure of certain judgments. It is not uncommon for judgments of the Supreme Court to subtitle discussion of foreign jurisprudence.[55] To avoid arbitrary judgments about the extent to which foreign jurisprudence was used, the dataset captures all explicit references to foreign cases, even if not discussed at length. This includes minor references, such as Lord Kerr's note in *In re JR38*, that Lord Reed's formulation of the fourfold proportionality test in *Bank Mellat* had 'followed the approach of Dickson CJ in the Canadian case *R v Oakes* [1986] 1 SCR 103'.[56] Citations within citations are common and these were also counted.[57] Joint judgments were not 'weighted' by repeat counting foreign case citations according to the number of judges subscribing to the judgment. For example, I did not multiply the Canadian case cited by the majority in *Miller* by the eight judges who are given as joint authors.[58] Weighting judgments in this way risked skewing the dataset and would have given rise to the argument that concurrences should be treated in the same way.[59]

F. The 'Influence' of Foreign Jurisprudence: Explicit and Implicit References

The 'influence' of foreign jurisprudence is the central thread of the enquiry. Discovering exactly how judges are utilising, employing, exercising, applying, exploiting, handling, managing, consuming or drawing from foreign jurisprudence are questions upon which all other research questions are parasitic. The influence of foreign jurisprudence must therefore be understood

[55] See, eg, O *(A Child) v Rhodes and Another (English PEN and Others Intervening)* [2015] UKSC 32; [2016] AC 219; *Montgomery v Lanarkshire Health Board* [2015] UKSC 11; [2015] AC 1450 [70]; *Versloot Dredging BV and Another v HDI Gerling Industrie Versicherung AG and Others* [2016] UKSC 45; [2016] Bus LR 371 [21].

[56] *In the Matter of an Application by JR38 for Judicial Review (Northern Ireland)* [2015] UKSC 42 [75].

[57] *O (A Child)* (n 55) [70]–[71]; *R (Bibi) v Secretary of State for the Home Department* [2015] UKSC 68; [2015] 1 WLR 5055.

[58] *R (Miller) v Secretary of State for Exiting the European Union* [2017] UKSC 5; [2017] 2 WLR 583 [141], citing *Re Resolution to Amend the Constitution* [1981] 1 SCR 753 on the role of constitutional conventions.

[59] The identical choice was made by Saunders and Stone in their analysis of Australian High Court judgments: Cheryl Saunders and Adrienne Stone, 'Reference to Foreign Precedents by the Australian High Court: A Matter of Method' in Groppi and Ponthoreau (n 9) 30. Saunders and Stone point out that other researchers have made the opposite choice. See, eg, Russell Smyth, 'Trends in the Citation Practice of the Supreme Court of Queensland over the Course of the Twentieth Century' (2009) 28(1) *University of Queensland Law Journal* 39, 49–50.

in the broadest sense.[60] It is analysed through any contribution made by foreign jurisprudence to judicial reasoning, from explicit citation to a passing reference or even a very casual consideration—including references that do not form part of the published judgment.

Non-explicit uses of foreign jurisprudence present obvious research challenges. In *The Use of Foreign Precedents by Constitutional Judges*, Groppi and Ponthoreau explained the omission of evidence about implicit foreign precedent citations on the basis that these would have required significant extra-judicial research, conducted by way of interviews and questionnaires. Yet a lack of express citations does not necessarily indicate a lack of knowledge or use of foreign jurisprudence on the part of judges. In fact, one of the authors in *The Use of Foreign Precedents by Constitutional Judges* wrote that 'the frequency of citations in itself does not tell us much about the reasons and effects of the references, so it is extremely difficult to evaluate the character of the use of foreign judicial practices and cases'.[61] For this research project, the opportunity of conducting interviews with active and former judges made it possible to gain some insight into the implicit uses of foreign jurisprudence. Nevertheless, given the implicit rather than explicit nature of judicial recourse to these sources, it is not possible to be systematic about the evidence. For that reason, no attempt has been made to quantify implicit uses of foreign jurisprudence.[62] The qualitative evidence in relation to these should be treated as illustrative rather than indicative.

There is also nothing to stop a judge from noting the position or attitudes of a foreign court or jurisdiction, without an explicit citation to a foreign law or case.[63] In some cases, the court makes no explicit citation of foreign judgments, but refers more generally to the legal position in other jurisdictions.[64] For example, in *R (Catt) v Commissioner of Police of the Metropolis*:

> In common with other jurisdictions, including the European Court of Human Rights and the courts of the United States, Canada and New Zealand, the courts

[60] The 'influence' of comparative law was also the focus of Burrows' study in the context of the English law of obligations: Burrows (n 43). Groppi and Ponthoreau employed the term 'use' in Groppi and Ponthoreau (n 9); Bobek (n 7) preferred the term 'inspiration'.

[61] Zoltán Szente, 'Hungary: Unsystematic and Incoherent Borrowing of Law: The Use of Foreign Judicial Precedents in the Jurisprudence of the Constitutional Court, 1999–2010' in Groppi and Ponthoreau (n 9) 266.

[62] Others have also resisted any attempt to quantify implicit uses of foreign jurisprudence. See, eg, John Bell, 'Comparative Law in the Supreme Court 2010–11' (2012) 1(2) *Cambridge Journal of International and Comparative Law* 20; Ian Cram, 'Resort to Foreign Constitutional Norms in Domestic Human Rights Jurisprudence with Reference to Terrorism Cases' [2009] *CLJ* 118.

[63] Cram (n 62) 129: 'failure to make an explicit attribution ... may occur for reasons to do with national pride ... or simply because there is no formal requirement to acknowledge help from foreign sources'.

[64] In *R (F)*, Lord Phillips mentioned the systems of several foreign jurisdictions and had evidently considered an argument made by counsel on the point: 'Those acting for the first

> of the United Kingdom have adopted as the test for what constitutes 'private life' whether there was a reasonable expectation of privacy in the relevant respect.[65]

Bobek included these sorts of 'unspecified references to a "foreign solution", invoking for instance the situation in country X, but not making any further substantiated reference to legislation, case law, or scholarly works' for the purposes of his study:[66]

> [E]ven allusions to 'foreign democratic legal systems'; 'a number of foreign democratic countries'; values shared by 'the Member States of the EU and other developed countries of the Western Europe'; or 'the founding principles of the contemporary Euro-Atlantic civilization' were eventually counted as further unspecified instances of invoking some foreign inspiration, in spite of the fact that the displayed referencing culture and the quality of 'comparative argument' leaves much to be desired.[67]

These 'uses' of foreign jurisprudence posed some difficulty in respect of my quantitative analysis. While it was easy to calculate explicit citations to foreign cases, quantifying the extent of reference to legal norms or values felt prone to oversight. On this point I found myself in sympathy with Cram, who undertook a study of resort to foreign jurisprudence in terrorism cases decided by the House of Lords. Cram suspected that the extent to which foreign jurisprudence is used is likely to be understated.[68] On any approach, the results seemed likely to be unsystematic, being based on my subjective reading of the cases. For that reason, I have resisted the temptation to attempt quantitative analysis of references to these sources. The quantitative data is therefore limited to explicit citations of foreign court decisions, leaving references to other sources of law to the qualitative analysis of decided cases.

G. Judgments and Judgment Writing

For each case, I recorded the contributions made by the individual justices. This included whether a written judgment was given, as well as whether

claimant have drawn attention to registration requirements for sexual offenders in France, Ireland, the seven Australian states, Canada, South Africa and the United States. Almost all of these have provisions for review': *R (F) and Another v Secretary of State for the Home Department* [2010] UKSC 17; [2011] 1 AC 331 [57] (Lord Phillips). In *Cox v Ministry of Justice* [2016] UKSC 10; [2016] AC 660 [23], Lord Reed noted that an idea has 'been emphasised in recent times in United States and Canadian authorities', but made no explicit reference to decisions emanating from those jurisdictions; *Angove's Pty Ltd v Bailey and Another* [2016] UKSC 47; [2016] 1 WLR 3179 [27].

[65] *R (Catt) v Commissioner of Police of the Metropolis and Another* [2015] UKSC 9; [2015] AC 1065 [4] (Lord Sumption).

[66] Bobek (n 7) 68.

[67] ibid 69.

[68] Cram (n 62) 129. Bobek adds that the use of foreign jurisprudence may be 'hidden behind the veil of domestic scholarship': Bobek (n 7) 72–73.

a written judgment could be described as a leading judgment, concurring, dissenting, or a concurring dissenting judgment. Identifying a lead judgment is significantly easier at the Supreme Court than it was at the House of Lords. As Baroness Hale has explained:

> One obvious change in the Supreme Court is that we can print the judgments in whatever order we choose, so the lead (what I call the 'donkey-work') judgment can come first regardless of seniority (although that may not always happen).[69]

I also recorded data on the Supreme Court's judgment writing as a whole. This includes figures relating to the number of single judgments (including a 'judgment of the court') versus cases where one or more of the unanimous panel wrote a concurrence. The latter would typically include (but would not be restricted to) cases in which the panel was unanimous as to the outcome, but not the reasoning.[70] For cases with at least one dissent, it was recorded whether the court gave a single majority judgment or if there was at least one concurrence in the majority. These insights made it possible to compare and update the existing scholarship on judgment writing at the Supreme Court (and, again, it was useful to test reliability with a comparison to those results).[71]

A 'judgment of the court', a single judgment with which all members of the panel agree or a single judgment with which others in the majority agree are sometimes referred to as examples of a 'plurality judgment',[72] but there is divergence on this point.[73] To avoid confusion, I have preferred to use 'single', 'single majority' and 'joint' judgments to indicate circumstances in which judges have either aligned themselves with another judgment or combined forces with another judge. The latter of these is sometimes described as a 'composite' judgment;[74] the majority judgment in *Miller* is a

[69] Brenda Hale, 'Judgment Writing in the Supreme Court', First Anniversary Seminar (London, 30 September 2010), www.supremecourt.uk/docs/speech_100930.pdf, 2.

[70] Paterson makes a distinction between 'unanimity' and 'univocal'. The former describes a panel that is unanimous as to the outcome. The latter applies 'where the Court is agreed not only as to the result but also as to the reasons for the outcome (even where there is more than one judgment'). Paterson (n 14) 14.

[71] The same classifications were adopted by Lee in his study of Supreme Court judgments in the 2015–16 legal year: Lee (n 19) 92.

[72] Dan Tranch and Laura Coogan, 'Baroness Brenda Hale: "I Often Ask Myself 'Why Am I Here?'"' *The Guardian* (16 September 2010), www.theguardian.com/law/2010/sep/16/uk-supreme-court-judiciary. This definition is compatible with the definition that guided Poole and Shah (n 1) in their quantitative analysis of the House of Lords, drawn from the *Harvard Law Review*: 'plurality opinions that announce the judgment of the court' are counted as 'opinions of the court'.

[73] Paterson (n 14) 14: Paterson defines a 'plurality judgment' as referring to 'the situation in which there is no majority judgment in the Court. In that situation the judgment which receives the most support is sometimes referred to as a plurality judgment'.

[74] ibid 11. As Paterson notes, composite judgments are rare. Single majority judgments are much more common and 'are almost always a collective work product of most of the Justices in the case'.

good example of this.[75] A concurrence was counted where, however briefly, a judge adds something beyond the basic formula agreeing with the outcome of the case.[76] In other cases, it includes passages of slightly greater length, but which serve only to add an observation or footnote to the judgment with which the Justice has otherwise associated himself. This was the approach adopted by Poole and Shah in their study of human rights cases in the House of Lords from 1994 to 2007. Poole and Shah's analysis of 'noise levels' (concurrences and dissents) was guided by the Harvard Rules, recording a concurrence 'as a "written opinion" whenever a reason, however brief, is given'.[77]

H. Limits

Some of my early ambitions had to be abandoned. In my doctoral work, I had attempted to code the cases according to the nature of the influence of foreign jurisprudence in any given case. On these decisions, I had taken a lead from the existing scholarship. A number of commentators have, for instance, suggested that judges use persuasive authority as a means of *judicial fig-leafing* or to support their own *predetermined conclusions*.[78] Other possibilities are that recourse to foreign jurisprudence has a *legitimation function*[79] or is a vehicle for adopting a more *theorised approach* to human rights.[80] Alternatively, a court may look to foreign case law for *pedagogical*

[75] *Miller* (n 58).

[76] This approach is in line with that adopted by Lee in his article on concurring speeches. Lee explained his use of 'concurrence' as 'a term of art to refer to "the publication of a separate speech beyond a basic formula concurring in the outcome of the case"': James Lee, 'A Defence of Concurring Speeches' [2009] *PL* 305, 306. Paterson took a more inclusive approach to concurrences, including 'an opinion or judgment which is not a lead or majority judgment of the court but one which either simply agrees with the majority judgment(s)'. Paterson (n 14) 11.

[77] Jaclyn Paterson's doctoral work followed a similar logic, acknowledging that this 'occasionally resulted in a single paragraph that went beyond the standard working being coded as a "concurring opinion"; the "enhanced paragraph" had to contribute some substantive reasoning to the appeal or associate/disassociate itself with a particular aspect of another judge's opinion'. Jaclyn Paterson, 'The Institutional Relations and Relationships of the United Kingdom Final Court of Appeal: An Empirical Analysis of the UK's Top Courts 2007–2011' (DPhil Thesis, Durham University, 2016), http://etheses.dur.ac.uk/11719.

[78] See, eg, Cram (n 62) 139–41; Wicks (n 45) 410.

[79] See, eg, Luc Heuschling, 'Comparative Law and the European Convention on Human Rights Cases' in Esin Örücü (ed), *Judicial Comparativism in Human Rights Cases* (United Kingdom National Committee of Comparative Law 2003) 47.

[80] Christopher McCrudden, 'Human Rights and Judicial Use of Comparative Law' in Örücü (n 80) 17; Christopher McCrudden, 'A Common Law of Human Rights?: Transnational Judicial Conversations on Constitutional Rights' (2000) 20(4) *Oxford Journal of Legal Studies* 499, 512.

reasons,[81] as a *warning*,[82] or as part of a *gap-filling* exercise.[83] To preserve a sense of continuity in the legal scholarship, those classifications have been used in this study. To these I have added *judicial respect*, *courtesy* and references made for *no discernible reason* at all. When I revisited and updated the data for the purposes of this book, I had in mind that a quantitative representation of the role played by foreign jurisprudence may be possible. It quickly became clear that my coding on these questions placed too great a weight on my own subjective interpretation of the cases. Thus, as in the original project, coding the cases in this way helped guide my qualitative analysis but made no contribution to the quantitative analysis. Again, I found it comforting that scholars publishing in the years since my doctoral research had apparently grappled with and come to the same conclusion on this question.[84]

I. Data Collection and Lessons in Empirical Legal Research

Information about each case was obtained from the official transcripts and law reports. Once collected and coded, the data was entered into a software package: Excel. The Excel spreadsheets also record basic information such as the full case name, neutral citation, date of hearing and the constitution of the judicial bench. In the interests of supporting empirical legal research, it is incumbent on me to admit that I would alter this approach in a future study of this kind. Having commenced the project in early 2010, I did not have the benefit of Epstein and Martin's invaluable book *An Introduction to Empirical Legal Research*.[85] I would be inclined to adopt their advice on this front in future, employing data entry systems and creating data files.[86] Just as Epstein and Martin warn, at all stages of the 'physical coding-transfer' I had an underlying unease about the potential for human error.[87] Given my data-entry choice, evaluating the data and performing reliability checks was very important. A number of error-checks were performed,

[81] Anne-Marie Slaughter, 'A Typology of Transjudicial Communication' (1994) 29 *University of Richmond Law Review* 99, 134; Gary J Jacobsohn, *Apple of Gold: Constitutionalism in Israel and the United States* (Princeton University Press 1995); Örücü (n 79) 10; McCrudden, 'A Common Law of Human Rights?' (n 80) 518.

[82] McCrudden, 'Human Rights and Judicial Use' (n 80) 10; McCrudden, 'A Common Law of Human Rights' (n 80) 518.

[83] Harold Cooke Gutteridge, *Comparative Law: An Introduction to the Comparative Method of Legal Study and Research* (Cambridge University Press, 1949) 40.

[84] Stanton (n 8) 273: 'although comments will be made on the kind of use to which comparative materials were put in the cases surveyed, no attempt will be made to quantify the different kinds of use'.

[85] Epstein and Martin (n 13).

[86] ibid 113 ff.

[87] ibid 113.

'cleaning' the dataset.[88] The simplest example might be using Excel sums to count the number of populated cells (=COUNTA) in respect of judicial contributions (having recorded a bench of 3, 5, 7, 9 or 11 Supreme Court Justices, this check could provide a quick assurance that the record of contributions in a given case matched the size of the bench). The more complex reliability exercises led me to compare samples with relevant results presented by other researchers. This also provided a certain level of reassurance in respect of the coding described above. Where comparable results were not available, I drew random samples from the dataset and, where I felt the risks were greatest, I repeated the data collection entirely. The result is confidence in the dataset, but the lessons learned from these exercises will not be forgotten. Epstein and Martin's confession struck a chord: 'we've both wasted many hours not following this guidance, and now do so religiously'.[89]

II. INTERVIEWS

Interview subjects were selected by a non-probability method, sometimes called 'purposive' or 'judgemental' sampling: it was always clear that questions about judicial reasoning at the UK Supreme Court would be best answered by the Justices of that court.[90] Difficulty with access to interviewees would have required a significant revision to the central research question, but the problem did not materialise; almost all interview requests were granted. This result was surprising, given the problems reported by many researchers seeking to interview elites, including the most senior judges.[91] For example, the author of one of the most recent studies has written:

> Problems start already at the level of identifying judges to interview: it was largely only those judges who themselves tend to be in favour of 'the foreign' and

[88] ibid 114, quoting Allen Rubin and Earl Babbie, *Research Methods for Social Work* (Brooks/Cole, 2011) 508: '"dirty" data will almost always produce misleading research findings'.

[89] Epstein and Martin (n 13) 115–16.

[90] See, eg, Bruce L Berg, *Qualitative Research Methods for the Social Sciences* (Pearson, 2007) 44; Frank E Hagan, *Research Methods in Criminal Justice and Criminology* (Allyn & Bacon, 2006). Feeling interviews to be impractical in the context of their study, Flanagan and Ahern opted for a system of questionnaires and electronic submission: Brian Flanagan and Sinead Ahern, 'Judicial Decision-Making and Transnational Law: A Survey of Common Law Supreme Court Judges' (2011) 60 *International and Comparative Law Quarterly* 1, 9. Interviews were feasible for this study and provided a distinct advantage: the possibility to follow up on interesting leads or to develop discussion in a way that is not possible in an electronic questionnaire. The point is also recognised by Elaine Mak, *Judicial Decision-Making in a Globalised World: A Comparative Analysis of the Changing Practices of Western Highest Courts* (Hart Publishing, 2013) 66.

[91] See, eg, Burton (n 4) 59: 'Organisations, such as the police and courts, are often deluged with research requests and those in authority may be reluctant to grant permission for their staff to devote time to what they see as unproductive academic research activities.'

> 'the international' that would typically consent to an interview on the subject. Those who do not care or are even mentally hostile to anything foreign are not inclined to share their views with a foreign researcher coming to talk to them about precisely that subject. Moreover, as Continental supreme jurisdictions are larger institutions, only several judges can in fact be interviewed, typically precisely those interested. Both of these factors generate a rather non-representative sample.[92]

Problems of this kind did not arise. There was never any expression of hostility towards the subject and the smaller number of Justices at the UK Supreme Court (compared to other continental courts) made it possible to ensure a representative sample. In the UK context at least, it is possible that the general willingness to be interviewed may reflect an increasing willingness on the part of judges to consider engagement with academics as a part of their judicial role.[93] Darbyshire reached similar conclusions from her experience of studying judges: 'Baby boomer judges seem to understand social research and academic freedom and most trust academics not to behave like journalists'.[94] Greater interaction with academics is also obvious from the judgments. It is no longer uncommon for judges to refer to academic work in judgments—a significant contrast to a time when academics were cited only once deceased.[95]

A. Primary Subjects

The primary subjects were the senior judiciary who were active between 2011 and 2012. Interviews with the judges were sought by letter and conducted in two rounds. The first-round letters were sent in August 2011 and the corresponding interviews took place between October and December of the same year. In total, 10 Justices of the Supreme Court and one Lady Justice of Appeal were interviewed. The decision to interview a single Court of Appeal judge was made early in the research period, when it was thought that more Court of Appeal judges may be interviewed as part of a broader study. Although the parameters were later revised to include only the use of foreign jurisprudence at the UK Supreme Court, it was felt that the evidence obtained through the interview with Lady Justice Arden was nevertheless helpful to retain on the basis that it provided a useful perspective from outside the Supreme Court.

[92] Bobek (n 7) 71. Mak reported a similar experience: Mak (n 90) 63.

[93] See, eg, Paterson (n 14) 5: 'My experience of elite "off the record" interviews both 40 years ago and now attests to the levels of trust that many interviewees are prepared to repose in an academic researcher that they may hardly know.'

[94] Penny Darbyshire, *Sitting in Judgment: The Working Lives of Judges* (Hart Publishing, 2011) 7.

[95] The point was also recognised by Bobek (n 7) 87–88.

The interviewees in round one were Baroness Hale of Richmond, Lord Phillips of Worth Matravers (then President of the Supreme Court), Lord Mance and Lady Justice Arden. The second-round letters were sent in March 2012, with the corresponding interviews taking place between April and July of the same year. The interviewees in the second round were Lord Dyson, Lord Reed, Lord Kerr of Tonaghmore, Lord Clarke of Stone-cum-Ebony, Lord Walker of Gestingthorpe, Lord Collins of Mapesbury and Lord Sumption. Requests were made for just 30 minutes, but the majority of the interviewees extended this time and provided useful information or thoughtful suggestions on developing the study. All interviews took place in the judicial offices of the relevant court. The interview design is detailed in Appendix 2.

Perhaps the most interesting findings related to the working practices of the judges—a subject that the judges generally considered to be obvious or uninteresting. Surprise was expressed, for example, when a question was posed about the use of the judicial assistants or about their own methods for finding sources of law. In fact, insight into the way that judges go about judging has inspired such a volume of scholarship that it might be categorised as a sub-discipline in itself.[96]

B. Questions

While necessary to retain structure and continuity in the questions for purposes of data analysis, the exploratory nature of the research required a broad scope for answers and it was important that the interviewees could fully explore these with minimal interruption or guidance. For these reasons, some questions were common to all interviews, while other questions varied according to the interview and the relevant experience or interest that the interviewee was able to offer. For example, judges who were already known to make liberal use of foreign jurisprudence were asked more probing questions about the reasons for those uses and their guiding motivations.

This aspect of the research has much in common with Mak's approach. Mak conducted interviews with judges from the UK Supreme Court and the Supreme Court of the Netherlands.[97] Mak's interviews were conducted prior to the interviews in this study, but the results were published after.[98]

[96] See, eg, Alan Paterson, *The Law Lords* (Macmillan, 1982); Blom-Cooper and Drewry (n 23); Darbyshire (n 94); Paterson (n 14).

[97] Mak conducted interviews with seven Justices of the UK Supreme Court and one retired Law Lord (as well as some judges at the Supreme Court of the Netherlands): Mak (n 90).

[98] Mak explains that the UK Supreme Court Justices were interviewed in November 2009; the first round of interviews conducted for the purposes of this research was October–November 2010.

For that reason, it was not possible to reflect and develop upon Mak's interview results ahead of the interviews conducted for this book.

In all cases, a 'semi-standardised' or 'guided semi-structured' method of interviewing was applied.[99] In other words, the questions posed to each interviewee were the same mixture of open questions, but the interviewees were able to develop certain points above others where it was felt more relevant to do so. It was crucial to the research aims that the judges were given the opportunity to expand on an answer or to volunteer further information. In those circumstances, time was given to following any interesting leads insofar that this did not detract from the consistency of the interviews or from an otherwise important point of discussion. This flexibility was necessary in order to ensure that the interviews were not self-fulfilling and to allow for the consideration of matters that may not otherwise have been raised. As one methodologist has described, the essence of the qualitative interview is the elicitation of stories:

> When people are least interrupted, when they can tell their stories in their own way ... they can react naturally and freely and express themselves fully ... [Interruptions and leading questions are likely to have the effect that] ... the adventure into the unknown, into unchartered and hitherto undisclosed spheres, has been destroyed.[100]

The interviews were therefore conducted in the spirit of conversation.[101] Where less was known about the particular area concerned, it was interesting to enable the judges to talk for longer, to give their views more fully and to hear the variety of ideas and feelings.[102]

Yet, it is also worth noting that these situations were not always intentional. As is common with elite interviews, there was a general tendency among the judges to steer the focus of the interview towards topics that they felt comfortable discussing. Such answers, however, are difficult to quantify and require strict attention to the precise language and comments given. The obvious limitation is that this kind of material restricts analysis to reporting the answers in their diversity, leading to anecdotal evidence or the 'cherry picking' of particular comments to fit a purpose. For that reason, careful

[99] The alternatives are given as either a 'standardised' or 'unstandardised' (or in words to similar effect). In contrast to the semi-standardised, these require a rigid schedule of predetermined questions or an open schedule, with questions located on the imaginary continuum: Berg (n 90) 92–95. Mak took the same approach in her interviews: Mak (n 90) 64.

[100] Pauline Young, quoted in Carol AB Warren and Tracy X Karner, *Discovering Qualitative Methods* (Roxbury, 2005) 12, citing Jennifer Platt, 'The History of the Interview' in Jaber D Gubrium and James A Holstein (eds), *Handbook of Interview Research* (Sage, 2002) 37.

[101] Sharyn Roach Anleu and Kathy Mack, *Performing Judicial Authority in the Lower Courts* (Palgrave Macmillan, 2017) 193. On interviews generally, see William S Harvey, 'Strategies for Conducting Elite Interviews' (2011) 11(4) *Qualitative Research* 431; Norman K Denzin and Yvonna S Lincoln, *The Sage Handbook of Qualitative Research*, 5th edn (Sage, 2018).

[102] The interview design is given in Appendix 2.

consideration was given to whether insight was valued above comparable data, and open questions were preferred to closed questions only where the balance fell with the former. Some attempt to focus the interview discussion was made by defining the topics (as given within the 'research parameters' discussed above) at the start of each interview. While these were primarily set out to ensure a common understanding of the terms and to enhance the comparability of answers, this technique also provided a useful way to communicate the research aims and develop a rapport with the interviewee, reducing the need for 'throwaway questions' or other such devices often suggested for those purposes.[103]

Despite the potential for disparity between interviews, the interviewees covered a number of common themes. These themes were usually a product of question design (drawing from questions common to all interviews) and where this was the case, it is interesting to compare and contrast the responses given by each of the judges. However, there are some surprising variations and some common themes were raised independently or as a corollary to the standard questions. For example, almost all of the judges interviewed raised the 'linguistic barrier' as part of their explanation about the limited use of jurisprudence outside the traditional common law countries.[104] Judges who did not raise the matter of their own accord were asked about this factor. Interestingly, those who raised the matter independently raised the linguistic barrier issue partly in response to a question regarding the overt reliance on the jurisprudence of Commonwealth jurisdictions. Of the judges who were prompted to consider the possible effect of a linguistic barrier on the use of foreign jurisprudence, most were dismissive about its relevance. A number of judges expressed the feeling that language would not be a problem and usually gave examples of competency in other languages.

Finally, an ethical issue arose as to the use of the interview evidence. It was not at first clear whether it would be appropriate to refer to each judge by name when using interview evidence in the analysis. It was concluded that the value to be drawn from comparing the interview findings with the case analysis would make it impossible to retain full anonymity.[105] Each interviewee was therefore offered a right of refusal over the recorded material and, to preserve that discretion, the full interview transcripts are not included. As Paterson found, the confidential atmosphere of each interview 'undoubtedly led to very candid discussions'.[106]

[103] See, eg, Berg (n 90) 101.

[104] The 'linguistic barrier' refers simply to the use of foreign jurisprudence precluded by unfamiliarity with the published language.

[105] This is in contrast to the approach taken by Mak. Mak does not name her interview subjects and offered this as a guarantee in her initial communication with the judges: Mak (n 90) 8.

[106] Paterson (n 14) 6.

Nevertheless, in common with Paterson's experience, the interviewees were very generous, and it was rare that discussions were indicated to be 'off limits'. Any requested revisions to the recorded discussion were minor.

C. Secondary Subjects

An important research aim was to expose the practical side of using foreign jurisprudence. Questions about the research behind the citations led to questions about those persons, other than the judges, who contribute to the research process. At the time, little information was available on those who support judicial work and it became clear that speaking with the judicial assistants (JAs) might provide the desired insight.[107] They are therefore the secondary subjects.

JAs support the work of judges by sourcing material, preparing briefs or undertaking specific items of research. Supreme Court JAs are usually appointed for one year, but some are in post for just one or two terms and, although very rarely, a JA may be in post permanently. Only one of the JA posts in the UK Supreme Court is filled permanently.[108] The positions are usually filled by early career solicitors or barristers, having completed—or being near the completion of—their training contracts or pupillages. Aside from some common duties, such as summarising the applications for permission to appeal into petition memos and the writing of press summaries, the work of JAs can vary significantly according to the judge by whom they are instructed.[109]

The individuals in post at any one time are not publicly listed. Contact was made with the assistance of the Supreme Court judges and their personal assistants. The meeting was agreed with the permission of Lord Kerr (as the Justice with overall responsibility for the JAs at the time) and arranged by email. Seven JAs were present at the meeting, which was conducted as a focus group. The focus group dynamic was not a conscious research choice, but was simply a product of the terms under which it was agreed that I could speak to the JAs.[110] Thus, the focus group took place in the JAs' open-plan offices at the UK Supreme Court in July 2012. All seven JAs were in post at the time of the focus group, although six were coming to the end of their annual contracts.

[107] Later publications shed more light on the work of the Supreme Court judicial assistants: Tetyana Nesterchuk, 'The View from Behind the Bench' in Andrew Burrows, David Johnston and Reinhard Zimmermann (eds), *Judge and Jurist: Essays in Memory of Lord Rodger of Earlsferry* (Oxford University Press, 2013); Paterson (n 14).

[108] The judicial assistant to Lord Phillips of Worth Matravers (and, at the time of writing, to Baroness Hale), Penelope Gorman, had progressed with Lord Phillips up from the Court of Appeal. See further Nesterchuk (n 107) 101.

[109] ibid 104.

[110] The consequences of this dynamic are explored further below.

D. The Reliability of Interview Evidence

The duration of each interview varied from 28 minutes to 64 minutes. It is evidently harder to cover any subject comprehensively in 28 minutes than is possible in 64 minutes. This is coupled with the general tendency of interviewees to maintain focus on what most interests them. When combined, these factors explain the different level of depth and consideration given to some of the subjects raised. It also explains the lack of any interview evidence on certain points from particular judges.

In all but two cases, the reliability of interview data was greatly increased by the use of a digital recording device.[111] Best efforts were made when transcribing the interviews; it is generally considered good practice to capture interviewees' comments as completely and accurately as possible.[112] In the majority of the interviews, recording devices made redundant the debate about memory aids and transcriptions before the interview has 'gone cold', although there remain important considerations about preserving the accuracy of mood and tone apart from the language itself. Mischler notes that an interview is a speech event as well as a special type of social interaction, requiring the contextual entirety of the dialogue to be recorded.[113] Thus, research methodologists generally agree that the interviewer's own questions, prompts and probes should be included and, accordingly, the transcripts reflect these fully. Transcriptions were not outsourced.[114] No more than one week was allowed to pass before each interview was fully transcribed.[115] In the two cases in which a recording device was not permitted, the interview was written up immediately after the event.

The nature of the focus group interview with the JAs posed some difficulties, which were not encountered during the transcription of the judicial interviews. The number of responses and the effect of differing distances from the recording unit led to the loss of some material. To some extent, it was possible to resolve these problems by reference to notes taken during the interview, but it is nevertheless acknowledged that minor errors or omissions were inevitable. These practical complications are additional to those fed by the nature of the focus group, as opposed to the one-to-one interviews conducted with the judges. While the focus group dynamic has the

[111] This is another contrast to Mak's experience. Mak explains that she did not use a recording device, but relied on writing up notes on the day of the interview: Mak (n 90) 64–65.

[112] Warren and Karner (n 100) 12; See also Platt (n 101) 37.

[113] Elliot G Mischler, *Research Interviewing: Context and Narrative* (Harvard University Press, 1986), cited by Warren and Karner (n 100) 152–53.

[114] Methodologists warn that transcriptions through 'hired hands', who may not have the benefit of memories of the interview, can lead to unsatisfactory results. See, eg, Warren and Karner (n 100) 152.

[115] In the vast majority of cases, the transcriptions were completed within a day or two of the interview.

potential to stimulate new thinking about a subject, an obvious drawback is that participants may be less willing to give a view on sensitive topics.[116]

It is worth noting that other researchers have been sceptical about the reliability of interview evidence as a foundation for data analysis generally. For example, Flanagan and Ahern point out that some commentators have questioned the validity of what is termed 'judicial self-reporting'.[117] They cite Epstein and King's cynicism:

> [A]sking someone to identify his or her motive is one of the worst methods of measuring motive. People often do not know, or cannot articulate, why they act as they do. In other situations, they refuse to tell, and in still others, they are strategic both in acting and in answering the scholar's question. This is obvious from the example of asking justices about how they reach decisions.[118]

The related risk is that self-selection bias might play a role in determining the subjects of any interview study. Flanagan and Ahern explain:

> [T]here may be a self-selection bias at work due to a judge's personal attitudes toward comparison. In principle, such an effect might cancel itself out, with those anxious to present favourable and unfavourable points of view experiencing an equal marginal inclination to respond. As it was voiced to the authors, however, the concern is that the effect would predominately work to attract responses from those favourable to comparison.[119]

Yet, as Flanagan and Ahern point out, 'as a method of investigating judicial decision-making, asking those with actual experience thereof offers unique advantages'.[120] Since it was possible to interview most of the Supreme Court Justices active during the time period for this study, it is hoped that the danger of 'self-selection bias' has been avoided.[121]

A final but important point is related to the extent to which it is possible to rely on responses that are subject to human fallibility. As Paterson found, 'very few Law Lords or Justices have a very accurate picture of decision-making data'.[122] Paterson's examples include:

> [T]he frequency with which they are on the winning or losing side where the court is sharply divided, their agreement rates with other judges, the proportion of judgments that are single, majority judgments, or whether their share of the lead judgment allocations is above or below the average for the Court.

116 See, eg, Richard A Krueger, *Focus Groups: A Practical Guide for Applied Research* (Sage, 2009).

117 Flanagan and Ahern (n 90) 8.

118 Lee Epstein and Gary King, 'The Rules of Inference' (2002) 69 *University of Chicago Law Review* 1, 93.

119 Flanagan and Ahern (n 90) 1.

120 ibid.

121 ibid 12.

122 Paterson (n 14) 8.

Paterson continues that 'even more intuitive statistics', including 'dissent rates, the average time taken between the hearing and judgment being handed down, and the average success rate for permission to appeal petitions or for full appeals, are matters where the Law Lords and Justices' "guestimates" may be considerably off the mark'.[123] Similar findings were made during the interviews conducted for this study. A number of the Justices interviewed were unable to make accurate guesses about the frequency with which foreign jurisprudence was cited at the Supreme Court. It should also be borne in mind that two of the Justices interviewed—Lord Sumption and Lord Reed—had only been in post for a short time.[124] It is for these reasons that the quantitative data is important. The interview evidence could be balanced against the evidence obtained through the empirical analysis, as well as providing insight beyond it. The final analysis reflects a 'spiralling' rather than 'linear' progression through the research.[125]

[123] ibid.

[124] Lord Sumption was sworn in on 1 January 2012 and was interviewed on 22 May 2012. Lord Reed was sworn in on 6 February 2012 and was interviewed on 8 May 2012.

[125] For further discussion of research methodology: Chava Frankfort Nachmias and David Nachmias, *Research Methods for the Social Sciences: Practice and Applications* (St Martin's Press, 1992); Berg (n 90) 23; Karl R Popper, *Conjectures and Refutations: The Growth of Scientific Knowledge* (Harper & Row, 1968); Barney Glaser and Anselm Strauss, *The Discovery of Grounded Theory: Strategies for Qualitative Research* (Cambridge University Press, 1987).

3

Legitimacy and Authority

THERE ARE NO rules governing the influence of foreign jurisprudence in UK human rights cases. Decisions of foreign courts are not authoritative in the precedential sense; UK courts are under no duty or obligation to follow the decisions of a foreign court.[1] In fact, there is no guidance on using foreign jurisprudence at all. The UK has no provision similar to section 39(1) of the South African Constitution, which provides that the Constitutional Court must consider international law and may consider foreign law. Indeed, as Cram has pointed out, the South African provision for consideration of foreign jurisprudence is 'the exception rather than the rule'.[2] Cram continued:

> More commonly, the citing of foreign norms is largely unregulated by constitutions, leaving the judges to exercise their discretion as to whether, and in which circumstances, the practice is appropriate.[3]

Some limited guidance is given to advocates by the Practice Direction on the Citation of Authorities, which both welcomes the use of foreign jurisprudence and also cautions against the overuse of those sources. Section 9.1 reads as follows:

> Cases decided in other jurisdictions can, if properly used, be a valuable source of law in this jurisdiction. At the same time, however, such authority should not be cited without proper consideration of whether it does indeed add to the existing body of law.[4]

Advocates are therefore directed to resist citation to foreign jurisprudence if unnecessary. Section 9.2 provides that any advocate who seeks to cite an authority from another jurisdiction must:

> ii. indicate in respect of each authority what that authority adds that is not to be found in authority in this jurisdiction; or, if there is said to be justification for adding to domestic authority, what that justification is;

[1] Recall that 'foreign jurisprudence' in this book refers to the domestic jurisprudence of foreign courts. It does not include within its scope the decisions of supranational courts such as the European Court of Human Rights in Strasbourg (the jurisprudence which UK domestic courts are obliged to 'take into account' per s 2 of the HRA 1998).

[2] Ian Cram, 'Resort to Foreign Constitutional Norms in Domestic Human Rights Jurisprudence with Reference to Terrorism Cases' [2009] *CLJ* 118, 119.

[3] ibid 118.

[4] Section 9.1 of *Practice Direction (Citation of Authorities)* [2001] 1 WLR 1001; [2001] 2 All ER 510.

iii. certify that there is no authority in this jurisdiction that precludes the acceptance by the court of the proposition that the foreign authority is said to establish.[5]

This guidance does not extend to the judiciary. There are no rules specifying the way that judges use foreign jurisprudence. In the absence of any guiding principles, the authority of foreign jurisprudence is merely persuasive. The most that could be claimed is that the lack of any limitation or prohibition on references to foreign jurisprudence might indicate 'a possible acquiescence on the part of the legislature'.[6] UK judges have not suggested a greater role for foreign jurisprudence. Lord Mance made clear his view that domestic courts could derive assistance from foreign jurisprudence in much the same way that they could derive assistance from any other non-binding authority:

> When judges look to comparative and international material, they may do so for information, inspiration, or confirmation, just as they use domestic decisions that are not binding on them. ... What Ronald Dworkin calls a 'relaxed doctrine of precedent' may embrace the past decisions not only of courts above him or at the same level in his jurisdiction but of courts in other states or countries.[7]

However, to say that foreign jurisprudence is merely 'persuasive' is to ignore the possibility that some sources may (legitimately or not) be more persuasive than others. For many, persuasive authority is a nebulous concept, 'well-known but imprecise',[8] about which we are 'still in the dark'.[9]

I. PERSUASIVE AUTHORITY

As a starting point, it is usually agreed that persuasive authority sits in direct contrast to binding or precedential authority. Whereas a court must follow or give reasons for departing from otherwise binding authority,[10] a court is neither obliged to follow nor to give reasons for departing from persuasive authority. Indeed, for Schwartz, it is the 'touchstone' of persuasive authority

[5] ibid s 9.2.

[6] Cram (n 2) 125.

[7] Lord Mance, 'Foreign Laws and Languages' in Andrew Burrows, David Johnston and Reinhard Zimmermann (eds), *Judge and Jurist: Essays in Memory of Lord Rodger of Earlsferry* (Oxford University Press, 2013) 87–88 citing Ronald Dworkin, *Law's Empire* (Hart Publishing, 1986) 25.

[8] Patrick H Glenn, 'Persuasive Authority' (1987) 32(2) *McGill Law Journal* 261, 264.

[9] Chris Flanders, 'Towards a Theory of Persuasive Authority' (2009) 62 *Oklahoma Law Review* 55, 57.

[10] The Supreme Court may depart from its own previous decisions (or those of its predecessor, the Appellate Committee of the House of Lords): *Practice Statement (Judicial Precedent)* [1966] 3 All ER 77; [1966] 1 WLR 1234.

that a court is not 'required to follow [its] result or reasoning'.[11] Schauer agrees: 'the distinction between [persuasive and binding authority] hinges on whether the decision maker has a choice to use the authority'.[12] If persuasive authority is not mandatory, it must essentially be optional.[13] But it is difficult to reconcile 'optional' with 'authoritative'. 'Authoritative' can be defined as 'proceeding from an official source and requiring compliance or obedience'.[14] Schauer has asked whether there is 'anything at all authoritative about an optional authority whose use is solely at the discretion of the judge?'[15] Flanders suggests that it may be 'puzzling to speak of persuasive *authority*' in the first place: 'Why not simply persuasive *sources*?'[16] Duxbury adds that 'a remark made obiter by a judge, say, or a work by a legal academic, is not a persuasive authority if we understand an authority to provide a reason for action which excludes a person's own reasoning regarding how to act in a particular situation'. [17]

The answer must be that something manifests as an 'authority' if a judge uses it as such. In the most straightforward sense, drawing from another argument in support of one's own is an appeal to authority. Law is a practice based on authority,[18] the appeal to which is signalled by citation:[19]

> [A] legal argument is often understood to be a better legal argument just because someone has made it before, and a legal conclusion is typically taken to be a better one if another court either reached it or credited it on an earlier occasion.[20]

A source therefore manifests itself as authority if it is followed or distinguished and—crucially—cited. Persuasive authority is 'authority' which attracts (rather than demands) adherence.[21] Schauer's conclusion, however,

[11] Timothy Schwartz, 'Cases Time Forgot: Why Judges Can Sometimes Ignore Controlling Precedent' (2007) 56 *Emory Law Journal* 1475, 1479.

[12] Frederick Schauer, 'Authority and Authorities' (2008) 94 *Virginia Law Review* 1931, 1945–46; Michael Bobek, *Comparative Reasoning in European Supreme Courts* (Oxford University Press, 2013) 33.

[13] Schauer (n 12) 1947.

[14] *Oxford Dictionaries*, www.oxforddictionaries.com/definition/english/authoritative. Other well-known writers have described authority in similar terms. See, eg, John Lucas, *The Principles of Politics* (Clarendon Press, 1966) 16: 'A man, or body of men, has authority if it follows from his saying "Let X happen", that X ought to happen', cited in Joseph Raz, *The Authority of Law: Essays on Law and Morality* (Oxford University Press, 1979).

[15] Schauer (n 12) 1947.

[16] Flanders (n 9) 66.

[17] Neil Duxbury, 'The Law of the Land' (2015) 78(1) *MLR* 26, 29.

[18] See, eg, Herbert LA Hart, 'Commands and Authoritative Legal Reasons' in *Essays on Bentham: Studies in Jurisprudence and Political Theory* (Clarendon Press, 1982) 243, 261–66; Frederick Schauer, 'The Questions of Authority' (1992) 81 *Georgetown Law Journal* 95, 95–96; Schauer (n 12) 1935.

[19] Schauer (n 12) 1934–35: 'Rather than being little more than the characteristic form of legal jargon, the law's practice of using and announcing its authorities—its citation practice—is part and parcel of law's character.' See generally Raz (n 14).

[20] Schauer (n 12) 1950.

[21] Glenn (n 8) 263.

was that 'persuasion is rarely part of the equation when persuasive authorities are being used'.[22] The problem is one of semantics:

> [B]eing persuaded is fundamentally different from doing, believing, or deciding something because of the prescriptions or conclusions of an authority. But if this is so, then the very idea of a persuasive authority is self-contradictory, for persuasion and authority are inherently opposed notions … The use of a source can be one or the other—it can be persuasive or it can be authoritative—but it cannot be both at the same time.[23]

It is the 'persuasive' element that is misleading. The problem for Schauer is that, on his analysis, a judge who draws from persuasive authority is learning from that source rather than taking it as authoritative. In that sense, he says, it is treated no differently in the decision-making process compared to the treatment of a persuasive argument from any source at all. But it is surely not the same thing for a judge to be persuaded by an argument 'heard from her brother-in-law or in the hardware store'[24] as it is for a judge to be persuaded by, say, the argument of a subject expert or the reasoning of a learned judge in a similar case before another court. Even if a judge is merely 'learning' from persuasive authority, it is clear that some sources are better suited to the job than others. To some extent, this is evidenced by explanations for citations from a small family of courts. Lord Phillips, for example, explained that 'some of the Canadian judgments are most impressive and can be very powerful support indeed for a judgment',[25] while Lord Sumption added that 'the quality and compelling character of the judgments can be very persuasive'.[26] Lord Dyson has used the same language: 'Sometimes, however, the passage [from a textbook or foreign case] sets out reasoning which the judge considers to be so compelling that he or she simply adopts it'.[27] Lord Reed recently stated that he 'always take[s] a particular interest in Australian case law and academic writing, because of their high quality' and that he is 'also a great admirer of the Canadian Supreme Court,

[22] Schauer (n 12) 1944–45.

[23] ibid 1944. Moreover, Schauer's conclusion is that 'persuasion is rarely part of the equation when persuasive authorities are being used' (at 1944–45).

[24] ibid 1943.

[25] Interview with the Rt Hon Lord Phillips of Worth Matravers, former President of the UK Supreme Court (Supreme Court, London, 23 November 2011).

[26] Interview with the Rt Hon Lord Sumption, Justice of the UK Supreme Court (Supreme Court, London, 28 May 2012). In *Patel v Mirza*, Lord Mance emphasised the 'great clarity' of McLachlin J (as she then was) in a judgment of the Canadian Supreme Court, drawing 'valuable insights' from that case. See *Patel v Mirza* [2016] UKSC 42; [2017] AC 467 [190]–[191]. In *Kennedy v Cordia (Services) LLP* [2016] UKSC 6; [2016] 1 WLR 597 [48], Lord Reed and Lord Hodge (in a joint judgment) felt that a judge of the South African Supreme Court had 'stated the matter well'.

[27] Lord Dyson, 'The Globalisation of Law', Pilgrim Fathers Lecture 2015 (Plymouth University, 6 November 2015), www.judiciary.gov.uk/wp-content/uploads/2015/11/pilgrim-fathers-lecture.pdf, 12; Lord Dyson, *Justice: Continuity and Change* (Hart Publishing, 2018) 161.

which tends to produce particularly stimulating judgments'.[28] In *SerVaas Inc v Rafidian Bank*, Lord Clarke referred to decisions from the US Court of Appeals Ninth Circuit as 'strong persuasive authority',[29] while Lord Rodger felt a decision of the High Court of Australia to be 'powerful authority' in *HJ (Iran) v Secretary of State for the Home Department*.[30]

The reasoning of a learned judge in a similar case, considering similar problems in a similar court, will be more persuasive and carry more authority than the arbitrary reasoning of friends, family, strangers[31] and academics.[32] The judgments of foreign courts can be valuable as '*tested* secondary sources';[33] 'it is generally more sensible, all things being equal, to take account of opinions which have had real-world consequences and which other judges have treated as legally sound'.[34] 'It is the participants, not the commentators, that one is likely to seek out if one wants advice on how to go about doing the job … foreign judges, though trading in other markets, are in the same business'.[35] Lady Justice Arden agreed:

> There is a big difference between a judgment and an article, which is not related to any specific case, because the point about a decision is that it has been used to alter people's rights and therefore it has had a considerable effect. It has been tested in the fire of actual practical use.[36]

As Justice Breyer put it, the 'experience [of foreign systems] may … cast an empirical light on the consequences of different solutions to a common problem'.[37]

A further manifestation of the importance attached to the nature of the source is the distinction between ratio decidendi and obiter dicta. While it is only the ratio of binding precedent that must be followed, obiter dicta (statements that do not go to the principle upon which a case is decided) have frequently been treated as more than merely persuasive authority by courts. In some well-known cases, obiter dicta were so persuasive as effectively to bind future courts. A good example is the development of the doctrine

[28] Lord Reed, 'Comparative Law in the Supreme Court of the United Kingdom', lecture at the Centre for Private Law, University of Edinburgh (13 October 2017), www.supremecourt.uk/docs/speech-171013.pdf.

[29] *SerVaas Incorporated v Rafidian Bank and Others* [2012] UKSC 40; [2013] 1 AC 593 [28] (Lord Clarke).

[30] *HJ (Iran) v Secretary of State for the Home Department; HT (Cameroon) v Secretary of State for the Home Department* [2010] UKSC 31; [2011] 1 AC 596.

[31] Schauer (n 12) 1943.

[32] ibid.

[33] Duxbury (n 17) 33.

[34] ibid.

[35] ibid 53–54.

[36] Interview with the Rt Hon Lady Justice Arden, Lord Justice of Appeal (Royal Courts of Justice, London, 7 December 2011).

[37] *Printz v US* (1997) 521 US 898, 977.

of promissory estoppel in *Central London Property Trust v High Trees House*.[38] As is well known, the case centred on the lease of a block of flats in London. In 1940, given the reduced occupancy rates at the outbreak of war, the landlord agreed to reduce the rental rate by half but did not specify the period for which this would apply. By 1945, the flats were at full occupancy and the landlord sued for the full rental rate. Denning J upheld the claim that the full rate was payable from the moment of full occupancy. However, he elaborated that a claim for the full rate from 1940 onwards would have been unsuccessful, since it would be inequitable for the landlord to resile from a representation on which the tenants had relied. This elaboration was made in an obiter statement but was subsequently followed in a number of cases which continued to develop the doctrine of promissory estoppel in English contract law.[39] A further example along these lines might be the obiter statement in *Hedley Byrne v Heller* that a duty of care could arise with respect to a negligent misstatement, giving rise to pure economic loss.[40] The statement was relied upon in a number of later cases despite not being strictly binding.[41] Dissenting judgments, too, can be a source of persuasion to a future court.[42] Lord Atkin's judgment in *Donoghue v Stevenson* drew upon Sir Balliol Brett MR's judgment in *Heaven v Pender*, which, while concurring in relation to the outcome, disagreed on the reasoning.[43] 'Today's dissent can often be tomorrow's authority'.[44]

In part, reliance on obiter dicta may be explained by the fact that the task of distinguishing the ratio of a case can be difficult.[45] This might be especially so where a case is comprised of multiple judgments.[46] Alternatively, the willingness to follow obiter dicta could be indicative of the greater persuasiveness of judicial pronouncements over other sources, such as academic

[38] *Central London Property Trust v High Trees House* [1947] KB 130.

[39] See, eg, *Combe v Combe* [1951] 2 KB 215; *Amalgamated Investment Co v Texas Bank* [1982] QB 84; *Collier v P & MJ Wright (Holdings) Ltd* [2007] EWCA Civ 1329; [2008] 1 WLR 643.

[40] *Hedley Byrne v Heller* [1964] AC 465.

[41] See, eg, *Esso Petroleum Co Ltd v Mardon* [1976] QB 801.

[42] On dissenting judgments generally, see John Alder, 'Dissents in Courts of Last Resort: Tragic Choices' (2000) 20 *OJLS* 221; Lord Kerr, 'Dissenting Judgments—Self-Indulgence or Self Sacrifice?', The Birkenhead Lecture (London, 8 October 2012), www.supremecourt.uk/docs/speech-121008.pdf; Alan Paterson, *Final Judgment: The Last Law Lords and the Supreme Court* (Hart Publishing, 2013) 110 ff.

[43] *Heaven v Pender* (1883) LR 11 QBD 503, 509; *M'Alister (Donoghue) v Stevenson* [1932] AC 562; cited in Lord Neuberger, 'No Judgment—No Justice', First Annual BAILII Lecture (London, 20 November 2012) [23].

[44] ibid.

[45] As one introductory text points out, 'judges do not actually separate their judgments into these two clearly defined categories'. See Gary Slapper, *How the Law Works* (Routledge, 2011) 87–88.

[46] See, eg, *Doherty v Birmingham City Council* [2006] EWCA Civ 1739; [2007] HLR 32, in which the Court of Appeal struggled to find a clear account of the majority ratio in the House of Lords decision in *Kay v Lambeth Borough Council* [2006] UKHL 10. Similar difficulties arose for the Court of Appeal when deciding *Secretary of State for the Home Department v AF and Others* [2008] EWCA Civ 1148; [2009] 2 WLR 423. See further Paterson (n 42) 210–11.

literature. This would also explain the greater persuasiveness of some Privy Council decisions.[47]

The idea that the source of a given statement could have a bearing on its authority sits in tension with the inclination amongst scholars to define persuasive authority as 'content-dependent'.[48] Since persuasive authority does not bind intrinsically, it is argued that 'the authority it holds flows from the persuasive content of the authority … [it] compels by what it says, not by what it is';[49] 'what carries weight is the reasoning, not the conclusion'.[50] Clearly, however, courts do consider the source of persuasive authority to be relevant to their analysis about the value of that authority. The well-known example about the reluctance of English courts to cite the academic work of living authors bears this out well.[51] It was evidently not the content of those sources that altered with death; it was the source itself and, presumably, the perceived authority of that source. Even when judges do cite the work of living academics, it is not always clear what the source of authority is. As Paterson wrote in his 1982 study of the Law Lords, it is unclear 'whether these academics influence the Law Lords by the authority of their reasoning or by reason of their authority'.[52]

But there is an important difference between the persuasiveness of, say, academic work and the persuasiveness of foreign jurisprudence. As Duxbury has explained, the jurisprudence of a foreign court 'can be simultaneously persuasive and authoritative: merely persuasive here, but an authority—a binding precedent—in the place from where it hails'.[53] The fact that foreign jurisprudence is an authority in one jurisdiction might even be a reason not to refer to it:

> [U]nlike other types of persuasive authority, [foreign precedents] do not have secondary status everywhere: somewhere, they bind. A judge might think that the best way to avoid blurring lines—to be sure that nobody can be under the

[47] In *Doughty Turner Manufacturing* [1964] 1 QB 518, the Court of Appeal felt that one of its own earlier decisions (*Re Polemis* [1921] 3 KB 560) could no longer be good law in light of the Privy Council decision in *Overseas Tankship (UK) Ltd v Morts Dock and Engineering Co Ltd ('The Wagon Mound')* [1961] UKPC 1. A rarer example of the weight attached to certain decisions of the Privy Council can be found in *R v James (Leslie)* [2006] EWCA Crim 14; [2006] QB 588, in which the Court of Appeal declined to follow a House of Lords decision in preference to the more recent Privy Council case. See further Richard Ward et al, *Walker & Walker's English Legal System* (Oxford University Press, 2011) 79.

[48] Vlad F Perju, 'The Puzzling Parameters of the Foreign Law Debate' (2007) 1 *Utah Law Review* 167, 179: 'The authority of a legal norm is content independent when it does not depend on that norm's background justification.'

[49] Flanders (n 9) 67; Schauer (n 12) 1935–1936.

[50] *Dingley v Chief Constable, Strathclyde Police* 1998 SC 548, 604 (Lord Prosser); cited in a different context in *Kennedy v Cordia* (n 26) [48].

[51] Frederick Schauer and Virginia J Wise, 'Legal Positivism as Legal Information' (1997) 82 *Cornell Law Review* 1080, 1088–89. This practice altered in 1945 when the House of Lords cited work by Arthur Goodhart; Alan Paterson, *The Law Lords* (Macmillan, 1982) 14–20.

[52] Paterson (n 51) 20.

[53] Duxbury (n 17) 30.

> misapprehension that another jurisdiction's precedent is binding here as well—is simply to refuse to consider (or at least to refuse to consider explicitly) the decisions of foreign courts.[54]

The importance attached to the source of the 'authority' is at the heart of the legitimacy debate. This is particularly clear from the US context. Posner explains:

> Problems arise only when the foreign decision is believed to have some (even if quite attenuated) persuasive force in an American court merely by virtue of being the decision of a recognized legal tribunal. This occurs, in short, when it is treated as an *authority*, albeit not a controlling one.[55]

In the UK, it is very clear that some sources are thought to be of greater relevance than others. This point was recognised by Bobek:

> Within the category of persuasiveness, the scale is a sliding one, depending on the case in question, its context, and its factual setting. Highly persuasive would typically be the judicial decisions from other common law jurisdictions, especially their highest courts. However, within the same category of persuasive precedent (albeit not with the same weight) also fall the decisions of any other courts in other jurisdictions, which might provide some inspiration or analogy in the case at hand, including decisions of Continental or other jurisdictions.[56]

The Court of Appeal, for example, has described decisions of the Privy Council as being of both 'strong' and 'high' persuasive authority,[57] while the Supreme Court has referred to decisions of the Grand Chamber of the Strasbourg Court as 'at least of the very highest persuasive authority'.[58] In *Cadder v HM Advocate*,[59] Lord Hope explained that 'the court is faced

[54] ibid.

[55] Richard Posner, 'No Thanks, We Already Have Our Own Laws' *Legal Affairs* (July/August 2004), www.legalaffairs.org/issues/July-August-2004/feature_posner_julaug04.msp.

[56] Bobek (n 12) 77.

[57] *Perrins v Holland and Others* [2010] EWCA Civ 840; [2011] Ch 270 [23]: 'the decision of the Privy Council in *Perera v Perera* [1901] AC 354 is strong persuasive authority for upholding the decision in *Parker v Felgate* (1883) 8 PD 171'; 'I doubt whether technically it is binding on this court, being contained in a decision of the Privy Council. None the less, it is of high persuasive authority' [49]. See also *R (HRH Sultan of Pahang) v Secretary of State for the Home Department* [2011] EWCA Civ 616 [35], in which the Court of Appeal sought to formally distinguish the Privy Council decision in *Liquidators of the Maritime Bank of Canada v Receiver-General of New Brunswick* [1892] AC 437, which was said to have been of 'high persuasive authority' and was followed by the Court of Appeal in *Mellenger v New Brunswick Development Corporation* [1971] 1 WLR 604.

[58] *HM Treasury v Mohammed Jabar Ahmed and Others (No 2) (FC)* [2010] UKSC 2; [2010] 2 AC 534, 596, referring to *Kadi v Council of the European Union (Joined Cases C-402/05P and C-415/05P)* [2009] AC 1225; Another example is *ANS and Another v ML (AP) (Scotland)* [2012] UKSC 30 [76]: 'variations are unsurprising bearing in mind that the judgments may be given by different chambers of the Strasbourg Court ... *Neulinger*, unlike the others, was a Grand Chamber decision and to that extent would normally be treated as having greater authority' (Lord Carnwath).

[59] *Cadder v Her Majesty's Advocate (Scotland)* [2010] UKSC 43; [2010] 1 WLR 2601.

with a unanimous decision of the Grand Chamber' and that 'this, in itself, is a formidable reason for thinking that we should follow it'.[60] Clearly, therefore, some persuasive authority is made more important by virtue of its 'pedigree'.[61] This is not surprising. In cases that engage provisions of international treaties, the decisions of associated supranational courts are of obvious relevance to a court attempting to reconcile international with domestic law. Similar cases would be those involving international conventions with no supranational court, where it surely makes sense to look for jurisprudence from other jurisdictions interpreting the same instrument. In these cases, a court may rely on the foreign jurisprudence in much the same way as domestic case law, seeking to identify the interpretation given to a particular clause in a similar vein to the identification of the core principle (or ratio) of a previous decision. However, a distinction between ratio and obiter is likely to be of less importance when referring to foreign jurisprudence in general, since the domestic court has no obligation to follow the foreign case in any event.

Judges may therefore refer to foreign jurisprudence simply because it is useful to do so. This is most evident in cases of interpretation since (to repeat an earlier conclusion) the reasoning of a learned judge in a similar case, considering similar problems in a similar court, will be of greater use than the jurisprudence of other courts dealing in different instruments. In fact, in such cases, the source (rather than the content) of the material is probably the very feature that renders it legitimate to use. This is relevant across most areas of law, but can be especially pertinent in human rights cases, where reconciling domestic and international law can require close scrutiny of persuasive sources. In this context, resort to foreign jurisprudence has the potential to pose 'awkward questions concerning judicial forays into the policy-making realm of the constitution and the erosion of parliamentary sovereignty'.[62]

II. THE INFLUENCE OF DOMESTIC v SUPRANATIONAL JURISPRUDENCE

In contrast to the lack of guidance about foreign jurisprudence, Parliament has legislated on the use of jurisprudence from some supranational courts. UK courts are obliged to follow supranational jurisprudence in some cases

[60] ibid [45]–[46] (Lord Hope). Where the Supreme Court has chosen not to follow a decision of the Grand Chamber, it has provided substantial justification. See, eg, *Posteh v Royal Borough of Kensington and Chelsea* [2017] UKSC 36; [2017] AC 624 [29]–[37].

[61] *cf* Flanders (n 9) 62, arguing that persuasive authority does not bind by virtue of its pedigree.

[62] Cram (n 2) 125.

or take them 'into account' in others.[63] The existence of such guidance has arguably increased the weight of those authorities as they are at least more persuasive than the decisions of foreign domestic courts. Indeed, many have recognised that the attention paid to the Strasbourg jurisprudence has often come close to the attention paid to binding authorities[64]—so close, in fact, that counsel have placed greater focus on the decisions of the Strasbourg Court in their arguments. As Baroness Hale put it:

> If you come and listen to a human rights case being argued in the Supreme Court, you will be struck by the amount of time counsel spend referring to and discussing the Strasbourg case law. They treat it as if it were the case law of our domestic courts.[65]

As Baroness Hale points out, this is strange because the 'Strasbourg case law is not like ours. It is not binding upon anyone, even upon them'.[66] The Strasbourg cases are therefore 'at best, an indication of the broad approach which Strasbourg will take to a particular problem'.[67]

The Strasbourg authority was never intended to be anything more than strictly persuasive authority. The words 'must take into account' were heavily debated during the legislative stages of the HRA 1998 and replacements like 'must follow' or 'shall be bound by' were rejected for precisely the reason that

> the word 'binding' is the language of precedent … [Strasbourg decisions] are a source of jurisprudence indeed, but not binding precedents which we necessarily should follow or even necessarily desire to follow.[68]

In the House of Lords debates, Lord Browne-Wilkinson concluded that 'the doctrine of stare decisis … does not find much favour north of the Border, finds no favour across the Channel and is an indigenous growth of dubious

[63] See, eg, Section 3 ECA 1972 which has the effect of binding UK courts to case law of the CJEU. Section 2 HRA 1998 does not bind domestic courts to the jurisprudence of the ECtHR, but at least obliges them to 'take into account' its decisions.

[64] See, eg, Helen Fenwick, *Civil Liberties and Human Rights* (Cavendish Publishing, 2007) 193: 'the obligation under s.2 as interpreted … comes close to affording binding force to the jurisprudence'; see also Roger Masterman, 'Section 2(1) of the Human Rights Act: Binding Domestic Courts to Strasbourg?' [2004] *PL* 725; Elizabeth Wicks, 'Taking Account of Strasbourg? The British Judiciary's Approach to Interpreting Convention Rights' [2005] *European Public Law* 405; Jonathan Lewis, 'The European Ceiling on Human Rights' [2007] *PL* 720; Jonathan Lewis, '*In Re P and Others*: An Exception to the "No More, Certainly No Less" Rule' [2009] *PL* 43; Francesca Klug and Helen Wildbore, 'Follow or Lead? The Human Rights Act and the European Court of Human Rights' (2010) 6 *European Human Rights Law Review* 621.

[65] Brenda Hale, '*Argentoratum Locutum*: Is Strasbourg or the Supreme Court Supreme? (2012) 12(1) *Human Rights Law Review* 65, 68; Lady Hale, 'What's the Point of Human Rights?', Warwick Law Lecture 2013 (Warwick, 28 November 2013), www.supremecourt.uk/docs/speech-131128.pdf.

[66] Hale, '*Argentoratum Locutum*' (n 65) 65.

[67] ibid 65.

[68] Hansard HL 18 November 1997, vol 583, col 515 (Lord Chancellor Lord Irvine of Lairg).

merit'.[69] Similarly, Lord Lester took the view that any stronger obligation than to 'take into account' would be inappropriate 'since such cases deal with laws and practices which are not those of the United Kingdom',[70] while Lord Irvine thought that it would give way to becoming 'more European than the Europeans'.[71] It was instead important to avoid 'putting the courts in some kind of straitjacket where flexibility is what is required'.[72] Accordingly, the White Paper prior to the enactment of the HRA 1998 clarified that the scheme of section 2 would require domestic courts to 'take account of relevant decisions ... (although these will not be binding)'.[73] A little later, the then President of the Supreme Court, Lord Phillips, said that 'if the wording "take into account" gives a message at all, it is that we are not bound by decisions of the Strasbourg court as binding precedent'.[74] In fact, in his view, had those words not been included, 'we might actually be treating them as stronger precedent than we do'.[75]

In fact, around the time that the HRA 1998 was coming into force, Stephen Sedley suggested that the HRA's status as a domestic statute 'opens the door to a wealth of jurisprudence and experience from other Commonwealth, common law and European jurisdictions, as well as from the Strasbourg Court itself, in its interpretation and application'.[76] He continued:

> It is through this rich prism that the Convention, in its turn will be read and applied in our courts: not as a monochrome exercise in textual interpretation and the application of received authority, but as a kaleidoscopic pattern combining the symmetry of law with the variety of experience.[77]

Nevertheless the dominant approach in the early years of the HRA 1998 seemed to be to give primacy to the Strasbourg jurisprudence. This has been a point of criticism in much of the academic commentary. For example, the early judicial guidance on the 2(1) HRA duty to 'take into account' relevant Strasbourg jurisprudence[78] seemed to require domestic courts

[69] ibid col 513.

[70] Hansard HL 19 January 1998, vol 584, col 1269.

[71] Hansard HL 18 November 1997, vol 583, col 514.

[72] ibid col 515.

[73] *Rights Brought Home: The Human Rights Bill*, Cm 3782 (October 1997) [2.4].

[74] Lord Phillips of Worth Matravers, Oral Submission to the Joint Committee on Human Rights, HC 873-ii, 15 November 2011, Question 64.

[75] ibid. This argument was developed more recently by Helen Fenwick and Roger Masterman, 'The Conservative Project to "Break the Link between British Courts and Strasbourg": Rhetoric or Reality?' (2017) 80(6) *MLR* 1111.

[76] Stephen Sedley, in Stephen Grosz, Jack Beatson and Peter Duffy, *Human Rights: The 1998 Act and the European Convention* (Sweet & Maxwell, 2000) vii.

[77] ibid vii.

[78] *R (Anderson) v Secretary of State for the Home Department* [2001] UKHL 23; [2003] 1 AC 837 [18] (Bingham LJ); *R (Alconbury) v Secretary of State for the Environment, Transport and the Regions* [2001] UKHL 23; [2003] 2 AC 295 [26] (Slynn LJ); *R (Ullah) v Special Adjudicator; Do v Immigration Appeal Tribunal* [2004] UKHL 26; [2004] 2 AC 323 [20] (Lord Bingham).

to 'follow' or 'keep pace' with the 'clear and constant' case law of that court. The approach led domestic courts to 'mirror' the Strasbourg Court's conclusions.[79] The UK courts risked becoming little more than 'Strasbourg surrogates'.[80] This loyalty to the Strasbourg jurisprudence prevailed for most of the HRA's first decade, but some reluctance to adhere so strictly to the Strasbourg Court's conclusions did begin to manifest itself during the final years of the Appellate Committee of the House of Lords. This is most evident from a series of possession proceedings cases, starting with *Qazi* and culminating in the Supreme Court decision in *Powell*.[81] As Paterson has written, in this series of 'fraught exchanges', the House of Lords was split between a group opposed to the ECHR destabilising a key part of the common law relating to property and an opposing group who were more content to follow Strasbourg.[82] In *Qazi*, although the House of Lords unanimously held that Article 8 was engaged, the majority (Lord Hope, Lord Scott and Lord Millett) held—contrary to the relevant Strasbourg jurisprudence—that Article 8 was not infringed. By the time the matter came back to the House of Lords in *Kay*,[83] the Strasbourg Court had decided *Connors v UK* the other way.[84] The majority (Lord Hope, Lord Scott and Lady Hale) in the House of Lords repeated their objections to the Strasbourg position. The saga went for another round with the Strasbourg Court's decision in *McCann*,[85] which took the minority view in *Kay*. When the matter came back in *Doherty*,[86] the majority (again Lord Hope and Lord Scott, along with Lord Rodger and Lord Walker)[87] explained the reluctance to follow the Strasbourg line on the basis that the Strasbourg Court had not 'fully appreciated the very real problems that are likely to be caused if [the court] were to depart from the majority view in *Kay*'.[88]

Once *Kay* was decided in Strasbourg (predictably endorsing the minority in the House of Lords),[89] this internal conflict took a sharp turn.

[79] Lewis, 'European Ceiling' (n 64) 720.

[80] *R (Prolife Alliance) v BBC* [2002] EWCA Civ 297; [2002] 2 All ER 756, 771–72; see also Masterman (n 64); Wicks (n 64).

[81] *Qazi v Harrow London Borough Council* [2003] UKHL 43; [2004] 1 AC 983; *Hounslow London Borough Council v Powell* [2011] UKSC 8; [2011] 2 AC 186. For an account of the cases and the state of the law relating to possession proceedings leading up to *Powell*, see, eg, Ian Loveland, 'The Shifting Sands of Article 8 Jurisprudence in English Housing Law' (2011) 2 *European Human Rights Law Review* 151.

[82] Paterson (n 42) 228.

[83] *Kay v Lambeth London Borough Council* [2006] UKHL 10.

[84] *Connors v UK* (2004) 40 EHRR 189.

[85] *McCann v UK* (2008) 47 EHRR 913.

[86] *Doherty v Birmingham City Council* [2008] UKHL 57; [2009] 1 AC 367.

[87] Although Paterson notes that Lord Walker expressed 'grave disquiet while concurring only because he felt bound by the principles of stare decisis to do so': Paterson (n 42).

[88] *Doherty* (n 86) [20] (Lord Hope).

[89] *Kay v UK* [2011] (Application No 37341/06) [2011] HLR 2, 21 September 2010.

By the time the matter returned in *Pinnock*,[90] the jurisdiction of the House of Lords had transferred to the Supreme Court, which, in the unanimous decision of a nine-strong court, retreated to a position of guarded loyalty to the Strasbourg jurisprudence. Lord Neuberger gave the single judgment, explaining that where there is

> a clear and constant line of decisions whose effect is not inconsistent with some fundamental substantive or procedural aspect of our law, and whose reasoning does not appear to overlook or misunderstand some argument or point of principle, we consider that it would be wrong for this court not to follow that line.[91]

A year later, a nine-strong Supreme Court endorsed the approach again in *Powell*.[92] These fluctuations in the approach of the top court are also clear outside of the possession proceeds saga. Prior to the retreat in *Pinnock* and *Powell*, the Supreme Court had decided *Horncastle*, which Chapter 8 argues represents one of the clearest examples of a 'departure' from the relevant Strasbourg jurisprudence.[93] The Court changed direction again in *Cadder*, considering itself compelled to follow the Strasbourg jurisprudence on the right to a fair trial. The current mood turns back the other way; a number of Supreme Court Justices have set out the view that the time has come to reconsider the *Ullah*-type loyalty to the Strasbourg jurisprudence.[94] The once well-ingrained temptation to 'mirror' the Strasbourg line appears to have been diluted. It appears that the weight of Strasbourg authority is tending back towards persuasive, in the optional sense.[95]

Even if not considered to be more than persuasive, it appears that the Strasbourg jurisprudence ranks higher than the jurisprudence of foreign domestic courts. Mak has argued that this is part and parcel of an 'acknowledgement by the British judges of a certain ideological affinity with the Strasbourg Court':[96]

> In comparison with other courts the Strasbourg case law is considered to fit the ideological framework of the British highest court regarding human rights

[90] *Manchester City Council v Pinnock* [2010] UKSC 45; [2011] 2 AC 104.

[91] ibid [48] (Lord Neuberger).

[92] *Hounslow London Borough Council v Powell* [2011] UKSC 8; [2011] 2 AC 186.

[93] *R v Horncastle and Another* [2009] UKSC 14; [2010] 2 AC 373; see also ch 8, text following n 67.

[94] Lord Wilson proposed reconsidering the *Ullah* principle in *Sugar v British Broadcasting Corporation* [2012] UKSC 4; [2012] 1 WLR 439 [59] (discussed further in ch 8). Extra-judicially, see, eg, Lord Sumption, 'The Limits of Law', 27th Sultan Azlan Shah Lecture (Kuala Lumpur, 20 November 2013); Lord Judge, 'Constitutional Change: Unfinished Business' (University College London, 4 December 2013); Hale, '*Argentoratum Locutum*' (n 65) 65; Lord Phillips, 'Strasbourg Has Spoken', in Burrows, Johnston and Zimmermann (n 7) 118.

[95] Paterson was tempted to conclude that the fluctuations in the approach of the top court in part reflect the political dynamics surrounding the 2010 general election. See further Paterson (n 42); and ch 8 from n 120.

[96] Elaine Mak, *Judicial Decision-Making in a Globalised World: A Comparative Analysis of the Changing Practices of Western Highest Courts* (Hart Publishing, 2013) 143.

> protection relatively well. A judge mentioned [in Mak's interviews] that the UK Supreme Court used to refer more often to the Supreme Court of Canada, which developed important human rights case law after the introduction of the Canadian Charter of Rights and Freedoms in 1982. However, this judge observed that the UK Supreme Court is now shifting its attention to Strasbourg, as it considers the Canadian Supreme Court's jurisprudence to be too liberal.[97]

An unofficial 'hierarchy' of persuasive authorities seemed to be well established among some of the Justices interviewed for this study. Lord Dyson, for example, explained that the approach in Convention cases would be to start with House of Lords or Supreme Court cases, if there were any. After those would come the Strasbourg jurisprudence and, after those, the foreign domestic courts. The latter were 'considerably down the list'.[98] The logic is intelligible: it 'reflects the fact that the Convention is an international instrument, the correct interpretation of which can be authoritatively expounded only by the Strasbourg court'.[99] The Convention and its jurisprudence are built into the structure of the HRA 1998 and therefore expressly tie domestic rights to those existing in the ECHR (in contrast to, say, the Canadian, Victorian and New Zealand experiences which do not draw from another treaty).[100]

The reliance on comparative research from supranational courts is also a reflection of the fact that the Supreme Court is a very busy court and does not always have time to conduct research into the approach of other jurisdictions. This was the theme of the explanation given by Lord Phillips when interviewed:

> With some exceptions, we basically don't have time to go to the other European countries and look at the way they've addressed [an issue]. There is quite enough case law in Strasbourg itself. We're looking at how Strasbourg deals with the decisions of courts in other member states and when you do that you are also looking to see how that particular court dealt with a problem and then how Strasbourg has viewed the approach of that court. And so, in some cases, we're looking quite closely at the domestic decision in the field of human rights.[101]

Of course, the human rights framework might yet change. If the link to the supranational jurisprudence is removed or diluted, a broader comparative outlook could become more important. A replacement British Bill of Rights

[97] ibid.

[98] Interview with the Rt Hon Lord Dyson MR, former Justice of the UK Supreme Court (Supreme Court, London, 1 May 2012).

[99] *Ullah* (n 78) [20] (Bingham LJ).

[100] Roger Masterman, 'Taking the Strasbourg Jurisprudence into Account: Developing a "Municipal Law of Human Rights" under the Human Rights Act' (2005) 54(4) *ICLQ* 907, 923.

[101] Interview with Lord Phillips (n 25).

might also be explicit about directing UK judges away from the jurisprudence of the Strasbourg Court.[102]

III. CONCLUSIONS

Recourse to the jurisprudence of foreign domestic courts is nowhere prohibited. Aside from some legislative steer to prioritise relevant supranational jurisprudence, there are no rules governing judicial comparativism. The absence of clear guiding principles leaves the judiciary with the discretion to use or ignore foreign judgments, in the same way as any persuasive authority. But foreign jurisprudence also represents an unusual kind of persuasive authority. It is unclear, for example, whether the usual distinction between persuasive and binding authority—that these carry authority by virtue of content and source respectively—works in the context of foreign jurisprudence. Both the content and source of a foreign judgment is likely to be relevant to its persuasiveness. In this respect, persuasion is a matter of degree. The relevance of foreign precedents is also likely to be context-dependent; there are different reasons as to why a court might be persuaded by foreign jurisprudence. This variable utility makes the persuasiveness of foreign jurisprudence a matter of kind. Understanding the influence of foreign jurisprudence therefore requires a deeper understanding of the purposes that these sources can serve. As Whitman has put it, '*some* kind of borrowing is surely taking place and we need *some* account of what is going on'.[103]

[102] Fenwick and Masterman (n 75) 1123; cl 2 of the Human Rights Act 1998 (Repeal and Substitution) Bill, introduced in 2012–13 by Charlie Elphicke MP, purported to grant the jurisprudence of foreign domestic courts at least as much weight as that of the Strasbourg Court: www.publications.parliament.uk/pa/bills/cbill/2012-2013/0031/2013031.i-ii.html. A motion for the Bill's Second Reading was moved on 1 March 2013, but was withdrawn at the end of the debate.

[103] James Q Whitman, 'The Neo-Romantic Turn' in Pierre Legrand and Roderick Munday (eds), *Comparative Legal Studies: Traditions and Transitions* (Cambridge University Press, 2003) 342.

4

The Purpose of Foreign Jurisprudence

THE LACK OF instruction about the use of jurisprudence from foreign domestic courts makes the guiding principles behind the use of these sources more obscure. Obscurity in judicial reasoning does not sit comfortably with the principles of transparency and predictability, which are integral to the usual understanding of the rule of law.[1] The lack of clear guiding principles has given rise to some debate about the legitimacy of using foreign jurisprudence in the first place. For instance, judges are occasionally suspected of using foreign jurisprudence which is likely to support their own predetermined conclusions,[2] or as a means of 'judicial fig-leafing', designed to obscure the reality of judicial choice.[3] Similar anxieties are prevalent about the 'substantial 'cherry picking' of which jurisdiction to cite, which McCrudden has explained as a concern that 'those jurisdictions chosen will be those which are likely to support the conclusion sought, leading to arbitrary decision-making, not legitimate judging'.[4]

Concerns about 'cherry picking' can be encapsulated in Judge Harold Leventhal's well-known remark that '[u]sing legislative history is like looking

[1] See generally Tom Bingham, *The Rule of Law* (Penguin, 2011); Lord Bingham, 'The Rule of Law' [2007] *CLJ* 67.

[2] See, eg, Ian Cram, 'Resort to Foreign Constitutional Norms in Domestic Human Rights Jurisprudence with Reference to Terrorism Cases' [2009] *CLJ* 118, 139–141; Elizabeth Wicks, 'Taking Account of Strasbourg? The British Judiciary's Approach to Interpreting Convention Rights' [2005] *European Public Law* 405, 410. See also Antonin Scalia, 'The Bill of Rights: Confirmation of Extent Freedoms or Invitation to Judicial Creation?' in Grant Huscroft and Paul Rishworth (eds), *Litigating Rights: Perspectives from Domestic and International Law* (Hart Publishing, 2002); James Allan, 'A Defence of the Status Quo' in Tom Campbell et al (eds), *Protecting Human Rights: Instruments and Institutions* (Oxford University Press, 2003). *cf* Christopher McCrudden, 'A Common Law of Human Rights?: Transnational Judicial Conversations on Constitutional Rights' (2000) 20(4) *OJLS* 499, 527: 'One possible explanation is that the use of foreign judgments is simply results-driven … [leading to a] suspicion that the selective use of foreign judgments is inevitably associated with a rights-expanding agenda. But this would be mistaken.'

[3] Richard Posner, 'No Thanks, We Already Have Our Own Laws' *Legal Affairs* (July/August 2004), www.legalaffairs.org/issues/July-August-2004/feature_posner_julaug04.msp; Sujit Choudhry (ed), *The Migration of Constitutional Ideas* (Cambridge University Press, 2006) 7.

[4] McCrudden (n 2) 507.

out over the crowd at a cocktail party to try to identify your friends'.[5] Part of the problem, of course, is that the burgeoning pool of foreign jurisprudence means that 'identifying friends' is almost always possible; a judgment might easily be manipulated by the 'unprincipled selection of foreign experience'.[6] As John Roberts, Chief Justice of the United States, said in his confirmation hearings before the US Senate, 'you can find anything you want [in foreign law]. If you don't find it in the decisions of France of Italy, it's in the decisions of Somalia or Japan or Indonesia or wherever'.[7] The implicit risk is that foreign jurisprudence invites manipulation.[8] Justice Scalia of the US Supreme Court repeatedly denounced any reference to foreign jurisprudence on this basis.[9] Dissenting in *Roper v Simmons*,[10] Scalia said that 'to invoke alien law when it agrees with one's own thinking, and ignore it otherwise, is not reasoned decision-making, but sophistry'.[11] For Justice Scalia then, citation of foreign jurisprudence was entirely opportunistic:

> When it agrees with what the justices would like the case to say, we use the foreign law, and when it doesn't agree, we don't use it ...[12]
>
> I want to do this thing; I have to think of some reason for it. I have to write something that—you know, that sounds like a lawyer. I have to cite something.[13]

Cram, Mak and Bell all appear to agree that in the House of Lords and now the Supreme Court, foreign jurisprudence is 'results-driven' and often used opportunistically.[14] The asymmetry in the use of comparative case law in some domestic decisions does little to rebut this suggestion. For instance, Lord Walker found a judgment of the Constitutional Court of South Africa 'very helpful' when giving judgment in *Williamson* and borrowed heavily

[5] Repeated at the Confirmation Hearing on the Nomination of John G Roberts Jr to be Chief Justice of the United States, 2005, 109th Congress 200, 200–01.

[6] Cheryl Saunders, 'Comparative Constitutional Law in the Courts: Is There a Problem?' (2006) 59(1) *Current Legal Problems* 91, 114.

[7] Confirmation Hearing on the Nomination of John G Roberts Jr (n 5) 200–01.

[8] Norman Dorsen, 'A Conversation between U.S. Supreme Court Justices' (2005) 3(3) *International Journal of Constitutional Law* 519; Vicki Jackson, 'Comparative Constitutional Federalism and Transnational Judicial Discourse' (2004) 2(1) *International Journal of Constitutional Law* 91. See also Jo Eric Khushal Murkens, 'Comparative Constitutional Law in the Courts: Reflections' (2008) *LSE Law, Society and Economy Working Papers* 15/2008, https://. papers.ssrn.com/abstract=1268487, 1 (abstract); Posner (n 3); *cf* Vicki Jackson, 'Yes Please, I'd Love to Talk with You' *Legal Affairs* (July/August 2004), www.legalaffairs.org/issues/July-August-2004/feature_jackson_julaug04.msp.

[9] Dorsen (n 8) 531 (Justice Scalia).

[10] *Roper v Simmons* (2005) 543 US 551, 627.

[11] ibid.

[12] Dorsen (n 8) 521 (Justice Scalia).

[13] ibid 531.

[14] Cram (n 2) 139–41. Elaine Mak concluded that there was a lack of a systematic approach in the use of foreign legal materials at the UK Supreme Court: 'Why Do Dutch and UK Judges Cite Foreign Law?' [2011] *CLJ* 420; John Bell, 'Comparative Law in the Supreme Court 2010–11' [2012] *Cambridge Journal of International and Comparative Law* 20.

from Justice Sachs' reasoning in that decision in order to conclude that the ban on corporal punishment did not violate Article 9 ECHR.[15] In that case, Lord Nicholls preferred to distinguish the decision of the Strasbourg Court in *Campbell and Cosans* in order to reach the same conclusion.[16] Yet this sort of example is only problematic if consistency in the treatment of foreign sources is thought to be a necessary condition for legitimate comparativism. Such a conclusion would ignore the possibility that judges may—legitimately—have different reasons for recourse to foreign jurisprudence. 'The question of real importance is—what is its purpose?'[17]

I. MANY MINDS

On a very basic level, to draw from foreign jurisprudence supports the simple premise that collective deliberation will produce a better solution.[18] Many minds may weed out bad judgments through an evolutionary process, while the multiple analyses may contribute different perspectives. In turn, these may lead to better deliberation and better conclusions. Those who support the practice of domestic courts using foreign jurisprudence in their judgments often cite the benefits of seeking guidance 'from the accumulated legal experience of mankind':[19] 'If I have a difficult case and a human being called a judge, though of a different country, has had to consider a similar problem, why should I not read what that judge has said? It will not bind me, but I may learn something'.[20] It is illogical, so the argument goes, to ignore the 'established body of findings to which others have contributed over the years'.[21] The argument is usually reinforced by analogy to scientific study. As Waldron explains:

> Existing science claims neither unanimity among scientists nor infallibility; nevertheless, it stands as a repository of enormous value to individual researchers as they go about their work, and it is unthinkable that any of them would try to proceed without drawing on that repository to supplement their own individual research and to provide a basis for its critique and evaluation.[22]

[15] *R (Williamson) v Secretary of State for Education and Employment* [2005] UKHL 15; [2005] 2 WLR 590 [67].

[16] *Campbell and Cosans v UK* (1982) 4 EHRR 293.

[17] Harold Cooke Gutteridge, *Comparative Law: An Introduction to the Comparative Method of Legal Study and Research*, 2nd edn (Cambridge University Press, 1949) 5.

[18] Anne-Marie Slaughter, 'A Typology of Transjudicial Communication' (1994) 29 *University of Richmond Law Review* 99, 132.

[19] Jeremy Waldron, 'Foreign Law and the Modern *Ius Gentium*' (2005) 119 *Harvard Law Review* 129, 140.

[20] Dorsen (n 8) 523 (Justice Breyer).

[21] Waldron (n 19) 139.

[22] ibid 132–33.

Foreign jurisprudence is therefore 'available to lawmakers and judges as an established body of legal insight, reminding them that their particular problem has been confronted before and that they like scientists should try to think it through in the company of those who have already dealt with it'.[23] Foreign jurisprudence might have a 'particular epistemic significance':[24]

> If a national court has to interpret a treaty provision, or apply a contentious common law principle, and it is brought to the court's attention that the court of another state party to that treaty, or of another common law jurisdiction, has already considered at length and in the same language how that provision or principle might best be understood, it would be somewhat odd (though not improper) if that national court were to refuse so much as to take a glance at the foreign court's ruling. Imagine, indeed, that you were struggling to decide an especially hard case and you had access to a sophisticated search engine which could not only discern the exact legal issue from your rudimentary search terms but which could also provide a straightforward and, if necessary, well translated summary of the legislation and major case law capturing how the issue has been addressed in as many other jurisdictions as you cared to consider. It would be surprising were you not at all inclined to look.[25]

The South African Constitutional Court's approach to foreign jurisprudence proceeds on these grounds. It has explained that: 'Comparative research is generally valuable, and is all the more so when dealing with problems new to our jurisprudence but well developed in mature constitutional democracies'.[26] Indeed, Rautenbach's empirical study of the South African Constitutional Court's use of foreign jurisprudence shows the Court to be among the heaviest users of comparative law in the world.[27]

The 'many minds' theory is sometimes criticised for being stylised or pitched at a high level of abstraction.[28] It has also been viewed with scepticism by those who see foreign jurisprudence as irrelevant to the interpretative task of the judge. The arguments in the US debate on foreign authority exemplify this well. On one view, it is the task of judges to interpret the

[23] ibid.

[24] Neil Duxbury, 'The Law of the Land' (2015) 78(1) *MLR* 26, 31.

[25] ibid.

[26] *Sanderson v Attorney General, Eastern Cape* 1998 (2) SA 38 (CC); Rabinder Singh, 'Interpreting Bills of Rights' [2008] *Statute Law Review* 82. The South African Constitution expressly says that '[w]hen interpreting the Bill of Rights, a court, tribunal or forum may consider foreign law' (s 39(1)(c) of the Constitution of the Republic of South Africa 1996), but that it 'must consider international law' (s 39(1)(b)).

[27] Christa Rautenbach, 'South Africa: Teaching an "Old Dog" New Tricks? An Empirical Study of the Use of Foreign Precedents by the South African Constitutional Court (1995–2010)' in Tania Groppi and Marie-Claire Ponthoreau (eds), *The Use of Foreign Precedents by Constitutional Judges* (Hart Publishing, 2013) 194, 411–12.

[28] Adrian Vermeule, 'Many-Minds Arguments in Legal Theory' (2008) *Harvard Public Law Working Paper* No 08-02, https://papers.ssrn.com/sol3/papers.cfm?abstract_id=1087017.

Constitution in light of the present day and it is appropriate to do so in the context and culture in which the issues arise. Justice Breyer, for instance, sees himself as interpreting the US Constitution 'in today's world' and that 'where similar relevant experience becomes more and more common we are more likely to learn from other countries'.[29] The primary objection to this approach usually stems from an 'originalist' view, whereby the task of interpreting the Constitution 'is to try to understand what it meant' and 'what it was understood by the society to mean when it was adopted'.[30] Using foreign jurisprudence as an aid to constitutional interpretation is said to undermine the authority of the original text and to risk importing a meaning that was not intended when the Constitution was drafted.

This concern is relevant in the US context, when foreign case law is being invoked to interpret the American Bill of Rights. This debate is greatly influenced by theories of constitutional interpretation.[31] In the UK, however, the influence of foreign jurisprudence is quite different. The source of human rights in the UK is not 'the UK Constitution' since no such document exists. Instead, the source is the common law, the ECHR or another international document. The influence of foreign jurisprudence in the development of common law rights would not be controversial, since the common law is usually understood to be a product of shared heritage. Recourse to foreign jurisprudence as an aid to the interpretation of an international human rights instrument would also be uncontroversial, since the rights at stake do not necessarily have a domestic provenance. The influence of foreign jurisprudence might therefore be more legitimate and expected in the UK constitutional context. The absence of a single human rights instrument in the UK may even encourage comparativism: 'without the constraints of a constitution or code, the legal systems of England and Scotland have a particular freedom to look to other systems'.[32]

II. DECORATION

The underlying tension between judicial interpretation and judicial law making often relates to concerns around the 'cherry picking' of jurisdictions from which citation occurs. Used in this way, foreign jurisprudence may be ornamental. A judge may be 'inclined to *bricolage*—to rummaging

[29] Dorsen (n 8) 537 (Justice Breyer).

[30] ibid 525 (Justice Scalia).

[31] Robert Reed, 'Foreign Precedents and Judicial Reasoning: The American Debate and British Practice' (2008) 124 *LQR* 253, 255.

[32] Lord Mance, 'Foreign Laws and Languages' in Andrew Burrows, David Johnston and Reinhard Zimmermann (eds), *Judge and Jurist: Essays in Memory of Lord Rodger of Earlsferry* (Oxford University Press, 2013) 87.

around just about anywhere for materials which might support particular arguments'.[33] Waldron notes that 'reference to official judgments, whether local or foreign, helps rescue judges from a feeling of intellectual nakedness',[34] whereas Posner describes the judicial search for quotations and citations of foreign jurisprudence (as well as previous decisions) as an effort 'to further mystify the adjudicative process and disguise the political decisions that are at the core of the Supreme Court's output'.[35] Slaughter has added that 'citation of [foreign decisions] seems most likely to reflect a calculation by the listening court that evidence of foreign support or parallel reasoning will strengthen its own decision'.[36] Indeed, it is not universally accepted that legal citations are necessarily connected to the outcome in any given case:

> Legal sophisticates these days worry little about the ins and outs of citation, tending instead to cast their lot with the legal realists in believing that the citation of legal authorities in briefs, arguments, and opinions is scarcely more than a decoration. Citation may be professionally obligatory, the sophisticates grudgingly acknowledge, but it persists largely as an ornament fastened to reasons whose acceptance rarely depends on the assistance or weight of the cited authorities ... it is a mistake to think that the cited authorities have very much to do with the substance of legal argument or the determination of legal outcomes.[37]

It must be true that the potential for ornamental citation is greater than ever before. Technological developments, in particular, have had a profound effect and the Internet has made available a burgeoning pool of materials. As Wilson and Horne have commented:

> from about the mid-1990s judgments started to become available on the internet. Previously, most unreported judgments effectively vanished. With the internet—coupled with the growing number of specialist series—almost every judgment is now freely available to counsel.[38]

Cram, too, has suggested that electronic databases are likely to have had a profound effect on the citation of foreign legal materials and 'it would be surprising if the results of database searches had not begun to filter through from counsels' submissions to court judgments'.[39] It would not be surprising if the jurisdictions from which judges draw were to be guided by sources

[33] Duxbury (n 24) 33.

[34] Waldron (n 19) 138.

[35] Posner (n 3). See also Dianne Marie Amann, '"Raise the Flag and Let it Talk": On the Use of External Norms in Constitutional Decision Making' (2004) 2(4) *International Journal of Constitutional Law* 597, 605: 'Foreign law has tended to appear as an expendable afterthought, a gratuitous remark on alien practice.'

[36] Slaughter (n 18) 119.

[37] Frederick Schauer, 'Authority and Authorities' (2008) 94 *Virginia Law Review* 1931, 1932.

[38] James Wilson and Alexander Horne, 'Judgment Matters' (2010) 160 *New Law Journal* 7446, www.newlawjournal.co.uk/nlj/content/judgment-matters.

[39] ibid.

selected and put before them by counsel.[40] The effect is recognised in the first paragraph of the *Practice Direction on the Citation of Authorities*:

> In recent years, there has been a substantial growth in the number of readily available reports of judgments in this and other jurisdictions, such reports being available either in published reports or in transcript form. Widespread knowledge of the work and decisions of the courts is to be welcomed. At the same time, however, the current weight of available material causes problems both for advocates and for courts in properly limiting the nature and amount of material that is used in the preparation and argument of subsequent cases.[41]

The research findings do not indicate a strong inclination on the part of the Supreme Court Justices towards ornamental citations. In fact, not all of the Justices felt that the vast numbers of cited authorities would always be an advantage. Lord Reed considered that numerous citations could often be 'a sign of the weakness of an argument'.[42] There is also a limit to the number of authorities that can realistically be used, as Lord Kerr explained:

> If you attend an appeal hearing that is going to last two or three days in the Supreme Court and which involves a number of human rights issues, you will see vast bundles of authorities, most of which are never referred to.[43]

The mere presence of foreign jurisprudence in the bundles would not therefore prompt the use of those sources by the Supreme Court.

The case law also hints at a reluctance to use comparative sources in this way. Consider, for example, Lord Carnwath's comments in *ANS v ML*:

> We were referred to numerous cases dating back over more than 20 years, dealing with the rights of children and parents in similar contexts ... In general little help is likely to be gained by detailed comparative or historical analysis. In the present case, as Lord Reed has shown, the relevant Strasbourg principles are readily apparent from the most recent cases, and the leading UK authorities, as cited in his judgment.[44]

When interviewed, Lord Clarke noted that the cases referred to in the judgments are 'very often the tip of the iceberg in terms of what is actually

[40] See, eg, *Starbucks (HK) Ltd and Another v British Sky Broadcasting Group and Others* [2015] UKSC 31; [2015] 1 WLR 2628 [38]; Alan Paterson, *The Law Lords* (Macmillan, 1982) ch 3; Alan Paterson, *Final Judgment: The Last Law Lords and the Supreme Court* (Hart Publishing, 2013) ch 2. Some time ago, Rudden identified 'four dialogues' that take place in the process of arriving at a decision: the dialogue between the Bar and Bench; the dialogue amongst the Bench; the dialogue with the past (or with precedent); and the dialogue with the future (whereby judges may consider the consequences of a decision such as any opening of 'floodgates'): Bernhard Rudden, 'Courts and Codes in England, France and Soviet Russia' (1974) 48 *Tulane Law Review* 1010.

[41] *Practice Direction (Citation of Authorities)* [2001] 1 WLR 1001; [2001] 2 All ER 510 [1].

[42] Interview with the Rt Hon Lord Reed, Justice of the UK Supreme Court (Supreme Court, London, 8 May 2012).

[43] Interview with the Rt Hon Lord Kerr of Tonaghmore, Justice of the UK Supreme Court (Supreme Court, London, 9 May 2012).

[44] *ANS and Another v ML (AP) (Scotland)* [2012] UKSC 30 [67] (Lord Carnwath).

considered ... one simply can't refer to every case that was referred to'.[45] It is not surprising, therefore, that the comparative authorities, which Lord Carnwath had implied were referred to by counsel in *ANS*, are not found in the published judgment.

If it were the case that citations represent little more than decoration, they could surely be left out altogether, as Lord Carnwath felt able to do here. Indeed, it is clear from the law reports that, frequently, counsel cite foreign cases that do not appear in the judgments. Some of the interviewed judges explained the discrepancy. Reflecting on the length of judgments, Lord Walker pointed out the size of the 'bundle' of authorities given to them by counsel (prior to the oral hearing), some of which included over 300 cited cases.[46] The numbers of citations was, he felt, 'terrifying, and one of the reasons that litigation is so expensive';[47] 'a judgment shouldn't be a textbook. It shouldn't try and refer to all the relevant cases'.[48]

Since judges decide cases on the basis of reasoned arguments, it is expected that there would be a strong correlation between materials referred to by counsel and those cited in the judgments. However, without access to the printed cases, it is impossible to quantify the full extent of counsel's submissions so as to prove this correlation.[49] The most that can be claimed is that there is a general perception that counsel at the Supreme Court would be likely to refer to foreign jurisprudence. Lord Clarke felt this to be obvious from the quality of counsel at the Supreme Court:

> The great thing about being in the Supreme Court is that we have, on the whole, very high quality counsel, who spend a great deal of time preparing every conceivable argument on every conceivable point and quite a few inconceivable points. And so they'd think nothing of filling the books with endless references to jurisprudence from all around the world.[50]

Baroness Hale also explained that this was always going to be more likely at the highest appellate court:

> You will find big variations as between this court and the Court of Appeal and the High Court, because obviously, any advocate preparing a case has got to think,

[45] Interview with the Rt Hon Lord Clarke of Stone-cum-Ebony, Justice of the UK Supreme Court (Supreme Court, London, 9 May 2012).

[46] Lord Walker also gave a rare insight into these bundles of authorities in *HJ (Iran) v Secretary of State for the Home Department; HT (Cameroon) v Secretary of State for the Home Department* [2010] UKSC 31; [2011] 1 AC 596 [87]: 'After all the carefully-researched debate that the Court has heard and participated in (we have had 23 bundles of authorities containing 250 different items).'

[47] Interview with the Rt Hon Lord Walker of Gestingthorpe, former Justice of the UK Supreme Court (Supreme Court, London, 15 May 2012).

[48] ibid.

[49] Law reports may provide a summary of the arguments, but these are not extensive. The reports also tend to list cases cited by counsel as additional to those cited in judgment, making the correlation between the two unclear.

[50] Interview with Lord Clarke (n 45).

'how interested will the Court be in this comparative material?' It costs money to cast your net wider and it's pretty tricky for them to predict the level of interest that there will be in a very busy court, whereas they can be pretty certain that, by the time it gets to us, we will want to know whether there is anything helpful in the rest of the world.[51]

III. COURTESY

If the citation of foreign jurisprudence does follow from references made by counsel, courtesy may be a factor. As Wilson and Horne explain, 'counsel feel able, and often obliged, to cite multiple authorities and judges, in turn, feel compelled to deal with all of them'.[52] Refusing to look at foreign precedents introduced by counsel might be considered 'churlish'.[53] Wilson and Horne considered the practice likely to be more acute in the lower courts, where a judge may prefer to deal with as many of the authorities as possible by way of a pre-emptive strike ('lest failure to do so results in an appeal').[54] Similar considerations apply at the most senior level. For example, Lord Reed described (during his interview) that foreign jurisprudence might come to his attention while reading into the academic literature. That jurisprudence, he explained, may not necessarily find its way into the judgment unless it were directly on point and important—in which case, it would just be 'good manners, apart from anything else, to acknowledge the idea you've found somewhere else'.[55] Mak also picked up on this theme in her interviews:

> The attitude of the British judges in particular has consequences for the use that is made of judgments from foreign courts ... If an argument is found in a foreign judgment and used in the reasoning of the case at hand, it is only courteous to mention the author, as one Supreme Court judge stated.[56]

Bell later agreed and argued that evidence of courteous citations could be found in the Supreme Court's case law:

> *Knowsley* very much reflects courtesy to counsel, who had presented the material at length and so merited a response, even if it was not very positive. Certainly Lord Mance's comments reflect a concern to show that he had considered the

[51] Interview with the Rt Hon Baroness Hale of Richmond, Justice of the UK Supreme Court (Supreme Court, London, 19 October 2011).

[52] Wilson and Horne (n 38) 7446.

[53] Duxbury (n 24) 33.

[54] Wilson and Horne (n 38) 7446.

[55] Interview with Lord Reed (n 42).

[56] Mak (n 14) 444–45; Elaine Mak, *Judicial Decision-Making in a Globalised World: A Comparative Analysis of the Changing Practices of Western Highest Courts* (Hart Publishing, 2013) 150–51.

> material, even if he felt he could come to a decision without having to make a final decision on the value of that material.[57]

There are other examples in the Supreme Court's case history to demonstrate this sort of approach. For example, in *HJ (Iran) v Secretary of State of the Home Department*, Lord Hope made a point of noting that 'the court was referred to a number of decisions in Australia, New Zealand, South Africa, the United States and Canada' and went on to spend five paragraphs reviewing those authorities, presumably to explain his conclusion that they did not 'reveal a consistent line of authority' on the point.[58]

Nevertheless, citations of this kind are not necessarily ornamental in the 'decorative' sense described by Schauer (see above). At the very least, it is a fundamental feature of judgment writing that reasons are given for the conclusions reached. The giving of principled reasons for judgments is a core aspect of the rule of law and judicial accountability.[59] It is no surprise, then, that a judge would address arguments put by counsel and seek to explain why the same view had or had not been taken (especially, perhaps, in the case of the latter).

A slightly different version of the courtesy point is that judges may cite foreign jurisprudence (or any jurisprudence) out of respect for a particular court or jurist. In other words, a judge might cite foreign jurisprudence in his judgment if it has been thought to provide a particularly well-reasoned account of the relevant issue, even where the conclusion in the domestic case is not in line with that authority. In these circumstances, it might look like foreign jurisprudence is being formally distinguished. When raised in the interviews with some of the judges, two possible explanations were given. The first was a speculation that it might be a means of showing respect to the jurist who had authored the judgment in question. The second was that it may simply be part and parcel of the duty to give reasons, especially if counsel had placed heavy emphasis on a particular source.

> Most likely [foreign jurisprudence is distinguished] because it has been cited and ... if you're turning away a party and holding that their case must be rejected, if they've relied on some foreign authority and made a big point of it then you have to deal with it.[60]

[57] Bell (n 14) 22, citing *Knowsley Metropolitan Borough Council v Willmore* [2011] UKSC 10; [2011] 2 AC 229.

[58] *HJ (Iran)* (n 46) [30]–[34].

[59] See, eg, Andrew Le Sueur, 'Developing Mechanisms for Judicial Accountability in the UK' (2004) 24 *Legal Studies* 73, 76. Le Sueur lists 'the common practice of giving reasons, well written judgments' as one of a number of practices that form accountability arrangements. Others would include the fact that most courts sit in public and the possibility that judgments are appealable to a higher judicial body.

[60] Interview with the Rt Hon Lady Justice Arden, Lord Justice of Appeal (Royal Courts of Justice, London, 7 December 2011).

This explanation ties in with the earlier discussions of showing respect to counsel, but sits uneasily alongside the effort to reduce the length of judgments.[61] A move to shorten judgments would, presumably, leave less room for ornamental citations of foreign jurisprudence. Indeed, none of the interviewed judges expressed the view that superfluous citations of foreign law would be a useful addition to a judgment. Lord Kerr's assessment was that:

> Ultimately, the outcome of these cases depends critically on your own powers of analysis. Reference to authority, be it domestic, supranational, international or whatever, is always going to be by way of supplement to your own reasoning in the case—hopefully to confirm the views that you have formed and, occasionally, to shape those views. But I see that very much in a secondary—an extremely important but nevertheless secondary—role.[62]

Thus, the dismissive view adopted by Schauer's legal realists does not provide a satisfactory explanation for citations of foreign jurisprudence at the UK Supreme Court. The Justices are not interested in padding out judgments by referencing foreign jurisprudence. Foreign jurisprudence citations are probably only relevant if they are directly on point and important.

IV. SUPPLEMENTS

Counsel may not always cite relevant jurisprudence. The citation of a foreign case may arise from supplemental research on the part of a judge. This might be especially likely where the reasoning of a foreign court provides a useful analytical lens. Evidence that the late Lord Rodger engaged in research of this kind can be drawn from Tetyana Nesterchuk's account of her role as his Judicial Assistant. Nesterchuk explained that written pieces of research to assist with the writing of the judgment would usually be commissioned at the post-deliberation meetings with Lord Rodger (after the oral hearing in any given case), but that Lord Rodger would often carry out his own research in parallel.[63] She continued:

> I soon discovered that I was linguistically ill-equipped to assist Lord Rodger who could read a number of languages, including French, German and Italian, and would often look up decisions from foreign jurisdictions to inform or supplement his judgments.[64]

[61] The most obvious example is the common use of single and plurality-style judgment (as discussed in ch 5, text from n 167), even if the reality is not quite as envisaged. Paterson's empirical research revealed that 'on average, sole leading judgments are longer than multiple leading judgments in the Supreme Court:. Paterson, *Final Judgment* (n 37) 106–07 and fn 161.

[62] Interview with Lord Kerr (n 43).

[63] Tetyana Nesterchuk, 'The View from behind the Bench' in Burrows, Johnston and Zimmermann (n 32) 109.

[64] ibid.

When interviewed, Lord Phillips implied that this was a relatively frequent occurrence at the Supreme Court:

> We do a bit of our own research on areas of foreign law ... that was particularly the case with Lord Collins. He would almost always go off and do some research and come up with a chunk of his judgment which didn't owe very much to counsel.[65]

Lord Collins explained in the interview that there were a number of factors that led him to conduct independent research of this kind. The first was to do with expense: while in big commercial cases few expenses are spared, in others, such as human rights cases, looking into foreign jurisprudence may not be included in the advocate's fee, but it may nevertheless be helpful for the court to hear about it. The second factor was a question of practicality: it was 'not for counsel to start looking at American law when they are not familiar' with the exercise—'these things take time'.[66]

Some judges felt this to be a bigger problem than others. Lord Kerr, for example, considered that if that jurisprudence was in any way controversial, it was important that counsel should be given the opportunity to make submissions on it:

> If counsel had not made submissions on this particular theme, and we subsequently discovered that there was a rich vein of jurisprudence to be mined from other jurisdictions, there would be two alternatives: if it was in any way controversial (if there were arguments to be made on either side of the particular theme) I think it's likely that we would invite submissions from counsel on it. More usually we would invite submissions in writing. Very occasionally, we have found ourselves in a situation (and I'm not now talking about foreign jurisprudence) where after deliberations between the Justices, issues have arisen which we feel where not sufficiently canvassed in the appeal hearing and we have reconvened to allow counsel to address those.[67]

But if the position was felt to be 'sufficiently clear so as not to require further submissions', the Supreme Court judges might 'conduct the research ... and take whatever course that jurisprudence led us to'.[68] This latter suggestion risks compromising transparency. At the extreme, the approach may be considered to render a trial unfair for the purposes of Article 6 ECHR, since the essence of a fair trial is that the parties are entitled to hear and reply to the case against them:

> Lawyers know that a court will take account of domestic precedents, and that their chances of winning a case are diminished if the opposing side uses those

[65] Interview with the Rt Hon Lord Phillips of Worth Matravers, former President of the UK Supreme Court (Supreme Court, London, 23 November 2011).

[66] Interview with the Rt Hon Lord Collins of Mapesbury, retired Justice of the UK Supreme Court (Supreme Court, London, 22 May 2012).

[67] Interview with Lord Kerr (n 43). The issue of judges referring to material that was not raised by counsel is given further discussion in ch 5, text from n 32.

[68] Interview with Lord Kerr (n 43)

> precedents more effectively than they do. But if a court omits to invite counsel to make use of foreign precedents and then reaches a decision which is significantly shaped by them, lawyers for the losing side might rue having devised a legal strategy which would have looked very different had they anticipated that the reasoning of foreign judges would have swayed the court as it did.[69]

When interviewed, Lord Clarke explained that 'one is generally reluctant ... to decide cases on arguments that were never run' and that the preference would be 'not to cite important authorities that were never mentioned'.[70] Lord Sumption explained that even reliance on written submissions 'would be very unsatisfactory on a brand new area'.[71] It would risk 'counsel passing like ships' and one would 'not [be] able to ask them about points which you need to clarify'.[72] Thus even where relevant material has been found independently of counsel's arguments, the Supreme Court will try to give counsel the opportunity to address them on it. If a Justice were to be influenced by foreign jurisprudence that had been considered independently of counsel's arguments, it would be referenced in the judgment. As Lord Kerr put it:

> If I, in writing a judgment, have been influenced by a foreign judgment, I will say so. I will not keep it in the background and allow it to inform my thinking but not refer to it in the judgment. I think that would be a very curious way of writing a judgment: allowing yourself to be influenced by a factor which you don't refer to.[73]

In any case, foreign jurisprudence is not generally used as a 'magical ace of trumps'.[74] Lord Collins felt 'sure that [he had] never been turned by foreign law'.[75] At best, he 'might have been confirmed in [his] feelings'.[76] Such research would be 'very much icing on the cake' (and preferably prior to the arguments 'so that you can put any tricky matters to them').[77] Lord Justice Sedley was of a similar mind when contributing to a 'roundtable' on comparative constitutionalism:

> Comparative constitutional law is of infinite interest but of little or no practical value in constitutional adjudication ... My sympathies are with the British

[69] Duxbury (n 24) 41.

[70] Interview with Lord Clarke (n 45).

[71] Interview with the Rt Hon Lord Sumption, Justice of the UK Supreme Court (Supreme Court, London, 28 May 2012).

[72] ibid.

[73] Interview with Lord Kerr (n 43).

[74] Tom Bingham, *Widening Horizons* (Cambridge University Press, 2010) 7–8. Equally, Waldron thought that a failure to consider foreign jurisprudence might be an 'embarrassment', but would 'hardly be fatal to a brief or an opinion': Jeremy Waldron, *Law and Disagreement* (Clarendon Press, 1999) 140. Duxbury's conclusion was that the likelihood of a case being decided solely by reference to foreign jurisprudence is 'extremely remote': Duxbury (n 24) 54.

[75] Interview with Lord Collins of Mapesbury (n 66).

[76] ibid.

[77] ibid.

> academic who has described the practice—not the theory—of comparative law as judicial tourism. Tourism is enjoyable and informative, but the artifacts which you bring back cannot be more than decorative. The real value of what you learn is to enhance your appreciation of your own culture. Like other British judges I refer to comparative sources in some of my judgments, a number of them on constitutional issues. But no judge I know anywhere in the world has ever decided a case differently because of persuasive decisions in other jurisdictions. Comparative sources will either amplify the decision which the judge has already decided is the correct one or, at worst, will be sidelined as unhelpful. This is not the isolationism of a Scalia. It is the cosmopolitanism of a Kennedy, a Breyer, a Ginsburg—tempered by judicial realism.[78]

V. CONSENSUS

A distinction ought to be made between piecemeal citations of foreign cases and citations of multiple foreign cases together presenting a common consensus. To conflate the two would commit the fallacy of composition. Identifying a consensus on a particular issue is one of the most obvious reasons for which judges draw from foreign jurisprudence.[79] For some, referring to a consensus position is the most legitimate way to use foreign jurisprudence. Waldron has gone so far as to argue that 'convergent currents of foreign statutes, foreign constitutional provisions, and foreign precedents sometimes add up to a body of law that has its own claim on us: the law of nations, or *ius gentium*, which applies to us simply as law, not as the law of any particular jurisdiction'.[80]

For those who see foreign jurisprudence as an opportunity to draw assistance from other judges facing similar problems, a consensus may represent a viewpoint that a judge would be remiss to ignore. A consensus might represent 'a dense network of checking and rechecking results'.[81] It is more than a simple accumulation of authorities and may therefore be more than the sum of its parts:[82] 'the fact that everyone in the world

[78] Stephen Sedley, 'Constitutional Court Judge' in 'Comparative Constitutionalism in Practice: Constitutional Court Judges' Roundtable' (2005) 3 *International Journal of Constitutional Law* 543, 569–70.

[79] Vlad F Perju, 'The Puzzling Parameters of the Foreign Law Debate' (2007) 1 *Utah Law Review* 167, 175; Waldron (n 19) 139; Some of the UK Supreme Court's foreign case citations have assisted the Court in identifying consensus or lack thereof, eg, in *R (N) v Lewisham London Borough Council* [2014] UKSC 62; [2015] 1 AC 1259 [88] (Lord Carnwath): 'Other common law countries have also attempted to grapple with this issue but there does not appear to be a settled or uniform approach.'

[80] Jeremy Waldron, *'Partly Laws Common to All Mankind': Foreign Law in American Courts* (Yale University Press, 2012) 3.

[81] Waldron (n 19) 145.

[82] ibid 145.

thinks one thing is at least worth finding out'.[83] For others, this approach is problematic. Identifying and relying upon a consensus in the foreign jurisprudence is to legitimate that authority on the basis of a nose-count; it is the mere fact of that conclusion being reached by a number of foreign jurisdictions that is the justification. Used in this way, the authority of foreign jurisprudence is content-independent and tends towards more than merely persuasive authority. A court draws value not from the reasoning towards the consensus position, but from the consensus itself.[84] In this situation, the difference between precedential decisions and decisions with merely persuasive authority turns out to be, as Flanders has put it, 'more a difference in degree than a difference in kind';[85] a kind of 'super persuasive' authority.[86]

The 'nose-counting' exercise is also problematic on the basis that it presumably relies on the consensus theory of truth. As Duxbury has argued, convergence among different jurisdictions 'is not necessarily evidence that an outlier jurisdiction must somehow be getting things wrong'.[87] Equally, similarities in the result may mask differences in the reasoning.[88] Among the most obvious criticisms is the simple possibility that a consensus can be engineered. A consensus among foreign jurisprudence 'carries no guarantee of moral authority' because the consensus itself 'could be the result of international arm-twisting, legitimacy-seeking, or simply a tendency to fall into patterns by imitating the behaviour of other states ("acculturation")'.[89]

An altogether different situation is the one in which the aim of the exercise is to identify the consensus itself. Such an exercise may be relevant, for example, to a court whose aim is to adjudicate in line with a particular agreement or regime. This point is pertinent to UK human rights cases since UK courts are duty bound by the HRA 1998 to decide cases compatibly with the ECHR.[90] Unlike the US Constitution, which places emphasis on interpreting an original meaning, it is well known that the ECHR is said to be a 'living instrument' that is to be interpreted 'in the light of

[83] Dorsen (n 8) 519 (Justice Breyer).

[84] Perju (n 79) 178–79; Posner (n 3); Schauer (n 37) 1944.

[85] Chris Flanders, 'Towards a Theory of Persuasive Authority' (2009) 62 *Oklahoma Law Review* 55, 59.

[86] ibid 82.

[87] Duxbury (n 24) 40–41.

[88] ibid.

[89] Ernest A Young, 'Foreign Law and the Denominator Problem' (2005) 119 *Harvard Law Review* 148, 157 (citing Ryan Goodman and Derek Jinks, 'How to Influence States: Socialization and International Human Rights Law' (2004) 54 *Duke Law Journal* 621, 638–56); Perju (n 79) 180. *cf* Flanders (n 85) 84: 'the more courts that have decided a matter in a certain way, the greater weight those decisions may be said to have, and not necessarily because consensus is a measure of truth'.

[90] Section 6(1) and 6(3) of the HRA 1998.

present-day conditions'.[91] A by-product of this is that the Strasbourg Court has frequently altered its decisions on the basis of an 'emerging consensus'. Keeping track of any evolving consensus is an exercise that has, on occasion, been passed down to the domestic courts of the UK.[92] When seeking to 'keep pace' with the Strasbourg jurisprudence in such cases, UK courts may find the domestic jurisprudence of other signatory states instructive. As the late Lord Bingham wrote:

> [T]he judge's task is not, as in an ordinary domestic case, to ascertain the meaning to be given to an expression in English law: it is to ascertain the autonomous meaning which an expression bears under the Convention.[93]

In the context of the Scottish courts, Murdoch reported that judicial comparativism had greatly increased since the Scotland Act 1998 and the HRA 1998.[94] Far from restraining judicial recourse to comparative law, those instruments had actually 'provide[d] a vessel for the use of comparative law analysis since domestic courts in giving effect to Convention rights ... have to consider comparative practices in other European (and post *Christine Goodwin*, in other non-European) states'.[95]

Similar considerations prevail when a court is interpreting an international convention with no supranational court. In those cases, the case law of foreign domestic courts is of even greater importance; the very purpose of these instruments is to harmonise standards on a particular issue.[96]

[91] *Tyrer v UK* (1978) 2 EHRR 1 [31].

[92] The duty of a domestic court to keep track of the development in Convention attitudes is most clearly exemplified by a series of judgments on the rights of transsexuals: *Rees v UK* (1987) 9 EHRR 56; *Cossey v UK* (1991) 13 EHRR 622; *Sheffield and Horsham v UK* (1999) 27 EHRR 163; *Bellinger v Bellinger* [2001] EWCA Civ 1140; [2002] 2 WLR 411. In the earlier cases, the Court held that the refusal of the UK government to alter the register of births or to issue birth certificates concerning the recorded gender of the individual could not be considered to be an interference with the applicant's Article 8 right, instead affording the UK a wider margin of appreciation, but stressed the importance of keeping appropriate legal measures in this area under review. In *Goodwin v UK* [2002] EHRR 583, the Strasbourg Court was satisfied that European (and international) consensus had progressed so that the 'fair balance' now tilted in favour of the applicants. The House of Lords in *Bellinger v Bellinger* [2015] UKHL 21 accordingly said that the case was an appropriate one for a declaration of incompatibility.

[93] Tom Bingham, 'The Human Rights Act' (2010) 6 *European Human Rights Law Review* 568, 572.

[94] Jim Murdoch, 'Comparative Law and the Scottish Judges' in Esin Örücü (ed), *Judicial Comparativism in Human Rights Cases* (United Kingdom National Committee of Comparative Law, 2003) 88.

[95] ibid 105. In *Goodwin*, it was reported that '[t]he Court ... attaches less importance to the lack of evidence of a common European approach to the resolution of the legal and practical problems posed [by the legal recognition of gender re-assignment], than to the clear and uncontested evidence of a continuing international trend in favour not only of the increased social acceptance of transsexuals but of legal recognition of the new sexual identity of post-operative transsexuals': *Christine Goodwin v UK (28957/95)* [2002] ECHR 583 [85].

[96] Duxbury (n 24) 37: 'since international inconsistency in treaty interpretation is something to be avoided wherever possible, a national court would do well to try to determine if, and

Consider, for example, the preamble to the 1951 Convention Relating to the Status of Refugees (hereinafter the 'Refugee Convention'), which recognises that 'a satisfactory solution of a problem of which the United Nations has recognised the international scope and nature cannot therefore be achieved without international co-operation'.[97] Similarly, the preamble to the United Nations Convention on the Rights of the Child includes: 'Recognizing the importance of international cooperation for improving the living conditions of children in every country'.[98] Where several jurisdictions are adjudicating with reference to a particular legislative instrument or agreement, the decisions of other jurisdictions may deserve recognition for exactly the same reasons that courts are minded to follow their own past decisions—that is, to uphold the same principles of predictability and stability which are embedded by the rule of law domestically.[99]

Critics may point out that this exercise is at odds with the cultural sensitivity of law. Back in 1974, Otto Kahn-Freund took stock of the increasing comparativism and warned that 'in the process of becoming fashionable a thing gets distorted, and it is liable to be misused'.[100] Kahn-Freund was not seeking to condemn the use of comparative law. On the contrary, he encouraged it, seeking only to caution that it must be undertaken with specific regard to a number of factors beyond the legal systems of the countries compared. Thus, scepticism about borrowing from other jurisdictions stems from the perceived contextual differences, which are thought to preclude the possibility for useful analysis.[101] Montesquieu was unconvinced that comparison between jurisdictions could ever be useful. His well-rehearsed feeling was that the law of any nation would (or should) vary according to a range of factors including (but not restricted to) that nation's history and politics, as well as the customs, religions and inclinations of its people. By its very nature, law was unsuited to a comparative exercise.[102] Law—or interpretations of the law—can alter from one jurisdiction to another. Law is a social science, subject to a number of external

how, the courts of other signatory jurisdictions have already interpreted a mutually binding treaty before it sets forth its own interpretation'.

[97] Convention Relating to the Status of Refugees, Geneva, 28 July 1951, 189 UNTS 150 (entered into force 4 October 1967), preamble.

[98] United Nations Convention on the Rights of the Child, adopted and opened for signature, ratification and accession by General Assembly Resolution 44/25 of 20 November 1989, preamble.

[99] Flanders (n 85) 84.

[100] Otto Kahn-Freund, 'On Uses and Misuses of Comparative Law' (1974) 37 *MLR* 1.

[101] Nicholas HD Foster, 'The Journal of Comparative Law: A New Comparative Resource', www.thejcl.com/pdfs/foster.pdf, 3.

[102] In *The Spirit of the Laws*, Montesquieu argued that the law of any jurisdiction 'should be so appropriate to the people for whom they are made that it is very unlikely that the laws of one nation can suit another'. See Anne M Cohler, Basia Carolyn Miller and Harold Samuel Stone (trans and eds), *The Spirit of the Laws* (Cambridge University Press, 1989) 8–9.

influences that flow from historical and cultural differences. In reality, local conditions produce difficulties 'which are often subtle and require … sophisticated analytical tools' to separate them from their 'culturally-determined realities'.[103] This line of thought has links with concerns propounded by participants in the legal transplants debate, who have been emphasising the importance of contextual analysis for some time.[104] As one commentator elegantly put it:

> Much as winemakers claim that a grape variety transplanted outside its native *terroir* produces a different wine notwithstanding that it remains the same plant, a transplanted law often functions in a different way in its new home.[105]

On the subject of legislative interpretation too, the emphasis is usually upon reading the statute as a whole and 'drilling down into the substratum of meaning'.[106] Comparative methodologists take the same view and usually argue that if comparativism is to be meaningful, it would necessarily engage with even the subtlest of contextual differences, since these may—even if indirectly—feed into the respective legislative regimes.[107]

Thus, the problem is not the reference to foreign jurisprudence per se. It is the elevation of foreign jurisprudence, often different in character to domestic law, to a position where it is treated as authoritative in domestic courts: 'The problem is not learning from abroad; it is treating foreign judicial decisions as authorities … as if the world were a single legal community'.[108] It would be a mistake to assume that convergent foreign precedents 'acquire, purely by virtue of their commonality, the status of positive law'.[109] The risk is not lost on the Justices of the Supreme Court. The late Lord Rodger, who is usually said to have been one of the most enthusiastic users of foreign jurisprudence at the Supreme Court, was aware of the issue and apparently voiced it among his colleagues. Lord Mance has written that Lord Rodger was 'insistent that the proper use of comparative law cannot permit the

[103] Foster (n 101). *cf* Slaughter (n 18) 127: 'Recognition of this commonality does not obviate cultural differences, but it assumes the possibility that generic legal problems such as the balancing of rights and duties, individual and community interests, and the protection of individual expectations, may transcend those differences.'

[104] See, eg, Alan Watson, *Legal Transplants: An Approach to Comparative Law*, 2nd edn (University of Georgia Press, 1993); Pierre Legrand, 'What "Legal Transplants"?' in David Nelken and Johannes Feest (eds), *Adapting Legal Cultures* (Hart Publishing, 2001) 55; Cram (n 2) 122.

[105] TT Arvind, 'The "Transplant Effect" in Harmonization' [2010] *ICLQ* 65, 66.

[106] Mary Arden, 'The Changing Judicial Role: Human Rights, Community Law and the Intention of Parliament' (2008) 67(3) *CLJ* 490.

[107] See, eg, Mark Van Hoecke and Mark Warrington, 'Legal Cultures, Legal Paradigms and Legal Doctrine: Towards a New Model for Comparative Law' (1998) 47(3) *ICLQ* 495, 496: 'law cannot be understood unless it is placed in a broad historical, socio-economic, psychological and ideological context'.

[108] Posner (n 3); Arden (n 106) 506.

[109] Duxbury (n 24) 54.

loose or selective citation of random foreign material; a full, informed, and up-to-date understanding is necessary'.[110]

VI. CONCLUSIONS

Judges use foreign jurisprudence because these sources are available to them in the same way as other persuasive authorities. Nevertheless, obscurity is created by the variety of purposes for which it is used and, in turn, by the anomaly of the consensus theory through which foreign jurisprudence tends towards binding rather than merely persuasive authority. The problem is to do with methodology. Suspicions about arbitrary decision making ultimately represent a complaint that the working methods behind the use of foreign jurisprudence are unclear.[111] As Cram has written:

> [F]requently no clear methodology is adopted to explain why certain sources were considered and others ignored, leaving its practitioners open to accusations of methodological sloppiness and a tendency to judicial activism. The latter charge arises because, critics argue, only those foreign norms that sit comfortably with the judge's moral preferences are ever likely to be invoked.[112]

A lack of transparency leaves the door open to charges of judicial activism and illegitimate law making, and, as Perju has highlighted, 'methodological challenges may be fatal to … the authority of foreign law in such situations':[113]

> The intuition is that methodological questions—such as which jurisdictions judges should consult, how to check sources and references, how they can escape the dangers of nominalism, and how to assess the relevance of a particular provision or line of reasoning outside of its broader legal, cultural, and historical context—are more difficult to answer in situations of piecemeal comparisons, with serious implications about the integrity of constitutional discourse.[114]

The criteria by which some jurisdictions are cited above other are not always clear.[115] Like many comparative scholars, Cram's conclusion is that

[110] Lord Mance (n 32) 88, citing 'The Use of Civil Law in Scottish Courts' in David L Carey Miller and Reinhard Zimmerman (eds), *The Civilian Tradition and Scots Law* (Duncker & Humblot, 1997) 225, 228–29; Alan Rodger, 'Roman Law in Practice in Britain' (1992) *Rechtshistorisches Journal* 261, 269–70; Alan Rodger, 'Savigny in the Strand' (1993–95) 28–30 *Irish Jurist* 1, 19, where Lord Rodger commended the work of 'scholars like Professor Treitel [in] providing the kind of detailed comparative treatment of particular topics without which, certainly, such a development [ie, the use of codified civil law sources] can never begin'.

[111] Duxbury (n 24) 40–41.

[112] Cram (n 2) 118, citing Yash Ghai, 'Sentinels of Liberty or Sheep in Woolf's Clothing? Judicial Politics and the Hong Kong Bill of Rights' (1997) 60 *MLR* 459, 479.

[113] Perju (n 79) 179.

[114] ibid.

[115] Cram (n 2) 140.

'[u]ntil the methodology for selection of foreign norms is made much more explicit, the suspicion will linger that the court's selection of foreign judgments is purely results-driven':[116]

> [S]ome greater level of justification is needed from the courts as to why Case A from the Ruritanian Supreme Court is relevant and possibly even dispositive of the dispute in hand whilst Case B from the Freedonian Constitutional Court can be dismissed as irrelevant and further why the domestic court does not even bother to look at Case C from the High Court of Syldavia.[117]

To extricate these principles, it will be necessary to draw together the ways in which judges use foreign jurisprudence, the effect of that practice on domestic human rights cases and the processes or influences involved. The answers to these may go a long way towards dispelling some of the well-worn complaints about judicial law making—or, if they must be rehearsed, they may at least refresh the debate. As Waldron has explained, 'we should not reject the idea of a theory of citation of foreign law simply because we see foreign law being cited opportunistically; we should reject it only if we think inconsistent and unprincipled citations is inevitable'.[118]

[116] ibid 141.
[117] ibid.
[118] Waldron (n 19) 131.

5

Foreign Jurisprudence in the UK Supreme Court

THIS CHAPTER SETS out some of the results from the quantitative and qualitative analysis of the judgments handed down by the UK Supreme Court during the first eight years of its activity (2009–17). Although this research focuses on human rights cases, the quantitative data includes results about references to foreign jurisprudence in all case types. A holistic view is important in order to understand the general trends in the use of foreign jurisprudence and to enable any context specific conclusions to be drawn about human rights cases.

I. THE EXTENT TO WHICH FOREIGN JURISPRUDENCE IS USED

The first claim in this book is that the Justices of the Supreme Court *are* using the jurisprudence of foreign domestic courts. Table 5.1 sets out the number of Supreme Court cases in which there was at least one reference to a decision of a foreign domestic court. Of the 533 cases handed down by the Supreme Court in its first eight years, explicit citations of foreign jurisprudence were found in 157, just under 30 per cent of the total.

Table 5.1: The proportion of UKSC cases in which at least one decision of a foreign domestic court is explicitly cited, by case type

	Total judgments handed down between 2009–17[1]	Total cases with citations of foreign jurisprudence	Cases citing foreign jurisprudence as a percentage of total cases
All cases	533	157	29%
Non-human rights cases	381	100	26%
Human rights cases	152	57	38%

[1] The total number of reported cases was 550. The total of 533 is the number of cases, combining appeals and procedural matters. A fuller explanation of the choices made in respect of the data sample is given in ch 2, text from n 14.

These results seem to support those who suggest that greater use is made of foreign jurisprudence in human rights cases.[2] Of the total 533 cases decided by the Supreme Court in the time period, 381 do not engage human rights issues and explicit citations of foreign jurisprudence can be found in 100 of those, or 26 per cent. The remaining 152 can be described as human rights cases and explicit citations of foreign jurisprudence can be found in 57 of those, or 38 per cent. However, these are fairly broad brush since the figures differentiate only between 'human rights cases' and 'non-human rights cases'. They do not consider human rights cases compared to, say, commercial law cases, corporate law cases and property or tort law cases. Tort law, in particular, is often given as a likely context for comparative law.[3] Another important reminder is that these numbers do not account for non-explicit citations of foreign jurisprudence or capture citations of Privy Council decisions.

The other obvious limitation to the overall picture is that it aggregates the results in particular legal years. Figure 5.1 distributes the results from Table 5.1 according to the legal year in which the cases were handed down, showing the number of cases citing foreign jurisprudence as a proportion of all decided cases.

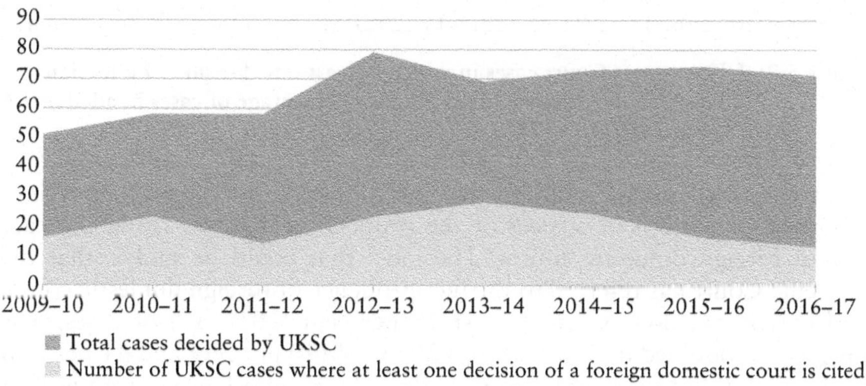

Figure 5.1: Cases citing foreign jurisprudence as a proportion of all cases decided each legal year

[2] See, eg, Tania Groppi and Marie-Claire Ponthoreau (eds), *The Use of Foreign Precedents by Constitutional Judges* (Hart Publishing, 2013) 416: 'The research clearly shows that citations of foreign case law prevail in … human rights decisions'; Christopher McCrudden, 'A Common Law of Human Rights?: Transnational Judicial Conversations on Constitutional Rights' (2000) 20(4) *OJLS* 499, 527, asking 'is there something specific to human rights that explains the apparently greater use of foreign case law in human rights cases?'. See also Jim Murdoch, 'Comparative Law and the Scottish Judges' in Esin Örücü (ed), *Judicial Comparativism in Human Rights Cases* (United Kingdom National Committee of Comparative Law, 2003) 96.

[3] Some insight on these can be gained from Elaine Mak, *Judicial Decision-Making in a Globalised World: A Comparative Analysis of the Changing Practices of Western Highest*

In this impression, 2013–14 saw the highest number of cases citing foreign jurisprudence: 28 out of a total 69 cases (41 per cent). This figure also shows that there is no obvious correlation between the number of cases citing foreign jurisprudence and the number of cases decided. The Supreme Court's busiest year, 2012–13, resulted in 79 judgments, but only 23 made explicit reference to the jurisprudence of a foreign court. The smallest proportion of cases citing foreign jurisprudence occurred in 2016–17 (13 out of 71 cases, or 18 per cent). When these proportions are set out as percentages, a more erratic picture emerges.

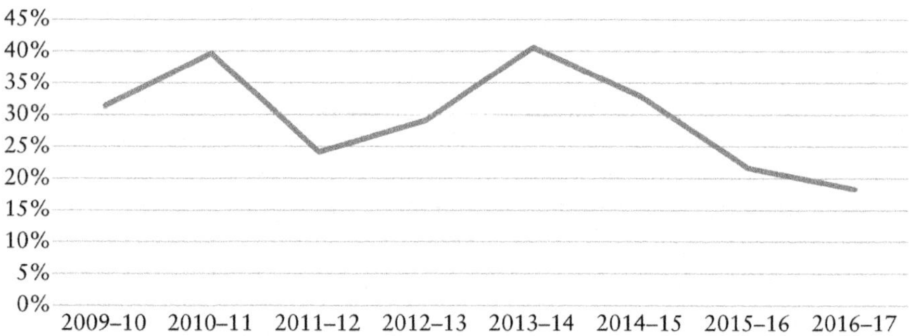

Figure 5.2: UK Supreme Court cases in which at least one decision of a foreign domestic court is explicitly cited, as a percentage of cases handed down in each year, 2009–17

The trend in Figure 5.2 indicates that the UK Supreme Court does not have a consistent pattern in respect of the proportion of cases citing the case law of foreign domestic courts. The most that could be said is that the Supreme Court has referred to the jurisprudence of foreign domestic courts and that it has done so in at least 18 per cent (2016–17) of cases. The proportion doubled in 2010–11 and 2013–14 (40 per cent and 41 per cent respectively), but we could also read these maximum figures as an indication that the Supreme Court is *less* rather than *more* likely to use foreign jurisprudence in any given case; even in the peak years, around three-fifths of the Court's cases made no (explicit) reference to the case law of foreign courts at all.

Courts (Hart Publishing, 2013) 180: 'British judges considered that citations of foreign law mostly occur in human rights cases and in private law cases … In contract and tort cases, the shared background with other common legal systems is thought to make legal comparison often useful … The use of foreign law is less frequent in criminal law cases.' See generally Keith Stanton, 'Comparative Law in the House of Lords and Supreme Court' (2013) 42 *Common Law World Review* 269; Andrew Burrows, 'The Influence of Comparative Law on the English Law of Obligations' in Andrew Robertson and Michael Tilbury (eds), *The Common Law of Obligations: Divergence and Unity* (Hart Publishing, 2016).

The pattern is a little different for human rights cases. Figure 5.3 overlays the proportion of human rights cases in which the Supreme Court made at least one reference to the decision of a foreign domestic court.

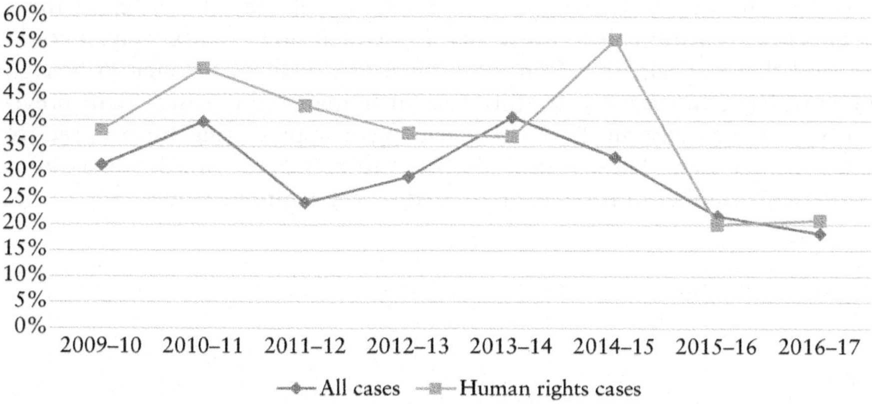

Figure 5.3: UK Supreme Court human rights cases in which at least one decision of a foreign domestic court is explicitly cited, compared with the same proportion in all cases, 2009–17

This overlay shows that reference to foreign jurisprudence is generally more likely in human rights cases. However, it also shows that human rights cases issues were not the main subject of comparativism in the year with the highest overall proportion of cases citing foreign jurisprudence. While Figures 5.1 and 5.2 show 2013–14 to be the year with the greatest number of judgments citing foreign case law, Figure 5.3 shows the number of *human rights* cases referring to foreign jurisprudence to be at the lowest in the same year. This picture also shows the unpredictability in the proportion of cases in which the Supreme Court is likely to make reference to foreign court decisions. While Table 5.1 gave the (mean) average for human rights cases citing at least one decision of a foreign domestic court as 38 per cent, Figure 5.2 shows a 30 per cent difference between either end of the scale. There was an initial spike in the 2010–11 year when explicit citations of at least one foreign decision were found in around 50 per cent of human rights cases, followed by a steady decline between 2011 and 2014. The numbers were surprising given the conclusion in Bell's study that there had been a paucity of cases citing foreign jurisprudence in 2010–11.[4] My data shows that 23 out of the 58 judgments handed down in 2010–11 cited at least one decision from a foreign court and that this included nine (of a total 21) human rights cases.

[4] John Bell, 'Comparative Law in the Supreme Court 2010–11' (2012) 1(2) *Cambridge Journal of International and Comparative Law* 20, 24.

The next spike, in 2014–15, reflects references to the jurisprudence of a foreign court in 56 per cent of decided cases. The surprise of this result is matched only by the dramatic downturn in the following year. The UK Supreme Court cited foreign courts in just 20–21 per cent of its cases in 2015–16 and 2016–17 respectively. The scale of the differences in these results makes it difficult to draw any firm conclusions. Tentatively, it could be said that the Supreme Court has been less inclined to refer to foreign jurisprudence in recent years (not just in human rights cases) than previously, but the spike in 2014–15 warns against predicting future practice from this dataset.[5] These results also need to be paired with the data about the overall number of foreign cases cited by the Supreme Court.

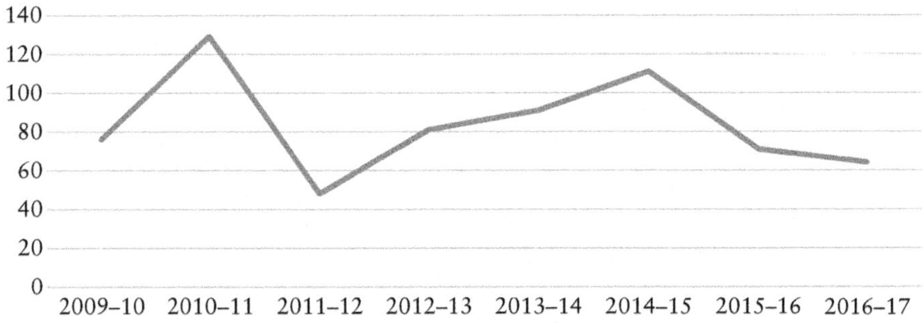

Figure 5.4: Total number of foreign cases cited by the UK Supreme Court, 2009–17

The fact that the Supreme Court refers to at least one foreign court decision in a certain proportion of cases tells us something about the willingness to draw assistance from abroad, but it does not tell us much about how far this goes. Figure 5.4 shows that the Supreme Court cited 671 decisions from foreign domestic courts between 2009 and 2017, peaking at 129 in 2010–11 and dropping to 48 in 2011–12.

While Figures 5.2 and 5.3 show that the Supreme Court generally referred to foreign jurisprudence in a lower proportion of its cases in 2015–16 and 2016–17, these were not the years in which the number of individual citations were lowest. In fact, Figure 5.5 shows no obvious correlation between the number of cases citing foreign jurisprudence and the number of foreign cases cited in each case. It appears that the Court cites, on average, between

[5] This can also be taken as a lesson from past work, making the importance of an extended data sample more obvious. My doctoral project was limited to an analysis of the first four years of the Supreme Court's work (2009–13). The data trend in that period led me to reflect on the 'decline' of judicial comparativism in human rights cases, whereas Figure 5.2 evidently shows a spike in 2014–15.

three and six foreign cases in any given case where it makes at least one reference to foreign jurisprudence.

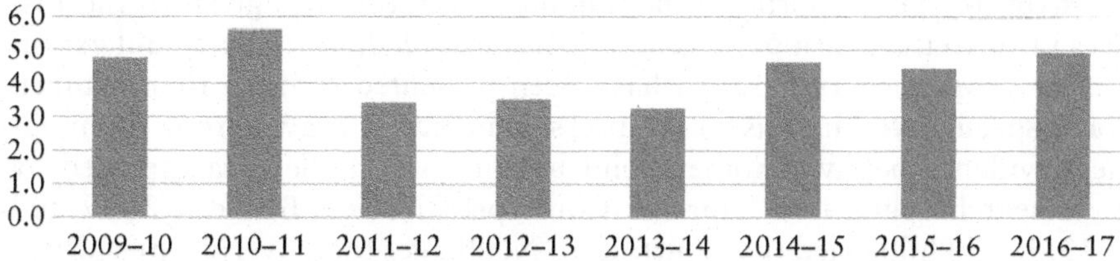

Figure 5.5: Average number of foreign cases cited for each UK Supreme Court decision citing foreign jurisprudence, 2009–17

In human rights cases, the picture is quite different. Figure 5.6 shows a big variation in the two years that were shown (in Figure 5.3) to have a lower proportion of cases citing foreign jurisprudence. In 2015–16, the Supreme Court seems to have made little use of foreign jurisprudence in general, while in 2016–17, it seems to have had more cause to cite foreign jurisprudence. The Court cited some 34 foreign cases in just eight decisions during 2016–17 (an average of 6.8 foreign case citations per decision), compared with just five foreign cases in three decisions during 2015–16 (1.7 foreign case citations per decision).

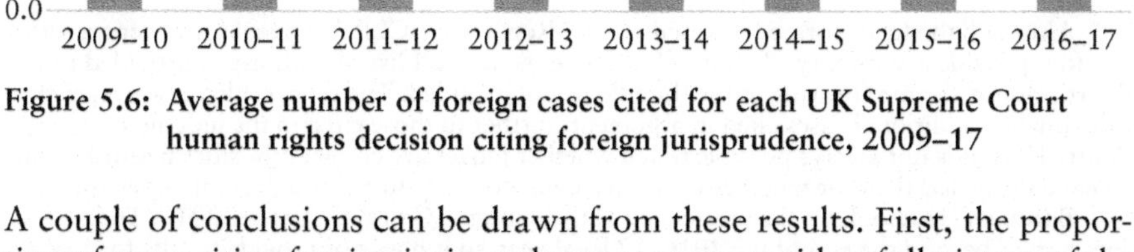

Figure 5.6: Average number of foreign cases cited for each UK Supreme Court human rights decision citing foreign jurisprudence, 2009–17

A couple of conclusions can be drawn from these results. First, the proportion of cases citing foreign jurisprudence cannot provide a full picture of the extent to which the Supreme Court uses these sources. Second, the lack of any obvious trend in either the proportion of cases citing foreign jurisprudence or the number of foreign cases that are cited makes it impossible to say that the use of these sources follows any overarching logic. The Supreme Court seems to be neither reluctant nor overly keen to have recourse to comparative law. The spikes in the use of foreign jurisprudence may be caused by any number of factors. A simple possibility is that counsel before the Supreme Court were more or less inclined to make reference to foreign jurisprudence in any given year. The influence of counsel's submissions on the use of foreign jurisprudence citation in a judgment is not always obvious from the law reports, as the 'bundles' of authorities given to the Justices prior to the hearing are generally not included,[6] but one would expect a large proportion of cases to have been presented through that channel. Some speculative analysis of counsel's influence is drawn from the interview evidence below. Another point to note is that the data captured by my research spans two Supreme Court presidencies. Between 2009 and 2013, Lord Phillips led the Court; Lord Neuberger took over the presidency between 2013 and 2017.[7] The difference in leadership style could have had an impact on the number of foreign case citations. For example, the reduction in the number of concurring judgments under Lord Neuberger might explain the reduction in references to foreign cases in the later years. This possibility is picked up in more detail below.

Finally, while it is evident that the Supreme Court refers to foreign jurisprudence, the number of references to foreign cases is relatively small when compared to the practice of other apex courts. With foreign case citations in about 30 per cent of its case law, the UK sits among the lesser users of foreign jurisprudence when compared to other common law courts. The New Zealand courts regularly engage with the jurisprudence of foreign domestic courts. In fact, some have suggested that the willingness to refer to foreign decisions 'is not the exception in New Zealand, but the rule'.[8] The South African Constitutional Court cited foreign jurisprudence in 52 per cent of its decisions following its establishment.[9] The High Court of Australia's citation practices were similar, with foreign jurisprudence in 51.3 per cent of its constitutional cases.[10] The Supreme Court of Canada and the Supreme Court of Israel come closer to the UK Supreme Court's

[6] Although the Incorporated Council of Law Reporting (ICLR)'s Appeal Cases report series do often provide a summary of counsel's arguments, the full list of authorities provided to the Court prior to the oral hearing in the 'bundle' is not included. The reports also resist repetition and only list 'additional cases cited in argument' further to those cited in the judgment(s) of the Court. Thus, it is not always possible to tell whether judges are citing authorities because counsel have presented them or whether they have come to the Court through some other route.

[7] Baroness Hale took up the presidency of the Supreme Court in October 2017. The dataset does not go beyond the end of the 2016–17 legal year, so it does not provide results for foreign jurisprudence citations under Lady Hale's leadership.

[8] Jeremy Waldron, *'Partly Laws Common to All Mankind': Foreign Law in American Courts* (Yale University Press, 2012) 18. Waldon cites *Taunoa v Attorney General* [2007] NZSC 70; [2008] 1 NZLR 429 as an example. In the determining questions about the application of the New Zealand Bill of Rights Act, the New Zealand Supreme Court cited cases from the US, Canada, South Africa, the UK, the European Court of Human Rights and the UN Human Rights Commission. The number of US cases alone outnumbered the number of New Zealand cases cited.

[9] Groppi and Ponthoreau (n 2) 411–12.

[10] ibid 412.

proportions, citing foreign jurisprudence in 37.9 per cent and 28 per cent of constitutional cases respectively.[11] Indeed, the only exception is the US, where the practice of citing foreign jurisprudence is very controversial.[12] The UK jurisprudence also ranks highly for foreign jurisprudence citations in other countries. In Australia, Ireland and the US, the UK jurisprudence is cited more often than the decisions of other foreign courts, and is frequently cited by the Canadian and Indian courts.[13] Bobek has gone so far as to ask whether references to the law of a select few common law nations, especially the British dominions like Australia, Canada and New Zealand, are references to foreign law at all.[14] Andenas and Fairgrieve too have suggested that the 'inherent characteristics of the common law have perhaps served to mask the fact that it is indeed based on a comparative law exercise'.[15]

A number of these courts also appear to cite greater numbers of foreign cases than the UK Supreme Court. For example, the Australian High Court cited foreign jurisprudence in 99 (out of 193) constitutional cases between 2000 and 2008, citing a total of 2,857 foreign cases (although the figure declined dramatically from 636 in 2000 to 93 in 2008).[16] That study included decisions of the European Court of Human Rights and the CJEU on the basis that Australia is not within the jurisdiction of either court. The inclusion of cases from those courts does not have a significant impact on their dataset (just 36 and five respectively), so the overall impression remains that the Australian High Court cites a much greater number of foreign cases than the UK Supreme Court. The UK Supreme Court appears to be closer in practice to the Canadian Supreme Court, but still makes comparatively fewer references to foreign law. A study of the Canadian Supreme Court

[11] ibid.

[12] See, eg, Cheryl Saunders, 'Comparative Constitutional Law in the Courts: Is There a Problem?' (2006) 59(1) *Current Legal Problems* 91; Norman Dorsen, 'A Conversation between U.S. Supreme Court Justices' (2005) 3(3) *International Journal of Constitutional Law* 519; Vicki Jackson, 'Comparative Constitutional Federalism and Transnational Judicial Discourse' (2004) 2(1) *International Journal of Constitutional Law* 91; Richard Posner, 'No Thanks, We Already Have Our Own Laws' *Legal Affairs* (July/August 2004), www.legalaffairs.org/issues/July-August-2004/feature_posner_julaug04.

[13] Cheryl Saunders and Adrienne Stone, 'Reference to Foreign Precedents by the Australian High Court: A Matter of Method' in Groppi and Ponthoreau (n 2) 33, figure 4; Cristina Fasone, 'The Supreme Court of Ireland and the Use of Foreign Precedents: The Value of Constitutional History' in Groppi and Ponthoreau (n 2) 120, graph 2; Angioletta Sperti, 'United States of America: First Cautious Attempts of Judicial Use of Foreign Precedents in the Supreme Court's Jurisprudence' in Groppi and Ponthoreau (n 2) 407, chart 3; Gianluca Gentili, 'Canada: Protecting Rights in a "Worldwide Rights Culture": An Empirical Study of the Use of Foreign Precedents by the Supreme Court of Canada (1982–2010)' in Groppi and Ponthoreau (n 2) 57, table 2; Valentina Rita Scotti, 'India: A "Critical" Use of Foreign Precedents in Constitutional Adjudication' in Groppi and Ponthoreau (n 2) 72, graph 5.

[14] Michael Bobek, *Comparative Reasoning in European Supreme Courts* (Oxford University Press, 2013) 91–93.

[15] Mads Andenas and Duncan Fairgrieve, *Courts and Comparative Law* (Oxford University Press, 2015) 5.

[16] Saunders and Stone (n 13) 32–34.

reported 966 foreign case citations within the 679 decisions cited between 2000 and 2008, of which there were 234 'constitutional' cases comprising 369 foreign jurisprudence citations.[17] These figures also included references to the European supranational courts, but, again, these did not account for a significant proportion of the foreign case citations (15 Strasbourg Court cases and two from the CJEU).[18]

II. THE INDIVIDUAL APPROACHES OF THE JUSTICES

It is clear from the case analysis and the interviews that the tendency to use foreign jurisprudence is likely to be connected to the background and inclination of individual judges.[19] It is also inevitable that judges might approach arguments with a number of preconceived perspectives,[20] which may include a willingness to look abroad. As Cardozo once said, it is hard for judges to remove themselves from 'the empire of [their] subconscious loyalties'.[21] Some of the existing literature suggests that judges from scholarly backgrounds—particularly those that have studied abroad—are much more likely to cite foreign jurisprudence than career judges.[22] Equally, Supreme Court judges might be likely to share some characteristics. Dickson opens his book *Human Rights and the United Kingdom Supreme Court* with this suggestion:[23]

> Life experience is particularly likely to influence Justices when they are confronted with human rights arguments, because those arguments will relate to what it is that every human being is entitled to expect from the state. The fact that all of the Justices will be of a certain age when appointed (the average age at appointment of those currently in post was 63) means that their approach to such arguments will be affected by long personal experience. Today's Justices will have begun attending primary school in the 1950s and will not have experienced military service, as many of their predecessors would have done, nor the pre-welfare state era. As adolescents, they will have lived through the sexual revolution of the 1960s and 1970s and will have benefited from free university education (even if prior

[17] Gentili (n 13) 53.

[18] ibid 57.

[19] A point recognised by other works: Bell (n 4) 21; Elaine Mak, 'Why Do Dutch and UK Judges Cite Foreign Law?' [2011] *CLJ* 420.

[20] For example, Arvind and Stirton have argued that there are measurable ideological differences between judges in the UK's top court: TT Arvind and Lindsay Stirton, 'Legal Ideology, Legal Doctrine and the UK's Top Judges' [2016] *PL* 418.

[21] Benjamin Cardozo, *The Nature of the Judicial Process* (Yale University Press, 1921), Lecture IV, 'Adherence to Precedent: The Subconscious Element in the Judicial Process. Conclusion', 138 ff.

[22] Wen-Chen Chang and Jiunn-Rong Yeh, 'Judges as Discursive Agent: The Use of Foreign Precedents by the Constitutional Court of Taiwan' in Groppi and Ponthoreau (n 2) 376.

[23] Brice Dickson, Human Rights and the UK Supreme Court (Oxford University Press, 2013) 1.

to university they attended private schools). As lawyers they will have built up considerable financial security and numerous esteem indicators. They will have acquired significant legal experience, including perhaps as a lower level judge, before the Human Rights Act was enacted in 1998.[24]

Lady Justice Arden considered that many judges would be 'self-starters' in comparative law: if judges had done a lot of work internationally or had studied abroad, they would be 'natural self-starters on this because they have no problem with different legal cultures'.[25] At the Supreme Court, Lord Mance explained that the extent to which a judge would be likely to use foreign jurisprudence was dependent on:

> how interested you got, how relevant you thought it might be and how difficult it was. Lord Collins, for example, used to focus quite heavily on American authority. He had access to databases and so on which I don't have access to and he mined that. He is obviously (from his academic work) very much interested in comparative law.[26]

Lord Mance was himself referred to as a more likely user of foreign jurisprudence by the other interviewed Justices. Talking about the possibility of an increase in the use made of foreign jurisprudence, Lord Dyson felt Lord Mance to be 'a shining example', being 'more adventurous'.[27] Baroness Hale, one of the lightest users of foreign jurisprudence at the Supreme Court, felt it obvious that the Justices may have different interests and 'do their own thing', giving the example of occasions on which the Court may get 'Mance on the German law of something'.[28] Lord Clarke implied that he was less likely to use foreign jurisprudence than some of his colleagues:

> I think we would be unlikely to go on a frolic of our own. I mean I would be unlikely myself to send my JA to go and look into the French text. But I might, I mean one might ... some people are keener on it than others ... Lord Mance is very interested in German Law for example.[29]

[24] ibid 13. Dickson notes a connected point made by Lord Neuberger in a 2011 lecture: 'yesterday's judges were children of the conventional and respectful 40s and 50s, whereas today's judges are children of the questioning and sceptical 60s and 70s'. See further Lord Neuberger of Abbotsbury, 'Who are the Masters Now?' Second Lord Alexander of Weedon Lecture (6 April 2011), http://webarchive.nationalarchives.gov.uk/20131203081513/http://www.judiciary.gov.uk/Resources/JCO/Documents/Speeches/mr-speech-weedon-lecture-110406.pdf, 15. Mak's work also confirms that the selection of foreign sources 'seems to be very much dependent on the personal background of the judges': Mak (n 19) 429.

[25] Interview with the Rt Hon Lady Justice Arden, Lord Justice of Appeal (Royal Courts of Justice, London, 7 December 2011).

[26] Interview with the Rt Hon Lord Mance, Justice of the UK Supreme Court (Supreme Court, London, 6 December 2011).

[27] Interview with the Rt Hon Lord Dyson MR, former Justice of the UK Supreme Court (Supreme Court, London, 1 May 2012).

[28] Interview with the Rt Hon Baroness Hale of Richmond, Justice of the UK Supreme Court (Supreme Court, London, 8 May 2012).

[29] Interview with the Rt Hon Lord Clarke, Justice of the UK Supreme Court (Supreme Court, London, 9 May 2012).

A good example of differences in approach is *Belhaj v Straw*.[30] In *Belhaj*, the Supreme Court was concerned with a doctrine in UK law, but analysed it by reference to the scope of the doctrine in other jurisdictions. Lord Mance and Lord Neuberger devoted a large proportion of their judgments to a survey of the French, German and Dutch case law, while Lord Neuberger was more sceptical about the value of the foreign jurisprudence.

Table 5.2 shows a breakdown of the citation practices according to each member of the Supreme Court who heard at least one case between 2009 and 2017. For each judge, the table gives: the total number of cases heard; the total number or cases heard where the Supreme Court cited foreign jurisprudence (whether the judge contributed a written judgment or not);[31] the number of those in which the named judge authored a judgment with at least one foreign case citation; and the latter figure expressed as a percentage.

Table 5.2: Judgments referring to foreign jurisprudence as a proportion of cases heard where at least one judge refers to foreign jurisprudence

Judge	Cases heard 2009–17	Number of cases heard in which FJ cited	Own judgments citing FJ	Own judgments citing FJ as a percentage of all cases heard and citing FJ
Lord Collins	54	24	12	50%
Lord Saville	14	4	2	50%
Lord Toulson	129	39	17	44%
Lord Hope	141	46	19	41%
Lord Phillips	75	30	10	33%
Lord Sumption	167	55	18	33%
Lord Neuberger	240	77	25	32%

(continued)

[30] *Belhaj v Straw* [2017] UKSC 3; [2017] AC 964.

[31] This view of the data reflects the reality that not all cases heard by the Supreme Court would benefit from reference to foreign jurisprudence. Results on the proportion of judgments in which an individual Supreme Court Justice had cited one or more foreign case out of the total cases heard or the total cases in which a written judgment was contributed would not take this into account. Calculating the proportion of citations in cases where foreign jurisprudence was cited by at least one member of the panel was thought to achieve a more accurate reflection of individual tendencies. Of course, counting explicit citations relies on the contribution of a written judgment, so these figures will inevitably leave out some cases where an individual judge might have cited foreign jurisprudence, but felt satisfied by the consideration of the source afforded by another colleague's judgment. This aspect of judicial individuality is likely to be another feature obscured by the increased proportion of single judgments. See, eg, James Lee, 'A Defence of Concurring Speeches' [2009] *PL* 305.

Table 5.2: *(Continued)*

Judge	Cases heard 2009–17	Number of cases heard in which FJ cited	Own judgments citing FJ	Own judgments citing FJ as a percentage of all cases heard and citing FJ
Lord Dyson	75	29	9	31%
Lord Mance	214	73	21	29%
Lord Hodge	126	36	10	28%
Lord Reed	199	48	13	27%
Lord Walker	106	36	9	25%
Lord Carnwath	153	34	8	24%
Lord Kerr	207	66	15	23%
Lord Rodger	61	26	5	19%
Baroness Hale	291	78	15	19%
Lord Wilson	162	46	8	17%
Lord Hughes	122	36	6	17%
Lord Clarke	232	77	12	16%
Lord Brown	92	34	2	6%
Lord Scott (ad hoc)	5	0	0	0%
Lord Carloway (ad hoc)	1	0	0	0%
Lord Gill (ad hoc)	5	0	0	0%
Sir Declan Morgan CJ (ad hoc)	1	0	0	0%
Lord Judge (ad hoc)	12	3	0	0%
Lord Thomas (ad hoc)	6	2	0	0%
Lord Hamilton (ad hoc)	2	2	0	0%

Thus, for example, Lord Toulson heard 129 cases between 2009 and 2017, of which 39 included at least one foreign case citation (not necessarily by Lord Toulson). In 17 of those 39 cases, Lord Toulson cited at least one foreign case. In other words, Lord Toulson was responsible for, or added to, the use of foreign jurisprudence in 44 per cent of the cases heard where foreign jurisprudence was used. Figure 5.7 shows that this proportion is at the upper end compared with others among the Supreme Court Justices.[32] Other than Lord Toulson, only Lord Hope, Lord Saville and Lord Collins came out as having cited foreign cases in more than 40 per cent of the cases heard and where the panel considered such sources relevant. Lord Saville

[32] Ad hoc panel members were omitted from this illustration. Table 5.2 shows that none of the supplementary panel made explicit reference to foreign jurisprudence in their judgments.

and Lord Collins came out as having made explicit reference to a foreign case in 50 per cent of such cases. These results were not surprising given the fact that Lord Toulson and Lord Collins, in particular, had a reputation for being willing to refer to foreign materials. In fact, the fluctuation between 2010–11 and 2011–12 shown by Figure 5.4 may be owed in part to Lord Collins' contributions in that period. In 2010–11, Lord Collins cited 88 foreign cases across seven judgments.

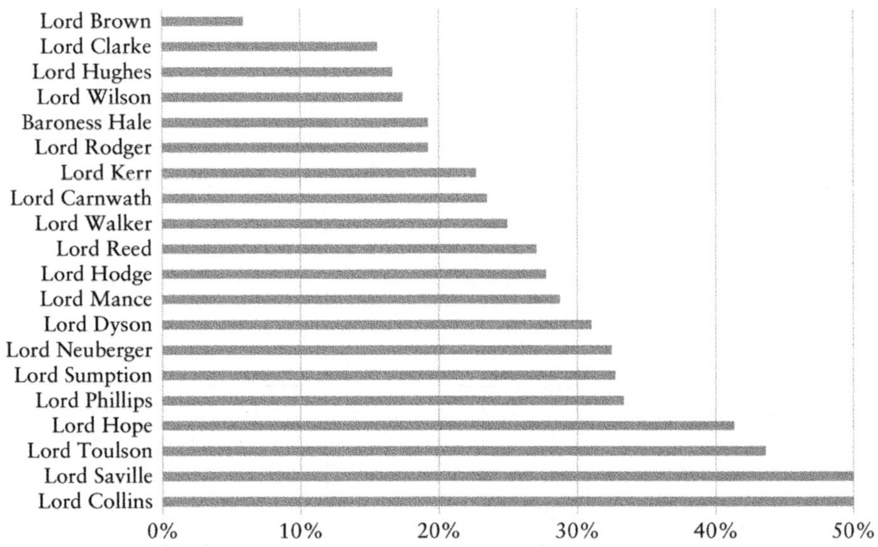

Figure 5.7: Judgments referring to foreign jurisprudence as a proportion of cases heard where at least one judge refers to foreign jurisprudence

The fact that certain judges are more willing to use foreign jurisprudence than others is further supported by the different approaches taken to resourcing those materials. For example, if counsel had not referred to foreign jurisprudence, a number of the Justices interviewed said that they might ask for it if they felt it was useful to do so. Lord Kerr explained:

> If we knew that there was a line of authority which bore on the questions that we had to answer and that we considered it was likely to be helpful in analysis, and we were alerted to it in sufficient time, then certainly we would ask counsel to address us on it. There have been occasions—very rare occasions—where we have pointed out to counsel that there was possibly some assistance to be derived from jurisprudence in other countries and invited them to research it themselves and to make submissions on it.[33]

[33] Interview with the Rt Hon Lord Kerr of Tonaghmore, Justice of the UK Supreme Court (Supreme Court, London, 9 May 2012); See, eg, *Cavendish Square Holding BV v Makdessi* [2015] UKSC 67; [2016] AC 1172 [166].

This is in tune with Mak's finding that the use of foreign jurisprudence is highly dependent on 'personal variables':[34]

> The judges of the Supreme Court for the UK feel that counsel should bring forward all legal materials which are relevant for deciding the case, including foreign judgments and academic resources concerning foreign law. The judges sometimes do conduct additional research themselves or ask a judicial assistant to look for useful sources. Some judges put more time and effort into this kind of research than others.[35]

Reference to material not cited by counsel is not unusual.[36] In *R (Bancoult) (No 2)*, for example, Lord Rodger was explicit about having conducted further research: 'Although not cited by counsel, there are two other passages which might tend to support the view that the right not to be banished from a British colony is indeed a fundamental principle of English Law'.[37] The issue was picked up by Paterson during his interviews for *The Law Lords* and revisited in *Final Judgment*.[38] He notes that:

> Among the counsel whom I have interviewed in the last 40 years, there has been a high degree of consensus on [this] point. Even at the level of the House of Lords or Supreme Court [counsel] do not consider it appropriate for the judges to decide appeals on points of law which have not been argued by counsel or at least put to them for comment.[39]

As Paterson points out, the differences between the Justices in relation to the expectation has surfaced in a number of the Supreme Court's cases.[40] In *Lumba*, for example, Lord Dyson seemed to see an element of Lord Phillips' dissent as a breach of the Convention:

> In my view it is not appropriate to depart from a decision which has been followed repeatedly for almost 30 years unless it is obviously wrong (which I do not believe to be the case), still less to do so without the benefit of adversarial argument.[41]

Others among the Justices, however, were less convinced that these steps would always be necessary. Paterson notes that 'Lord Phillips and Lady Hale

[34] Elaine Mak, 'Reference to Foreign Law in the Supreme Courts of Britain and the Netherlands: Explaining the Development of Judicial Practices' (2012) 8(2) *Utrecht Law Review* 20, 27.

[35] ibid 30.

[36] For a critical view, see Neil Duxbury, 'The Law of the Land' (2015) 78(1) *MLR* 26, 41.

[37] *R v Secretary of State for Foreign and Commonwealth Affairs ex parte Bancoult (No 2)* [2008] UKHL 61; [2009] 1 AC 453 [88].

[38] Alan Paterson, *The Law Lords* (Macmillan, 1982) 38–45; Alan Paterson, *Final Judgment: The Last Law Lords and the Supreme Court* (Hart Publishing, 2013).

[39] Paterson, *Final Judgment* (n 38) 20.

[40] ibid 22.

[41] ibid, citing *Walumba Lumba (Congo) v Secretary of State for the Home Department* [2011] UKSC 12; [2012] 1 AC 245 [25] (Lord Dyson).

were sceptical as to the strength of the convention when interviewed',[42] while Lord Reed felt it would be 'a question of judgement what you decide to do'.[43]

Some indication of the willingness to conduct or commission research on foreign jurisprudence can be seen in some of the Supreme Court's case law. In *HM Treasury v Ahmed*,[44] Lord Rodger wrote in his judgment that he had found it 'instructive in this regard to see how certain other Commonwealth countries' had approached the instrument in question.[45] Mak reported another example:[46] the *Jewish Free School* (*JFS*) case.[47] *JFS* concerned a policy to impose a criterion for admission to the Jewish Free School that a child applicant be recognised as being Jewish by the Office of the Chief Rabbi of the United Congregation of the Commonwealth. The issue was whether the policy constituted discrimination under section 1(1)(a) of the Race Relations Act 1976. The Supreme Court judgments cite, inter alia, jurisprudence from Israel, New Zealand and the US.[48] The source of the jurisprudence is not obvious from the reported judgment, but Mak's evidence from her own interviews is that '[s]everal members of the panel indicated that extra comparative legal research had been carried out at the request of the judges themselves'.[49] A similar indication was given in the interviews conducted for this study.

III. ACCESSING FOREIGN JURISPRUDENCE

Since the Justices do sometimes consider foreign jurisprudence as a product of their own research in this way, it is interesting to consider how this unfolds. Baroness Hale confirmed that there were several avenues to the use of foreign jurisprudence:

> We might ask counsel, we might know about it anyway, we might look it up, or we might get one of our legal assistants to look it up and see if there is anything.[50]

42 Paterson, *Final Judgment* (n 38) 21.

43 ibid 22.

44 *Her Majesty's Treasury v Mohammed Jabar Ahmed and Others (No.2) (FC)* [2010] UKSC 2.

45 ibid [199].

46 Mak (n 34) 31.

47 *R (E) v Governing Body of JFS* [2009] UKSC 15; [2010] 2 AC 728.

48 Respectively: *No'ar K'halacha v Ministry of Education HCJ 1067/08* (unreported) 6 August 2009, SC Israel; *King-Ansell v Police* [1979] 2 NZLR 531; *Bob Jones University v US* (1983) 461 US 574.

49 Mak (n 34) 31. See, eg, *Cavendish Square Holding* (n 33) [165]–[166] (Lord Mance): 'I note in parenthesis that many national European legal systems already appear to contain similar provisions ... *At the court's request*, Cavendish also included as an appendix to its case a valuable examination of the law of, and relevant academic commentary from, other common law countries: Australia, Canada, New York and other United States' states and sources, Scotland, New Zealand, Singapore and Hong Kong' (emphasis added).

50 Interview with Baroness Hale (n 28).

Practical considerations play an important part. As Lord Kerr explained:

> First of all we need to have been referred to the jurisprudence of foreign courts, or to have some means of entry to it, which arises extraneously from the litigation of the appeal.[51]

Lord Sumption concluded that 'the main barrier is not knowing where to start on the research'.[52] Lord Collins explained that it was also likely to be a question of resources:

> By contrast with the United States, we don't have banks of law clerks here. Those Justices who are interested in the way things are done abroad will get their law clerks to research it and those who are not won't. Here, by contrast, we are largely dependent on counsel for our legal materials. We have some judicial assistants but on the whole I don't think that they are used much for research.[53]

The judicial assistants (JAs) are qualified barristers or solicitors in the UK. All JAs bar one (at the time of writing) are appointed for one-year posts and are generally available to assist their assigned Justice(s) in their work. The JAs do not write judgments, but have had a growing input in other ways.[54] For example, it is no longer uncommon for JAs to see and comment on draft judgments of their own Justice or sometimes even those of other Justices.[55] Their role may also include conducting research on cases, and a Justice could certainly ask his JA to look into foreign jurisprudence if it appeared relevant. This might be of particular relevance if a Justice relies on his assistant to carry out online searches. Although not specifically discussing foreign jurisprudence, one of Lord Brown's JAs has written that she was frequently asked to conduct research of this kind:

> Either in the morning before the oral hearing or in the lunchtime break, Lord Brown would often think of a case that contained useful guidance on the matter that was before the Court. If the parties had not relied on this particular authority, it would be my job to find it and print enough copies for the Justices and the parties if Lord Brown decided to bring it up in oral argument. I would also give my view on the relevance of this new authority and highlight any important passages.[56]

Lord Reed explained that his JA might make notes through her own initiative and that she might choose to give references to foreign jurisprudence, but that

[51] Interview with Lord Kerr (n 33).

[52] Interview with the Rt Hon Lord Sumption, Justice of the UK Supreme Court (Supreme Court, London, 28 May 2012).

[53] Interview with the Rt Hon Lord Collins of Mapesbury, retired Justice of the UK Supreme Court (Supreme Court, London, 22 May 2012).

[54] Penny Darbyshire, *Sitting in Judgment: The Working Lives of the Judges* (Hart Publishing, 2013) 383; Paterson, *Final Judgment* (n 38) 254–56.

[55] Paterson, *Final Judgment* (n 38) 254–57.

[56] Tetyana Nesterchuk, 'The View from behind the Bench' in Andrew Burrows, David Johnston and Reinhard Zimmermann (eds), *Judge and Jurist: Essays in Memory of Lord Rodger of Earlsferry* (Oxford University Press, 2013) 107.

so far he had not specifically asked her to research foreign jurisprudence.[57] The amount of foreign jurisprudence that would be likely to come from the JAs is limited. For the most part, the JAs are often too busy to undertake extensive research of this kind without having been prompted for it. It is also not the case that the UK Supreme Court Justices each have their own JA as, for example, do the Justices of the US Supreme Court or the courts of other countries.[58] An obvious different between the UK Supreme Court and other top courts is that JAs are recruited from within the UK legal system. This is in stark contrast to the South African Constitutional Court, which recruits between 15 and 20 young lawyers from around the world to serve as 'foreign law clerks'.[59] In addition to one foreign law clerk, each judge on the South African Constitutional Court is assisted by two South African law clerks.[60] A limiting factor in the UK Supreme Court is that it is normal for the JAs to be shared between two Justices. At the time of the interviews, Lord Reed and Lord Kerr shared a JA.[61] Lord Kerr confirmed that there were limited opportunities for either the JAs or the judges to undertake this kind of extraneous research:

> [P]artly because I share [a JA], but mainly because we are so busy; the opportunity to cast a wide net over potentially relevant foreign jurisprudence just doesn't exist.[62]

Others among the Justices interviewed expressed similar sentiments about time pressures in reference to their own research. Digesting the precise meaning of foreign jurisprudence takes time:

> If I get say six decisions of the German Supreme Court or Constitutional Court, it takes some time to read them—they are not short! You could easily spend three or four hours reading those decisions once you've got them. And you've got to find them first.[63]

[57] Interview with the Rt Hon Lord Reed, Justice of the UK Supreme Court (Supreme Court, London, 8 May 2012).

[58] David S Law and Wen-Chen Chang, 'The Limits of Global Judicial Dialogue' [2011] *Washington Law Review* 523.

[59] Some advertisements specify that applicants should show an interest in comparative law, See, eg, 'Invitation for Applications for Foreign Law Clerks: Constitutional Court of South Africa, February 2017', www.iacl-aidc-blog.org/2017/03/21/invitation-for-applications-for-foreign-law-clerks-constitutional-court-of-south-africa-february-2017.

[60] Website of the Constitutional Court of South Africa, 'About Law Clerks', https://www.concourt.org.za/index.php/law-researchers/about-law-clerks. The South African Constitutional Court is also influenced by American interns: Christa Rautenbach, 'South Africa: Teaching an "Old Dog" New Tricks? An Empirical Study of the Use of Foreign Precedents by the South African Constitutional Court (1995–2010)' in Groppi and Ponthoreau (n 2) 200.

[61] Focus group interview with the judicial assistants of the UK Supreme Court (Supreme Court, London, 22 May 2012).

[62] Interview with Lord Kerr (n 33).

[63] Interview with Lord Mance (n 26).

Nevertheless, several of the Justices admitted that they would be likely to conduct their own research into areas of foreign jurisprudence that were felt to be of interest. Technological developments, in particular, have had a profound effect on this; the ability to conduct research and communicate online has made available a burgeoning pool of materials. This complements a growing tradition of international conferences and symposiums, which facilitate a direct exchange of ideas between judges and practitioners from all over the world. As Cram has said, 'just as those parties appearing before the courts interact increasingly with others beyond national boundaries ... so are courts confronted with the existence and practices of other legal systems',[64] and it is not surprising that these have filtered into their judgments. Lord Dyson explained:

> We are living in an increasingly interdependent world. Jurists read each other's judgments with ease on the internet. They meet at international conferences to discuss issues of common interest. The good sense of learning from each other and taking the best that each of us has to offer is now well appreciated.[65]

Baroness Hale commented that 'you only have to push a few buttons' to find any material that may be of interest.[66] In most cases, this involved using the various legal databases such as Westlaw International or LexisLibrary (previously LexisNexis). The Supreme Court also has its own library, which may be asked to source relevant materials for consideration. The library is well stocked with law reports from various foreign jurisdictions and produces a monthly broadsheet, including some comparative law material.

Research into relevant comparative law is likely to be easier at the Supreme Court than in other courts. In the Court of Appeal, Lady Justice Arden explained that the time pressures would often be too great to allow for much research of this kind on the part of the judges:

> You have to have something which gets you started with the foreign law, because you simply do not have time to go and, as it were, sit down with Lexis Australia or Lexis South Africa, and work out what relevant cases there might be. There has to be somebody who has done some work first.[67]

For these reasons, academic work is an important channel for comparative jurisprudence. Lord Phillips explained that 'academics have the advantage of being able to spend much [more] time on looking at a particular area of the law than [the Supreme Court]' and the Justices would all be likely to read

[64] Ian Cram, 'Resort to Foreign Constitutional Norms in Domestic Human Rights Jurisprudence with Reference to Terrorism Cases' [2009] *CLJ* 118, 121.

[65] Lord Dyson, 'The Globalisation of Law', Pilgrim Fathers Lecture 2015 (Plymouth University, 6 November 2015), www.judiciary.gov.uk/wp-content/uploads/2015/11/pilgrim-fathers-lecture.pdf accessed 21 September 2016 [41]; Lord Dyson, *Justice: Continuity and Change* (Hart Publishing, 2018) 171.

[66] Interview with Baroness Hale (n 28).

[67] Interview with Lady Justice Arden (n 25).

'the leading academics on a particular topic to see what they have to say'.[68] Thus, where foreign jurisprudence has been identified by academics in leading works, the Supreme Court would be alerted to it.[69] A good example of academic work being used in this way can be drawn from the *HJ (Iran)* case considered in Chapter 7.[70] In that case, Lord Dyson did not 'find it necessary to examine the Australian authorities to which [the Supreme Court] were referred'.[71] Instead, it was 'sufficient' to refer to an academic paper exploring the impact of the troublesome *S395/2002* case on the refugee jurisprudence of Australia and the UK five years on.[72] Lord Dyson was satisfied that the paper showed that 'the reasoning of the majority judgments is being generally applied in Australia'.[73] Lord Walker also noted comparative academic work on this point and reproduced a lengthy paragraph from the paper to which Lord Dyson referred.[74] The implicit suggestion here is that cases not digested by academic work are not as likely to be used as those that are. Lord Reed took this view to explain the reasons why some jurisdictions were cited more than others:

> There is a practical problem about finding foreign jurisprudence. I've got a French textbook on human rights law, which obviously cites French case law. But not many people have got foreign textbooks on their shelves.[75]

This reliance on academic research may also inform the consideration as to why certain jurisdictions are cited above others. According to Lord Mance, one wouldn't look up jurisprudence from smaller foreign courts, for example. If foreign sources are used, 'it would be because it was in some particular international field and had received a degree of notoriety'.[76] 'That sort of case', he explained, 'would be a case that had achieved international note and had therefore appeared in human rights textbooks and you would be referred to it because it was there in a footnote'.[77] Similar explanations can be made about reference to authority that had previously been cited by a domestic judge.[78] Foreign jurisprudence might otherwise be

[68] Interview with the Rt Hon Lord Phillips of Worth Matravers, former President of the UK Supreme Court Supreme Court (Supreme Court, London, 23 November 2011).

[69] ibid.

[70] See ch 7, text from n 107.

[71] *HJ (Iran) (FC) v Secretary of State for the Home Department* [2010] UKSC 31; [2011] 1 AC 596 [112] (Lord Dyson).

[72] *Appellant S395/2002 v Minister for Immigration* (2003) 216 CLR 473.

[73] *HJ (Iran)* (n 71), citing Jenni Millbank, 'From Discretion to Disbelief: Recent Trends in Refugee Determinations on the Basis of Sexual Orientation in Australia and the United Kingdom' (2009) 13 *International Journal of Human Rights* 391.

[74] ibid 92.

[75] Interview with Lord Reed (n 57).

[76] Interview with Lord Mance (n 26).

[77] ibid.

[78] See, eg, *R (Lord Carlile of Berriew QC) v Secretary of State for the Home Department* [2014] UKSC 60; [2015] AC 945, where the Supreme Court of Fiji was cited

difficult to find: 'You probably wouldn't come across it unless you had been to a conference, in Africa with the Commonwealth Magistrates and Judges Association, or something like that, and it had been mentioned'.[79]

The influence of international conferences or judicial exchanges is one of the easiest explanations for judicial comparativism. The so-called 'transjudicial dialogue' usually encompasses 'dialogue' both in the sense that judges may communicate through their judgments and in the more obvious sense of judges communicating through a direct—face-to-face—exchange of ideas. Broadly speaking, dialogue of this kind can be summarised simply as meetings that bring about an awareness of each other's decisions.[80] Such meetings are of obvious relevance for national and supranational courts, especially where national judges may wish to seek guidance as to the supranational court's jurisprudence. Thus, it is not surprising that these meetings are common between the Justices of the UK Supreme Court and the judges of the Strasbourg and Luxembourg Courts. Interestingly, Paterson also notes that the Supreme Court interacts with the Strasbourg Court much more frequently than with the CJEU in Luxembourg:

> [T]here is far more interaction—oral and written—between the two courts than there is with Luxembourg. Members of each court visit the other and discussions ensue of actual cases and points of debate. Written exchanges are also frequent, and not just in judgments but also through lectures, and even occasional emails.[81]

Paterson explains that the difference may be due to the style of the judgments in either court: 'the outputs from the Luxembourg court are short, stilted and enigmatic, adhering to a civilian style which appears as though drafted by a committee with no spark of individualism'.[82] Similar explanations were given by several of the Justices of the Supreme Court interviewed for this study.

Conferences and judicial exchanges are also common between national domestic courts. Some Justices of the UK Supreme Court might participate in a few international visits each year, usually lasting three to four days. Some of the Justices interviewed did consider that international conferences and symposiums of this kind would be likely to contribute to an awareness of foreign jurisprudence. Lord Walker, for example, felt that personal

(*Matalulu v Director of Public Prosecutions* [2003] 4 LRC 712) via a quote from Lord Bingham's judgment in *R (Corner House Research) v Director of the Serious Fraud Office* [2009] 1 AC 756.

[79] Interview with Lord Mance (n 26).

[80] Anne-Marie Slaughter, 'A Typology of Transjudicial Communication' (1994) 29 *University of Richmond Law Review* 99, 103.

[81] Paterson, *Final Judgment* (n 38) 224.

[82] ibid 223. Paterson notes (at fn 72) that no dissents or concurrences are permitted at the CJEU. See also Lord Neuberger, 'Some Thoughts on Judicial Reasoning across Jurisdictions', 2016 Mitchell Lecture (Edinburgh, 11 November 2016), www.supremecourt.uk/docs/speech-161111.pdf.

relationships between judges would affect the attention paid to the jurisprudence from a particular court:

> In my case that certainly is a factor. When I was at the bar and as a first instance judge, I did virtually no networking; I simply just got on with my work. It is really only since I got to the top appeal court that I have started travelling. I first went to Australia in 2005 to give a lecture and I'm going for the 5th time this summer. So that's five times in seven years. I've been to New Zealand a couple of times. You do get to know people and it does make a big difference that you read a judgment and you know who it is that is writing it. I think that, right or wrongly, that is a very important factor in how much interest you take.[83]

Lord Walker later added to these examples, mentioning the official judicial exchange visits with the Canadian judiciary in London (in 2005) and in Ottawa (in 2008). Lord Walker headed the British 'team' on these occasions, which included Lady Hale, Lord Kerr, Lord Reed, Lord Dyson, Dame Janet Smith, Rabinder Singh QC (then still at the Bar) and Professor David Feldman of Downing College, Cambridge (but then also a judge on the Constitutional Court of Bosnia and Herzegovina). Lord Walker reflected that this was 'a wonderful experience … and the start of friendships with two outstanding judges, the Chief Justice and Justice Rosalie Abella'. Lord Walker felt that Canadian law had 'in some ways diverged from English law (especially in the law of trusts)', but that on human rights, 'they have quite a lot to teach us'.[84]

However, none of the Justices interviewed appeared to consider that these sorts of meetings would usually be a primary source of foreign jurisprudence. It was felt to be only in very exceptional cases that dialogues of this kind would substantially affect judicial reasoning. Rarely was an example given during the interviews in which a Justice could link discussion with judges from other jurisdictions with the reasoning in a later judgment. Only one such example could be recalled, regarding the well-known *Daly* case from the early years of the HRA 1998.[85] Lord Dyson recounted a story about a visit to the Supreme Court of Israel during which a roundtable discussion took place on the concept of proportionality. Lord Dyson felt that Lord Steyn's judgment in *Daly* drew heavily from that meeting. Lord Dyson recalled Lord Steyn to have said something along the lines of 'this has been a very useful discussion, especially as I have now to write a judgment concerning this issue'.[86] Other judges have given more explicit

[83] Interview with the Rt Hon Lord Walker of Gestingthorpe, former Justice of the UK Supreme Court (Supreme Court, London, 15 May 2012).

[84] Email from Lord Walker to the author, 23 November 2017.

[85] *R (Daly) v Secretary of State for the Home Department* [2001] UKHL 26; [2001] 2 AC 532.

[86] Interview with Lord Dyson MR (n 27).

acknowledgments about the influence of these exchanges in the years since the interviews were conducted. For example, in a lecture at the University of Edinburgh, Lord Reed reported that his discussion of the concept of proportionality in *Bank Mellat* had been 'influenced by discussion with Prof Dr Gertrude Lübbe-Wolff', then a judge at the German Federal Constitutional Court.[87]

Aside from the *Daly* example, the general feeling appears to be that international meetings would usually be very interesting, but would not necessarily contribute substantively to the work of a judge in his home court.[88] In part this may be explained by a convention that discussion of topics that are known to be coming up in the Supreme Court is avoided, but there are a number of other reasons as well. First, the meetings are pitched at varying levels. Some of the Justices who had not participated in the more serious conferences felt more sceptical about the value of international judicial exchanges. Second, it was evident that some of the Justices were more enthusiastic about these meetings than others. While some of the Justices recounted that they had led delegations to other courts and found these meetings to be useful, others explained that they were not as keen on participating in this way, preferring instead 'to get on with the business of judging'.[89] Third, visits tend to be to those courts that are already familiar to the Justices of the Supreme Court, such as Canada and South Africa, where there is already an established relationship. The established relationships and familiarity with certain courts also perpetuates the tendency to refer to the jurisprudence of those jurisdictions.

IV. THE INFLUENCE OF COMMON LAW JURISDICTIONS

Not too long ago, the late Lord Bingham wrote about the earlier reluctance of English courts to draw from foreign jurisprudence, feeling the 'unquestioning belief in the superiority of the common law and its institutions' to be at the root of the matter:[90]

> When I started in practice, it was an almost universal article of faith that English law and legal institutions were without peer in the world, with very little to be usefully learned from others ...[91]

[87] *Bank Mellat v HM Treasury* [2013] UKSC 39; [2014] AC 700; Lord Reed, 'Comparative Law in the Supreme Court of the United Kingdom', Lecture at the Centre for Private Law (University of Edinburgh, 13 October 2017), www.supremecourt.uk/docs/speech-171013.pdf.

[88] Similar findings are reported by Mak: Mak (n 3) 85.

[89] Interview with Lord Clarke (n 29).

[90] Tom Bingham, 'There is a World Elsewhere: The Changing Perspectives of English Law' (1992) 41 *ICLQ* 513, 514.

[91] ibid 514.

This attitude lingers in the US. Several of the participants in the foreign authorities debate there have expressed scepticism about the value in borrowing from certain jurisdictions not previously famous for the quality of their human rights decisions.[92] Whether true or not, there is a perception that different ideological positions on human rights are taken by different jurisdictions and (if that is true) that drawing from one particular jurisdiction's approach to human rights may be regarded as a sign of a particular orientation towards human rights generally.[93] McCrudden found that 'it is [in the main] the judiciaries of liberal democratic regimes that cite each other'.[94] 'The citation of, for example, Chinese cases by the [UK] House of Lords [did] not seem likely'.[95]

Perhaps the most compelling explanation for the use of foreign jurisprudence in human rights cases is that a particular regime requires it or that there exists a common alliance. On this basis, it would not be surprising if jurisprudence under Bills of Rights from jurisdictions in similar legal traditions, and that are of recent origin, were to have been especially relevant in this respect. Many countries with legal systems rooted in the common law have adopted Bills of Rights not dissimilar to the UK HRA 1998. Indeed, the framers of the HRA are often thought to have taken inspiration from some of those jurisdictions. For example, it is often pointed out that the Labour Party was strongly influenced by the Canadian position when it decided to campaign for human rights legislation.[96] Hence Feldman's suggestion that the decisions of the Supreme Court of India under that country's 1947 Constitution, those of the Court of Appeal of New Zealand on the New Zealand Bill of Rights Act 1990, and those of the South African Constitutional Court on the rights under South Africa's 1993 and 1996 African Constitutions may all contain 'useful insights'.[97] The point was repeated frequently in the early literature on the HRA. Before the coming into force of the Act, Starmer considered jurisprudence of this kind to be 'invaluable' in assisting the interpretation of Convention rights.[98] A few years later, Lester and Clapinska wrote

[92] Dorsen (n 11) 528 (Justice Breyer): 'I may have made what one might call a tactical error in referring to a case from Zimbabwe—not the human rights capital of the world.'

[93] ibid; Richard Clayton, 'Judicial Deference and "Democratic Dialogue": The Legitimacy of Judicial Intervention under the Human Rights Act 1998' [2004] *PL* 33, 47; Leighton McDonald, 'New Directions in the Australian Bill of Rights Debate' [2004] *PL* 22.

[94] McCrudden (n 2) 517–18.

[95] ibid.

[96] See, eg, Lord Irvine, 'The Legal System and Law Reform under Labour' in David Bean (ed), *Law Reform for All* (Blackstone, 1996), referred to in Clayton (n 93) 45.

[97] David Feldman (ed), *English Public Law* (Oxford University Press, 2004) 397.

[98] Keir Starmer, *European Human Rights Law: The Human Rights Act 1998 and the European Convention on Human Rights* (Legal Action Group, 1999) 27.

that: 'The developing principles contained in the constitutional case law of courts in other common law countries ... are likely to be at least *as persuasive* as the Strasbourg case law'.[99] Indeed, some of the literature confirmed that these jurisdictions frequently refer to UK jurisprudence,[100] but there had been little empirical research to confirm that the UK courts follow the same pattern. Mak did not gather quantitative data on foreign judgment citations, but the results of her interviews with UK Supreme Court Justices led her to conclude that 'the first criterion for the selection of foreign judgments concerns legal tradition, in the sense of the shared background with other common law systems. Sources most often referred to come from Commonwealth legal systems and from the US legal system'.[101]

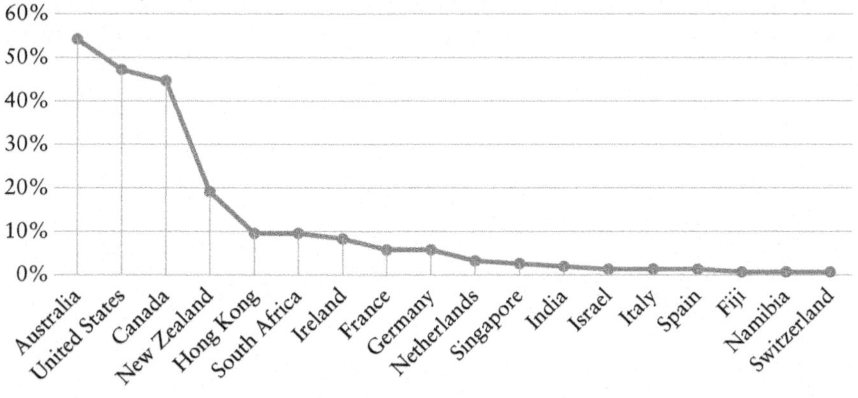

Figure 5.8: Number of UK Supreme Court cases citing at least one decision from given jurisdiction, as a percentage of all cases making reference to foreign jurisprudence, 2009–17

Figure 5.8 corroborates Mak's account, showing that Australia, the US and Canada were the most commonly cited jurisdictions between 2009 and 2017, referenced in 54 per cent, 47 per cent and 45 per cent of all cases making reference to foreign jurisprudence respectively. Other common law

[99] Lord Lester and Lydia Clapinska, 'Human Rights and the British Constitution' in Jeffrey Jowell and Dawn Oliver (eds), *The Changing Constitution*, 5th edn (Oxford University Press, 2004) 83.

[100] See, eg, Groppi and Ponthoreau (n 2).

[101] Mak (n 3) 206.

jurisdictions followed, with fewer cases referring to courts working in civil law or mixed legal traditions. The pattern in Figure 5.8 is repeated in the results about the total number of foreign cases cited. Figure 5.9 sets the data about citation frequency (Figure 5.8) against citation numbers. In that arrangement, it is possible to see that the US accounts for the most foreign cases cited, but that the second and third-greatest numbers of citations are drawn, again, from Australia and Canada. As a proportion of all explicit citations of foreign jurisprudence at the Supreme Court, Figure 5.9 shows that the jurisprudence of common law courts is the clear favourite. Of the total 671 foreign decisions cited by the Supreme Court between 2009 and 2017, cases from Australia, the US and Canada accounted for 492 citations (73 per cent of all cases cited). There were 93 citations from New Zealand, South Africa and Ireland (14 per cent). Among the civil law systems, France and Germany were the most cited, together accounting for 53 citations (8 per cent). The remaining 33 citations (5 per cent) were spread between nine jurisdictions.

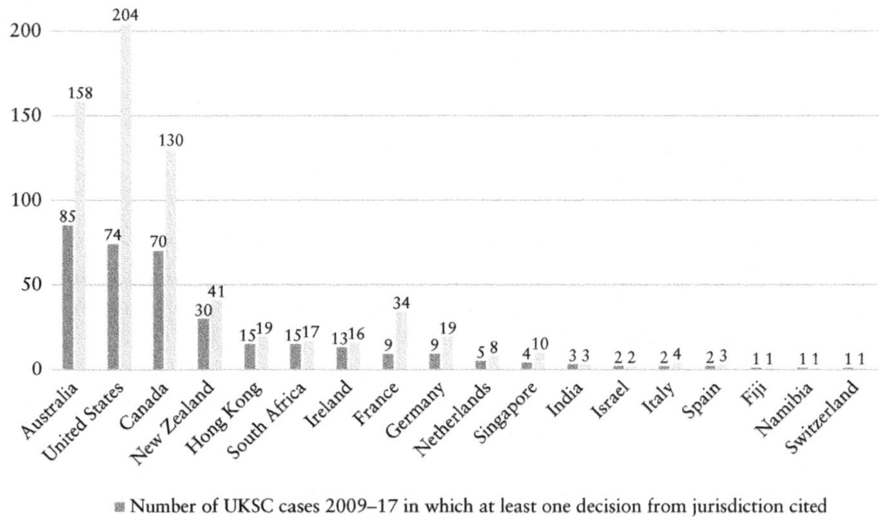

Figure 5.9: UK Supreme Court cases with at least one reference to given jurisdiction compared with total number of foreign cases cited

Figure 5.10 shows that the pattern is fairly consistent between human rights cases and non-human rights cases, although there are far fewer references to decisions of the Australian courts in human rights cases.

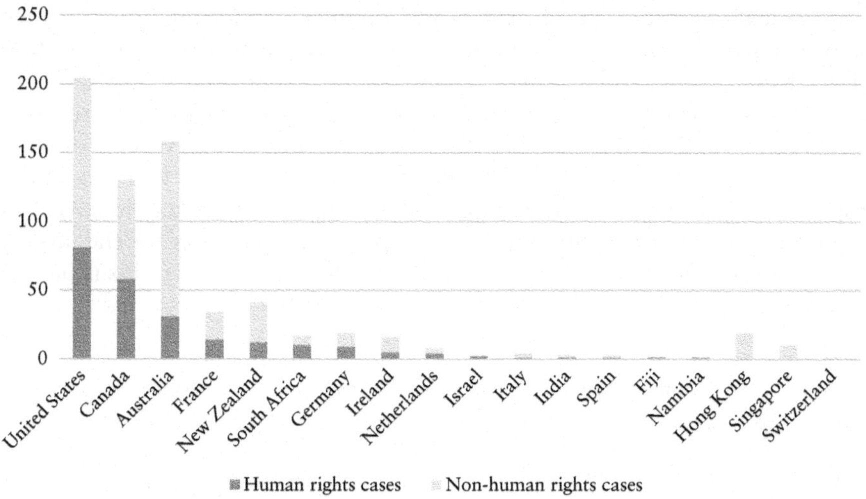

Figure 5.10: Case citations from each jurisdiction, arranged by number cited in human rights cases

The reason for this might simply be that Australian jurisprudence is more commonly referred to in the law of obligations. The results of Burrows' survey of tort cases decided by the House of Lords and the Supreme Court between 1989 and 2014 showed references to common law jurisdictions in 64 per cent of cases and to civil law jurisdictions in 10 per cent of cases.[102] Australia came out as the most commonly cited jurisdiction, followed by US and Canadian jurisprudence. *Montgomery v Lanarkshire Health Board* is a good example,[103] concerned with medical negligence. The Supreme Court in *Montgomery* referred to cases from Australia, Canada and the US. Lord Reed has since explained that reference to this jurisprudence was 'to identify respects in which the then leading authority on informed consent to medical treatment was unconvincingly reasoned and out of date'.[104] The foreign cases 'particularly the Australian cases' assisted the Court in 'identifying a principled and practical approach for the United Kingdom to adopt'.[105]

Whatever the area of law, it is indisputable that the Supreme Court generally cites foreign jurisprudence from a small family of courts.[106] In the

[102] Burrows (n 3) 26.
[103] *Montgomery v Lanarkshire Health Board* [2015] UKSC 11; [2015] AC 1450.
[104] Lord Reed (n 87) 3.
[105] ibid.
[106] Groppi and Ponthoreau also found that the practice of citing foreign jurisprudence in courts of other jurisdictions is usually confined to a particular group or 'family' of courts: Groppi and Ponthoreau (n 2) 430.

UK context, Figure 5.11 illustrates the number of foreign jurisprudence citations from courts in common law systems (Australia, Canada, Fiji, Hong Kong, India, Ireland, Israel, New Zealand, Singapore and the US), civil law systems (France, Germany, Italy, the Netherlands, Spain and Switzerland) and mixed legal systems (Namibia and South Africa) for each year between 2009 and 2017. This makes clear that the fluctuations in the Supreme Court's citations numbers are largely due to references to common law courts. Given that common law jurisprudence accounts for the largest proportion of foreign case citations at the UK Supreme Court, this is hardly surprising.

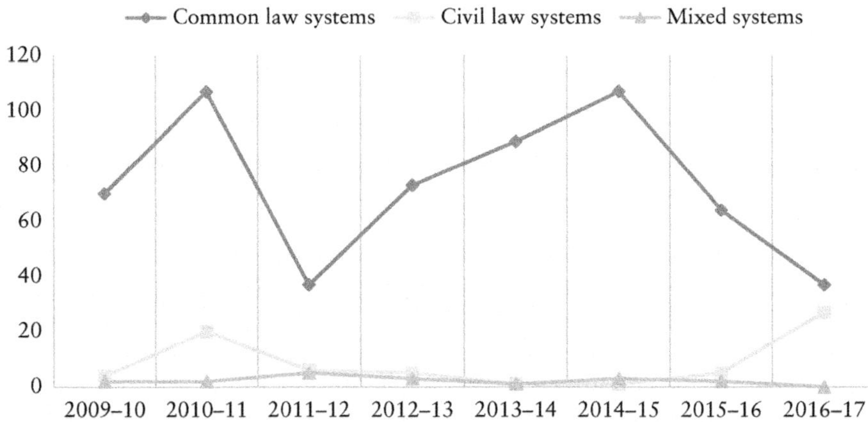

Figure 5.11: Total number of foreign case citations from civil law, common law and mixed systems in the UK Supreme Court 2009–17, by year

Figure 5.12 seems to show that the citation practice in human rights cases is more evenly spread than in other areas of law. In fact, the increase in the number of foreign case citations from 2015–16 to 2016–17 strikes a balance between cases from common and civil law jurisdictions. This reflects the unusual reference list in the Supreme Court's decision in *Belhaj*, which was handed down on 17 January 2017. The Supreme Court made an unusual number of references to decisions of the French (five), German (six) and Dutch (three) courts, as well as to the jurisprudence of US courts on the doctrine of foreign act of state.[107]

[107] *Belhaj* (n 30). Sanger has described the survey of foreign jurisprudence as both 'remarkable' and 'distracting'; a 'paradigm of transnational judicial dialogue'. See Andrew Sanger, 'UK Government Cannot Hide from Complicity in Human Rights Abuses' [2017] *CLJ* 223, 226.

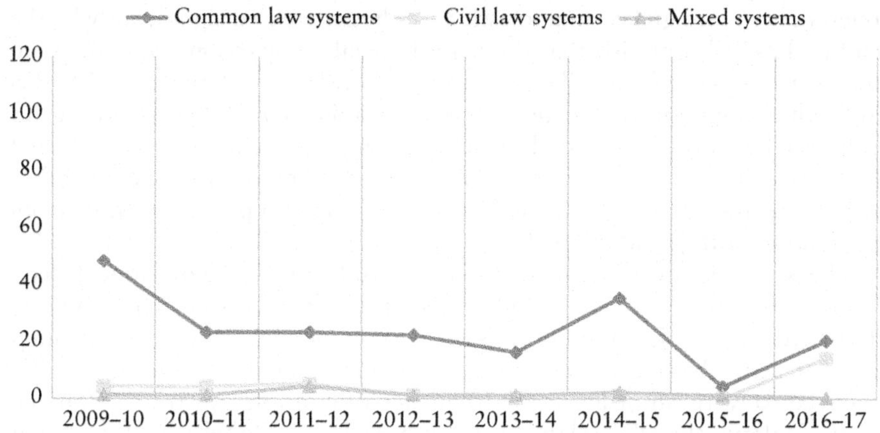

Figure 5.12: Total number of foreign case citations from civil law, common law and mixed systems in human rights cases before the UK Supreme Court 2009–17, by year

The unusual balance in 2016–17 is made more obvious by the bar chart given in Figure 5.13. The general preference for recourse to jurisprudence from common law or mixed legal systems between 2009 and 2016 suggests that 2016–17 is likely to be an outlier.

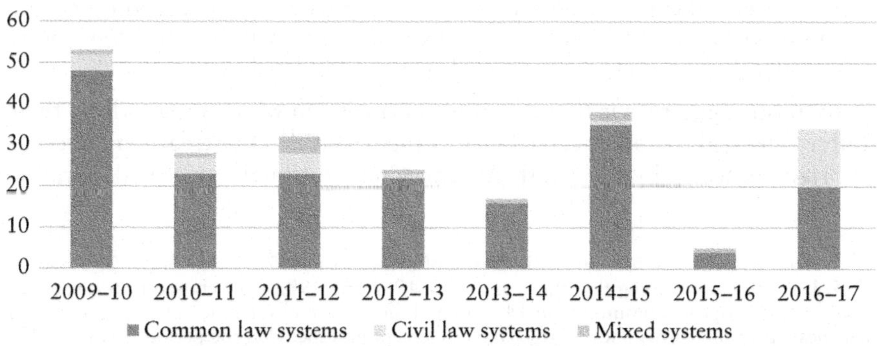

Figure 5.13: Total number of foreign case citations from civil law, common law and mixed systems in human rights cases before the UK Supreme Court 2009–17, by year

The pattern of citation is not much different from that observed by Örücü in her study of decisions published in the *All ER* rendered in 1972, 1982, 1992 and between 1990 and 1995.[108] Örücü found that the proportion of

[108] Esin Örücü, 'Comparative Law in British Courts' in Ulrich Drobnig and Sjef van Erp (eds), *The Use of Comparative Law by Courts: 14th International Congress of Comparative Law* (Kluwer, 1999) 253.

references to foreign law in domestic cases had increased significantly by the end of 1995,[109] but also that the main judicial comparisons were between members of the common law family, with frequent references to the US and other Commonwealth jurisdictions. Further, since 1993, references to common law jurisdictions had 'increased four-fold', while references to civil law jurisdictions had doubled.[110] Flanagan and Ahern also concluded that judges are likely to refer to a small family of courts, in particular those from Commonwealth jurisdictions.[111]

The same pattern prevailed in Siems' study of Court of Appeal decisions between 1984 and 2006:[112] common law courts were cited in 16 per cent of cases, while citations to non-common law courts were around 0.5 per cent. Among the common law courts that were most frequently referred to were (in order of the frequency of citation) Australia, Canada, New Zealand, the US, Ireland and South Africa.[113] Bobek also found that citations of foreign jurisprudence continue to be drawn from mainly common law jurisdictions.[114] It was for that reason that the focus of Bobek's chapter on England and Wales was on how to classify such 'intra-common law referencing'.[115]

The reasons for citing any particular jurisdiction are not made obvious in the judgments. As Cram found:

> English judges, it seems, do little to explain why the insights of a particular jurisdiction might be relevant to the interpretation of domestic law and why those derived from other jurisdictions were not. The reader of these law reports searches in vain for an account of the criteria by which the included jurisdictions were deemed includable and why the excluded were considered excludable.[116]

A common suggestion is that the jurisdictions from which judges draw their sources must, above all else, be 'fit for comparison'.[117] The treatment of comparative authority by the South African Constitutional Court is illustrative

[109] From references to foreign law in 26 out of 602 cases in 1972 to 119 out of 285 cases in 1995. It is worth explaining that the years 1972, 1982 and 1992 were chosen to test whether entry to the European Community in 1972 altered the pattern of references. Örücü recognised that these intervals allowed for a large chance element and included the period between 1990 and 1995 in part to correct this (but also since it was the most recent period and one that she felt to be long enough to attempt meaningful analysis and reliable hypotheses).

[110] Örücü (n 108) 253.

[111] Brian Flanagan and Sinead Ahern, 'Judicial Decision-Making and Transnational Law: A Survey of Common Law Supreme Court Judges' (2011) 60 *ICLQ* 1.

[112] Mathias Siems, 'Citation Patterns of the German Federal Supreme Court and the Court of Appeal of England and Wales' (2010) 21 *King's Law Journal* 152.

[113] ibid. See also Martin Gelter and Mathias Siems, 'Networks, Dialogue or One-Way Traffic? An Empirical Analysis of Cross-citations between Ten of Europe's Highest Courts' (2012) 8 *Utrecht Law Review* 88, 93.

[114] Bobek (n 14) 75.

[115] ibid.

[116] Cram (n 64) 140.

[117] See McCrudden (n 2) 501; Clayton (n 93) 33, 47; McDonald (n 93) 22.

of this point.[118] The Court has explained that: 'Comparative research is generally valuable, and is all the more so when dealing with problems new to our jurisprudence but well developed in *mature constitutional democracies*' (emphasis added).[119] On that basis, it is hardly surprising that 'it is [in the main] the judiciaries of liberal democratic regimes that cite each other'.[120] In fact, Allan has gone so far as to suggest that, given a shared understanding of constitutional principles, common law jurisdictions can be 'understood to *share* a common law constitution, grounded in broadly liberal conceptions of legitimate governance'.[121] This sort of motivation seemed to underpin the references to eight foreign jurisdictions in *Starbucks (HK) Ltd v British Sky Broadcasting Group*:

> In addition to domestic cases, it is both important and helpful to consider how the law has developed in other common law jurisdictions—important because it is desirable that the common law jurisdictions have a consistent approach, and helpful because every national common law judiciary can benefit from the experiences and thoughts of other common law judges.[122]

Cram was tempted to conclude his own study by suggesting that 'the judges in the House of Lords and Court of Appeal conceive, in the main, of the Canadian and United States Supreme Courts as similarly placed institutions functioning under similar circumstances within a framework of broadly similar rules and underlying values'.[123] This is a conclusion that is supported by the interview evidence from this research. As Baroness Hale explained:

> The common law world is preferred to elsewhere and that is partly because it is all in English and partly because we are dealing in similar instruments, similar modes of thought and similar styles of judgment.[124]

Others among the interviewed Justices agreed. The then President of the Supreme Court, Lord Phillips, felt that there would be:

> more use when we are a looking at courts in the long established democracies than some of the countries which have not had the benefit of developing over years with democratic and independent judiciaries.[125]

[118] Section 39(1)(b) of the Constitution of the Republic of South Africa 1996 expressly declares that '[w]hen interpreting the Bill of Rights, a court, tribunal or forum *may* consider foreign law', but that it '*must* consider international law' (emphasis added).

[119] *Sanderson v Attorney General, Eastern Cape* 1998 (2) SA 38 (CC); see also Rabinder Singh, 'Interpreting Bills of Rights' [2008] *Statute Law Review* 82.

[120] McCrudden (n 2) 517.

[121] Trevor RS Allan, *Constitutional Justice: A Liberal Theory of the Rule of Law* (Oxford University Press, 2001).

[122] *Starbucks (HK) Ltd and Another v British Sky Broadcasting Group and Others (No 2)* [2015] UKSC 31; [2015] 1 WLR 2628 [50].

[123] Cram (n 64) 141.

[124] Interview with Baroness Hale (n 28).

[125] Interview with Lord Phillips (n 68).

Lord Phillips added that whether or not foreign jurisprudence would be used depended very much on 'the nature of the authority' and that some decisions of foreign courts have been really 'carefully thought out', giving the example of some Canadian judgments.[126] Explaining what it takes to be 'carefully thought out', Lord Phillips said that 'you have to be an outstandingly good jurist'.[127] Asked if that was something perceived from reading the cases or if that is known before, he answered: 'We have a very good idea of who the really outstanding jurists in the Commonwealth are'.[128] Lord Collins gave similar answers to these questions, expressing a requirement for confidence in the jurisdiction that one is drawing from:

> [Foreign jurisprudence] won't necessarily be of direct assistance, unless it is a court of great authority and it is something that hasn't come up here, like the Supreme Court of Canada.[129]

In fact, this apparently provides one of the barriers to the use of foreign jurisprudence from other countries:

> It is very difficult to judge the quality of foreign decisions if you don't know the people and their reputation ... I suppose in itself you can say 'well the Supreme Court—American Supreme Court or Canadian Supreme Court or Australian High Court—they wouldn't have got there unless they were pretty good'. You get a feel for it. When precedents are cited here, even of English judges, there are some who have got much greater reputation than others. For example, one might pay more attention to what Lord Bingham or Lord Hoffmann has said than to another judge whose reputation is not so high.[130]

Nevertheless, a continued tendency to cite common law jurisprudence in human rights cases is surprising given the fact that the dominant force in human rights cases has been the ECHR. That the UK has moved steadily towards convergence with the rest of Europe is hardly contentious. Indeed, the UK was among the first members of the Council of Europe to ratify the Convention and English lawyers made a substantial contribution to the drafting of the document. Moreover, a major factor said to be involved in the reluctance of the French judges to rely on Strasbourg decisions is their national pride in front of a new instrument, which is supposed to be dominated by English legal conceptions.[131] More significantly, cases from jurisdictions outside the Convention borders are 'unlikely to point to the direction in which the common law should be developed to ensure compatibility

[126] ibid.
[127] ibid.
[128] ibid.
[129] Interview with Lord Collins (n 53).
[130] ibid.
[131] Jean-François Burgelin and Agnès Lalardrie, *L'application de la Convention par le juge judiciaire français, Mélanges Pettiti* (Bruylant, 1998) 160, referred to in Luc Heuschling, 'Comparative Law and the European Convention on Human Rights Cases' in Örücü (n 2) 36.

with the Convention rights'.[132] Unlike the Canadian, Victorian and New Zealand experiences, the Convention and its jurisprudence are built into the structure of the HRA 1998.

The use of common law jurisprudence is especially surprising given the cautionary statements made in the early days of the HRA 1998. For example in *Sheldrake*, Lord Bingham set out that even though courts had on a number of occasions 'gained valuable insights from the reasoning of Commonwealth judges',[133] the UK 'must [now] take its lead from Strasbourg'.[134] In *Gillan*, Lord Bingham thought it was 'perilous ... to seek to transpose the outcome of Canadian cases',[135] by reason of their being 'decided under a significantly different legislative regime'.[136] In *Marper*, Lord Steyn rejected the idea that domestic traditions bear any relevance to the scope of Convention rights at all.[137] The court in *British American Tobacco* recognised that 'it is instructive ... to see how another respected jurisdiction has dealt with a related but confined problem', but also considered that comparison (with the jurisprudence of the US First Amendment) should be undertaken with care:[138]

> [T]he balance between State legislation and federal legislation in the United States is a subject of renowned complexity. Decisions on such matters can have limited effect on our consideration of the balance to be struck in considering a restriction of a limited Convention rights and the measure of a discretion to be afforded to Parliament and ministers under our own rather different constitutional system.[139]

Since it is the Strasbourg jurisprudence that provides the authoritative interpretation on Convention rights, there is little incentive to use foreign jurisprudence if an authoritative judgment is to be found in the Strasbourg case law. Bobek identified 'a correlation between the amount of the mandatory foreign sources and the likeliness of any further, non-mandatory foreign inspiration', concluding that 'the exponential growth of the European and international *must* sources takes away much of the free space and energy for the *may* ones'.[140] Indeed, the influence of the Strasbourg jurisprudence

[132] Roger Masterman, 'Taking the Strasbourg Jurisprudence into Account: Developing a "Municipal Law of Human Rights" under the Human Rights Act' [2005] 54 *ICLQ* 907, 923.

[133] *Sheldrake v Director of Public Prosecutions* [2004] UKHL 43; [2004] 3 WLR 876 [33].

[134] ibid.

[135] *R (Gillan) v Commissioner of Police for the Metropolis* [2006] UKHL 12; [2006] 2 AC 307 [23].

[136] ibid.

[137] *R (Marper) v Chief Constable of Yorkshire* [2004] UKHL 39; [2004] 1 WLR 2196 [27].

[138] *R (British American Tobacco UK Ltd) v Secretary of State for Health* [2004] EWHC (Admin) 2493; [2005] ACD 27.

[139] ibid [36].

[140] Bobek (n 14) 195.

is so clear as to be evident in some jurisdictions that are not signatories to that instrument. Groppi and Ponthoreau found that the decisions of the Strasbourg Court 'are experiencing an increasing influence' even in jurisdictions that are not signatories to the ECHR:[141]

> The many reasons explaining this phenomenon … include the accessibility for English-speaking countries of the [European Court of Human Rights] decisions and the fact that human rights are a more fertile ground for foreign citations.[142]

Implicit in the idea that common law jurisprudence is likely to provide less assistance in human rights cases, for the reason that they were 'decided under a significantly different legislative regime',[143] is the conclusion that jurisprudence from courts interpreting the same legislative regime would be of greater relevance. This makes the paucity of explicit references to other courts that *are* signatories to the ECHR, at first glance, surprising. It might have been thought that the jurisprudence of European domestic courts interpreting the same instrument would be of heightened interest to the Supreme Court. As Bobek has written:

> After the UK joined the European Communities, some people might have hoped (and others feared) that the UK would now join Continental Europe. This should be evidenced by a change in the (comparative) attention of the English courts: less comparative consideration would be given to the common law world and more considerations to Continental Europe.[144]

If the courts have followed this sort of approach, the use of foreign jurisprudence from common law jurisdictions should be on the decline. Without placing too much weight on the unusual citation pattern in 2016–17 (see Figure 5.13), this is difficult to substantiate without comparable data on explicit citations of foreign jurisprudence in the early years of the HRA 1998. The closest of the existing studies is that conducted by Cram, encompassing judicial references to a foreign court's jurisprudence in cases concerning rights to liberty and a fair trial since October 2000. Cram found just five cases referencing other nations' constitutional courts, but does not give a figure for the overall number of cases captured by his research.[145] From those five cases, Cram also found that citations were most likely to be drawn from common law jurisdictions.[146] Another study reviewed the decisions of the House of Lords in its final year (2009). In that year, Bobek counted

[141] Groppi and Ponthoreau (n 2) 420.
[142] ibid.
[143] *Gillan* (n 135) [23] (Lord Bingham).
[144] Bobek (n 14) 93.
[145] Cram (n 64) 132.
[146] ibid 140: 'The United States and Canada supplied by far the most frequent sources to which our judges refer, although the jurisprudence of five other jurisdictions is also represented in this survey.' See also Siems (n 112) 152.

that 'legal materials from outside of the UK' were referred to in 24 per cent of cases. These were 'almost exclusively of common law provenience', with just one referenced to materials from outside the common law world.[147]

An obvious explanation is that the analysis of explicit citations distorts the picture. In fact, the Supreme Court *does* consider the jurisprudence of European domestic legal orders, but the Justices can usually rely on the Strasbourg Court to outline the position of national legal systems. Sir Nicholas Bratza, the then President-elect of the European Court of Human Rights, has explained that it is 'the wider role of the Court' to '[examine] the law and practice in other Member States in resolving issues of general importance for the development of the Convention'.[148] Mahoney and Rondak, too, concluded that the Strasbourg Court's references to comparative law 'are a well-established part of the Court's judicial analysis and figure consistently in the Grand Chamber, as well as chamber, judgments'.[149] Bell has pointed out that this applies to the jurisprudence of supranational courts generally:

> [I]t is through [the decisions of the supranational courts] that the state of the law in other European countries comes to the notice of the UK justices. Strasbourg and Luxembourg consider the different ways a common problem is handled by national courts and select a permitted range of acceptable solutions (often by deferring to national decisions, rather than imposing a single right answer). As a result, it is not necessary for lawyers or justices to look directly at national law.[150]

Another explanation for the tendency to draw from common law courts is that linguistic barriers preclude meaningful comparison with non-English-speaking jurisdictions.[151] Mak observed this as a factor impacting on the citation of non-common law jurisdictions:

> With regard to a comparison with non-common law jurisdictions, the judges in general conduct research by themselves, i.e. without the help of judicial assistants. Therefore, the selection of this kind of foreign sources seems to be very much dependent on the personal background of the judges, in particular concerning the languages they master and the data they have access to.[152]

[147] Bobek (n 14) 89.

[148] Nicolas Bratza, 'The Relationship between the UK Courts and Strasbourg' [2011] *European Human Rights Law Review* 505, 507.

[149] Paul Mahoney and Rachael Kondak, 'Common Ground: A Starting Point or Destination for Comparative-Law Analysis by the European Court of Human Rights?' in Andenas and Fairgrieve (n 15) 119.

[150] Bell (n 4) 24; Bobek (n 14) 93. See also Jane Wright, 'Interpreting Section 2 of the Human Rights Act 1998: Towards an Indigenous Jurisprudence of Human Rights' [2009] *PL* 595, 614–615, arguing that while 'customary for the ECtHR to recite international materials on any question ... the reasoning of the ECtHR is generally premised upon European authorities'.

[151] Lord Reed (n 87) 3.

[152] Mak (n 34) 30.

Other comparative law scholars have been persuaded that different languages and styles are likely to be a significant barrier to judicial comparativism.[153] Discussion of this suggestion was one of the common themes from the interviews. As mentioned in Chapter 2, it is interesting that the judges held different views about the significance of linguistic barriers and that these views broadly correlated with whether or not the judge had raised the matter of his own accord or if he was directly questioned on it. Thus, when asked about the propensity to use jurisprudence from the main common law courts, Lord Mance replied that:

> For language reasons, it is easier to use common law courts. Unless you speak the language pretty fluently it's not so easy to use most other European courts. Although if you do speak the language, it is interesting to be able to do so.[154]

Lord Mance went on to explain that he is comfortable reading German and that he often found the German jurisprudence to be useful.[155] Lord Collins raised similar issues:

> There is a language issue in all of this. There is also unfamiliarity with the legal system. On the whole we don't get presented with anything from France or Germany or Italy. I suppose, if there is a really important issue and the French Conseil d'Etat or the German Constitutional Court has dealt with it, maybe we would be told about it. But then we would just be told what they did.[156]

Baroness Hale explained the problem to be one of confidence: confidence in any translation that one may use and confidence in one's own standard in the relevant language:

> The linguistic barrier is, I think, a very strong one because good translation is difficult to come by and very expensive. We may all think that we understand French and at least one of my colleagues has good German but nevertheless you've got to be very confident that you have good legal French and good legal German.[157]

The point was put most simply by Lord Clarke:

> With the best will in the world you have to speak very good French to understand legal French ... I once spent six months on a farm in France and spoke quite good

[153] Norman Weiss, 'The Impact of the European Convention on Human Rights on German Jurisprudence' in Örücü (n 2) 60–61; Mak (n 3) 114–15.

[154] Interview with Lord Mance (n 26).

[155] In one judgment, another Supreme Court Justice made reference to jurisprudence from the German Federal Constitutional Court: *R (HS2 Action Alliance Ltd) v Secretary of State for Transport and Another* [2014] UKSC 3; [2014] 1 WLR 324. Two references to judgments of the German Federal Constitutional Court are made by Lord Reed at [106] and [111], approving a principle applied by the German court (that the rulings of the CJEU should not be read as undermining national constitutions).

[156] Interview with Lord Collins (n 53).

[157] Interview with Baroness Hale (n 28).

> French at the end, but that doesn't really qualify you to read dense texts at the Conseil d'Etat.[158]

Similar reservations have been made by judges in other courts. In the South African context, Justice Kriegler expressed difficulty with judicial recourse to German cases on the basis that German is 'not an easy language'.[159] If it was not possible to 'get to the guts of what it's about', Justice Kriegler felt that it would not be possible to understand what the German court was 'really saying'.[160] However, Justice Kriegler evidently felt more comfortable with recourse to German cases where translations were available.[161]

Others among the UK Supreme Court Justices attributed much less influence to language as a barrier to the use of jurisprudence from non-English-speaking jurisdictions. Lord Sumption, for example, felt that 'the linguistic barrier is not terribly important': 'Most judges speak French'. In fact, Lord Sumption considered that it was 'the duty of every civilised man to read another language, if not more than one'.[162] Lord Kerr was also dismissive of the idea that judges were prevented from using such materials by a lack of language proficiency and gave an altogether different explanation:

> It is certainly not a linguistic barrier [that prevents use of case law from European domestic courts], because it is always possible to get a translation of the particular judgment. It's just that we have, generally, a wealth of material to get through and … if you attend an appeal hearing that's going to last two or three days in the Supreme Court and which involves a number of human rights issues, you will see vast bundles of authorities—most of which are never referred to.[163]

Although acknowledging language as a factor, Lord Walker's explanation for the lack of citations of jurisprudence from European domestic courts proceeded along slightly different lines:

> I think it is much more [to do with] habits of judgment writing. English judgments are far too long, and most continental judgments are—to our taste—a good deal too short. I remember being shown a judgment of the Supreme Court of the

158 Interview with Lord Clarke (n 29).

159 Ursula Bentele, 'Mining for Gold: The Constitutional Court of South Africa's Experience with Comparative Constitutional Law' (2009) 37(2) *Georgia Journal of International and Comparative Law* 219, 242–43, cited in Rautenbach (n 60) 201.

160 ibid.

161 ibid. Rautenbach cites *Du Plessis v De Klerk* [1996] 3 SA 850 (CC) 41 as an example of Justice Kriegler's willingness to refer to the German and Canadian jurisprudence on the basis that both had 'developed a strong culture of individual human rights, which finds expression in the decisions of their courts'.

162 Interview with Lord Sumption (n 52). In another context, Lord Sumption is reported to have lamented the loss of a 'general culture' among the newest generation of barristers and solicitors: 'It is very unfortunate, for example, that many of them cannot speak or read a single language other than their own.' Lord Sumption in conversation with Stephen Turvey and Matthew Lawson for *Counsel Magazine* (July 2012), www.lpalegal.com/news/conversation-with-lord-sumption 017.

163 Interview with Lord Kerr (n 33).

> Netherlands and it was so short and so devoid of reasoning. No doubt all the reasoning was there, but it was concealed in their discussions and not really set out in their judgment.[164]

A final alternative reason for reference to common law jurisdictions in human rights cases might be a shift in perceptions of rights ownership. Where the court is concerned with the development of common law rights, recourse to the jurisprudence of commonwealth countries is unremarkable. In *Kennedy v The Charity Commission*, Lord Mance reiterated that the domestic law should be the 'natural starting point'; the approach should 'certainly not [be] to focus exclusively on the Convention rights, without surveying the wider common law scene'.[165] Lord Toulson has been more direct, condemning the 'baleful and unnecessary tendency to overlook the common law'.[166] The 'common law resurgence' and the question of 'British' rights are considered in more detail in Chapter 8.[167]

V. THE EFFECT OF CHANGING JUDGMENT STYLES

There is a close connection to be made between the use of foreign jurisprudence and judgment types. One feeling about the shift from the House of Lords to the new Supreme Court was that there might be new opportunities to develop the methods adopted by the House of Lords 'so as to operate in a more modern and accessible way':[168]

> The Justices do now compile and deliver their judgments slightly differently from the way their predecessors did, with the first judgment no longer always being that of the most senior judge but rather that of the judge who has written the most detailed judgment explaining why the decision has gone a certain way; any dissenting judgments are usually placed after the judgments of all the judges in the majority. Moreover, Justices are increasingly issuing joint judgments.[169]

[164] Interview with Lord Walker (n 83).

[165] *Kennedy v The Charity Commission* [2014] UKSC 20; [2015] AC 455 [46].

[166] ibid [133].

[167] Roger Masterman and Se-shauna Wheatle, 'A Common Law Resurgence in Rights Protection' (2015) 1 *European Human Rights Law Review* 57; Mark Elliott, 'Beyond the European Convention: Human Rights and the Common Law' (2015) 68(1) *Current Legal Problems* 85, 92–95. See generally Dickson (n 23) 20–34; Richard Clayton, 'The Empire Strikes Back' [2015] *PL* 3; Phillip Sales, 'Rights and Fundamental Rights in English Law' [2016] *CLJ* 86; Eirik Bjorg, 'Common Law Rights: Balancing Domestic and International Exigencies' (2016) 75(2) *CLJ* 220.

[168] Dickson (n 23) 3.

[169] ibid. Dickson (at 4) also notes changes surrounding the decisions as to whether more than five judges should hear the appeal. The criteria, he notes, has been made more explicit. He takes this to be an indication 'that the Court wishes to be more transparent about the way it operates and that it envisages a larger bench being convened reasonably frequently'. Moreover: 'Decisions by larger benches have the potential to allow the Court to present a more powerful and united front to the outside world.'

Dickson's last point touches on one of the most interesting findings from this research: that the Supreme Court now commonly hands down joint judgments. Baroness Hale referred to what she described as 'plurality' judgments in an interview for the UK Supreme Court Blog, published in *The Guardian* newspaper in 2010:

> The idea of plurality judgments as the norm is very radical. It would mean that the majority who agreed on the result would have one judgment which reflected their common views (with possible post-scripts from adherents) rather than numerous judgments reasoning in almost identical ways towards the same result.[170]

In a speech shortly after that interview, Baroness Hale explained that the parliamentary procedure in the House of Lords made these kinds of judgments difficult:[171]

> In the House of Lords, we could have a considered opinion of the whole appellate committee, individual opinions with which the others simply agreed, or a series of individual opinions; but jointly authored or plurality opinions were difficult and rarely tried.[172]

The trend from the early years of the Supreme Court's activity is towards a significant change in that pattern. In her speech, Baroness Hale gave figures collected by one of the JAs from that year:

> Richard Reynolds, one of this year's judicial assistants (to whom I am greatly indebted for his researches on this subject), has surveyed our first 57 decided cases. He found that in 20, there was a 'judgment of the court'; and in a further 11, there was either a single judgment (with which all the other Justices agreed), or a single majority judgment (with which all the Justices in the majority agreed), or an 'effectively' single or single majority judgment (because separate judgments were simply footnotes or observations). So 31, or more than half, came out as plurality or effectively plurality judgments.[173]

This is consistent with the results of the data collection conducted for the purposes of this study, although I followed a slightly different method. Table 5.3 provides the results. For 'single judgments', I include the shaded categories: a leading judgment with which all members of the court agree, single majority judgments and judgments of the court (though these appear to have given way to single judgments in recent years, from 20 in 2009–10

[170] Dan Tranch and Laura Coogan, 'Baroness Brenda Hale: "I Often Ask Myself 'Why Am I Here?'"' *The Guardian* (16 September 2010), www.theguardian.com/law/2010/sep/16/uk-supreme-court-judiciary.

[171] See also Alan Paterson, *Lawyers and the Public Good* (Cambridge University Press, 2012) 159, 164 ff.

[172] Brenda Hale, 'Judgment Writing in the Supreme Court' (First Anniversary Seminar, 30 September 2010), https://www.supremecourt.uk/docs/speech_100930.pdf, 1.

[173] ibid 2.

Table 5.3: Numbers of single judgments, concurring judgments and dissenting judgments at the UK Supreme Court, 2009–17

	2009–10	2010–11	2011–12	2012–13	2013–14	2014–15	2015–16	2016–17	2009–13	2013–17	2009–17
Unanimous as to outcome	45	43	44	67	65	50	62	57	199	234	433
Judgment of the court	20	13	5	3	2	0	0	0	41	2	43
Single judgment	1	2	12	45	39	32	47	45	60	163	223
Unanimous court, one or more concurring judgments	24	28	27	19	24	18	15	12	98	69	167
At least one dissent	12	17	14	15	6	26	13	14	58	59	117
Dissenting judgments with single majority judgment	3	1	0	3	2	5	5	6	7	18	25
Dissenting judgments with concurrence in majority	9	16	14	12	4	21	8	8	51	41	92
Total (reported) cases	*57*	*60*	*58*	*82*	*71*	*76*	*75*	*71*	*257*	*293*	*550*

to zero in the three years since the start of 2014–15).[174] Of the total 550 cases reported by the Supreme Court between 2009 and 2017,[175] the Court was unanimous as to the outcome in 433. There were 43 judgments of the Court, 223 single judgments with which other members of the Court agreed and 25 single majority judgments, making 291 overall 'single judgments'. This proportion represents a significant increase in the proportion of single judgments in the House of Lords.[176]

One explanation might be that the move to the Supreme Court has simply promoted a greater sense of collegiality. For example, Paterson has described the establishment of 'team-working' practices under Lord Phillips and Lord Neuberger as far greater than had been the case at the House of Lords.[177] Alternatively, the difference could be down to a broader change in personnel.[178] A number of judges who were known to have supported multiple opinions have left the Court, while the new appointments appear to have been more willing to collaborate on judgments, or else to resist adding concurrences.[179] Darbyshire has a more practical take: '[j]urisprudentially, judges claim they are sparing us the pain of extracting the ratio decidendi from multiple judgments' but '[p]ractically, single judgments have become a labour saving device'.[180]

It might have been thought that the greater the number of judges, the more difficult it would be to come to a single unanimous judgment. But the trend towards a greater use of single judgments has developed notwithstanding the increase in panel sizes at the Supreme Court.[181] In fact, it is possible to run the argument the other way. The Supreme Court sits in enlarged panels when the Court is being asked to depart from a previous decision, where there is a conflict between decisions of the House of Lords,

[174] The same classifications were adopted by Lee in his study of Supreme Court judgments in the 2015–16 legal year: James Lee, 'The United Kingdom Supreme Court' in Emmanuel Guinchard and Marie-Pierre Granger (eds), *The New EU Judiciary* (Kluwer, 2017) 92.

[175] This analysis reflects on the total number of reported cases (550), which is greater than the total number of distinct 'cases' (533) analysed for the use of foreign jurisprudence. For a fuller explanation of research methods, see ch 2, text from n 14.

[176] Poole and Shah had actually predicted the continuation of 'noise' at the Supreme Court: Thomas Poole and Sangeeta Shah, 'The Law Lords and Human Rights' (2011) 74(1) *MLR* 79, 105.

[177] Paterson, *Final Judgment* (n 38) 141.

[178] Lee (n 174) 92.

[179] ibid; Paterson, *Final Judgment* (n 38) 105–08. During Paterson's interviews, it emerged that Lord Clark, Lord Kerr, Lord Dyson and Lord Carnwath were generally supportive of single majority judgments.

[180] Darbyshire (n 54) 344–45.

[181] Dickson (n 23) 3: 'In its first three "legal" years, 2009–12 ... 29 per cent of all the cases dealt with involved more than five Justices, and 45 per cent of the cases involving more than five Justices concerned human rights issues. In the last three years of the Appellate Committee of the House of Lords, by way of contrast, only two of the 180 cases involved more than five Law Lords (just over 1 per cent), each of which raised human rights issues.'

the Judicial Committee of the Privy Council and/or the Supreme Court to be reconciled, where the case is of high constitutional importance or great public importance, or raises an important point in relation to the ECHR.[182] It would not be surprising if the importance of the case also led the Court to prioritise clarity in the reasons for the decision: 'the ability to join in writing or agreeing a single judgment ensures that, when possible, the opinion of the court can be given simply and clearly'.[183] Indeed, *Miller* has (so far) been the only case to be heard by a panel of 11 judges, and the eight judges in the majority gave a single judgment.[184] By changing its working methods in this way, 'the Court aims to create more transparency';[185] 'working with majority opinions leads to more consistency and gives clearer guidance to the lower courts [or the parties] on how to operate in the future'.[186]

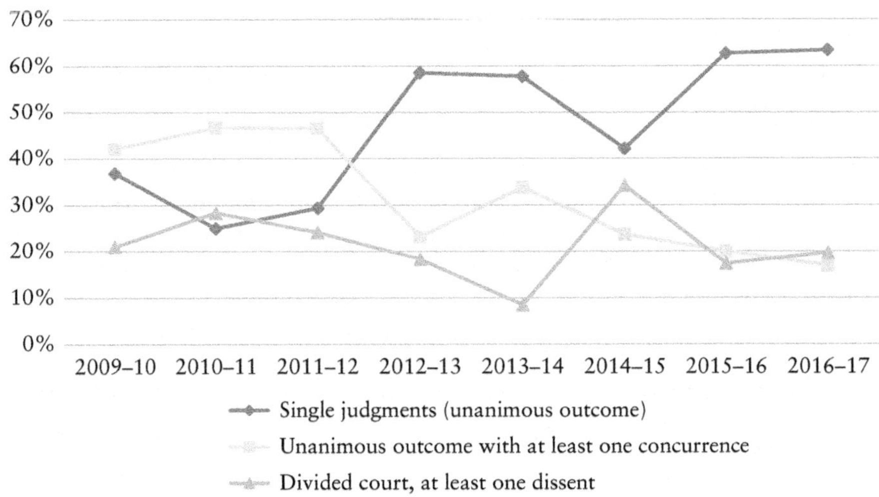

Figure 5.14: Percentage of single judgments, concurrences and dissents at the UK Supreme Court, 2009–17

[182] The Supreme Court website, www.supremecourt.uk/procedures/panel-numbers-criteria.html.

[183] Lord Neuberger (n 82) [37].

[184] *R (Miller) v Secretary of State for Exiting the European Union* [2017] UKSC 5; [2017] 2 WLR 583.

[185] Mak (n 19) 430.

[186] ibid. Indeed, this is itself an area where the Supreme Court may have learned from courts of other jurisdictions. When Baroness Hale made the case for developing towards plurality judgments in *OBG Ltd v Allan*, it was clear that some support was derived from the practices applied abroad: 'there would be much to be said for our adopting the practice of other supreme courts in having a single majority opinion to which all have contributed and all can subscribe without further qualification or explanation'. *OBG Ltd v Allan, Douglas v Hello! Ltd (No 3), Mainstream Properties Ltd v Young* [2007] UKHL 21; [2008] 1 AC 1 [303], cited in Lee (n 31) 305.

These concerns also reflect the leadership of the court. Lord Neuberger was explicit about pursuing this aim:

> In general, I have been keen to reduce the number of concurring judgements ... they are sometimes valuable, but often they are what I have called vanity judgments. A vanity judgment is one which is intended to agree with the lead judgment, but not to add anything other than saying 'I have understood this case' or 'I think I can express is better' or 'I am interested in the point' or simply 'I am here too'. Such judgments ... are at best a waste of time and space, and, at worst, [cause] confusion and uncertainty—although they are popular with academics.[187]

Figure 5.14 shows that, with the exception of 2013–14, concurring majority judgments fell to their lowest point during Lord Neuberger's presidency. There has been a corresponding increase in the proportion of single judgments (including judgments of the court and single majority judgments). The trend started before the end of Lord Phillips' presidency, but the proportion of single judgments remained high throughout Lord Neuberger's term. Dissent rates have been fairly steady, aside from a dip in 2013–14 (8 per cent) and a spike in 2014–15 (34 per cent), as have the rates of concurrences in cases with at least one dissent. There has been a clear decline in the number of concurrences where the Court is unanimous as to the outcome (from above 40 per cent in the first three years to 17 per cent in 2016–17).

Not all commentators agree that single judgments are a positive development. Writing in 1998, Robertson expressed a concern that an expectation of single judgments might reduce 'the extent of genuine argument and discussion of issues in a way that not only academic lawyers but many leading counsel find distinctly unhelpful'.[188] A further drawback has been pointed out by Paterson relating to a 'loss of individualism in our Justices':[189]

> Single judgments representing the outcome of the internal debates within the Supreme Court which are not publicly rehearsed, remove the humanity of individual difference and potentially undermine transparency ... Fewer dissents and concurrences in return for more single judgments mean more judgments devised by a committee and consequently more compromise.[190]

Paterson cites Lord Rodger of Earlsferry as a supporter of this view, setting out evidence obtained through interview:

> If the powers that be have their way, and the new Supreme Court of the United Kingdom adopts more single judgments, then there will be less scope in future

[187] Lord Neuberger (n 82) [39].

[188] David Robertson, *Judicial Discretion in the House of Lords* (Oxford University Press, 1998) 77–78. More recently, see, eg, Paterson, *Final Judgment* (n 38) 91–95; Darbyshire (n 54) 387–90.

[189] Paterson, *Final Judgment* (n 38) 315.

[190] ibid; Brice Dickson, 'Close Calls in the House of Lords' in James Lee (ed), *From House of Lords to Supreme Court: Judges, Jurists and the Process of Judging* (Hart Publishing, 2011) 284; Lee (n 31) 205.

> for humour or indeed for any other expressions of the judges' individuality. By definition the author of a composite judgment is not writing just as himself and will alter his voice accordingly ... The much touted efficiency savings of a single judgment will be clearly bought if, as a result, we lose individual hallmark contributions of [the] quality [of Lords Macnaghten, Wilberforce and Bingham].[191]

There is a clear tension between single judgments and judicial individuality.[192] An increase in single judgments might also reduce the likely number of citations from foreign courts, since the citation of these sources is dependent on the inclination of the judge writing the judgment. Interestingly, one of the judges interviewed by Mak 'indicated that the use of foreign jurisprudence need not be hampered by the increased use of majority opinions' because 'an individual judge might still choose to write a separate opinion about foreign law if ... not satisfied with the majority opinion'.[193] Nevertheless, if a single judgment were to be handed down which has been authored by a Justice who is less keen on comparative law, one could speculate that the explicit citation of foreign jurisprudence would be less likely overall.[194] Against this, it could be argued that not all single judgments represent a single voice; some single judgments are the product of a combined effort on the part of a number of judges, as in *Miller.*[195] But the scope for reference to foreign jurisprudence could be even smaller in these circumstances: 'the need for unanimity often results in the deletion of all but the essential'.[196]

The effect of single judgments on the use of foreign jurisprudence would be difficult to measure. A simple count of foreign case citations in single judgments versus judgments with a dissent or at least one concurrence in the majority might be artificial. As explained in later chapters, some of the judges indicated in the interviews that foreign jurisprudence would be helpful for 'insight',[197] especially where the law is 'uncertain'.[198] A number of the judges also acknowledged a tendency to seek reassurance from foreign jurisprudence, wishing to learn from the experience of other courts 'about the impact of particular laws', [199] which might in turn lead a judge to be 'encouraged or emboldened' by what other jurisdictions have done.[200] It would not be surprising, therefore, if foreign jurisprudence would be most

191 Paterson, *Final Judgment* (n 38) 315–16.

192 James Lee, 'The Judicial Individuality of Lord Sumption (2017) 40(2) *University of New South Wales Law Journal* 862, 869; Lee (n 31) 305, 331.

193 Mak (n 19) 430; Mak (n 34) 26.

194 Although it should be noted that all judges have the opportunity to read and revise a single judgment.

195 *Miller* (n 184). The eight judges in the majority collaborated to produce a single judgment.

196 Lord Neuberger (n 82) [15].

197 Interview with Lord Mance (n 26).

198 Interview with Lord Phillips (n 68).

199 Interview with Lord Kerr (n 33).

200 Interview with Lord Collins (n 53).

likely to find its way into the more difficult cases, which, in turn, would be more likely to produce multiple judgments.[201] This would fit with the citation of foreign jurisprudence in the controversial assisted suicide cases: *Pretty*,[202] *Purdy*,[203] and *Nicklinson*.[204] In these circumstances, where the judges may find it harder to reach a consensus, separate judgments are more likely.[205]

VI. CONCLUSIONS

The quantitative analysis makes clear that the Supreme Court does make reference to foreign jurisprudence. It is also clear that the proportion of cases in which foreign jurisprudence is cited has remained fairly constant across the first eight years of the Court's activity, although there are some fluctuations to note—especially in 2010–11 and 2013–14.

One of the clearest findings is that the Supreme Court continues to prefer the jurisprudence of common law courts. Not only is the Supreme Court likely to cite common law authorities most often, it is also likely to cite more of those decisions per case. The dataset also reveals some surprising results. For example, one finding from the data analysis was that there were few citations of German jurisprudence: just 19 cases—including nine human rights cases—cited German jurisprudence out of the possible 533 handed down between 2009 and 2017. Given the reputation that Lord Mance, in particular, has in terms of enthusiasm for German law, it was expected that the number would be greater. Having said this, Figure 5.9 shows that French and German cases were the next most cited after the common law jurisdictions.

For similar reasons, it was surprising to see that Lord Rodger did not come out as one of the more frequent users of foreign jurisprudence. Lord Rodger's enthusiasm for using comparative law is well documented, including in contributions by Lord Mance and Tetyana Nesterchuk (a former JA) in a volume of essays published in Lord Rodger's memory.[206] One possible

[201] The controversial nature of a case is more likely to produce multiple judgments, whether or not foreign jurisprudence is relevant. Lord Kerr thought spikes in dissent and consensus between 2010–11 and 2011–12 were more likely to 'reflect the controversial nature of the cases rather than any more marked inclination on the part of the justices to dissent': Lord Kerr, 'Dissenting Judgments—Self-Indulgence or Self Sacrifice?', the Birkenhead Lecture (London, 8 October 2012), www.supremecourt.uk/docs/speech-121008.pdf accessed 12 November 2017.

[202] *R (Pretty) v Director of Public Prosecutions and Secretary of State for the Home Department* [2001] UKHL 61; [2002] 1 AC 800.

[203] *R (Purdy) v Director of Public Prosecutions* [2009] UKHL 45; [2010] 1 AC 345.

[204] *R (Nicklinson) v Ministry of Justice* [2014] UKSC 38; [2015] AC 657.

[205] *cf Miller* (n 184), in which the eight judges in the majority issued a single judgment.

[206] Lord Mance, 'Foreign Laws and Languages' in Burrows, Johnston and Zimmermann (n 56); and Nesterchuk (n 56).

implication of these results is that foreign jurisprudence is used more extensively than is apparent from the law reports. It is perhaps for this reason that Lady Justice Arden commented during interview that there is 'far more use of comparative law than appears on the face of the judgments ... it's informing the judges behind the scenes'.[207] There is another obvious explanation for the surprisingly low number of explicit citations from these judges, otherwise known to be enthusiastic about comparative law: foreign jurisprudence may not always be being used as 'authority' or cited out of courtesy to counsel (as mooted in Chapter 4). Instead, it is possible that foreign jurisprudence is being used more determinatively, as an analytical lens, to help with a process of reflection on a problem, but which does not necessarily contribute to the outcome of a case. As Lord Mance put it:

> [W]hen judges look to comparative and international material, they may do so for information, inspiration, or confirmation, just as they use domestic decisions that are not binding on them.[208]

The potential for using foreign jurisprudence simply as a heuristic device is explored further in Chapter 6.

Whether used implicitly or explicitly, it was clear from the interviews that practical considerations are some of the main forces driving the manner and frequency with which foreign jurisprudence is used at the Supreme Court. The Court continues to rely on counsel for references to legal materials that are to be used in the process of judicial reasoning, although it would not be unusual for judges to ask counsel to address comparative material if it was felt to be useful.[209] Beyond this, judges might be willing to undertake their own research, but this is likely to be closely connected to the individual approach of each judge. It is worth noting that those judges who did express greater willingness to embark upon research of this kind also tended to be heavier users of foreign jurisprudence.[210]

When foreign jurisprudence is sourced independently of counsel's submissions, online databases and collections in libraries provide the most obvious avenue. To a lesser extent, the JAs might also raise comparative material, but this would be less usual. Accessibility and time pressures are additional factors. The Supreme Court does have a little more time for research on complex points of law than the lower courts, but, as several of the Justices

[207] Interview with Lady Justice Arden (n 25).

[208] Lord Mance (n 206) 87.

[209] See, eg, *Cavendish Square Holding* (n 33) [166] (Lord Mance): '*At the court's request*, Cavendish also included as an appendix to its case a valuable examination of the law of, and relevant academic commentary from, other common law countries ...' (emphasis added).

[210] Further analysis of the correlation between personal attributes and the frequency of foreign jurisprudence citations is given by Michael Bobek in his study of the supreme courts in Europe: Bobek (n 14) 57.

explained during the interviews, there are limits to what can be done.[211] As a result, it is not surprising that citations of foreign jurisprudence remain unsystematic.

> We do all sorts of things for all sorts of reasons, just as things come to us in all sorts of ways. There is a large random element to all of this.[212]

An effective time-saving measure is to refer to the works of leading academics in the relevant field. This, in turn, is likely to influence the jurisdictions that are used since the discretion is with the author rather than the judge. Other related influences, despite having less practical significance, are the various judicial exchanges and international meetings or conferences. These meetings may perpetuate the tendency to resort to jurisprudence from a small family of courts, but there is little evidence to suggest that new material is introduced as a result of such meetings. Even where this appears to be more likely, it is better to explain uses of foreign jurisprudence as part of a prior willingness to draw from selected foreign jurisprudence rather than as a product of judicial exchanges per se. Indeed, Lord Steyn's use of the Israeli perspective in *Daly* comes as no particular surprise given the general openness to foreign jurisprudence exhibited by some of his earlier judgments. For example, in *McFarlane v Tayside Health Board*,[213] Lord Steyn explained that he would have used foreign jurisprudence mainly to assist in his own reflections about the case. Lord Steyn also argued that comparative law has the 'inestimable value of sharpening our focus on the weight of competing considerations'.[214]

For that purpose, it is most likely that judges simply refer to jurisprudence from the jurisdictions that they feel most confident with, either because there is an impression about the quality of the jurists from a particular court or because it is easier to consider decisions from English-speaking jurisdictions. As Markesinis and Fedtke have written, 'one must not ignore the very pragmatic limitation that language limitations may restrict the extent of these "fishing expeditions"'.[215] Despite the fact that not all the interviewed judges agreed that language would be a barrier to foreign jurisprudence, it is not surprising that, where there are citations of foreign jurisprudence, there is an enduring allegiance to the courts of established

[211] *cf* Bobek (n 14) 44–45: '[c]omparative analysis is, in terms of time, expertise, and resources, a demanding exercise' and 'it is at the level of supreme jurisdictions where human resources (analytical backup) and also procedural tools (lesser docket, selection of cases) may be available. These allow judges to concentrate on contentious legal issues in greater detail'.

[212] Interview with Baroness Hale (n 28).

[213] *McFarlane v Tayside Health Board* [2000] 2 AC 59.

[214] ibid [81] (Lord Steyn).

[215] Basil Markesinis and Jörg Fedtke (eds), *Judicial Recourse to Foreign Law: A New Source of Inspiration?* (University College London Press, 2006) 71.

common law jurisdictions.[216] Flanagan and Ahern reported similar results from their electronic questionnaires:

> A large majority of judges, 81 per cent, indicated that a democratic form of government was a prerequisite for the citation of the law of another jurisdiction in a judgment about domestic rights. Conversely, 17 per cent of judges indicated they set *no* jurisdictional prerequisites. Only a single judge indicated a set of traits that did not include democracy, namely, that it be a common law jurisdiction. Other than democracy, the most cited prerequisite was that it be a common law jurisdiction (26 per cent), followed by commonality of language (14 per cent). There were seven comments to the effect that, were a jurisdiction to possess the 'same language' and 'common law' traits, it would be more readily comparable, but that, democracy aside, such traits were not a sine qua non.[217]

The effect of the HRA 1998 might have been thought to promote greater interest in the position of European domestic courts, but, as in other areas, practical considerations usually drive the Supreme Court to rely on the Strasbourg jurisprudence to inform them on such matters. Undoubtedly, changes in judgment styles since the last years of the House of Lords have also had an effect. It is clear that the Justices are inclined to work towards single judgments,[218] which would be likely to yield fewer citations of foreign jurisprudence.

These are changes that must be balanced against the value of foreign jurisprudence. The potential to derive assistance from foreign jurisprudence was of obvious value to the interviewed judges. Writing in memory of Lord Rodger, Lord Mance expressed the feeling that it was his ability and willingness to take a comparative view of matters that formed an important part of Lord Rodger's legacy as a judge. It is worth reproducing the passage at length:

> Part of Lord Rodger's legacy as a judge will lie in the weight he attached to looking at matters from all angles and from the viewpoint of others. That is the essential role of the comparativist, for whom languages are correspondingly important. Too often in the highest court, issues arise which one feels must have been considered in other major legal systems. Too often, difficulties of obtaining appropriate information or an appropriate interlocutor to explore or explain a foreign system stand in the way of cross-fertilization of this sort. Lord Rodger's knowledge and experience straddled different legal systems and was, in that respect, unique.

[216] Allan et al have made similar findings in the context of the use of foreign jurisprudence in New Zealand: James Allan, Grant Huscroft and Nessa Lynch, 'The Citation of Overseas Authority in Rights Litigation in New Zealand: How Much Bark? How Much Bite?' (2007) 11 *Otago Law Review* 433, 438.

[217] Flanagan and Ahern (n 111) 21.

[218] Paterson found that the proportion of single judgments has increased greatly since the House of Lords and that there has been 'a parallel growth in judgments by one Justice with which one or more colleagues will join or agree. See further Paterson, *Final Judgment* (n 38) 102–07.

> His departure invites the thought that the Supreme Court should itself aim to acquire a comparative legal and linguistic expertise that its present admirable judicial assistants do not generally bring. Other European courts, supranational and national, have within their organization young lawyers, often with the highest academic qualifications ... Their role is to research issues where comparative legal input could be relevant and to liaise with their homologues in similar positions.[219]

Lord Mance continued:

> There have been numerous cases at the highest level where this might have proved of interest ... [and] [i]n all these cases, it could have been valuable to have a direct in-house facility for comparative law research. It is an idea worth pursuing after Alan Rodger's much-mourned departure from the court.[220]

219 Lord Mance (n 206) 96–97.
220 ibid 97.

6

Foreign Jurisprudence as a Heuristic Tool

IT WAS CONCLUDED in Chapter 4 that the legitimacy of using foreign jurisprudence must be contingent—at least in part—upon the reason for which it is used. That conclusion is not controversial: Saunders has suggested that legitimacy is intimately connected to the purposes for using foreign jurisprudence.[1] In fact, for Saunders, the latter was said to assume the former. Thus, Saunders' thesis was that the legitimacy of using any foreign jurisprudence would necessarily vary according to the purpose for which a court employs it.[2]

The conditions in which the use of foreign jurisprudence might be problematic can be summarised as those in which the result is the adoption of foreign norms or the development of domestic jurisprudence in reliance on those norms. The crux of the problem is the enduring debate about sovereignty. If a court uses foreign jurisprudence to develop domestic law in a direction not envisaged by the legislature, it effectively assumes legislative sovereignty.[3] This is particularly clear in the US debate about the legitimacy of recourse to foreign jurisprudence. Cram explains:

> [One] strand of US exceptionalism objects to foreign norm citation on sovereignty grounds. The suggestion here is that where the Constitution does not authorize or formally give a status to foreign norms, resort to such norms by the court is improper, occurring as it does without a proper mandate from the people or their representatives ... These difficulties are further compounded where the judiciary enjoy a power of review over primary legislation and when the foreign source is being used by the domestic court to strike down a measure that has been passed by the democratically elected legislature. It is unsurprising therefore when resort to comparative legal resources is labeled as foreign interference and something to be resisted.[4]

[1] Cheryl Saunders, 'Comparative Constitutional Law in the Courts: Is There a Problem?' (2006) 59(1) *Current Legal Problems* 91.

[2] ibid.

[3] See, eg, Roger Alford, 'Misusing International Sources to Interpret the Constitution' (2004) 98 *American Journal of International Law* 57, 59; Roger Alford, 'In Search of a Theory for Constitutional Comparativism' (2005) 52 *ULCA Law Review* 639.

[4] Ian Cram, 'Resort to Foreign Constitutional Norms in Domestic Human Rights Jurisprudence with Reference to Terrorism Cases' [2009] *CLJ* 118, 123–24.

Criticisms of this kind are perpetuated by the relative lack of transparency about the methods or purposes involved in the use of foreign jurisprudence. In a limited number of cases, explanations for the citation of foreign materials can be derived from the context of a judgment. However, in by far the greatest proportion of cases, little to no explanation is given as to why the foreign jurisprudence has been cited.

Further uncertainty is created by the disparity between the data collected from the judgments and the evidence obtained through interviews, which suggested that judges use foreign jurisprudence to a greater extent than is detectable from the judgments themselves. If that is so, it is worth clarifying the reasons for these additional recourses to foreign jurisprudence. Certainly, the evidence from the interviews described in Chapter 4 was that the citations of foreign materials are not likely to be purely decorative or ornamental. If this were to be the case, foreign jurisprudence would always be detectable on the face of the judgment.

The thesis in the following three chapters is that there are three main purposes for using foreign jurisprudence in human rights cases before the UK Supreme Court (and, often, in Supreme Court cases generally). The first is the purpose considered by this chapter: that foreign jurisprudence is used as a 'heuristic tool'.[5] Foreign jurisprudence represents an opportunity for reflection on a given issue. Although this may be prompted by a lack of relevant or helpful domestic jurisprudence, the 'gap-filling' thesis propounded in much of the literature is not supported. The Supreme Court is not concerned with filling gaps per se; rather, the Justices are using foreign jurisprudence as an analytical lens[6] through which to theorise on the domestic issue. Such an analytical lens is especially useful when the Court is making significant changes to the law, going beyond the merely incremental. In such cases, it is not surprising that a judge may refer to foreign jurisprudence as a way to test the non-trivial change, checking for bear traps, flood gates, neglected dimensions or unintended consequences. As heuristic devices, these recourses to foreign jurisprudence may not result in a substantive contribution to the reasoning in any one case and so would not necessarily convert into explicit citations in a published judgment. Chapters 7 and 8 detail the other two main purposes for which it is argued that the Supreme Court uses foreign jurisprudence in human rights cases: to identify and maintain consensus or uniformity; and instrumentally, to support conclusions at odds with the relevant domestic (or Strasbourg) jurisprudence.

[5] The phrase 'a heuristic tool' is borrowed from Lord Reed's judgment in *Bank Mellat v HM Treasury* [2013] UKSC 39; [2014] AC 700 [74]. Elsewhere, Lord Reed has suggested that foreign law may be treated as a 'relevant fact': Robert Reed, 'Foreign Precedents and Judicial Reasoning: The American Debate and British Practice' (2008) 124 *LQR* 253, 255.

[6] The term 'analytical lens' is used in Esin Örücü (ed), *Judicial Comparativism in Human Rights Cases* (United Kingdom National Committee of Comparative Law, 2003).

I. GAP FILLING

Gutteridge wrote in 1949 that 'at some future date more extensive use will, no doubt, be made of foreign law for the purpose of assisting our judges to fill the gaps that are still to be found in our law'.[7] Some years later, a strong theme remains that foreign jurisprudence may offer a useful perspective where the indigenous jurisprudence is lacking or unsettled. In such circumstances, it is usually argued that foreign jurisprudence can contribute solutions to similar legal problems. It is a functionalist approach, which proceeds on the basis of 'usefulness and need'. The logic is intelligible: 'only a fool would refuse quinine just because it didn't grow in his back garden'.[8] Lord Bingham referred to such circumstances in his 2009 Hamlyn Lecture:

> There are perhaps two situations in which foreign authority may exert a significant if not a decisive influence. One is where domestic authority points towards an answer that seems inappropriate or unjust. The other is where domestic authority appears to yield no clear answer.[9]

Bell was evidently persuaded by the possibility in his study of the Supreme Court's 2010–11 decisions, considering that *R v Chaytor* provided an example of foreign case law being used in this way (although Bell's definition of foreign jurisprudence included Privy Council decisions, unlike this book, which considers only the case law of foreign domestic courts).[10] The gap-filling thesis also formed one of Feeley's five purposes for using comparative law, alongside being educated about other legal systems, assisting domestic law reform, assisting in the transnational spread of norms and bringing about greater harmony and unity across legal systems.[11] Alternatively, foreign judgments might be used 'as a warning', where 'the foreign law is "the other", which must be avoided'.[12]

It is fairly clear that counsel would tend to approach foreign jurisprudence in this way, making use of it as evidence for a movement in the domestic position or to persuade a court about the way in which domestic

[7] Harold Cooke Gutteridge, *Comparative Law: An Introduction to the Comparative Method of Legal Study and Research*, 2nd edn (Cambridge University Press, 1949) 40. More recently, see, eg, Saunders (n 1) 114.

[8] Rudolph von Jhering, quoted in Konrad Zweigert and Hein Kötz, *An Introduction to Comparative Law*, Tony Weir trans, 3rd edn (Oxford University Press, 1998) 17.

[9] Tom Bingham, *Widening Horizons* (Cambridge University Press, 2010) 7–8.

[10] John Bell, 'Comparative Law in the Supreme Court 2010–11' [2012] *Cambridge Journal of International and Comparative Law* 20, 23; *R v Chaytor and Others* [2010] UKSC 52; [2011] 1 AC 684.

[11] Malcolm Feeley, 'Comparative Criminal Law for Criminologists: Comparing for What Purpose?' in David Nelken (ed), *Comparing Legal Cultures* (Dartmouth, 1997), cited in Cram (n 4) 128.

[12] Christopher McCrudden, 'A Common Law of Human Rights?: Transnational Judicial Conversations on Constitutional Rights' (2000) 20(4) *OJLS* 499, 518.

jurisprudence ought to be construed and developed. Legal practitioners are trained to give evidence for their arguments and the accessibility of foreign jurisprudence through the Internet has enlarged the pool of potential authorities. As McCrudden has written:

> For the human rights advocate the role of comparison is that of persuasion to an essentially moral position. Lawyers in the human rights context often use comparison to legitimate their argument that a particular interpretation of an existing human rights norm should be adopted, or as part of the process of generating further norms.[13]

It is clear that some Justices of the Supreme Court expect counsel to behave in this way. Lord Kerr explained:

> I suppose there must be a tendency on the part of counsel to have resort to foreign jurisprudence that deals with the point if there isn't any unambiguous answer to be found in domestic jurisprudence.[14]

Whether or not judges articulate 'gap filling' as a purpose, there are examples of cases in which foreign jurisprudence has been used in this way. For instance, the development of the common law breach of confidence action, so as to protect the privacy right enshrined under Article 8 ECHR, owes much to a decision of the Australian High Court.[15] The approach has been similar where the jurisprudence of the Strasbourg Court (which the HRA 1998 obliges domestic courts to 'take into account') is silent or unhelpful.[16] As Baroness Hale has confirmed (extra-judicially):

> [T]here is nothing in the [Human Rights] Act ... to support the reluctance ... to seek such guidance as we can from the jurisprudence of foreign courts ... especially on subjects where Strasbourg has not recently spoken.[17]

One of the best examples is given by two cases handed down prior to the move to the Supreme Court. In *Secretary of State for the Home Department v MB*,[18] the issue turned on the minimum requirements for a fair hearing

[13] Christopher McCrudden, 'Judicial Comparativism and Human Rights' in Esin Örücü and David Nelken (eds), *Comparative Law: A Handbook* (Hart Publishing, 2007) 371, 376.

[14] Interview with the Rt Hon Lord Kerr of Tonaghmore, Justice of the UK Supreme Court (Supreme Court, London, 9 May 2012).

[15] *Australian Broadcasting Corporation v Lenah Game Meats* [2001] HCA 63; Roger Masterman, 'Section 2(1) of the Human Rights Act: Binding Domestic Courts to Strasbourg?' [2004] *PL* 725, 726; Gavin Phillipson, 'Transforming Breach of Confidence? Towards a Common Law Right of Privacy under the Human Rights Act' (2003) 65 *MLR* 726, 731.

[16] Section 2 of the HRA 1998 obliges domestic courts to 'take into account' relevant Strasbourg jurisprudence in cases that raise a Convention point. See Francesca Klug, 'The Human Rights Act 1998, *Pepper v Hart* and All That' [1999] *PL* 246, 251: domestic courts will therefore draw from foreign jurisprudence, especially where there is 'little or no steer from the Strasbourg organs'.

[17] Brenda Hale, 'Who Defines Convention Rights?' (2010) 5(2) *JUSTICE Journal* 10, 13.

[18] *Secretary of State for the Home Department v MB* [2007] UKHL 46; [2008] 1 AC 440.

in control order cases for the purposes of Article 6 ECHR. In brief, the question was whether the disclosure of closed material to a special advocate would enable a controlled person to have a fair trial. When *MB* was before the House of Lords, the Strasbourg Court's approach to the level of disclosure required to render a hearing fair was unclear. As Baroness Hale wrote: 'Strasbourg [had] not yet had to deal with a case exactly on all fours with the present'.[19] The Grand Chamber had not yet decided *A v UK*, which considered breaches of procedural guarantees in Article 5(4) ECHR (providing similar requirements about the lawfulness of a decision, as determined by a court).[20] In the absence of clear and constant Strasbourg authority, the House was forced to attempt to identify some of the guiding principles from the existing Strasbourg case law. In doing so, Lord Bingham made heavy reference to the approach of the Canadian and US courts on the issue. The references to those jurisdictions did not themselves provide the 'magical ace of trumps',[21] but it is clear that the House found them to be a useful resource and used them to confirm that the Strasbourg case law had developed along the same lines. It was after quoting passages from the Canadian and US Supreme Courts[22] that Lord Bingham noted that '[s]tatements to similar effect, less emphatically expressed, [were] to be found in the Strasbourg case law'.[23]

By the time *Secretary of State for the Home Department v AF (No 3)* reached the House of Lords,[24] the Grand Chamber judgment in *A v UK* had been handed down.[25] As Baroness Hale later explained (extra-judicially):

> Although *A v United Kingdom* was concerned with detention, and the control order cases were not, the House of Lords in *AF (No 3)* considered it inevitable that Strasbourg would take the same view of the procedural requirements for confirming control orders.[26]

While the Canadian and US authorities were again cited (when referring to *MB*), the effect of the decision in *A v UK* prompted Lord Rodger's well-known conclusion: '*Argentoratum locutum, iudicium finitum*—Strasbourg has spoken, the case is closed'.[27]

[19] ibid [67] (Baroness Hale).

[20] *A v UK* [2009] EHRR 301; Article 5(4) reads: 'Everyone who is deprived of his liberty by arrest or detention shall be entitled to take proceedings by which the lawfulness of his detention shall be decided speedily by a court and his release ordered if the detention is not lawful.'

[21] Bingham (n 9) 7–8.

[22] *Charkaoui v Canada (Citizenship and Immigration)* [2007] 1 SCR 350; *Hamdi v Rumsfeld* (2004) 542 US 507.

[23] *MB* (n 18) [30]–[31] (Lord Bingham).

[24] *Secretary of State for the Home Department v AF and Another* [2009] UKHL 28; [2010] 2 AC 269.

[25] *A v UK* (n 20).

[26] Brenda Hale, '*Argentoratum Locutum*: Is Strasbourg or the Supreme Court Supreme? (2012) 12(1) *Human Rights Law Review* 65, 67.

[27] *AF* (n 24) [98] (Lord Rodger).

The *MB* and *AF (No 3)* cases demonstrate that a wider net might be thrown where the Strasbourg position is unclear, but it is difficult to link such examples to an attitude of using foreign jurisprudence as 'gap fillers' generally. If the gap-filling explanation were accurate, the assumption would be that the use of foreign jurisprudence would significantly decline—or be non-existent—where domestic law is settled, unless its suitability is questioned in some way;[28] while it is said that only a fool 'would refuse quinine just because it didn't grow in his back garden', it is also said that '[n]o one bothers to fetch a thing from afar when he has one as good or better at home'.[29] The first problem is that it is not easy to find examples of cases where foreign jurisprudence would have been cited *but for* the existence of relevant domestic law. The judges are hardly likely to highlight such possibilities in their judgments, which they are in any case aiming to reduce in complexity and length. The second problem is that, even in cases where the attitude is possible to discern, the matter is not necessarily put so clearly. Lord Rodger's short statement in *AF (No 3)* is unusual. As Lord Mance has written, the 'brevity and wit were here a misleading guide to the approach which Lord Rodger might have taken in other contexts'.[30] Further obscurity is created by the fact that the House of Lords in the later cases did repeat the citations of the foreign jurisprudence used in *AF*, which is not unexpected given that the House was considering the identical issue and was reviewing the reasoning in the earlier case. Indeed, when reviewing the cases handed down by the Supreme Court between 2009 and 2017, it was notable that many references to foreign jurisprudence were prompted by discussion of previous cases in which those sources had been considered, rather than as a result of a fresh contribution.[31]

[28] McCrudden (n 12) 523. *cf* Albert Kiralfy, 'The Persuasive Authority of American Rulings in England' (1948–49) XXIII *Tulane Law Review* 209, 210; Saunders (n 1) 101.

[29] Von Jhering (n 8) 17.

[30] Lord Mance, 'Foreign Laws and Languages' in Andrew Burrows, David Johnston and Reinhard Zimmermann (eds), *Judge and Jurist: Essays in Memory of Lord Rodger of Earlsferry* (Oxford University Press, 2013) 95.

[31] Other examples include: *Smith and Others (FC) v Ministry of Defence* [2013] UKSC 41; [2014] AC 52 [87], where Lord Hope considered a decision of the Australian High Court by reference to an earlier domestic case: 'In *Mulcahy v Ministry of Defence* [1996] QB 732, 746 Neill LJ said that it seemed to have been recognised in the Australian cases that warlike activities fell into a special category. He concluded … that an English court should approach a claim of negligence … in the same way as in the High Court of Australia did in the Shaw Savill case.' In *The Catholic Child Welfare Society and Others v Various Claimants (FC) and the Institute of the Brothers of the Christian Schools and Others* [2012] UKSC 56; [2013] 2 AC 1 [67]–[68], Lord Phillips made reference to Canadian decisions when considering the domestic jurisprudence: 'In *Lister v Hesley Hall Ltd* [2002] 1 AC 215 … Lord Steyn … referred to *Bazley v Curry* 174 DLR (4th) 45 and *Jacobi v Griffiths* 174 DLR (4th) 71 as "luminous and illuminating" judgments which would henceforth be the starting point for consideration of similar cases.' See also *Belhaj v Straw* [2017] UKSC 3; [2017] AC 964.

The gap-filling thesis is therefore very hard to confirm in the UK context. In fact, if there were to be cases where judges were inclined to look abroad notwithstanding a relevant body of (albeit unhelpful or unsupportive) domestic jurisprudence, the risk would be that citations would begin to look opportunistic. The point is a regular feature of the debate about the use of foreign jurisprudence in US constitutional cases. For example, arguing against references to foreign material in *Knight v Florida*,[32] Justice Thomas suggested:

> [T]he only reason why this material was resorted to was there was no support in the American constitutional tradition or in this Court's precedent ... [for the conclusion reached] ... [Had there been] any such support in our own jurisprudence, it would be unnecessary for proponents of the claim to rely on European Court of Human Rights, the Supreme Court of Zimbabwe, the Supreme Court of India, or the Privy Council.[33]

The most vocal critic was Justice Scalia of the US Supreme Court: if domestic jurisprudence is lacking, '[t]hat's the end of the question ... What good would reading Canadian opinions do, unless it was my job to be the moral arbiter, which I don't accept?'[34]

The ferocity of the US debate is not mirrored in the UK, where recourse to foreign jurisprudence has not been the subject of great concern. Besides, the argument that recourse to foreign norms would imply greater creativity on the part of a judge is not itself logically sound. It is entirely possible that the use of foreign jurisprudence could be motivated by a desire to elucidate an issue, rather than signalling the opportunity to support an otherwise illegitimate conclusion.[35] It is not difficult to read Lord Bingham's judgment in *MB* as taking this sort of approach.[36]

In any case, the idea that foreign jurisprudence has some substantive influence on the outcome of the case where there is a dearth of domestic law is a little extreme. The Justices of the UK Supreme Court provided some insight during the interviews. While Lord Dyson seemed to agree with Lord Bingham's Hamlyn Lecture formulation—that foreign jurisprudence was especially useful where there was 'not a great deal of domestic [material]' or if a case raised a 'relatively new point',[37] Lord Kerr was evidently less convinced about the impact of foreign jurisprudence on gap-filling situations:

> Just because there is a dearth of authority doesn't mean to say that we have to close the gap by recourse to foreign jurisprudence. Very often, cases come here

32 *Knight v Florida* (1999) 120 S Ct 459.

33 ibid 460 (Thomas, J).

34 Norman Dorsen, 'A Conversation between U.S. Supreme Court Justices' (2005) 3(3) *International Journal of Constitutional Law* 519, 535 (Justice Scalia).

35 It is presumed that Justice Scalia and Justice Thomas would consider a conclusion that was not supported by domestic jurisprudence to be illegitimate.

36 *MB* (n 18).

37 Interview with the Rt Hon Lord Dyson MR, former Justice of the UK Supreme Court (Supreme Court, London, 1 May 2012).

> because there is no clear—or unambiguous—answer, and that is entirely as it should be. We have to try to come up with the proper principled response to whatever problem is presented to us. Now, we would be unwise to neglect to have recourse to whatever assistance we can derive in order to help us in that process. But I think it would be wrong to overestimate the influence that foreign jurisprudence has in circumstances where there isn't any clear national or domestic authority.[38]

This reflects the responsibility of the top court in addressing difficult questions. As Duxbury has noted, 'the court which is heavily indebted to foreign precedent ... risks the accusation of failing to do its own homework':[39]

> [T]hat other countries' courts have tackled a problem already, and have apparently tackled it well, does not mean that our courts need not—indeed, they may be failing to take a sufficiently serious approach to their task if they do not—devise their own distinctive answer to that problem.[40]

II. AN ANALYTICAL LENS

A more realistic version of the gap-filling thesis is that an absence of relevant domestic (or supranational) authority might prompt judges to use foreign jurisprudence as an analytical lens through which to test ideas and reflect on their own analysis of the law. Judges themselves often claim such a role for foreign jurisprudence. As an example, Emeritus Justice Laurie Ackermann, formerly a Justice of the Constitutional Court of South Africa, has described the purpose of recourse to foreign jurisprudence as 'seeking information, guidance, stimulation, clarification, or even enlightenment ... One is doing no more than keeping the judicial mind open to new ideas'.[41] It is common for legislators to work in this way and judges, too, 'might acknowledge that a foreign precedent, or a collection of foreign precedents, casts light on a

38 Interview with Lord Kerr (n 14).

39 Neil Duxbury, 'The Law of the Land' (2015) 78(1) *MLR* 26, 40–41.

40 ibid. This is equally the case in the private law sphere. When considering the law of illegality in *Patel v Mirza*, Lord Mance noted that the basis for invoking other jurisdictions was 'slender'. The Australian and New Zealand authorities could not give the Court much insight or information 'as to whether or not the approach there has proved unproblematic for the profession or the courts'. Even the 'authoritative' Canadian Supreme Court decision (*Hall v Hebert* [1993] 2 SCR 159) could not be taken to support the wholesale abandonment of a clear-cut test and was limited to 'explain[ing] and redefine[ing] the principle *ex turpi causa* in a manner which (consistently with the way in which the common law usually develops) offers every prospect of avoiding the evident anomalies which an over formalistic approach has in the past evidenced'. *Patel v Mirza* [2016] UKSC 42; [2017] AC 467 [207].

41 Laurie H Ackermann, 'Constitutional Comparativism in South Africa: A Response to Sir Basil Markesinis and Jörg Fedtke' (2005) 80 *Tulane Law Review* 169, 183.

legal problem in a way that domestic precedent does not'.[42] Justice Breyer of the US Supreme Court is well known to support such an approach:

> I would say that I understand that a judge cannot read everything. But if the lawyers find an interesting and useful foreign case, and if they refer to that case, the judges will likely read it, using it as food for thought, not as binding precedent. I think that is fine.[43]

Aharon Barak, former President of the Supreme Court of Israel, similarly described the possibility that comparative law 'awakens judges to the potential latent in their own system' and 'allows for greater self-knowledge'.[44] Saunders has explained:

> [F]oreign law has potential to contain, rather than expand, the discretion of a judge, identifying directions that others have taken and enabling evaluation of their consequences, while leaving the judge free to craft a domestic solution … A 'comparative legal approach' can give judges insight into their own prejudices and assist in eliminating personal preferences.[45]

In the Court of Appeal, Lady Justice Arden explained that she had 'most often' used foreign jurisprudence 'as part of [her] own thinking about the case, [looking] at what other courts have done and at the examples they have come up with'. This might include looking 'at situations [the other courts] have had to deal with and the difficulties there might be if the rule was X rather than Y'.[46] A good example is the decision in *Dunnage v Randall*,[47] in which the Court of Appeal was asked to consider whether the personal characteristics of a defendant should be taken into account when determining the standard of care for the purposes of liability in negligence. Lady Justice Rafferty made reference to a number of foreign cases from Australia, Canada, New Zealand and the US.[48] Lady Justice Arden, too, made a point of stating that 'the citation of foreign materials [had] assisted [her] to weight up the arguments in this case'.[49] This was so despite the fact that '[d]ifferent common law systems may take a different view on the policy issues'; it was 'still valid to look at these authorities so long as that point is borne in mind'.[50]

[42] Duxbury (n 39) 27.
[43] Dorsen (n 34) 524 (Justice Breyer).
[44] Aharon Barak, 'Foreword: A Judge on Judging: The Role of a Supreme Court in a Democracy' (2002) 116 *Harvard Law Review* 19, 111; Aharon Barak, 'Comparison in Public Law' in Basil Markesinis and Jörg Fedtke, *Judicial Recourse to Foreign Law: A New Source of Inspiration?* (University College London Press, 2006) 288.
[45] Saunders (n 1) 114–15.
[46] Interview with the Rt Hon Lady Justice Arden, Lord Justice of Appeal (Royal Courts of Justice, London, 7 December 2011).
[47] *Dunnage v Randall* [2015] EWCA Civ 673; [2016] 2 WLR 839.
[48] ibid.
[49] ibid [154] (Lady Justice Arden).
[50] ibid.

The feeling continues in the Supreme Court. Lord Mance explained that foreign jurisprudence 'gives you insights and helps ensure that you've thought about all possible aspects of a problem'.[51] Lord Mance used similar language in *Patel v Mirza,*[52] considering that 'valuable insight' on the law of illegality could be found in a judgment of the Canadian Supreme Court: 'a number of points emerge[d] with great clarity' from the judgment of Justice McLachlin (as she then was) in that case.[53] Lord Collins justified his use of foreign jurisprudence in similar terms:

> In formulating my conclusions, it is useful just to see how other people have done it and whether there is anything to be learned from other people. Not only where there are gaps; in theory there are never gaps. Something that is done abroad won't be persuasive authority in the sense that you'll follow it, you'll just see what conclusion they have come to.[54]

This sort of motive was clearly the driving force in *Jones v Kaney*,[55] the case in which Lord Collins all but reprimanded counsel for their failure to cite what he considered to be relevant foreign authorities. So unusual were his comments that it is worth quoting the passage at some length:

> It is highly desirable that at this appellate level, in cases where issues of legal policy are concerned, the court should be informed about the position in other common law countries. This court is often helped by being referred to authorities from other common law systems, including the United States ... On this appeal the claimant did not rely on the United States material, although it is helpful to his case. The defendant's counsel drew attention to some of the United States cases on the basis of research which (it was said) was 'slightly hampered by the renovation of the Middle Temple's American room'. But there is an outstanding collection of United States material in the Institute of Advanced Legal Studies in London University, and (provided the barristers or solicitors concerned are prepared to make the expenditure) all of the material is readily available online.[56]

The vast American jurisprudence on 'precisely the same arguments of policy which [had] been argued before [the UK Supreme Court]' was, to Lord Collins, of obvious assistance. This was despite the fact that the culture relating to expert evidence was different in the US, because 'the underlying principle is the same'.[57] Thus, as Bell concluded, the Commonwealth and US

[51] Interview with the Rt Hon Lord Mance, Justice of the UK Supreme Court (Supreme Court, London, 6 December 2011).

[52] *Patel* (n 40) [190], referring to *Hall v Hebert* [1993] 2 SCR 159.

[53] ibid *Patel* [191]; In *Bilta (UK) Ltd (in Liquidation) v Nazir (No 2)* [2015] UKSC 23; [2016] 1 AC 1 [174], Lord Toulson and Lord Hodge recommended that 'in any future review the court would undoubtedly wish to examine the law in other countries and particularly the judgments of the High Court of Australia in *Nelson v Nelson*, all of which merit reading'.

[54] Interview with the Rt Hon Lord Collins of Mapesbury, retired Justice of the UK Supreme Court (Supreme Court, London, 22 May 2012).

[55] *Jones v Kaney* [2011] UKSC 13; [2011] 2 AC 398.

[56] ibid [74].

[57] ibid [77].

jurisprudence in *Jones v Kaney* was effectively cited as a way of 'checking that no relevant argument had been ignored'.[58]

Belhaj v Straw is another example.[59] Both Lord Mance and Lord Sumption undertook a detailed survey of jurisprudence from French, German, Dutch and US courts. Lord Mance recognised that the 'reasoning and nuances of United States law have not been constant and are not necessarily transposable to English law',[60] but evidently felt the US cases to be a helpful analytical lens. In explaining the point, Lord Mance quoted from Lord Wilberforce's judgment in *Buttes Gas*:

> When the judicial approach to an identical problem between the same parties has been spelt out with such articulation in a country, one not only so closely akin to ours in legal approach, the fabric of whose legal doctrine in this area is so closely interwoven with ours, but that to which all the parties before us belong, spelt out moreover in convincing language and reasoning, we should be unwise not to take the benefit of it.[61]

Lord Neuberger was less enthusiastic about the usefulness of the comparative exercise: courts of this jurisdiction 'should exercise great caution before relying on, let alone adopting, the reasoning of foreign courts'; 'Decisions of courts in states with a civil law system and with a coherent written constitution seem to me to be as likely to mislead as to help when it comes to analysing the boundaries of a common law rule developed on a case by case basis over the years'.[62] Nevertheless, Lord Neuberger accepted that 'any practical explanation by a court for or against judicial abstention is worth considering' and that the reasoning of the courts referred to by Lord Mance and Lord Neuberger were 'unsurprisingly, comprehensible and principled'.[63]

In the human rights context, it is worth remembering that UK judges have been, until recently, relatively unfamiliar with human rights adjudication and with the duties imposed upon them by the HRA 1998. For example, prior to the HRA, the balancing act required by the qualified rights had almost exclusively been the jurisdiction of the supranational court. A positive duty to 'take into account' one particular pool of otherwise persuasive jurisprudence, to read domestic law compatibly with an international convention and to declare any incompatibilities that could not be so remedied,[64] have all led domestic courts to grapple with greater depth and detail on questions hitherto unfamiliar to the role of the judge. It would not be surprising if judges were to consider the jurisprudence of other similar

[58] Bell (n 10) 21.
[59] *Belhaj* (n 31).
[60] ibid [57].
[61] *Buttes Gas and Oil Co v Hammer (No 3)* [1982] AC 888, 936–37.
[62] *Belhaj* (n 31) [133].
[63] ibid.
[64] Sections 2, 3 and 4 of the HRA 1998, respectively.

systems, particularly those with similar human rights instruments, in order to draw any assistance that they may provide when theorising about a particular problem at home. One of the major justifications for comparativism is that it can aid not only in applying the undertheorised jurisprudence, but can also encourage the domestic court to adopt a more theorised approach to human rights.

Yet explanations about the reference to foreign jurisprudence such as in *Jones v Kaney* and *Belhaj v Straw* are relatively rare. Where foreign jurisprudence has been used as an analytical lens, it will not necessarily be obvious from the text of the judgment. Lady Justice Arden explained that 'comparative law in that sense is very useful but it is not obvious on the face of the judgment because it wouldn't be relevant to cite it'.[65] This kind of use is a good example of the reasons why this book attempts to look beyond explicit citations. If foreign jurisprudence is referred to but omitted from the list of citations in a judgment, it represents an implicit rather than explicit use of foreign jurisprudence. It is therefore not a use that will be captured by a quantitative analysis of the cases. It is also a use that, if ignored, would significantly distort any conclusions about the influence of foreign jurisprudence in UK courts.

III. REASSURANCE

Closely connected to the gap-filling and analytical lens theories is the idea that foreign jurisprudence can provide reassurance. Slaughter has argued that '[r]eferences to the activity of fellow courts in other states can act as … a security blanket',[66] while Justice Barak talked of comparative law 'grant[ing] comfort to the judge and giv[ing] him the feeling that he is treading on safe ground'.[67] Along these lines, Flanagan and Ahern felt that judges in foreign jurisdictions were likely to 'form a reference group' to domestic judges adjudicating on constitutional rights.[68]

This purpose is distinct from the gap-filling and analytical lens theories because it constructs judicial comparativism as a sort of yardstick: by seeing that courts in other jurisdictions have come to the same or similar

[65] Interview with Lady Justice Arden (n 46).

[66] McCrudden (n 12) 519, quoting Anne-Marie Slaughter, 'A Typology of Transjudicial Communication' (1994) 29 *University of Richmond Law Review* 99, 116.

[67] Aharon Barak, 'Constitutional Human Rights and Private Law' (1996) 3 *Review of Constitutional Studies* 218, 242; Michael Bobek, *Comparative Reasoning in European Supreme Courts* (Oxford University Press, 2013) 91: 'English judges consider the use of the decisions from other common law jurisdictions to be "useful", to give them reassurance, illumination, inspiration, or comfort.'

[68] Brian Flanagan and Sinead Ahern, 'Judicial Decision-Making and Transnational Law: A Survey of Common Law Supreme Court Judges' (2011) 60 *International and Comparative Law Quarterly* 1.

conclusions about a particular problem, a judge can feel more confident in his own conclusions, which are reached independently of the jurisprudence from those jurisdictions.[69] In other words, the gap-filling and analytical lens theories capture uses of foreign jurisprudence in the very early stages of a judgment, while the use of foreign jurisprudence for the purpose of reassurance is likely to come a little later, once the judge has come to at least some tentative conclusion.[70] Despite this difference, the circumstances that give rise to using foreign jurisprudence in this way are likely to be similar to those suggested to give rise to gap-filling or to seeking an analytical lens. If a judge requires reassurance, it is likely to be because the domestic law is unsettled or underdeveloped. The then President of the Supreme Court, Lord Phillips, explained the relevance of foreign jurisprudence in this way:

> I think we like to look elsewhere: if we've got an area where we are uncertain; an area where we are developing the law; an area where, particularly, where we would like to develop the law in a particular direction, then you are particularly keen to see if you can get any support for what your thinking is from foreign jurisdictions.[71]

This sort of explanation also tends towards a view of foreign jurisprudence as an instrumental tool used to legitimate one's own decision. It lends support to those who feel that the legitimacy of judicial comparativism is often compromised by the tendency on the part of judges to 'cherry pick' decisions of foreign jurisdictions according to those that best support their own conclusions. The most cynical view of this is that in using foreign jurisprudence in this way, judges neglect to take a balanced view of the position in foreign jurisdictions. For the reasons given elsewhere, that argument is not accepted as an explanation for the Supreme Court's approach to foreign jurisprudence. For the instant purpose, the important observation is that the Supreme Court might use foreign jurisprudence in areas of uncertainty or where the law is under development. In those situations, Lord Phillips continued, 'to see how similar jurisdictions, dealing with similar problems have developed their jurisprudence is a valuable thing to do'.[72]

[69] Similar findings are reported by Elaine Mak, 'Reference to Foreign Law in the Supreme Courts of Britain and the Netherlands: Explaining the Development of Judicial Practices' (2012) 8(2) *Utrecht Law Review* 20, 33–34.

[70] See, eg, Lord Bingham's oft-cited judgment in *Fairchild v Glenhaven Funeral Services Ltd* [2002] UKHL 22; [2003] 1 AC 32 [31]: 'if ... a decision is given in this country which offends one's basic sense of justice and if considerations of international sources suggest that a different and more acceptable decision would be given in most other jurisdictions ... this must prompt anxious review of the decision in question'.

[71] Interview with the Rt Hon Lord Phillips of Worth Matravers, former President of the UK Supreme Court Supreme Court (Supreme Court, London, 23 November 2011).

[72] ibid.

Using foreign jurisprudence as a type of checking mechanism was common among the explanations of the other Justices interviewed. Although Lord Kerr felt it 'difficult to be prescriptive about the use to which [foreign jurisprudence] is put', it was possible to 'envisage two main strands':[73] The first strand was that 'even if it does not necessarily provide a template that one would wish to follow', analysis conducted by a foreign court, or the court's line of reasoning 'does provide a yardstick against which you can measure your own process of reasoning'. Lord Kerr's second strand echoed Lady Justice Arden's explanation that it was helpful to get an empirical view of the effect of certain developments,[74] 'in relating to the experience of the courts about the impact of particular laws'.[75] Lord Collins agreed: 'You might be, I suppose, encouraged or emboldened by what someone else has done'.[76]

For most of the Justices, it seemed that the extent to which foreign jurisprudence is used in this way would likely be connected to the arguments made by counsel. For example, Lord Reed explained that counsel using foreign jurisprudence essentially present the Supreme Court with:

> material from analogous legal systems. The argument is that the point has been considered by a superior court in that jurisdiction, and what they had to say about it is at least interesting and may give [the court] an idea about how the common law should be developed in this country.[77]

Therefore, foreign authorities are cited 'in order to persuade us to develop the common law in a particular way ... to show us that another leading common law court ... has taken [a] step without the heavens falling in'.[78] In human rights cases specifically, the justification is that the Court is concerned with considering the underlying values. As Baroness Hale put it:

> It is obviously of interest to us in this court if a foreign court has been interpreting a human rights instrument which is not unlike the European Convention, to look at its approach. That is because human rights are all about values—underlying values—and it's good to see how similar societies, similar legal systems, see those underlying values. If you find that the same result has been reached on the same set of facts, by a completely different route, it gives you some view of the underlying values.[79]

[73] Interview with Lord Kerr (n 14).

[74] Interview with Lady Justice Arden (n 46).

[75] Interview with Lord Kerr (n 14).

[76] Interview with Lord Collins (n 54).

[77] Interview with the Rt Hon Lord Reed, Justice of the UK Supreme Court (Supreme Court, London, 8 May 2012).

[78] ibid. The same point is made in Duxbury (n 39) 26, 33, citing *Re Spectrum Plus* [2005] UKHL 41; [2005] 2 AC 680 at [18]–[25] (Lord Nicholls) as an example.

[79] Interview with the Rt Hon Baroness Hale of Richmond, Justice of the UK Supreme Court (Supreme Court, London, 8 May 2012).

IV. CONCLUSIONS

In the early or formative stages of a judgment, particularly where the domestic law is unsettled or underdeveloped, the stock argument about judicial discretion is an obvious problem. If the domestic jurisprudence is unsettled or there is an absence of clear guiding principles, the discretion of the judge is in any event approaching its outer limits,[80] and reference to foreign jurisprudence for the purpose of 'gap filling' is likely to attract attention. As the US debate shows, using foreign jurisprudence for this purpose may invite the accusation that a judge has made opportunistic citations of foreign jurisprudence in order to bolster a point that is otherwise not supportable in domestic law. However, it has been argued in this chapter that the 'gap-filling' thesis does not explain the UK Supreme Court's use of foreign jurisprudence. Certainly, none of the Justices interviewed fully accepted the theory.

Rather, it is more realistic to consider that foreign jurisprudence provides the Supreme Court with a fresh perspective—an analytical lens—through which to reflect on its own reasoning about a problem. In this way, foreign jurisprudence is used mainly as a heuristic device. This is what appeared to be happening in the House of Lords control order cases *MB* and *AF (No 3)*, and this is what seemed to drive Lord Collins' insistence on the consideration of American decisions in *Jones v Kaney*.[81] The evidence from the interviews supports this construction. None of the judges interviewed felt this use of foreign jurisprudence to be problematic, largely because no particular reliance is placed on these materials in any event. Lord Collins was 'sure that [he had] never been turned by foreign law'.[82] At best, he 'might have been confirmed in [his] feelings'.[83]

As Saunders has suggested, the reality is simply that 'such cases must be determined ... with or without the insights offered by comparative law' and 'in at least some such cases, foreign experience can help to elucidate the issues and options for their resolution'.[84] In some circumstances, this may translate into using foreign jurisprudence as a heuristic device: a yardstick against which to measure a judge's own thinking about a problem. In these circumstances, foreign jurisprudence simply provides an opportunity for reflection and becomes 'part of the process of reaching a more fully theorised ... agreement'.[85] When interviewed, Lord Kerr gave reasons along

[80] Saunders (n 1) 114.
[81] *MB* (n 18); *AF* (n 24); *Jones v Kaney* (n 55).
[82] Interview with Lord Collins (n 54).
[83] ibid.
[84] Saunders (n 1) 114.
[85] McCrudden (n 13) 374. This follows discussion drawn from Cass R Sunstein, *Legal Reasoning and Political Conflict* (Oxford University Press, 1996), in which Sunstein described the process of deciding cases on their facts without necessarily agreeing on any particular theory supporting the decision as giving rise to 'incompletely theorised' agreements.

these lines for dismissing the significance that might be attributed to the use of foreign jurisprudence. Lord Kerr's words are worth repeating:

> Ultimately ... the outcome of these cases depends critically on your own powers of analysis. Reference to authority, be it domestic, supranational, international or whatever, is always going to be by way of supplement to your own reasoning in the case. Hopefully to confirm the views that you have formed and, occasionally, to shape those views. But I see that very much in a secondary—an extremely important but nevertheless secondary—role.[86]

These uses of foreign jurisprudence are also likely to be the more obscure in the judgment, since it would not usually be relevant to cite them explicitly unless they had contributed something of substance to the instant case. This finding goes some way towards explaining the anomalies in the dataset discussed in Chapter 5, where it was explained that the data collected on explicit citation did not show some Supreme Court Justices—known for their enthusiasm for comparative law—to be heavy users of foreign jurisprudence. Where judges use foreign jurisprudence as a heuristic device, as an analytical lens, yardstick, or benchmark against which to measure thinking, or when seeking reassurance, it is easy to understand the lack of explicit citations.[87] It was perhaps purposes of this kind that prompted Lady Justice Arden's comment (although not speaking for the Supreme Court) that there is 'far more use of comparative law than appears on the face of the judgments ... it's informing the judges behind the scenes'.[88] If a foreign court has already adopted the solution, it is useful to check the consequences. This is likely to be especially important where the Court is making more than an incremental development to the law. As heuristic devices, these recourses to foreign jurisprudence may not result in a substantive contribution to the reasoning in any one case and so would not necessarily convert into explicit citations in a published judgment. Just as there is no obligation to use persuasive authorities, neither is there an obligation to cite them.

If foreign jurisprudence is used in this way, concerns about legitimacy and cherry picking fall away. In seeking to shed light on matters of salience that might have escaped the court's attention, the courts are treating foreign jurisprudence as illustrative rather than as normatively persuasive statements of legal principle. This is in keeping with one of the major justifications for comparativism: that it can encourage the domestic court to adopt a more theorised approach to human rights. As McCrudden

[86] Interview with Lord Kerr (n 14).

[87] The point has also been recognised by Bobek (n 67) 72: 'The reasons for the absence of an express reference may be multiple ... [including] the [possibility that] comparative argument was from the very beginning intended for internal use only, ie, as a tool of internal persuasion within the court, but never even intended to be displayed in the reasoning of the court.'

[88] Interview with Lady Justice Arden (n 46).

recognised: 'Even where the *result* of the foreign judicial approach has not been adopted, it has often been influential in sharpening the understanding of the court's view of domestic law'.[89] Foreign jurisprudence may 'perform a cognitive function ... the confrontation of both legal systems may force some consideration and better understanding of the nature of domestic law'.[90]

[89] Christopher McCrudden, 'Human Rights and Judicial Use of Comparative Law' in Örücü (n 6) 17; McCrudden (n 12) 512.

[90] Luc Heuschling, 'Comparative Law in French Human Rights Cases' in Örücü (n 6) 44; Rabinder Singh, 'Interpreting Bills of Rights' [2008] *Statute Law Review* 82. Foreign judgments provide 'more of a benchmark of the rightness' for the Justices: Bell (n 10) 23.

7

The Pursuit of a Common Enterprise

IN CHAPTER 6, it was argued that judges use foreign jurisprudence as a heuristic device. Foreign jurisprudence might elucidate issues or provide a useful yardstick against which judges can reassure themselves about their own conclusions, especially where domestic jurisprudence is unsettled or underdeveloped. By seeing that courts in other jurisdictions have come to the same or similar conclusions about a particular problem, a judge can feel more confident in his own independent conclusions. It is a receptive use of foreign jurisprudence—a one-way transaction, based on the functionalist theory of 'usefulness and need'.[1] But recourse to foreign jurisprudence can also promote greater harmonisation or integration within a group of countries. This may be in response, for instance, to a common agreement or a shared heritage. One of Slaughter's conclusions was that the use of foreign jurisprudence would be likely where there was an 'awareness of a common enterprise'.[2] That awareness 'could flow either from a particular self-conception or a common substantive focus'.[3] For example:

> [T]he courts of some subset of countries may see their primary function as the protection of individual rights against the government. From this perspective, it is not surprising that one of the most active areas of transjudicial communication outside the European Community is among courts specifically charged with the interpretation and application of international instruments concerning human rights.[4]

In these situations, foreign jurisprudence is used as part of an information-gathering exercise,[5] with the aim of seeking to maintain uniformity with other jurisdictions.

[1] See, eg, Konrad Zweigert and Hein Kötz, *An Introduction to Comparative Law*, Tony Weir trans, 3rd edn (Oxford University Press, 1998) 17.

[2] Anne-Marie Slaughter 'A Typology of Transjudicial Communication' (1994) 29 *University of Richmond Law Review* 99, 128; Ian Cram, 'Resort to Foreign Constitutional Norms in Domestic Human Rights Jurisprudence with Reference to Terrorism Cases' [2009] *CLJ* 118, 121–122.

[3] Slaughter (n 2) 128.

[4] ibid.

[5] Elaine Mak, 'Why Do Dutch and UK Judges Cite Foreign Law?' [2011] *CLJ* 420, 443.

I. USING FOREIGN JURISPRUDENCE TO PROMOTE UNIFORMITY

In the context of human rights, this discussion tends to draw from the ongoing debate about universalism. For some, this is problematic. It is said that the citation of foreign jurisprudence assumes reliance on a fictional shared understanding. Posner, for example, has remarked that 'to cite foreign law as authority, is to flirt with the discredited (I had thought) idea of a universal natural law; or to suppose fantastically that the world's judges constitute a single, elite community of wisdom and conscience'.[6] If the citation of foreign jurisprudence does suppose that there is some common understanding about human rights, the unyielding debate between universalism and cultural relativism will continue to pose awkward questions for judges that tend towards comparativism. A connected issue is that judicial comparativism may pose greater risks in such circumstances, since the inclusion of common principles in these texts may act to disguise divergent views about their application as well as any theory supporting them.[7]

The debate is further complicated by the shift in focus away from universal instruments and towards regional systems of more selective integration. For example, the Universal Declaration on Human Rights greatly influenced the drafters of the ECHR, which is arguably the primary text for human rights regulation in the European legal order. As McCrudden has pointed out, one of the attractive aspects of regional instruments 'is that states that appear to share more common cultural and ethical roots can come together to establish human rights regimes that go beyond the state, but stop short of the global'.[8] For McCrudden, this 'gives rise to the question as to whether *regionally shared conceptions of human rights* are emerging, for example, a European *ius commune*'.[9] This understanding would presumably lead UK domestic judges to consider relevant European jurisprudence in cases which engage a Convention point ahead of, say, Commonwealth jurisprudence. Yet the evidence suggests that the reality is quite the reverse. As Lord Mance has written:

> When interpreting legislation to give effect to international treaties, the need for international consistency provides a strong justification [for the use of foreign jurisprudence]. In areas such as fundamental rights, international instruments invite international discourse, though sometimes raising the question how far different social backgrounds and standards justify differences in application. Within Europe, the frameworks of the European Union and the European Convention on Human Rights encourage uniformity. Indeed, the role of the Court of Justice

[6] Richard Posner, 'No Thanks, We Already Have Our Own Laws' *Legal Affairs* (July/August 2004), www.legalaffairs.org/issues/July-August-2004/feature_posner_julaug04.msp.

[7] Christopher McCrudden, 'Judicial Comparativism and Human Rights' in Esin Örücü and David Nelken (eds), *Comparative Law: A Handbook* (Hart Publishing, 2007) 371, 373.

[8] ibid.

[9] ibid.

> and the European Court of Human Rights in establishing the 'true' effect of the European Treaties and European Convention means that such uniformity may be achieved even without consensus among national courts.[10]

Aspirations towards adopting uniform positions can therefore play a role in limiting the use of foreign jurisprudence.

II. UNIFORMITY UNDER THE HUMAN RIGHTS ACT

It is a common feature of judicial reasoning under the HRA 1998 that the Convention must be understood and applied uniformly amongst all contracting states. In *Ullah*, Lord Bingham stressed that while Member States could legislate so as to provide for

> rights more generous than those guaranteed by the Convention, national courts should not interpret the Convention to achieve this: the Convention must bear the same meaning for all states party to it.[11]

Accordingly, his Lordship felt that the task of domestic courts was 'no more, but certainly no less' than keeping pace with Strasbourg. This restrained approach was adopted in a line of cases after *Ullah*. In *R (Clift)*, Lord Hope added that '[a] measure of self-restraint is needed, lest we stretch our own jurisprudence beyond that which is shared by all the States Parties to the Convention'.[12] Lord Brown gave endorsement to this cautious approach in *Al-Skeini*, further suggesting that 'no more, but certainly no less' could be read as 'no less, but certainly no more'.[13]

A major justification for this approach is based on 'the general desirability of a uniform interpretation of the Convention in all member states',[14] designed to avoid confusion and relativism. The net result of this interpretation is that UK courts initially took a deferential approach to the case law of the ECtHR in Strasbourg. Masterman argued that the loyalty domestic courts were showing to the Strasbourg line would have the result of binding domestic courts to Strasbourg.[15] In similar terms, Lewis described the approach as 'the mirror principle' and felt the result to be that domestic

[10] Lord Mance, 'Foreign Laws and Languages' in Andrew Burrows, David Johnston and Reinhard Zimmermann (eds), *Judge and Jurist: Essays in Memory of Lord Rodger of Earlsferry* (Oxford University Press, 2013) 87.

[11] *R (Ullah) v Special Adjudicator; Do v Immigration Appeal Tribunal* [2004] UKHL 26 [20]; *Kay and Others v London Borough of Lambeth* [2006] UKHL 10; [2006] 2 AC 465.

[12] *R (Clift) (FC) v Secretary of State for the Home Department* [2006] UKHL 54; [2007] 1 AC 484 [49] (Lord Hope).

[13] *R (Al-Skeini and Others) v Secretary of State for Defence* [2007] UKHL 26; [2008] 1 AC 153 [106]. *cf In Re P and Others* [2008] UKHL 38; [2009] 1 AC 173 [50] (Lord Hope).

[14] *In Re P and Others* [2008] UKHL 38 [36].

[15] Roger Masterman, 'Section 2(1) of the Human Rights Act: Binding Domestic Courts to Strasbourg?' [2004] *PL* 725.

human rights law would effectively be 'nothing more than Strasbourg's shadow'.[16] The reasons for this approach are intelligible, reflecting 'the fact that the Convention is an international instrument, the correct interpretation of which can be authoritatively expounded only by the Strasbourg Court'.[17] As Masterman suggested, the jurisprudence of jurisdictions that are not signatories to the ECHR is 'unlikely to point to the direction in which the common law should be developed to ensure compatibility with the Convention rights'.[18]

The courts are sometimes steered towards Strasbourg jurisprudence by legislation other than the HRA 1998. For example, in *P v Cheshire West and Cheshire Council*,[19] the Supreme Court had to consider the criteria for judging whether the living arrangements made for a mentally incapacitated person amount to a deprivation of liberty. In answering the question, the Supreme Court read section 64(5) of the Mental Capacity Act 2005 as giving the Strasbourg jurisprudence 'added significance',[20] feeling that they were 'more closely tied to [the Strasbourg Court's] interpretation of the Convention than … under section 2(1) of the Human Rights Act 1998':

> In cases under the Human Rights Act 1998, the courts have frequently to consider how far their duty, in section 2(1), to 'take into account' the jurisprudence of the European Commission and Court of Human Rights goes. That problem does not trouble us in this case. Section 64(5) of the Mental Capacity Act states that: 'In this Act, references to a deprivation of a person's liberty have the same meaning as in article 5(1) of the Human Rights Convention.' As the object was to avoid the violation identified in *HL* 40 EHRR 761, it seems clear that we are expected to turn to the jurisprudence of the Strasbourg Court to find out what is meant by a deprivation of liberty in this context.[21]

The Supreme Court would not be precluded from forming its own view of how it would decide the matter where (as here) there was not directly relevant Strasbourg jurisprudence but, 'short of a clear indication' in the Strasbourg jurisprudence, the Supreme Court felt it better to be 'cautious about extending a concept as sensitive as "deprivation of liberty" beyond the meaning which it would be regarded as having in ordinary usage'.[22]

[16] Jonathan Lewis, 'The European Ceiling on Human Rights' [2007] *PL* 720, 730; Lord Justice Laws, 'The Limitations of Human Rights' [1998] *PL* 254; Roger Masterman, 'Taking the Strasbourg Jurisprudence into Account: Developing a "Municipal Law of Human Rights" under the Human Rights Act' [2005] 54 *ICLQ* 907; Stephen Grosz, Jack Beatson and Peter Duffy, *Human Rights: The 1998 Act and the European Convention* (Sweet & Maxwell, 2000) 20.

[17] *Ullah* (n 11) [20] (Lord Bingham); *Kay* (n 11) [87].

[18] Masterman (n 16) 907, 923.

[19] *P (by His Litigation Friend the Official Solicitor) v Cheshire West and Chester Council and Another* [2014] UKSC 19; [2014] AC 896.

[20] ibid [91] (Lord Carnwath and Lord Hodge).

[21] ibid [19] (Lady Hale).

[22] ibid [91] (Lord Carnwath and Lord Hodge).

Even where it would be of interest to the Supreme Court to review the position of the other states signatory to the Convention, it is clear that the Court prefers to accept the results of the Strasbourg Court's research on the point. The practical reasons were considered in Chapter 5: the Supreme Court simply does not have time 'to go to the other European countries and look at the way they've addressed [an issue]'.[23] Baroness Hale also explained the lack of citations from the domestic courts of other European states along these lines, suggesting that it was simply 'easier' to look at the Strasbourg Court's findings about the state of the national law in the various contracting states than for the Supreme Court to undertake its own analysis:

> It is not easy for us to find out what Europe is doing on a particular point; it is much easier for Strasbourg. We may know about it [but] I don't think that we, as a matter of policy, would ask ourselves what is going on in France or Germany or wherever. We might decide to do it in a particular case, but mainly we rely on what Strasbourg tells us about the way in which things are developing elsewhere.[24]

The approach is surprising, given the well-recognised problems with the quality and consistency of the Strasbourg Court's decisions. As Amos has written, the Strasbourg case law 'can be unclear, confusing, and admitting of many possible interpretations'.[25] The best examples are those where the Strasbourg Court has simply got it wrong, such as in *Osman v UK*.[26] In other cases, the judges have commented on the lack of clarity or the mixed messages given by the complexity of several judgments.[27] Another possibility is that Strasbourg's review of the European jurisprudence is itself outdated. It is implicit in the construction of the ECHR as a 'living instrument' that interpretations and the consensus among Member States may evolve.[28] The Strasbourg Court has thus explained that the Convention 'is first and foremost a system for the protection of human rights' and

[23] Interview with the Rt Hon Lord Phillips of Worth Matravers, former President of the UK Supreme Court Supreme Court (Supreme Court, London, 23 November 2011). The full quote was given in ch 3.

[24] Interview with the Rt Hon Baroness Hale of Richmond, Justice of the UK Supreme Court (Supreme Court, London, 19 October 2011).

[25] Merris Amos, 'The Principle of Comity' [2009] *Yearbook of European Law* 503, 525. See also Lord Hoffmann, 'Human Rights and the House of Lords' (1999) 62 *MLR* 159, 162–64, expressing 'doubts ... about the suitability, at least for this country, of having questions of human rights determined by an international tribunal made up of judges from many countries'.

[26] *Osman v UK* (2000) 29 EHRR 245. See also Lord Steyn, '2000–2005: Laying the Foundations of Human Rights Law in the United Kingdom' 2005 *European Human Rights Law Review* 349, 361.

[27] See, eg, *R (Countryside Alliance) v Her Majesty's Attorney General* [2007] UKHL 52; [2008] 1 AC 719 [139]; *R (Al Skeini) v Secretary of State for Defence* [2007] UKHL 26 [67]; and other examples cited by Amos (n 25) 525.

[28] *Tyrer v UK* (1978) 2 EHRR 1 [31]. It was argued in a previous thesis that the 'living instrument' places a duty on domestic courts to keep track of the development in Convention jurisprudence.

that 'the Court must [therefore] have regard to the changing conditions in Contracting States and respond, for example, to any emerging consensus as to the standards to be achieved'.[29] Nevertheless, the language of 'uniformity' and 'consensus' led domestic courts to defer to the Strasbourg Court. The risk was put clearly by Sedley: 'in trying to stay level, we shall fall behind'.[30] If consistency and uniformity are the aim, the Supreme Court should be willing to engage in research to that end, including the use of foreign jurisprudence as necessary. This would at least be relevant where the Strasbourg jurisprudence is unhelpful or unclear: 'to collaborate fully with the Court, national tribunals have to keep on top of the developments in the Court's practice, and even anticipate how it might resolve an issue'.[31]

There has been some evidence of the willingness to engage with foreign jurisprudence in this way, especially when seeking to confirm the conclusions of the Strasbourg jurisprudence. A good example of this is the Supreme Court's decision in *Cadder.*[32] *Cadder* was, in effect, an appeal against the High Court of Justiciary in *HM Advocate v McLean.*[33] Both cases involved persons detained under section 14 of the Criminal Procedure (Scotland) Act 1995 and admissions made by the detainee during police interviews without prior access to legal advice. In *McLean*, the High Court of Justiciary had concluded that reliance on admissions made by a detainee in such circumstances was not incompatible with the detainee's right to a fair trial under Article 6 ECHR. The appellant in *Cadder* contended that *McLean* had been wrongly decided. The question for the Supreme Court was therefore whether the use of material obtained in a police interview without legal representation did in fact render a subsequent trial unfair.

Pursuant to their duty under section 2(1) of the HRA 1998, the Justices of the Supreme Court took into account the relevant Strasbourg jurisprudence as a starting point: *Salduz v Turkey.*[34] In common with the detainees in both *McLean* and *Cadder*, Salduz had not had the benefit of legal advice when in police custody. The Grand Chamber of the Strasbourg Court in that case held (unanimously) that there had been a violation of Article 6(1) and 6(3)(c) ECHR. Turning to the question of whether the Supreme Court must follow *Salduz v Turkey*, the Supreme Court applied the 'clear and constant'

[29] *Stafford v UK* (2002) 35 EHRR 32 [68].

[30] Stephen Sedley, *Ashes and Sparks: Essays on Law and Justice* (Cambridge University Press, 2011) 384.

[31] Colin Warbrick, 'The View from the Outside' in Helen Fenwick, Roger Masterman and Gavin Phillipson (eds), *Judicial Reasoning under the UK Human Rights Act* (Cambridge University Press, 2007) 37.

[32] *Cadder v HM Advocate* [2010] UKSC 43; [2010] 1 WLR 2601.

[33] *HM Advocate v McLean* [2009] HCJAC 97; 2010 SLT 73.

[34] *Salduz v Turkey* [2008] ECHR 1542.

test derived from *Alconbury.*[35] The Court felt the test to be satisfied by evidence that *Salduz v Turkey* had been followed in a subsequent line of cases. To illustrate this point, Lord Hope referred to a list of authorities provided by JUSTICE (intervening). Although the five cases cited from that list were decisions of the ECtHR,[36] it appears from a later section of the judgment (quoted below) that the full list provided by JUSTICE had also included foreign jurisprudence from the domestic courts of other Member States. It was by reference to a selection of this material that Lord Hope drew further support:

> As JUSTICE has shown by the materials referred to in its written intervention, the majority of those member states which prior to *Salduz v Turkey* did not afford a right to legal representation at interview (Belgium, France, the Netherlands and Ireland) are now recognising that their legal systems are, in this respect, inadequate.[37]

Lord Hope went on to review the approach of a selection of foreign domestic courts more closely:

> In the Netherlands the Supreme Court has held that a suspect arrested by the police must be offered the opportunity to consult a lawyer before being interviewed and that an arrested minor was entitled to have the assistance of a lawyer while being interviewed ... In France the Conseil Constitutionnel has held that articles 62 and 63 of the Code of Criminal Procedure, which authorise the questioning of a person remanded in police custody ... but do not allow the person held against his will to have the benefit of legal assistance while undergoing questioning, are unconstitutional because they could not be reconciled with articles 9 and 16 of the Declaration of 1789 des droits de l'homme et du citoyen ... The Conseil d'Etat in its turn has drawn the government's attention to the fragility, in the light of article 6 of the Convention, of article 706 -88 of the Code de procédure pénale, which prevents access to legal assistance at this stage.[38]

[35] *R (Alconbury) v Secretary of State for the Environment, Transport and the Regions* [2001] UKHL 23; [2003] 2 AC 295 [26] (Slynn LJ), 'Although the Human Rights Act 1998 does not provide that a national court is bound by [Strasbourg] decisions it is obliged to take account of them so far as they are relevant. In the absence of some special circumstances it seems to me that the court should follow any clear and constant jurisprudence of the European Court of Human Rights.'

[36] *Cadder* (n 32) [47] (Lord Hope). The cases referred to are as follows: *Sükran Yildiz v Turkey* (Application No 4661/02) (unreported), 3 February 2009; *Amutgan v Turkey* (Application No 5138/04) (unreported), 3 February 2009 [17]–[18]; *Plonka v Poland* (Application No 20310/02) (unreported), 31 March 2009 [35]; *Pishchalnikov v Russia* (Application No 7025/04) (unreported), 24 September 2009 [70]; *Dayanan v Turkey* (Application No 7377/03) (unreported), 13 October 2009 [32]–[33]; *Fatma Tun v Turkey* (Application No 18532/05) (unreported), 3 October 2009 [14]–[15].

[37] *Cadder* (n 32) [49] (Lord Hope).

[38] ibid. The decisions referred to from the Supreme Court of the Netherlands, the French Conseil Constitutional and the Conseil d'Etat are, respectively: *LJN BH3079 NJ* (Netherlands Law Reports) 30 June 2009; *Decision No 2010-14/22 QPC* (unreported) 30 July 2010; and *Section de L'intérieur, Projet de loi relatif à la garde à vue*, 7 October 2010 (No 384.505).

Lord Hope concluded that 'if Scotland were not to follow the example of the others it would be almost alone among all the member states in not doing so'.[39] Moreover, the system of detention under sections 14 and 15 of the 1995 Act was devised in view of a balance to be struck between the public interest and the rights of the accused that was irreconcilable with the Convention rights.[40] This view had been reached 'without any attempt at comparative jurisprudence on [the] issue' and as a result of 'shutting their eyes to the way thinking elsewhere was developing'.[41]

Many considered the Supreme Court to have taken too slavish an approach to the Strasbourg case law in *Cadder*, with enormous repercussions for the Scottish legal system and the many victims whose cases were overturned.[42] Lord Hope explicitly recognised the unpopularity of the decision in a lecture given to the Scottish Young Lawyer's Association in April 2011:

> As Lord Bingham has said, our task is to apply the law, not to decide cases according to our personal preferences. Of course, the decision was not popular, especially among those who must answer to the electorate. But, as Justice Stephen Breyer of the US Supreme Court has said, do not imagine that our decisions are popular. It is not our job to be popular.[43]

Nevertheless, Lord Hope did alter his approach to the issue in another Article 6 case later in the same judicial year: *Ambrose v Harris*.[44] In *Ambrose*, the issue was whether the questioning of a suspect by police prior to being taken into custody constituted a violation of the suspect's right to a fair trial under Article 6 of the Convention. Lord Hope felt that the consequences of the Supreme Court establishing such a rule would be 'profound' and relied on the absence of clear Strasbourg jurisprudence to avoid that result: 'if Strasbourg has not yet spoken clearly enough on this issue, the wiser course must surely be to wait until it has done so'.[45] The others in the majority took the same approach. Lord Clarke also noted the implications for the investigation of crime,[46] agreeing that 'Strasbourg jurisprudence, to date,

[39] *Cadder* (n 32) [49] (Lord Hope).

[40] ibid [51] (Lord Hope).

[41] ibid. Lord Rodger's judgment in *Cadder* did not replicate this review of foreign jurisprudence, although it is clear that Lord Roger's reasons are given as supplementary to those outlined by Lord Hope. Indeed, on the separate but important issue as to the consequences of allowing the appeal, both Lord Hope and Lord Rodger drew heavily from a judgment of Chief Justice Murray of the Irish Supreme Court. The relevant section is reproduced in each of their judgments; see, eg, [99]–[103] (Lord Roger).

[42] See, eg, Alan Paterson, *Final Judgment: The Last Law Lords and the Supreme Court* (Hart Publishing, 2013) 244.

[43] Lord Hope of Craighead, 'Scots Law Seen from South of the Border' [2012] *Edinburgh Law Review* 58, 74.

[44] *Ambrose v Harris (Procurator Fiscal, Oban)* [2011] UKSC 53; [2011] WLR 2435.

[45] ibid [15].

[46] ibid [116]: 'such a requirement could hamper proper and effective investigations in situations which are often dynamic, fast moving and confused'.

does not support the ... contention ... that the European court has gone as far as to say that the right [to a fair trial] emerges as soon as a suspect is to be questioned by the police in whatever circumstances'.[47]

The interesting feature of the majority reasoning in *Ambrose* is that the absence of Strasbourg guidance was supplemented by an analysis of relevant jurisprudence from Canada and America.[48] When expressing his reasons for rejecting Lord Kerr's dissenting view, Lord Hope denied that there was 'any support in the Strasbourg cases, or in such international authorities as we have been shown',[49] and explained his own analysis of the Canadian and American jurisprudence in those terms. In particular, Lord Hope relied on the well-known American case *Miranda v Arizona*.[50] Lord Hope devoted five paragraphs to the *Miranda* judgment,[51] finding that the basis for the ruling in that case was that police custody creates particular pressures which mean that the person's will is more likely to be overcome when he is being questioned under conditions of that kind. The observation from the relevant Strasbourg jurisprudence, *Salduz v Turkey*,[52] was that 'the rationale of the generally recognised international human rights standards relates in particular to the protection of the accused against abusive coercion on the part of the authorities', which Lord Hope felt 'fit[ted] in with this line of reasoning'.[53] Thus, Lord Hope's view was that 'this feature is likely to be absent when questions are being put at the locus or in the person's home'.[54]

Further, Lord Hope inferred support for the *Miranda* judgment from the Strasbourg Court's jurisprudence; although recognising that the Strasbourg Court had not referred to *Miranda* in any of its judgments, Lord Hope felt that it could be 'assumed that the court will not have overlooked it in its search for generally accepted international human rights standards'.[55] Lord Hope continued:

> It is not unreasonable to think that *Miranda* and subsequent cases that the ruling in that case [has] given rise to in the United States will influence the thinking of the Strasbourg court.[56]

Lord Kerr, in his dissent, analysed the foreign jurisprudence rather differently:

> [O]ne must be careful about making assumptions about the *Miranda* experience or believing that it can be readily transplanted into European jurisprudence in

[47] ibid [115].
[48] *R v Grant* [2009] 2 SCR 353 and *Miranda v Arizona* (1966) 384 US 436, respectively.
[49] *Ambrose* (n 44) [59].
[50] *Miranda* (n 48).
[51] *Ambrose* (n 44) [50]–[54].
[52] *Salduz* (n 34).
[53] *Ambrose* (n 44) [54].
[54] ibid.
[55] ibid [52].
[56] ibid [53].

> any wholesale way. The implications of that decision must be considered in the context of police practice in the United States of America. Nothing that has been put before this court establishes that it is common practice in America to ask incriminating questions of persons suspected of a crime other than in custody. Indeed, it is my understanding that as soon as a person is identified as a suspect, police are trained that they should not ask that person any questions until he or she has been given the Miranda warnings.[57]

A cynical observation is that the use of foreign jurisprudence in *Ambrose* was a vehicle for the Supreme Court's reluctance to decide the case in a way that was perceived to be advancing on the Strasbourg jurisprudence. Some support for this suspicion is given by Lord Kerr's later explanation about the majority reasoning in *Ambrose* (extra-judicially):

> I have no objection to a mode of analysis which takes account of the fact that Strasbourg has not spoken, provided that this is by way of incidental observation or subsidiary reasoning, rather than being the sole basis for the decision to refuse to recognise the right. And, while this is not quite how the majority expressed themselves, their approach can perhaps be said to be consistent with that way of dealing with the question. I make that tentative claim because there can be detected in the judgments of my colleagues, particularly from their consideration of jurisprudence from America and Canada, clear indications that, irrespective of Strasbourg's silence, they did not consider that article 6 could have the breadth of application that was claimed for it.[58]

As Lord Kerr points out, it is that continued reference to the absence of clear Strasbourg case law that made the use of comparative jurisprudence unconvincing. Indeed, the majority reasoning (and Lord Hope in particular) read the conclusion in *Miranda* into the Strasbourg jurisprudence. Thus, Lord Kerr concluded that he would be 'much more comfortable with the decision' if the 'absence of Strasbourg jurisprudence on the point [could] be relegated to a subsidiary status'.[59] The example indicates that foreign jurisprudence may be influential in anticipating the conclusions of the Strasbourg Court and confirming the consensus on a position. Where there is relevant Strasbourg jurisprudence, however, the Supreme Court might be likely to pay less attention to foreign jurisprudence.

III. THE ABSENCE OF A SUPRANATIONAL COURT

Identifying a consensus among foreign jurisdictions on a particular issue will be especially important where there is no relevant supranational

[57] ibid [167].

[58] Lord Kerr, 'The Modest Underworker of Strasbourg?' Clifford Chance Lecture (London, 25 January 2012), https://www.supremecourt.uk/docs/speech_120125.pdf, 17.

[59] ibid 18.

court jurisprudence. The hypothesis is relatively straightforward. Where an instrument is given an authoritative interpretation by a supranational court, domestic courts faced with questions of interpretation will look to that jurisprudence in the first instance. The approach taken by UK courts to the Strasbourg Court case law provides a good example. By contrast, where there is no supranational court to give an authoritative interpretation of a convention, domestic courts do not have an obvious body of jurisprudence to consult. Courts are nevertheless still concerned to maintain consistency in the interpretation of an international convention, since the very purpose of these instruments is to harmonise standards on a particular issue. The need for a consistent approach will provide 'strong justification' for recourse to foreign jurisprudence.[60] As Dickson has explained:

> The courts take account of Strasbourg's thinking on human rights because they have been directed by Parliament to do so. Parliament has likewise transposed other international human rights standards into UK law and the courts are obliged to apply them too. The only difference is that for these other standards there is no international court the decisions of which the UK Parliament can direct UK courts to take into account. At best these other standards are overseen by treaty-monitoring bodies which are not courts, or by national courts in other countries which have transposed the standards into their domestic law. Parliament has chosen not to direct UK courts to take account of what those treaty-monitoring bodies or national courts may have said about the standards, although Article 32 of the Vienna Convention on the Law of Treaties 1969 does say that in the interpretation of treaties 'recourse may be had to supplementary means of interpretation' when, after applying the approach to interpretation set out in Article 31, the meaning is still 'ambiguous or obscure or leads to a result which is manifestly absurd or unreasonable'. The House of Lords often looked at these other sources of its own motion, especially when interpreting treaties the effectiveness of which depended on the same interpretation being adopted by all States Parties to the treaty (eg treaties on international transport).[61]

Consider, for example, the preamble to the 1951 Convention Relating to the Status of Refugees (hereinafter the 'Refugee Convention'), which recognises that 'a satisfactory solution of a problem of which the United Nations has recognized the international scope and nature cannot therefore be achieved without *international co-operation*' (emphasis added).[62] Similarly, the preamble to the UN Convention on the Rights of the Child includes: 'Recognizing the importance of *international cooperation* for improving

[60] Lord Reed, 'Comparative Law in the Supreme Court of the United Kingdom', Lecture at the Centre for Private Law (University of Edinburgh, 13 October 2017), www.supremecourt.uk/docs/speech-171013.pdf, 12.

[61] Brice Dickson, *Human Rights and the United Kingdom Supreme Court* (Oxford University Press, 2013) 34–35. See also Shaheed Fatima, *Using International Law in Domestic Courts* (Hart Publishing, 2005) 141.

[62] Convention Relating to the Status of Refugees, Geneva, 28 July 1951, 189 UNTS (entered into force on 4 October 1967), preamble.

the living conditions of children in every country' (emphasis added).[63] The limitations associated with using foreign jurisprudence where there is relevant Strasbourg jurisprudence are presumably non-existent in these circumstances, not least because the Strasbourg Court is also assumed to be developing its jurisprudence in line with the international context.[64] Baroness Hale explained as much in *P v Cheshire West and Cheshire Council*:

> The whole point about human rights is their universal character. The rights set out in the European Convention are to be guaranteed to 'everyone' (article 1). They are premised on the inherent dignity of all human beings whatever their frailty or flaws. The same philosophy underpins the United Nations Convention on the Rights of Persons with Disabilities (CRPD), ratified by the United Kingdom in 2009. Although not directly incorporated into our domestic law, the CRPD is recognised by the Strasbourg court as part of the international law context within which the guarantees of the European Convention are to be interpreted.[65]

These uses of comparative law are distinct from the 'gap-filling' theories discussed in Chapter 6. There it was explained that one of the most obvious reasons for using foreign jurisprudence is to draw assistance where domestic jurisprudence is unhelpful or non-existent. Thus, one of the reasons that comparativists give for the use of foreign jurisprudence is based on 'gap-filling'—offering a useful perspective where the indigenous jurisprudence is lacking or unsettled.[66] The argument in this section is different. Far from resorting to foreign jurisprudence where there is a dearth of domestic jurisprudence, in some cases, foreign jurisprudence may appropriately be of equal or greater importance than the domestic case law, irrespective of the nature or absence of domestic jurisprudence.

[63] Convention on the Rights of the Child, adopted and opened for signature, ratification and accession by General Assembly Resolution 44/25 of 20 November 1989 (entered into force on 2 September 1990), preamble.

[64] See, eg, *Neulinger v Switzerland* (2010) 28 BHRC 706 [131] in relation the UN Convention on the Rights of the Child; *Zoumbas v Secretary of State for the Home Department* [2013] UKSC 74; [2013] 1 WLR 3690 [11]; *ZH (Tanzania) (FC) v Secretary of State for the Home Department* [2011] UKSC 4; [2011] 2 AC 166 [21] ff.

[65] *P (by His Litigation Friend the Official Solicitor) v Cheshire West and Chester Council and Another* [2014] UKSC 19; [2014] AC 896 [36]. Baroness Hale provided the example of *Glor v Switzerland* (Application No 13444/04), 30 April 2009 [53]. The Court reiterated that the Convention must be interpreted in the light of present-day conditions and continued: 'It also considers that there is a European and Worldwide consensus on the need to protect people with disabilities from discriminatory treatment (see, for example, Recommendation 1592 (2003) towards full inclusion of people with disabilities, adopted by the Parliamentary Assembly of the Council of Europe on 29 January 2003, or the United Nations Convention on the Rights of Persons with Disabilities, which entered into force on 3 May 2008).'

[66] See, eg, Harold Cooke Gutteridge, *Comparative Law: An Introduction to the Comparative Method of Legal Study and Research*, 2nd edn (Cambridge University Press, 1949) 40; Cheryl Saunders, 'Comparative Constitutional Law in the Courts: Is There a Problem?' (2006) 59(1) *Current Legal Problems* 91, 114; Rudolph von Jhering, quoted in Zweigert and Kötz (n 1) 17.

A. The Background from Non-Human Rights Cases

As most human rights issues before the Supreme Court are likely to fall within the framework of the ECHR (and consequently the HRA 1998), the use of foreign jurisprudence under conventions with no supranational court is likely to be most relevant in non-human rights cases. As Baroness Hale explained in her interview:

> If we are interpreting an international treaty, which has got nothing to do with human rights, and which may not have a supranational body which is the final arbiter, that's the situation in which what other countries are doing with that treaty is particularly important ... in a way, it's the non-human rights cases that may be more important.[67]

Baroness Hale considered that in such cases it was 'quite important to know what the other countries who are signatories to that Convention are doing'.[68] Others among the Supreme Court Justices agreed. Lord Reed considered that in these cases, 'a bit of knowledge of a foreign system can be helpful in not looking at international conventions in too parochial a way'.[69] Both Lord Mance and Lord Phillips, the then President of the Supreme Court, felt that greater weight is 'undoubtedly' attached to comparative material in these cases.[70] Lord Phillips added:

> If you are looking at any law under an international convention, you'll look very closely at decisions in other countries. There are not all that many cases and so you'll be looking around the world to see where there had been similar jurisprudence.[71]

A number of examples can be found to corroborate this in the case law of the Supreme Court. One is the judgment in *Schutz (UK) Ltd v Werit UK Ltd.*[72] *Schutz* involved an issue of statutory interpretation where the statutory language had been designed to conform with an international convention. The basic issue was whether the actions of one party constituted the 'making' of a patented item according to section 60(1) of the Patents Act 1977 (which would infringe the patent at issue) or simply 'repairing' the item (which would not infringe the patent). Lord Neuberger considered various factors which ought to be taken into account in ascertaining the proper interpretation of the word 'makes' in the 1977 Act, one of the significant ones being the conformity with an international convention. Lord

[67] Interview with Baroness Hale (n 24).
[68] ibid.
[69] Interview with the Rt Hon Lord Reed, Justice of the UK Supreme Court (Supreme Court, London, 8 May 2012).
[70] Interview with the Rt Hon Lord Mance, Justice of the UK Supreme Court (Supreme Court, London, 6 December 2011); interview with Lord Phillips (n 23).
[71] ibid Lord Phillips.
[72] *Schutz (UK) Ltd v Werit UK Ltd* [2013] UKSC 16; [2013] Bus LR 565.

Neuberger (with whom Lord Walker, Baroness Hale, Lord Mance and Lord Kerr agreed) explained that:

> [T]he fact that the word 'makes' is in a section of the 1977 Act which is intended to conform with the provisions of an international convention is particularly significant where ... the convention contains a set of principles which are intended to apply consistently across signatory states.[73]

Lord Neuberger went on to cite a number of German authorities, on the basis that they were 'not only decisions of a highly expert, experienced and respected court on the very point which is raised in this case',[74] but also because they were decisions of a court of another signatory state to the Convention being interpreted. For those reasons, Lord Neuberger explained that the Supreme Court 'should therefore accord them considerable respect, and sympathetically consider the extent to which we should adopt any points of principle or practice which they raise'.[75] And although this did not amount to an obligation to 'follow the approach of the German courts', Lord Neuberger concluded that it was 'sensible for national courts at least to learn from each other' and that they should 'seek to move towards, rather than away from, each other's approaches'.[76]

This practice of citing foreign jurisprudence relating to international conventions has been consistent in the jurisprudence of the UK's highest court for some years. There are numerous examples of this prior to the transfer of jurisdiction to the new Supreme Court. One such example was recalled by Baroness Hale during her interview of October 2011. In *Deep Vein Thrombosis v Air Travel Group Litigation*,[77] the House of Lords were interpreting the Warsaw Convention (regulating the 'international carriage of persons, baggage, or cargo performed by aircraft for reward') in order to determine whether deep vein thrombosis fell within the scope of that instrument.[78] The case is not a human rights case, but does provide useful insights into the use of foreign jurisprudence under international conventions where there is no supervisory body.

In that case, the House of Lords referred to case law from Canada, Australia and the US. In fact, the UK jurisprudence played a relatively minor part and accounted for just nine out of the 26 cases cited in the judgments. By contrast, the House of Lords referred to 13 cases from the US, two from Canada and two from Australia. There is some evidence that German

[73] ibid [37] (Lord Neuberger).
[74] ibid [39] (Lord Neuberger).
[75] ibid.
[76] ibid.
[77] *In Re Deep Vein Thrombosis and Air Travel Group Litigation* [2005] UKHL 72; [2006] 1 AC 495.
[78] Convention Relating to Unification of Certain Rules in International Carriage by Air, signed in Warsaw on 12 October 1929, effective on 13 February 1933.

jurisprudence was considered, although not cited.[79] Indeed, Lord Scott of Foscote (with whom the other members of the House of Lords agreed) expressly acknowledged the importance of adopting an interpretation of the Warsaw Convention that was consistent with the interpretation adopted by other signatory countries. Heavy reliance was placed on a decision of the Australian High Court and the House of Lords' conclusions were consistent with the outcome of that case.[80]

This approach is not without its dangers. One significant possibility is that courts reasoning by reference to foreign jurisprudence on the interpretation of an international convention run the risk of distorting the language of the international convention itself. Lord Scott of Foscote gave a clear explanation of this risk in the *Deep Vein Thrombosis* case, which is worth reproducing:

> The language of the Convention itself must always be the starting point. The function of the court is to apply that language to the facts of the case in issue. In order to do so and to explain its decision, and to provide a guide to other courts that may subsequently be faced with similar facts, the court may well need to try to express in its own language the idea inherent in the language used in the Convention. So a judge ... will often describe in his or her own language the characteristics that an event or happening must have in order to qualify [under an international convention provision]. But a judicial formulation ... should not, in my opinion, ever be treated as a substitute for the language used in the Convention. It should be treated for what it is, namely, an exposition of the reasons for the decision reached and a guide to the application of the Convention language to facts of a type similar to those of the case in question.[81]

Baroness Hale agreed with Lord Scott's judgment and added a few words only to associate herself with those cautionary remarks about 'the dangers of interpreting words of the decision of a court, which is interpreting the words of the Convention, as if the court's words were those of the Convention'.[82] The sentiment was repeated by Lord Hope in *JS (Sri Lanka)*, which is discussed in further detail below. In that case, Lord Hope noted:

> There is always a risk, as one court after another seeks to formulate the principles that are to be applied in the interpretation of an international instrument, of making things worse, not better. A misplaced word here or there can make all the difference between an interpretation that will be respected internationally because it accords with the true purpose of the instrument and one that will not.[83]

[79] Lord Scott of Foscote recognised that claims under the article of the Warsaw Convention in question (Article 17) based on the airline's failure to warn passengers about deep vein thrombosis had been 'rejected in Australia, Canada, Germany and the United States': *In Re Deep Vein Thrombosis and Air Travel Group Litigation* [2005] UKHL 72; [2006] 1 AC 495 [19].

[80] *Povey v Qantas Airways Ltd* [2003] VSCA 227; [2005] HCA 33.

[81] *In Re Deep Vein Thrombosis* (n 78) [12] (Lord Scott of Foscote).

[82] ibid [49] (Baroness Hale).

[83] *R (JS (Sri Lanka)) v Secretary of State for the Home Department* [2010] UKSC 15; [2011] 1 AC 184 [41].

The observations made in this chapter are therefore subject to these important qualifications. The argument made here is not that courts are applying the foreign jurisprudence in international convention cases with less scrutiny than in other areas; it is simply that in these cases, domestic courts have a tendency to consider foreign jurisprudence more readily. Indeed, it is perhaps in recognition of that tendency that the judges have expressed awareness of the risks described above.

B. Refugee Convention Cases

The 1951 Refugee Convention provides a useful example. Because there is no supranational body acting as the final arbiter on the interpretation of the Refugee Convention, the interpretation of the Refugee Convention falls to the domestic courts of almost 150 signatory countries.[84] It is not surprising to see citations of foreign cases in these judgments. Baroness Hale explained the usefulness of foreign jurisprudence in such cases:

> There is no supranational body which is the final arbiter of what [the Refugee Convention] means, so again it is of very great interest to know what other countries are doing in relation to certain problems … I think we take some trouble to look at those.[85]

Lord Bingham's judgment in *Fornah* (decided by the House of Lords) put the matter in similar terms:

> Since the Convention is an international instrument which no supra-national court has the ultimate authority to interpret, the construction put upon it by other states, while not determinative … is of importance.[86]

Yet, given the divergence of judicial systems in the signatory states, interpretation is not always easy.[87]

Of the 533 judgments handed down by the Supreme Court between the start of its work in October 2009 and the end of the judicial year in July 2017, the Refugee Convention was cited in 25. Of the 25 cases in which

[84] See generally Lord Dyson, 'The Globalisation of Law', Pilgrim Fathers Lecture 2015 (Plymouth University, 6 November 2015), www.judiciary.gov.uk/wp-content/uploads/2015/11/pilgrim-fathers-lecture.pdf, [5] ff; Lord Dyson, *Justice: Continuity and Change* (Hart Publishing, 2018) 158 ff.

[85] Interview with Baroness Hale (n 24).

[86] *Fornah v Secretary of State for the Home Department* [2006] UKHL 46]; [2007] 1 AC 412 [10]. See also *R v Secretary of State for the Home Department ex parte Adan* [2001] 2 AC 477. Article 38 provides that disagreement about the meaning of the Convention could be resolved by the International Court of Justice, but, in practice, the court is never asked to make such rulings: Lord Dyson, 'The Globalisation of Law' (n 84) [8]; Lord Dyson, *Justice* (n 84) 159.

[87] See, eg, *ex parte Adan* (n 86).

the words 'Refugee Convention' are found, five concern the interpretation of the Convention's provisions.[88] It is interesting but not surprising (given the approach to the interpretation of international conventions described above) to note that foreign jurisprudence is cited in each of these five cases. The first of these cases was *JS (Sri Lanka)*, in which the main issue was the interpretation and application of Article 1F(a) of the Refugee Convention.[89] Article 1F(a) provides that a person would not be recognised as a refugee under the Convention where there are serious reasons for considering that he 'has committed a crime against peace, a war crime, or a crime against humanity, as defined in the international instruments'.[90] It was the first in a series of cases at the Supreme Court concerning Article 1F.

The respondent in *JS (Sri Lanka)* was a Sri Lankan Tamil who, for a number of years, was a member of the Liberation Tigers of Tamil Eelam. The Secretary of State had refused his claim for asylum on the basis of the membership of an organisation responsible for war crimes and crimes against humanity. The Secretary of State appealed against the decision of the Court of Appeal, which had quashed the decision that Article 1F(a) applied in this case. The questions for the Supreme Court were whether the respondent could be regarded as having committed a crime within the meaning of Article 1F(a) and, more specifically, if an individual is a member of an organisation that is committing war crimes, what—beyond membership of such an organisation—must be established before an individual is himself personally to be regarded as a war criminal?[91] The leading domestic authority was the decision of the Immigration Appeal Tribunal (IAT) in *Gurung v Secretary of State for the Home Department*,[92] which had been endorsed (obiter) by the Court of Appeal in another case.[93] The effect of the IAT's decision in *Gurung* was that a person was a war criminal (ie, could be excluded from refugee status under Article 1F) if the individual was a member of an 'extremist terrorist organisation', despite not having personally participated in the criminal activities of the group.[94] Thus, counsel for the Home Secretary sought to persuade the Supreme Court that the

[88] *JS (Sri Lanka)* (n 83); *HJ (Iran) (FC) v Secretary of State for the Home Department* [2010] UKSC 31; [2011] 1 AC 596; *R (ST (Eritrea)) (FC) v Secretary of State for the Home Department* [2012] UKSC 12; [2012] 2 AC 135; *RT (Zimbabwe) and Others v Secretary of State for the Home Department* [2012] UKSC 38; [2013] 1 AC 152; *Al-Sirri (FC) v Secretary of State for the Home Department* [2012] UKSC 54; [2013] 1 AC 745.

[89] *JS (Sri Lanka)* (n 83).

[90] Article 1F(a) of the Refugee Convention.

[91] *JS (Sri Lanka)* (n 83) [1].

[92] *Gurung v Secretary of State for the Home Department* [2003] Imm AR 115.

[93] *MH (Syria) v Secretary of State for the Home Department* [2009] EWCA Civ 226; [2009] 3 All ER 564.

[94] Although the IAT in *Gurung* recognised that mere membership of a terrorist organisation was not sufficient to bring an individual within Article 1F, it added that if an organisation had become predominantly terrorist in character, 'very little more will be necessary': *Gurung* (n 92) [102]–[105].

respondent's membership of the Liberation Tigers of Tamil Eelam was a factor justifying his exclusion from refugee status according to Article 1F(a).

In the course of the arguments, counsel in both the Court of Appeal and the Supreme Court made extensive references to the case law of foreign jurisdictions. Counsel for the Home Secretary argued that there had been a significant degree of international consensus as to the correct approach to Article 1F(a) of the Refugee Convention prior to the Court of Appeal's decision and that the Court of Appeal had not paid enough attention to that material. The Canadian courts were said to have 'the most developed jurisprudence in relation to Article 1F(a) in the common law world' and the Court of Appeal had 'failed to explain why it was *departing* from the approach in those cases' (emphasis added) as applied in *Gurung*.[95] In reply, counsel for the respondent sought to rule out the Canadian jurisprudence (on the basis of age) and drew the Supreme Court's attention to (more recent) Commonwealth cases, which had endorsed the Court of Appeal's approach.[96]

The Supreme Court ultimately distanced itself from the approach of one of the Canadian cases, *Ramirez*,[97] in which it had been suggested that mere membership may be sufficient for an organisation whose aims, methods and activities are predominantly terrorist in character. It was instead concluded that each case should be considered according to its specific facts. In this respect, the *JS (Sri Lanka)* case is a good example of the risk awareness described above; the tendency to consult the approach of other jurisdictions does not extend to a tendency to follow it as well.[98]

Nevertheless, it is noteworthy that the Supreme Court drew some support for 'departure' from the *Ramirez* approach by reference to other Canadian cases as well as jurisprudence from other jurisdictions. As Lord Kerr explained:

> The Canadian cases ... seem for the most part to at least imply that the participative element involves either a capacity to control or at least to influence events. They appear to contemplate a minimum requirement that the mind of the individual be given to the enterprise so that some element of personal culpability is involved. A notable exception to this theme is to be found in the obiter statements ... in *Ramirez v Canada* ... where it is suggested that voluntary knowing participation can be assumed from membership of a brutal organisation. These statements have not been relied on by the Secretary of State in this case and, in my judgment, wisely so. The broad thrust of authority in this area is to contrary effect.[99]

[95] *JS (Sri Lanka)* (n 83) 33 A–B.
[96] ibid 35 D–E.
[97] *Ramirez v Canada (Minister of Employment and Immigration)* (1992) 89 DLR (4th) 173.
[98] *JS (Sri Lanka)* (n 83) [41].
[99] ibid [57].

Lord Brown also drew from a decision of the German Federal Administrative Court when considering the issue as one of 'complicity' from an international criminal law perspective (the clear outcome of this case is that the Rome Statute of the International Criminal Court is now the starting point for considering whether an applicant was disqualified from asylum by virtue of Article 1F(a) of the Refugee Convention). Lord Hope endorsed this point, again referencing the German Administrative Court.[100]

Lord Brown also cited a US case to support his conclusions that 'Article 1F disqualifies those who make "a substantial contribution to" the crime, knowing that their acts or omissions will facilitate it', agreeing that 'Article 1F responsibility will attach to anyone "in control of the funds" of an organisation known to be "dedicated to achieving its aims through such violent crimes", and anyone contributing to the commission of such crimes "by substantially assisting the organisation to continue to function effectively in pursuance of its aims"'.[101] He continued:

> This approach chimes precisely with that taken by the Ninth Circuit in *McMullen v Immigration and Naturalization Service* (1986) 788 F 2d 591: '[Article 1F] encompasses those who provide [the gunmen etc] with the physical, logistical support that enable modern, terrorist groups to operate'.[102]

Despite the conclusion that each case ought to be considered on its specific facts, the Supreme Court judgment in *JS (Sri Lanka)* provides a useful illustration of the use of foreign jurisprudence in cases concerning the interpretation of international conventions with no supranational court. Several others follow in this theme. For example, although the Supreme Court judgment in *ST (Eritrea)* made less use of foreign jurisprudence than *JS (Sri Lanka)*, the foreign cases cited were again used to address questions of interpretation.[103] Considering the balance that the framers of the Refugee Convention intended to strike between the protection of victims of oppression and the desire of sovereign states to maintain control over their

[100] ibid [49] (Lord Hope): 'Lord Brown JSC puts the test for complicity very simply ... I would respectfully endorse that approach. The words "serious reasons for considering" are, of course, taken from Article 1F itself. The words "in a significant way" and "will in fact further that purpose" provide the key to the exercise. Those are the essential elements that must be satisfied to fix the applicant with personal responsibility. The words "made a substantial contribution" were used by the German Administrative Court, and they are to the same effect.'

[101] ibid [35]. Note that *McMullen v Immigration and Naturalization Service* (1986) 788 F 2d 591 had also been cited in *Gurung* (n 92).

[102] *JS (Sri Lanka)* (n 83) [35].

[103] *ST (Eritrea)* (n 88). In *ST (Eritrea)*, the question was whether the appellant was entitled to the protection of Article 32 of the Refugee Convention, which prevents contracting states from expelling refugees who are lawfully in their territory. Counsel for the appellant argued that the Convention had to be interpreted in the light of its purpose and that the purpose of Article 32 was to ensure that a refugee who had been admitted to the appeal process of a contracting state was not removed to a country that could not provide the full panoply of rights to which a refugee was entitled under the Convention.

territory, Lord Hope cited jurisprudence from Australia and the US.[104] In doing so, he was mindful that 'however generous and purposive its approach to interpretation may be, the Court's task remains one of interpreting the document to which the contracting parties have committed themselves by their agreement'. Moreover:

> [P]arties to an international agreement are not to be treated as having agreed something that they did not agree, unless it is clear by necessary implication from the text *or from uniform acceptance by states* that they would have agreed or have subsequently done so. (Emphasis added)[105]

These cases provide clear examples of the Supreme Court using foreign jurisprudence as a means of limiting their discretion: it is by reference to those sources that the Court ensures that it does not inflate the agreements reached between the various contracting parties. This awareness and tendency to exercise restraint in these sorts of cases is demonstrative of the judges' role as interpreters rather than law makers.

There *are* circumstances in which it may be appropriate to interpret such instruments purposively, such that it reflects a change in attitudes or traditions among the contracting parties. It is in these cases that identifying uniformity and consensus is most important and the Supreme Court has shown willingness to use foreign jurisprudence in this way. The *HJ (Iran)* case provides the clearest example of this.[106] The issue in *HJ (Iran)* was the test to be applied when considering whether a gay person (claiming asylum under the Refugee Convention) has a 'well-founded fear of persecution' in his or her home state, based on membership of that particular social group, so as to come within the meaning of the term 'refugee' for the purposes of the Convention.[107] The two appellants were gay men from Iran and Cameroon, claiming to have a well-founded fear that they would be persecuted if they were to be returned to their home countries. The respondent Secretary of State had refused asylum in both cases and appeals against that decision had been dismissed by the IAT. In the Court of Appeal, the Secretary of State accepted that practising homosexuals are a particular 'social group' for the purposes of Article 1A of the Convention. The issue was then how those with a 'well-founded fear of persecution' could be identified. The Secretary of State considered that the issue was whether the applicant could

[104] The cited cases are: *Applicant A v Minister for Immigration and Ethnic Affairs* (1997) 190 CLR 225; and *Rodriguez v United States* (1987) 480 US 522.

[105] *ST (Eritrea)* (n 88) [41] (Lord Hope).

[106] *HJ (Iran)* (n 88).

[107] Article 1A(2) of the Refugee Convention provides that the term 'refugee' shall apply to a person who 'owing to well-founded fear of being persecuted for reasons of race, religion, nationality, membership of a particular social group or political opinion, is outside the country of his nationality and is unable or, owing to such fear, is unwilling to avail himself of the protection of that country'.

reasonably be expected to tolerate the need for discretion in their home country. In other words, the two appellants could reasonably be expected to conceal their identities as gay men and thus avoid the persecution feared. Counsel for the appellants argued that a requirement to conceal sexual identity in order to avoid harm was incompatible with the Convention.

As Lord Hope recognised, the difficulty was that the High Contracting Parties did not perceive persecution for reasons of homosexuality as a problem when the Convention was being drafted.[108] Nevertheless, the reality before the Supreme Court was that there is now a 'huge gulf in attitudes to and understanding of gay persons between societies on either side of the divide' and that 'more and more gays and lesbians are likely to have to seek protection here, as protection is being denied to them by the state in their home countries'.[109] Yet it was 'crucially important that they are provided with the protection that they are entitled to under the Convention—*no more … but certainly no less*' (emphasis added).[110] The issue, therefore, was identifying the protection that this social group was entitled to.

In the arguments on this point, counsel had cited cases from Australia, Canada, the US, South Africa and New Zealand. The Court of Appeal had,[111] in particular, been referred to a decision of the High Court of Australia.[112] Lord Justice Buxton had accepted that the judgments in that case contained a number of statements to the effect that if an applicant's way of life would be subjected to persecution in his home country, he cannot be denied asylum on the basis of a conclusion that he could avoid that persecution by modifying that way of life. In the Supreme Court, therefore, counsel for the appellant sought to persuade the Justices that the comparative jurisprudence illustrated the 'proper approach'.[113] By contrast, counsel for the Secretary of State acknowledged that the comparative case law was 'informative', but argued that it was not 'dispositive'.[114] Examples of inconsistent case law from Australia were given to show that the approach in other jurisdictions was neither unanimous nor uniform. Indeed, Lord Walker noted that the Supreme Court had been given '23 bundles of authorities containing 250 different items'.[115] Lord Hope devoted a section of his judgment to explaining this: five paragraphs under the heading 'Comparative Jurisprudence' dealt with the approach in Australia, South Africa, New Zealand, Canada

[108] *HJ (Iran)* (n 88) [2] (Lord Hope): 'It was the practice for leaders in these countries simply to insist that homosexuality did not exist.' See further S Chevlan, 'Put Your Hands up (If You Feel Love)' [2011] *Journal of Immigration, Asylum and Nationality Law* 56, 57.

[109] *HJ (Iran)* (n 88) [3] (Lord Hope).

[110] ibid.

[111] *Z v Secretary of State for the Home Department* [2004] EWCA Civ 1578 [2005] Imm AR 75.

[112] *Appellant S395/2002 v Minister for Immigration* (2003) 216 CLR 473.

[113] *HJ (Iran)* (n 88) 603.

[114] ibid 617.

[115] ibid [87] (Lord Walker).

and the US.[116] His Lordship ultimately agreed that the comparative jurisprudence did not 'reveal a consistent line of authority' and that it did not indicate 'an approach which is universally accepted internationally'.[117] Nevertheless, the respect paid to these sources is evident. By way of example, a judgment of the New Zealand Refugee Status Appeals Authority was said to have contained 'impressive analysis of the relevant principles'.[118]

After lengthy analysis, all members of the Supreme Court agreed that the Court of Appeal had misunderstood a particular Australian case that had provided the thrust of support for adopting the 'reasonable tolerability' test. As Lord Collins put it, the test 'was based on a misunderstanding of the passage in the judgment of McHugh and Kirby JJ in *Appellant S395/2002 v Minister for Immigration* (2003) 216 CLR 473'. Reviewing the passage again, Lord Collins concluded:

> [T]he idea of reasonable toleration was plainly being mentioned in the context of what amounts to persecution and not in the context of what they described as 'taking avoiding action' or where members of the group 'hide their membership or modify some attribute or characteristic of the group' to avoid persecution.[119]

Moreover, drawing on a number of other comparative cases, Lord Collins clarified that a person concealing sexual identity because of a well-founded fear of persecution does not cease to have that well-founded fear even if the concealment is successful.[120] Lastly, Lord Collins pointed out that 'a similar, though not identical, approach has been adopted in Canada and the United States'.[121]

Lord Rodger, in particular, paid significant attention to the comparative jurisprudence, also recognising the Court of Appeal's misunderstanding of the judgment in *S395/2002*. Like the other members of the Supreme Court, Lord Rodger considered the requirement to actively avoid persecution from the perspective of the Australian case. It was of assistance that the point made by the English authority had been made 'with considerably more elaboration' in the Australian judgment:

> [McHugh and Kirby JJ] begin by pointing out ... that 'persecution does not cease to be persecution for the purpose of the Convention because those persecuted can eliminate the harm by taking avoiding action within the country of nationality'. In the remainder of para 40 they point out that, if the position were otherwise,

[116] ibid [30]–[34] (Lord Hope).
[117] ibid [30] (Lord Hope).
[118] ibid; *Refugee Appeal No 74665/03* [2005] INLR 68.
[119] *HJ (Iran)* (n 88) [102]–[103] (Lord Collins).
[120] ibid [103] (Lord Collins). The cases referenced on this point were: *Applicant NABD of 2002 v Minister for Immigration and Multicultural and Indigenous Affairs* (2005) 216 ALR 1; *SZATV v Minister for Immigration and Citizenship* (2007) 233 CLR 18; *Refugee Appeal No 74665/03* (n 118).
[121] ibid [104] (Lord Collins).

the Convention would not protect those who chose to exercise their right, say, to express their political opinion openly.[122]

In fact, Lord Rodger's reasoning appears to rely heavily on the Australian jurisprudence—his Lordship reproduces large sections of the judgments in the course of his analysis,[123] before expressly confirming the weight of that authority:

> The decision of the High Court is accordingly *powerful authority, which I would respectfully follow*, for the proposition that, if a person has a well-founded fear that he would suffer persecution on being returned to his country of nationality if he were to live openly as a gay man, then he is to be regarded as a refugee for purposes of the Convention, even though, because of the fear of persecution, he would in fact live discreetly and so avoid suffering any actual harm. The High Court has followed the same line of reasoning in subsequent cases. (Emphasis added)[124]

Further, Lord Rodger acknowledged that the 'same approach has been followed in New Zealand'.[125] His Lordship concluded the point on this evidence:

> For present purposes I take the decision of the [New Zealand Refugee Status Appeals] authority … as clear support for the High Court of Australia's approach that an applicant cannot be denied asylum on the basis that he would, in fact, take effective steps, by suppressing his sexual identity, to avoid the harm which would otherwise threaten him.[126]

Similar support was drawn from the comparative case law when dismissing the approach taken by the Court of Appeal. Lord Rodger's view was that it was not possible to proceed 'on the basis that a man or woman could find it reasonably tolerable to conceal his or her race indefinitely to avoid suffering persecution. Such an assumption about gay men and lesbian women is equally unacceptable'.[127] Lord Rodger felt that most significantly, 'it is unacceptable as being inconsistent with the underlying purpose of the Convention', citing Canadian jurisprudence as authority for that point.[128] A similar analysis was conducted by Lord Dyson, who agreed that '[l]ike Lord Rodger JSC, I would follow this approach which has been substantially followed in Australia'. His Lordship's final reason for rejecting the reasonable tolerability test is instructive:

> [T]here is no support for the Court of Appeal approach in any other jurisprudence. This is important in view of the implicit rejection of it in a number of other

[122] ibid [55] (Lord Rodger). The Australian case referred to is *Appellant S395/2002* (n 112).
[123] *HJ (Iran)* (n 88) [55], [66]–[72] (Lord Rodger).
[124] ibid.
[125] ibid [72] (Lord Rodger).
[126] ibid.
[127] ibid [76] (Lord Rodger).
[128] ibid; *Atta Fosu v Canada (Minister of Citizenship and Immigration)* 2008 FC 1135.

jurisdictions, including at least Australia and New Zealand, and the fact that it is desirable that, so far as possible, there should be international consensus on the meaning of the Convention.[129]

IV. CONCLUSIONS

It has been argued in this chapter that the Supreme Court may use foreign jurisprudence as part of an information-gathering exercise, particularly where there is a desire to interpret a common legislative scheme consistently among contracting states. As a starting point, it is clear that the Supreme Court approaches the Strasbourg jurisprudence in this way. Notions of consistency and uniformity are prevalent in the HRA jurisprudence and are in fact a significant barrier to explicit citations of foreign jurisprudence where relevant Strasbourg decisions exist. As was suggested in Chapter 5, this is in part because the Supreme Court relies on the Strasbourg Court to inform it about developments in contracting states through the analysis in the Strasbourg Court's own jurisprudence. The risk in this approach is that the Supreme Court is placing heavy reliance on the Strasbourg Court's own review of the position in the various contracting states to the Convention. If the goal is to identify a common consensus or maintain the uniformity of interpretation, it will be important to remember that reliance on the Strasbourg jurisprudence may not always provide the most valuable or up-to-date analysis.

The influence of the Strasbourg jurisprudence is all the more evident when the approach in ECHR cases is compared with cases turning on the interpretation of instruments that have no associated supranational court. In such cases, one of the primary aims is to establish a common understanding or position among contracting states. Dickson has made a similar point. After an analysis of the Convention cases in which the Supreme Court (and House of Lords before it) adopted the 'mirror principle' approach to the Strasbourg jurisprudence, Dickson points out that it is in non-HRA 1998 cases that the Supreme Court is more willing to assert itself:

> A good example of judicial creativity in *non-Convention* human rights law is the decision of the Supreme Court in *HJ (Iran) v Secretary of State for the Home Department*, where the Justices held that gay men who would risk persecution if they were returned to their home country and did not conceal their sexuality were entitled to be considered for asylum in the United Kingdom. (Emphasis added)[130]

In such cases, it is clear that the Supreme Court is willing to pay significant attention to the foreign jurisprudence. In doing so, the Court keeps similar concerns in mind to those usually offered as a reason for restraint or deference in claims engaging the ECHR. Indeed, the importance of ensuring

[129] *HJ (Iran)* (n 88) [127] (Lord Dyson).
[130] Dickson (n 61) 43.

that the Court does not interpret the relevant provision so as to provide for rights over and above the common understanding of other signatory States is arguably of even greater importance than in the ECHR context. In these cases, there is no supranational court to correct overgenerous interpretations and to prevent courts from imposing obligations on contracting states that they did not mean to undertake.

The use of foreign jurisprudence in cases concerning international conventions with no supranational court therefore proceeds on the basis of identifying a consensus as to interpretation. It is clear that identifying a consensus on a particular issue is one of the most obvious reasons why judges might draw from foreign jurisprudence.[131] Here, a consensus is more than a simple accumulation of authorities—it represents 'a dense network of checking and rechecking results'.[132] Where there is no supervisory body for a particular instrument, identifying and maintaining a consensus position serves to ensure that the instrument will continue to be interpreted in the same way in different jurisdictions. Many of the Supreme Court Justices interviewed spoke on the subject in these terms, highlighting the importance of consensus in such cases. Lord Mance explained:

> It is a very traditional and well-recognised fact that courts try to achieve a purposive uniform international construction if they can. In that context, there is an imperative to arrive at a uniform interpretation that will mean that there is no particular advantage of suing in one country rather than another.[133]

In fact, Lord Mance explained that the 'imperative' extends so far that judges will be 'prepared to suppress certain hesitations about the actual intention in order to achieve uniformity'.[134]

It is against that background that the risks outlined in several judgments (discussed above) are best understood. To repeat Lord Scott's clear statement, 'a judicial formulation ... should not ... ever be treated as a substitute for the language used in [a] Convention'. Lord Mance felt this to be obvious during the interview: 'if you disagree, of course, then you disagree'.[135] The Refugee Convention cases discussed in this chapter are illustrative of this attitude. While foreign jurisprudence was cited in each of those cases and was of evident assistance to the Supreme Court, it is clear that the tendency to have recourse to this material in the first instance did not necessarily give rise to a tendency to apply it as well.

'Foreign jurisprudence' in these cases extends beyond foreign *cases*. When interviewed, Lord Collins felt this to be an important clarification,

[131] Vlad F Perju, 'The Puzzling Parameters of the Foreign Law Debate' (2007) 1 *Utah Law Review* 167, 175; Jeremy Waldron, 'Foreign Law and the Modern *Ius Gentium*' (2005) 119 *Harvard Law Review* 129, 139.

[132] ibid 129, 145.

[133] Interview with Lord Mance (n 70).

[134] ibid.

[135] ibid.

explaining that it was 'not so much foreign law but foreign practice' which would be of greater weight in an international convention case: 'if it is an international convention you ought to have uniformity of *practice* if possible'.[136] However, it is clear that further complications may arise where there are many signatories to a convention, since it is likely to be more difficult to establish an interpretation based on state practice in those circumstances. This is in addition to the fact that, despite a shared agreement or a common membership of a legal system, a legal order does not necessarily require homogeneity. Further, it is important to distinguish between what countries are doing under an international convention and what they are doing as a matter of discretion over and above the relevant convention obligations.[137] As Lord Brown put it in a Refugee Convention case before the House of Lords:

> It is one thing to invite this House to construe the Convention as a living instrument generously and in the light of its underlying humanitarian purposes; quite another to urge your Lordships effectively to rewrite it.[138]

Given the Supreme Court's ability to maintain this awareness and balance in these cases, it is not obvious (other than for purely practical reasons) why there is such reluctance to engage in research of this kind into the jurisprudence of the European States signatory to the ECHR. Moreover, taking a more proactive approach to the interpretation of the Convention could provide the Court with an opportunity to conduct its own review, using the findings as support for its reasoning where required. After all, the use of foreign jurisprudence to illustrate reasons for a decision was among the clearest explanations given by the Justices interviewed. Reference to foreign jurisprudence does not necessarily indicate reluctance on the part of a judge to do his or her own 'homework'.[139] Extra-judicially, Lord Dyson has explained that recourse to foreign jurisprudence or the work of academics would 'often' be 'cited to reinforce a conclusion that has already been reached by independent detailed reasoning': the 'willingness of judges to borrow from each other is now an accepted and, in my view, welcome fact of judicial life':[140]

> There is much that we can learn from each other, and not merely in relation to the interpretation of international treaties. In recent years, the development of the common law of England has benefited hugely from decisions of courts of other common law jurisdictions.[141]

[136] Interview with the Rt Hon Lord Collins, retired Justice of the UK Supreme Court (Supreme Court, London, 22 May 2012).

[137] *R (Hoxha) v Special Adjudicator* [2005] 1 WLR 1063.

[138] ibid 1088.

[139] Neil Duxbury, 'The Law of the Land' (2015) 78(1) *MLR* 26, 40–41.

[140] Lord Dyson, 'The Globalisation of Law' (n 84) [120]; Lord Dyson, *Justice* (n 84) 161.

[141] ibid.

8

Instrumental Uses of Foreign Jurisprudence

ONE OF THE most frequent criticisms made of the judicial use of foreign jurisprudence is that it mainly performs a legitimation function, supporting a judge's conclusions where the relevant authority could not have done so. Such criticisms are usually linked to the fear that judges are liable to 'cherry pick' jurisprudence for that instrumental purpose. The US debate on that theme and Justice Scalia's well-known denunciation of the use of foreign decisions for those reasons were considered in Chapter 4. In the UK, the problem is much less pronounced and comparatively little attention has been paid to the judicial use of foreign jurisprudence in the English courts. Nevertheless, as Cram has written, 'resort to comparative legal materials nonetheless poses similarly awkward questions concerning judicial forays into the policy-making realm of the constitution and the erosion of parliamentary sovereignty'.[1]

The risks are obvious: if a judge is not able to support a conclusion with domestic statute or common law, the conclusion has the potential to provide for an outcome that was not intended by Parliament. Thus, reliance on foreign jurisprudence might be thought to provide a smokescreen for a judge's own law making. However, the interviewed Justices largely dismissed the idea that they might engage in the 'cherry picking' of sources to suit preconceived conclusions. Lord Kerr answered the charge as follows:

> I wouldn't accept that criticism at all. We don't really look for validation or endorsement from foreign jurisprudence. That would be a most curious way of adjudication, quite honestly: to reach a view and then to cast about to try to find some other court that has reached the same view. I just find that completely alien to my own personal experience.[2]

Lord Mance was also dismissive of the idea, maintaining that the use of foreign jurisprudence was not 'selective' and that, if it were used, it would

[1] Ian Cram, 'Resort to Foreign Constitutional Norms in Domestic Human Rights Jurisprudence with Reference to Terrorism Cases' [2009] *CLJ* 118, 125.

[2] Interview with the Rt Hon Lord Kerr of Tonaghmore, Justice of the UK Supreme Court (Supreme Court, London, 9 May 2012).

be necessary also to ensure that one had accounted for foreign jurisprudence that worked against one's conclusions:

> I think the criticism which is often made, 'you look abroad only to find what suits what you already think', is unfair actually. If one was conscious of two streams of authority, I do not believe that one would think of simply selecting the one which you liked. That wouldn't be respectable. If you are going to address foreign law, you have to address it warts and all. And if you disagree with some aspects of it, you have to face up to that. I think the criticism of selectivity is a little unfair. Even if you were simply faced with authorities that were all against a particular position, you would not suppress them, you would face up to them. You would say, 'the following were cited' (normally they would have been cited but even if they came to your notice without being cited, and any were directly in point, you'd still feel the need to address it). This is part of one's desire to produce something which is intellectually sustainable and which you yourself respect. Selectivity is a cynical view of judging and I don't think it really corresponds to the way we think or operate.[3]

Others among the interviewed Justices were less determined to dismiss the idea of selective citation. Lord Phillips, for example, felt this approach would be 'fairly natural' and commented on this as part of his explanation of the reasons for using foreign jurisprudence:

> If we've got an area where we are uncertain, an area where we are developing the law, an area where ... we would like to develop the law in a particular direction, then you are particularly keen to see if you can get any support for what your thinking is from foreign jurisdictions. One is always glad to find some foreign jurisprudence that actually supports one's own decision.[4]

The use of foreign jurisprudence is not necessarily 'selective', but it may be used instrumentally for some particular purpose. The purpose is most frequently articulated as the giving of reasons. Baroness Hale has explained:

> In a sense, you are trying to give the best possible explanation that you can for the conclusions that you have arrived at. Obviously if that is a set of reasons that satisfy you, you hope that it will satisfy your colleagues and you hope, if it is a Strasbourg case—or a case that could go to Strasbourg—that it satisfies Strasbourg.[5]

[3] Interview with the Rt Hon Lord Mance, Justice of the UK Supreme Court (Supreme Court, London, 6 December 2011).

[4] Interview with the Rt Hon Lord Phillips of Worth Matravers, former President of the UK Supreme Court Supreme Court (Supreme Court, London, 23 November 2011).

[5] Interview with the Rt Hon Baroness Hale of Richmond, Justice of the UK Supreme Court (Supreme Court, London, 19 October 2011). Baroness Hale made similar suggestions in the context of *R v Horncastle and Another* [2009] UKSC 14; [2010] 2 AC 373, discussed further below from n 68. Baroness Hale, '*Argentoratum Locutum*: Is the Supreme Court Supreme?', Nottingham Human Rights Lecture 2011 (Nottingham, 1 December 2011), www.supremecourt.gov.uk/docs/speech_111201.pdf: 'the Court went to a great deal of trouble to explain to Strasbourg why we thought they were wrong, and that a fair trial could still be had in those circumstances'.

I. TO CONFIRM OR BOLSTER CONCLUSIONS

The use of foreign jurisprudence for the purpose of giving reasons can give the impression that the sources are used for legitimation, bolstering a predetermined conclusion. In other words, that foreign jurisprudence is used to support a conclusion that a judge or court is anyway inclined to reach. In particular, this may occur where the court is supporting a conclusion that is likely to be controversial, either because the issue in the case is morally charged or because the outcome would be surprising on the basis of other relevant jurisprudence. In this way, foreign jurisprudence may be used as evidence to justify a particular conclusion.

The use of foreign jurisprudence for confirmation or bolstering is to be distinguished from the categories of 'reassurance' and 'consistency' discussed in Chapters 6 and 7 respectively. Using foreign jurisprudence for reassurance would be an internal exercise, designed to lend comfort or confidence to the judge (and as such may not attract explicit citation). Using foreign jurisprudence for consistency entails gathering evidence from elsewhere as a starting point (usually on a point of interpretation) and ensuring that the approach in the instant case is in line with the approach taken in those other jurisdictions. Using foreign jurisprudence for confirmation or to bolster conclusions is quite different in the sense that it performs a justificatory function. Here foreign jurisprudence represents evidence that the conclusions in the instant case are reasonable, especially where they are likely to be surprising or unpopular.

The use of foreign jurisprudence for this purpose might also extend to the Strasbourg Court. During the interview, Baroness Hale cited a House of Lords judgment as an example:[6]

> A good example, I suppose, is the *Pretty* case, in which the House of Lords quoted a case that they had had in Canada. I think that that was bolstering the conclusion that they had already wanted to reach … and in fact it was also quoted in Strasbourg.[7]

The facts of the case are well known. Dianne Pretty suffered from the degenerative and incurable motor-neurone disease and sought assurances from the Director of Public Prosecutions that her husband would not be prosecuted under section 2(1) of the Suicide Act 1961 for aiding and abetting her suicide. Mrs Pretty claimed a right to her husband's assistance in committing suicide and, if the 1961 Act effectively prohibited that assistance, that the Act would be incompatible with the ECHR. The House of Lords made

[6] *R (Pretty) v Director of Public Prosecutions and Secretary of State for the Home Department* [2001] UKHL 61; [2002] 1 AC 800.

[7] Interview with Baroness Hale (n 5).

extensive use of a judgment from the Supreme Court of Canada: *Rodriguez v Attorney General of Canada*.[8] *Rodriguez* involved a woman with a similar disease who had also sought to end her life with medical assistance. The Canadian Supreme Court had upheld the equivalent provision of the Canadian Criminal Code, although several of the Justices of that court had concluded that the relevant section of the Canadian Charter of Fundamental Rights did confer a right to personal autonomy, extending even to decisions on life and death. Counsel for Mrs Pretty sought to rely upon those statements by analogy with Article 8 ECHR. The House of Lords, however, found that the case better supported the alternative conclusion: that the Suicide Act was not incompatible with the Convention.

The curious feature of the case is that *Rodriguez* was cited extensively at all. The issue had been clearly determined by relevant Strasbourg jurisprudence, which the House of Lords were bound to 'take into account' under the HRA 1998. Lord Bingham reviewed the relevant Strasbourg jurisprudence and concluded that it did not support Mrs Pretty's contention.[9] Yet he also felt it necessary to review the Canadian case closely, copying several passages into his own judgment.[10] Lord Bingham explained the relevance of the Canadian case on the basis that it was the 'most detailed and erudite discussion known to me of the issues in the present appeal'.[11] Lord Steyn made the contribution of the foreign jurisprudence more obvious:

> Given the fact that Mrs Pretty's case is based on the European Convention I have concentrated on European developments. It is, however, noteworthy that in the United States and Canada arguments similar to that of Mrs Pretty ultimately failed.[12]

The language of Lord Steyn implies that the foreign jurisprudence was considered as an additional point, which supported the decision reached primarily on the European jurisprudence. It served to bolster the conclusion that had already been determined.

Lord Hope offered a subtle variation, explaining that the Canadian case may have been of greater importance if it provided evidence of an international consensus, which could make a 'strained' reading of Article 8 appropriate:

> Mrs Pretty has a right of self-determination. In that sense, her private life [according to Article 8 ECHR] is engaged even where in the face of a terminal illness she seeks to choose death rather than life. But it is an entirely different thing to imply

[8] *Rodriguez v Attorney General of Canada* [1994] 2 LRC 136.
[9] *Pretty* (n 6) [24].
[10] ibid [19]–[23].
[11] ibid [19] (Lord Bingham).
[12] ibid [2002] 1 AC 800 [55] (Lord Steyn); citing *Vacco v Quill* (1997) 521 US 793; *Washington v Glucksberg* (1997) 521 US 702; *Rodriguez v Attorney General of Canada* [1994] 2 LRC 136.

> into these words a positive obligation to give effect to her wish to end her own life by means of an assisted suicide. I think that to do so would be to stretch the meaning of the words too far … A strained reading might have been appropriate if there was evidence of a consensus of international opinion in favour of assisted suicide. But there is none. As Sopinka J said in *Rodriguez v Attorney General of Canada* [1994] 2 LRC 136, 176A, no new consensus has emerged in society opposing the right of the state to regulate the involvement of others in exercising power over individuals ending their lives.[13]

The implication is that Lord Hope might have been tempted to 'stretch' the meaning of Article 8, but for the lack of evidence of international consensus. Put another way, it was the lack of that evidence in the foreign jurisprudence which bolstered the conclusion to dismiss Mrs Pretty's appeal. *Pretty* thus provides an example of foreign jurisprudence being used to justify a conservative approach to the Strasbourg position.[14]

A more interesting issue arises where the Supreme Court uses foreign jurisprudence in a claim where the Strasbourg case law is clear and constant, but where it nevertheless wishes to reach a different conclusion. In these cases, the purpose is to support a conclusion at odds with the otherwise relevant Strasbourg authority. These uses are surprising given the relatively deferential attitude towards the Strasbourg Court.

Section 2(1) of the HRA 1998 provides that domestic courts 'must take into account' the relevant Strasbourg jurisprudence when addressing 'a question which has arisen in connection with a Convention right'.[15] In the absence of any normative guidance about the precise meaning of the words 'take into account', domestic courts initially guided themselves to 'follow any clear and constant' Strasbourg jurisprudence 'in the absence of special circumstances'.[16] In fact, as a result of that provision, the courts have often been criticised for taking too slavish an approach to the Strasbourg case law. It is said that the judicial interpretation of section 2(1) as requiring domestic courts to 'follow' or 'keep pace' with the 'clear and constant' Strasbourg jurisprudence[17] has led to a treatment of the Strasbourg case law as something more than persuasive authority.[18] In the early years of the

[13] *Pretty* (n 6) [2002] 1 AC 800 [100]–[101] (Lord Hope).

[14] The Strasbourg Court unanimously found no violation with the Convention when Mrs Pretty's case was appealed: *Pretty v UK* (2002) 35 EHRR 1.

[15] Section 2(1) of the HRA 1998.

[16] *R v Secretary of State for the Environment, Transport and the Regions ex parte Alconbury Developments Ltd and Others* [2001] UKHL 23; [2003] 2 AC 295; *R (Ullah) v Special Adjudicator; Do v Immigration Appeal Tribunal* [2004] UKHL 26 [20] (Lord Bingham); *R (Animal Defenders International) v Secretary of State for Culture, Media and Sport* [2008] UKHL 15; [2008] 1 AC 1312.

[17] *R (Anderson) v Secretary of State for the Home Department* [2001] UKHL 23; [2003] 1 AC 837 [18] (Lord Bingham); *Alconbury* (n 16); [2003] 2 AC 295 [26] (Lord Slynn); *Ullah* (n 16) [20] (Lord Bingham).

[18] Amos describes the Strasbourg jurisprudence as having been 'warmly received': Merris Amos, *Human Rights Law*, 2nd edn (Hart Publishing, 2014) 19.

HRA, Kearns suggested that loyalty to the jurisprudence of the Strasbourg Court is 'a practice that is becoming gradually habitual for our judiciary ... the effects of which would be difficult to reverse'.[19] Krisch agreed, writing that 'the dominant position among the judges is ... one of close attention and loyalty to Strasbourg judgments'.[20] Perhaps the most well-known example of this attitude in the case law comes from the *AF* case, where Lord Rodger's short concurring paragraph adds just this:

> Even though we are dealing with rights under a United Kingdom statute, in reality, we have no choice: *Argentoratum locutum, iudicium finitum*—Strasbourg has spoken, the case is closed.[21]

But there are signs of change. The fluctuations in the top court's approach was noted in Chapter 3, with reference to the possession proceedings cases.[22] The willingness to reject the Strasbourg jurisprudence also filtered down to the Court of Appeal. In *R (on the Application of the Children's Rights Alliance for England)*, as a postscript to his decision, Laws LJ added the following:[23]

> I hope the *Ullah* principle may be revisited. There is a great deal to be gained from the development of a municipal jurisprudence of the Convention rights, which the Strasbourg court should respect out of its own doctrine of the margin of appreciation, and which would be perfectly consistent with our duty to take account of (not to follow) the Strasbourg cases.[24]

This is in tune with the Supreme Court's approach in *Sugar v BBC*.[25] Lord Wilson outlined his view of the manner in which the *Ullah* interpretation of the duty under section 2 of the HRA 1998 had developed:

> It was in *Ullah* that, in para 20, Lord Bingham suggested that it was the duty of the House to keep pace with the evolving jurisprudence of the European Court of Human Rights ('the ECtHR') 'no more, but certainly no less'. It was in *Al Skeini* that, in para 106, Lord Brown suggested that its duty was to keep pace with it 'no less, but certainly no more'. I would welcome an appeal ... in which it was appropriate for this court to consider whether, of course without acting extravagantly, it might now usefully do more than to shadow the ECtHR in the manner hitherto

[19] Paul Kearns, 'United Kingdom Judges in Human Rights Cases' in Esin Örücü (ed), *Judicial Comparativism in Human Rights Cases* (United Kingdom National Committee of Comparative Law Birmingham, 2003) 82.

[20] Nico Krisch, 'The Open Architecture of European Human Rights Law' (2008) 71 *MLR* 183, 202–03.

[21] *Secretary of State for the Home Department v AF and Another* [2009] UKHL 28; [2010] 2 AC 269 [98] (Lord Rodger).

[22] See ch 3, nn 81 ff.

[23] *R (Children's Rights Alliance for England) v Secretary of State for Justice* [2013] EWCA Civ 34; [2013] 1 WLR 3667.

[24] ibid [62]–[64].

[25] *Sugar v British Broadcasting Corporation* [2012] UKSC 4; [2012] 1 WLR 439.

suggested—no doubt sometimes in aid of the further development of human rights and sometimes in aid of their containment within proper bounds.[26]

II. THE ABSENCE OF STRASBOURG JURISPRUDENCE

Several factors may encourage domestic courts to decide matters independently of Strasbourg. Masterman posited a series of circumstances that the case law indicates might underpin a departure from the 'mirror' or *Ullah* principle. Some of these include: where applying the Strasbourg jurisprudence would compel a conclusion which would be 'fundamentally at odds' with the UK's separation of powers;[27] where there are 'special circumstances';[28] and where the court can think of a 'good reason' that the Strasbourg jurisprudence should not be applied.[29] Other more interesting opportunities are where the area is governed by common law and the court is minded to exercise its discretion to depart from the Strasbourg line;[30] where the court wishes to enter into a 'dialogue' with the Strasbourg Court (on the basis that the applicable case law may be wrong or badly informed, or both);[31] and where the domestic court prefers to follow non-Strasbourg authority.[32] In all such situations, the Supreme Court must be prepared to decide the case without the benefit of clear Strasbourg jurisprudence.

The most obvious problem with the Strasbourg jurisprudence is that it has the potential to be outdated. Implicit in the construction of the ECHR as a 'living instrument'[33] is the presumption that domestic courts may properly conclude that Convention jurisprudence has lost its relevance with age. The Convention itself does not require reliance on its own jurisprudence. This is virtually a mirror image of the classical common law approach: instead of a doctrine of precedent, the Strasbourg Court has operated a doctrine of evolutionary law in which the most recent case law is usually the most persuasive.[34] As Feldman put it, 'should there be reason to believe that the

26 ibid [59] (Lord Wilson).

27 *Alconbury* (n 16) [76].

28 ibid [26].

29 *R v Secretary of State for the Home Department ex parte Amin* [2004] 1 AC 653 [44].

30 *Rabone and Another v Pennine Care NHS Trust (Inquest and Others Intervening)* [2012] UKSC 2; [2012] 2 AC 72 [113]–[114].

31 *Horncastle* (n 5) [11].

32 *R (Daly) v Secretary of State for the Home Department* [2001] UKHL 26 [27]–[28]. The remainder of Masterman's list can be read at Roger Masterman, 'The Mirror Crack'd' *UK Constitutional Law Blog* (13 February 2013), http://ukconstitutionallaw.org/2013/02/13/roger-masterman-the-mirror-crackd.

33 *Tyrer v UK* (1978) 2 EHRR 1 [31].

34 Francesca Klug, 'The Human Rights Act: A "Third Way" or "Third Wave" Bill of Rights' [2001] *European Human Rights Law Review* 361, 366.

European Court would not follow one of its own previous decisions, that would be a good reason for domestic courts and tribunals to interpret a provision differently'.[35] Other commentators, too, noted the need to keep 'constantly up to date':[36]

> [I]t would appear to be insufficient simply to identify a previous decision of the ECtHR on the matter in issue and to follow it; some consideration would also be required, if that decision were not a recent one, of whether it held good in the face of changes in society that had occurred in the meantime.[37]

The possibility that the HRA 1998 and the ECHR might have this effect was not at first popular with the judiciary. In *Anderson*, for example, Lord Brown opined that 'it would seem somewhat presumptuous for us, in effect, to pre-empt [the] decision [of the Strasbourg Court]'.[38] Similarly, in *N*, Lord Hope explained that: 'It is for the Strasbourg Court, not for us, to decide whether its case law is out of touch with modern conditions'.[39]

However, the courts have shown a willingness to undertake these sorts of exercises. The decision in *Re P* is a good example.[40] The issue in that case was the effect of a blanket ban on unmarried adoptions in Northern Ireland.[41] It was argued that the discrimination against unmarried couples violated Article 14 of the Convention (read in conjunction with Article 8). No case had yet reached Strasbourg on the precise issue of discrimination that was raised in *Re P*. Two cases raising similar issues had been handed down, which the House considered in turn. In *Fretté v France*, the Strasbourg Court had decided by a majority of four to three that it was within the margin of appreciation allowed to member states of the Council of Europe to discriminate against homosexuals as applicants to be adoptive parents.[42] A few years later, however, 'the court appear[ed] to have changed course':[43] In *EB v France*, the Grand Chamber decided that the rejection of an application by a single homosexual woman did constitute discrimination according to Article 14.[44] On the back of this analysis, Lord Hoffmann concluded that it was now not at all unlikely that if the issue in this case were to

[35] David Feldman, 'The Human Rights Act 1998 and Constitutional Principles' [1999] 19(2) *Legal Studies* 165, 192.

[36] Merris Amos, *Human Rights Law* (Hart Publishing, 2006) 18.

[37] Neil Sheldon, 'The Effect of the Human Rights Act on Domestic Precedent' [2001] *Judicial Review* 208, 210.

[38] *Anderson* (n 17) [66].

[39] *N v Secretary of State for the Home Department* [2005] UKHL 31; [2005] 2 WLR 1124 [25] (Lord Hope).

[40] *In Re P and Others* [2008] UKHL 38; [2009] 1 AC 173.

[41] Article 14 of the Adoption (Northern Ireland) Order 1987 provided that an adoption order could only be made on the application of more than one person if the applicants were a married couple.

[42] *Fretté v France* (2002) 38 EHRR 438.

[43] *Re P* (n 40) [25] (Lord Hoffmann).

[44] *EB v France* (2008) 47 EHRR 509.

go to Strasbourg, the court would hold that discrimination against a couple who wish to adopt a child on the grounds that they are not married would violate Article 14. In fact, Lord Hoffmann felt the blanket rule in *Re P* to be 'quite irrational'[45] and referred to a recent decision of the South African Constitutional Court which had made similar points.[46] Interestingly, this reference to the South African Court came prior to Lord Hoffmann's analysis of the relevant Strasbourg jurisprudence. Lord Hope, too, noted that the more recent Strasbourg case (*EB*) was consistent with the points made by the South African Constitutional Court.[47]

Another obvious excuse for divergence is created by the operation of the 'margin of appreciation' doctrine. The judges of the Strasbourg Court are:

> acutely conscious that on several key issues, the European-wide consensus which generally provides the mainspring of their decision-making does not exist … precisely because of the prevalence of divergent moral standards and religious traditions in the affiliated states.[48]

The approach of the Strasbourg Court has therefore been that the lesser the consensus among contracting states,[49] the better placed national authorities are to decide on the matter and the more deferential the Strasbourg Court has to be in its review.[50] The doctrine arguably signifies that there are issues on which there is no relevant Strasbourg authority at all.[51]

It is relatively clear that judges are willing to view the matter in this way, for example, by reaching a conclusion that goes further than the Strasbourg Court had previously done. This appeared to justify the House of Lords' conclusion in *Re P*,[52] concerning the joint adoption of a child by an unmarried couple discussed above. In Lord Hoffmann's view, it would make 'no difference' if the Strasbourg Court were to revert to its earlier position and say that these are delicate questions which should therefore be left to the national margin of appreciation. Accordingly, his Lordship did not feel that the House should be inhibited from declaring the 1987 Order incompatible 'by the thought that [they] might be going further than the Strasbourg Court'.[53] Repeating the tenets delivered by Lord Bingham in *Ullah* (that the duty of domestic courts is to 'keep pace' with Strasbourg jurisprudence

[45] *Re P* (n 40) [16] (Lord Hoffmann).
[46] *Du Toit v Minister for Welfare and Population Development* (2002) 13 BHRC 187.
[47] *Re P* (n 40) [54] (Lord Hope).
[48] Ian Leigh and Laurence Lustgarten, 'Making Rights Real: The Courts Remedies, and the Human Rights Act' (1999) 58 *CLJ* 509, 544.
[49] *Fretté v France* (n 42) [41]: where the law 'appears to be in a transitional stage, a wide margin of appreciation must be left to the authorities of each State'.
[50] George Letsas, 'Two Concepts of the Margin of Appreciation' (2006) 26 *OJLS* 705, 722.
[51] See, eg, Francesca Klug 'A Bill of Rights: Do We Need One or Do We Already Have One?' [2007] *PL* 701, 708.
[52] *Re P* (n 40).
[53] ibid [37].

'no more ... no less'), Lord Hoffmann emphasised that: 'These remarks were not ... made in the context of a case in which the Strasbourg Court has declared a question to be within the national margin of appreciation'.[54] His Lordship explained that 'none of these considerations can apply in a case in which Strasbourg has deliberately declined to lay down an interpretation for all member states, as it does when it says that the question is within the margin of appreciation'.[55] For that reason, his Lordship concluded that 'the question is one for the national authorities to decide for themselves and it follows that different member states may well give different answers'.[56] Moreover, 'it is for the court in the United Kingdom to interpret Articles 8 and 14 and to apply the division between the decision-making powers of courts and Parliament in the way which appears appropriate for the United Kingdom'.[57] Lord Mance evidently agreed, adding that:

> It would be contrary to the Strasbourg court's purpose, and circular, if national authorities were to take the view that they should not consider any question other than whether a particular solution was within the United Kingdom's margin of appreciation. Under the 1998 Act, United Kingdom authorities (legislators and courts) have domestically to address the impact of the domestically enacted Convention rights in the particular context of the United Kingdom.[58]

A third opportunity for divergence is given by the nature of the Strasbourg authority itself. Although some commentators have argued that Strasbourg's decisions are so important as to be considered as authority even in instances in which they did not 'argue the point through in a coherent and thorough manner',[59] the prevailing attitude among the judiciary has been that there is 'room for dialogue' where an English court 'considers that the ECtHR has misunderstood or been misinformed about some aspect of English law' and 'it may wish to give a judgment which invites the ECtHR to reconsider the question'.[60] As Warbrick argued, there is 'space for national courts to reconsider Strasbourg cases which appear "wrong", either because they are founded on a misunderstanding of national law or because they are poorly reasoned'.[61]

[54] ibid [31].
[55] ibid [36].
[56] ibid.
[57] ibid [37].
[58] ibid [129].
[59] Ian Loveland, 'Making it up as They Go Along? The Court of Appeal on Same Sex Spouses and Succession Rights to Tenancies' [2003] *PL* 222, 233.
[60] *R v Lyons (No 3)* [2002] UKHL 44; [2003] 1 AC 976 [46].
[61] Although Warbrick was also careful to suggest that 'a strong case would need to be made that this were the case': Colin Warbrick, 'The View from the Outside' in Helen Fenwick, Roger Masterman and Gavin Phillipson (eds), *Judicial Reasoning under the UK Human Rights Act* (Cambridge University Press, 2007) 37.

There are some examples of this approach at the Supreme Court. In *R (Smith) v Secretary of State for Defence*,[62] for example, Lord Collins referred to 12 decisions of foreign domestic courts: one decision from Canada, one from Australia and 10 from the US. The references to foreign jurisprudence are surprising at first glance, since the case concerned the meaning of 'jurisdiction' in the ECHR and it is not obvious that the jurisprudence of those countries that are not signatories to the Convention are likely to provide assistance on the interpretation of a term in that instrument. Lord Collins later explained that the reason for reference to US authorities was to show that other constitutional systems have had to grapple with extra-territorial reach and the meaning of jurisdiction. In this way, the foreign jurisprudence was helpful to confirm his feelings about the result, since the matter had been 'treated in a very superficial way by Strasbourg'.[63]

Some commentators have suggested that departing from Strasbourg jurisprudence on these grounds usually indicates a desire to avoid the conflicting Strasbourg jurisprudence per se. For instance, Amos has argued that the means by which conflicting Strasbourg jurisprudence is usually avoided is by a finding that the reasoning of the Strasbourg Court (or the Commission) was inadequate,[64] while Elizabeth Wicks identified one of the prevalent judicial approaches under section 2 of the HRA 1998 to be 'assessing relevance by reference to own perception of merits'.[65] In other words, 'the Strasbourg jurisprudence is being used merely to substantiate domestic reasoning: it is not taken into account as a factor in reaching the decision; merely as a factor in justifying the decision'.[66]

III. 'DEPARTING' FROM STRASBOURG

This evaluative approach to Strasbourg jurisprudence has developed a step further. UK courts are willing not only to reject that jurisprudence as determinative of a particular issue, but also to reject its conclusions outright. This represents a departure from the deferential start to the relationship with the Strasbourg Court, and the sense that the UK courts appeared to be

[62] *R (Smith) v Secretary of State for Defence and Another* [2010] UKSC 29; [2011] 1 AC 1.

[63] Interview with the Rt Hon Lord Collins of Mapesbury, retired Justice of the UK Supreme Court (Supreme Court, London, 22 May 2012). The Supreme Court has since departed from *Smith (No 1)* in *Smith (No 2)*: *Smith and Others (FC) v Ministry of Defence* [2013] UKSC 41; [2014] AC 52. In that case, the Supreme Court made little to no discernible reference to foreign jurisprudence, taking its lead from the more recent Strasbourg jurisprudence handed down by the Grand Chamber: *Al-Skeini v UK* (2011) 53 EHRR 589.

[64] Merris Amos, 'The Principle of Comity' [2009] *Yearbook of European Law* 503; Merris Amos, 'The Dialogue between United Kingdom Courts and the European Court of Human Rights' [2012] 61(3) *ICLQ* 557.

[65] Elizabeth Wicks, 'Taking Account of Strasbourg? The British Judiciary's Approach to Interpreting Convention Rights' [2005] *European Public Law* 405, 419.

[66] ibid 405, 423.

acting as 'merely agents or delegates of the ECHR and Council of Europe'.[67] These cases are illuminating in relation to both the relationship between the Strasbourg Court and the UK courts, as well as on the influence of foreign jurisprudence in domestic human rights cases.

A. *R v Horncastle*: Departure and Dialogue

Since Strasbourg jurisprudence is not binding (section 2 of the HRA 1998 only obliges domestic courts to take it into account), it is not technically appropriate to talk of 'departing' from the Strasbourg Court's case law. In this context, therefore, 'departure' serves only to represent cases in which the decision of the UK court is not in line with the relevant or 'clear and constant' Strasbourg jurisprudence. In these cases, the Supreme Court has tended towards giving reasons for declining to follow the Strasbourg case law. This may simply be an attempt to enter into a 'dialogue' with the Strasbourg Court or it may be illustrative of the hesitancy to 'depart' from its jurisprudence without clear reasoning. Many would describe the first case considered here—*Horncastle*—as an example of the former. Indeed, Lord Phillips appeared to have this in mind when explaining that the detailed reasons would be 'likely to give the Strasbourg court the opportunity to reconsider'.[68] What follows is an alternative perspective: *Horncastle* is considered as a case that is illustrative of both the strength attached to the (clear and constant) Strasbourg jurisprudence, and of the willingness to depart from it. The use of foreign jurisprudence in the reasoning is illuminating on both points.

Horncastle was the first Convention rights case in which the Supreme Court 'departed' from seemingly clear and constant Strasbourg jurisprudence.[69] The case concerned two defendants convicted of serious offences on the basis of evidence from an absent witness ('hearsay' evidence). In the first, the witness had died after making a full written statement. In the

[67] Lord Irvine of Lairg, 'A British Interpretation of Convention Rights', Lecture at University College of London's Judicial Institute (London, 14 December 2011), https://www.ucl.ac.uk/drupal/judicial-institute/sites/judicial-institute/files/british_interpretation_of_convention_rights_-_irvine.pdf.

[68] *Horncastle* (n 5) [11] (Lord Phillips).

[69] ibid. *Horncastle* was the seventh case to raise Convention rights issues in the Supreme Court's first term after *R (E) v Governing Body of JFS and Another (Rev 3)* [2009] UKSC 1; [2009] 1 WLR 2353; *R (L) v Commissioner of Police of the Metropolis* [2009] UKSC 3; [2010] 1 AC 410; *R (BA (Nigeria)) v Secretary of State for the Home Department* [2009] UKSC 7; [2010] 1 AC 444; *R (A) (FC) v London Borough of Croydon and One Other Action* [2009] UKSC 8; [2009] 1 WLR 2557; *R (Barclay and Others) v Secretary of State for Justice and Others* [2009] UKSC 9; [2010] 1 AC 464; *R (A) v B* [2009] UKSC 12; [2010] 2 AC 1. While the Supreme Court also appeared to avoid applying the Strasbourg jurisprudence (*Tsfayo v United Kingdom* [2009] 48 EHRR 18) in *R (A) (FC) v London Borough of Croydon*, it was clear that the Court did not have to decide the related point in order to dispose of the appeal (Lord Walker at [67]). Thus, it was not necessary to fully reason that point and a number of the

second, the witness feared for her life if she were to attend the hearing. In each case, the evidence had been admitted pursuant to the provisions of the Criminal Justice Act 2003.[70] In both cases, it was argued that the appellant's conviction was based, to a 'sole or decisive' extent, on the statements of the absent witnesses. On this basis, it was submitted that the lack of an opportunity to cross-examine the witnesses violated the appellants' rights under Article 6 ECHR, rendering their convictions unsafe.

The relevant Strasbourg jurisprudence was a decision of the Chamber in *Al-Khawaja and Tahery v UK*.[71] *Al-Khawaja and Tahery* concerned similar facts to *Horncastle*. Mr Al-Khawaja claimed that the admission of a statement given by a complainant who had later died was in violation of his rights under Article 6(3)(d) ECHR. Mr Tahery claimed the same in relation to the admission of a statement given by a witness who later refused to give evidence because of fear. In each case, the Court of Appeal had held that the statements were admissible and that the convictions were safe.[72] The Strasbourg Court sitting as a Chamber disagreed and held that there would always be a breach of Article 6 if a conviction is based 'solely or decisively' on hearsay evidence.[73] Counsel for the defendants placed heavy reliance on *Al-Khawaja and Tahery*, but also provided extensive lists of Strasbourg jurisprudence supporting the argument that the Strasbourg Court had 'established a clear and constantly applied principle to the effect that the admission of a statement from an absent witness whose testimony provides sole or decisive evidence at a criminal trial will breach article 6(1)(3)(d)'.[74]

There is nothing in the judgment given by Lord Phillips (giving the judgment of the Court) to suggest that the Supreme Court felt that the Strasbourg jurisprudence was not clear and constant. Instead, Lord Phillips acknowledged the argument that the Supreme Court 'should treat the judgment of the Chamber in *Al-Khawaja* as determinative of the success of these appeals' and responded by providing reasons for declining to do so.[75] It is worth setting out the paragraph in full:

> The requirement to 'take into account' the Strasbourg jurisprudence will normally result in the domestic court applying principles that are clearly established by the

Justices preferred to 'leave the point open', not least because the Strasbourg jurisprudence was not 'clear and constant', but was 'still developing' (Lord Walker at [67]; see also Lord Hope at [62]).

[70] Section 116(1)(2)(a) of the Criminal Justice Act 2003; section 116(1)(2)(e) of the Criminal Justice Act 2003, respectively.

[71] *Al-Khawaja and Tahery v UK* (2009) 49 EHRR 1.

[72] *R v Al-Khawaja* [2005] EWCA Crim 2697; [2006] 1 WLR 1078; *R v Tahery (Alireza)* [2006] EWCA Crim 529.

[73] ibid. The UK subsequently requested that the decision be referred to the Grand Chamber. On 5 June 2009, the panel of the Grand Chamber adjourned consideration of that request pending the judgment of the Supreme Court in the present case.

[74] *Horncastle* (n 5) 423.

[75] ibid [10].

> Strasbourg court. There will, however, be rare occasions where the domestic court has concerns as to whether a decision of the Strasbourg court sufficiently appreciates or accommodates particular aspects of our domestic process. In such circumstances it is open to the domestic court to decline to follow the Strasbourg decision, giving reasons for adopting this course. This is likely to give the Strasbourg court the opportunity to reconsider the particular aspect of the decision that is in issue, so that there takes place what may prove to be a valuable dialogue between the domestic court and the Strasbourg court. This is such a case.[76]

Clearly, then, Lord Phillips was not suggesting that the Strasbourg case law was anything other than clear and constant. Rather, the Supreme Court would 'decline to *follow*' (emphasis added) it on the basis that the Strasbourg Court had not 'sufficiently appreciate[d] or accommodate[d] particular aspects of our domestic process'.[77]

To speak of 'following' implies that declining to follow the Strasbourg jurisprudence would amount to a departure. This much is reinforced by the addition of a condition that the court 'gives reasons' for doing so.[78] And Lord Phillips did indeed give detailed reasons for declining to follow the Strasbourg authority. After outlining the common law approach to a fair trial in some detail, Lord Phillips set out examples of hearsay exceptions in other Commonwealth jurisdictions:

> Other established common law jurisdictions, namely Canada, Australia and New Zealand have, by both common law and statutory development, recognised hearsay evidence as potentially admissible, under defined conditions, in circumstances where it is not possible to call the witness to give evidence, even where the evidence is critical to the prosecution case. ... *This demonstrates that*, under the common law and statutory exceptions to the hearsay rule recognised in those jurisdictions *there is no rigid rule excluding evidence if it is or would be either the 'sole' or 'decisive' evidence*, however those words may be understood or applied.[79]

The strength of these examples was further supported by a detailed analysis of the position in those jurisdictions, prepared by Lord Mance and annexed to the judgment.[80]

Not all the comparative jurisprudence supported the admission of hearsay evidence. It was explained that in the US, the 'right under the Sixth Amendment "to be confronted with the witnesses against him" had recently been interpreted in an absolute sense';[81] the effect was 'to exclude any "testimonial" evidence whatever in respect of which there has been or can be no cross-examination'.[82] But rather than take this as a balance against

76 ibid [11].
77 ibid.
78 ibid.
79 ibid [41] (emphasis added).
80 ibid Annex 1.
81 ibid [44] (Lord Phillips).
82 ibid [45] (Lord Phillips).

the position adopted by the Commonwealth jurisdictions set out in Lord Mance's annex, Lord Phillips used the extremity of the US to show that the Strasbourg Court had not itself gone that far:

> Article 6(3)(d) has not been interpreted by the Strasbourg Court in the same way that the US Supreme Court has now interpreted the Sixth Amendment. The Strasbourg Court has accepted that there are circumstances that justify the admission of statements of witnesses who have not been subject to 'confrontation' with the defendant.[83]

From that basis, Lord Phillips called once more upon the Commonwealth jurisprudence to make the argument clear:

> The possibility remains, however, that by propounding the 'sole or decisive test' the Strasbourg Court has condemned as rendering a trial unfair the admission of hearsay evidence in circumstances where the legislature and courts of this jurisdiction and of other *important Commonwealth jurisdictions* (Canada, Australia and New Zealand) have determined that the evidence can fairly be received. This is a startling proposition.[84]

It was on this basis that Lord Phillips felt it necessary to embark upon a 'careful analysis of the Strasbourg jurisprudence'.[85] The detailed analysis of the Strasbourg case law incorporated judgments before *Al-Khawaja* and made important distinctions between the approach of civil law and common law jurisdictions. Lord Phillips used the example of the French Criminal Procedure, referred to by Lord Rodger in an earlier House of Lords decision,[86] and spent four paragraphs illustrating the differences.[87] The conclusion was that the Strasbourg jurisprudence in relation to Article 6(3)(d) had 'developed largely in cases relating to civil law rather than common law jurisdictions and this [was] particularly true of the sole or decisive rule'.[88] Further, 'that case law appears to have developed without full consideration of the safeguards against an unfair trial that exist under the common law procedure'.[89] Thus, the Supreme Court held that 'it would not be right for this court to hold that the sole or decisive test should have been applied rather than the provisions of the 2003 Act, interpreted in accordance with their natural meaning'.[90] Lord Phillips continued:

> In so concluding I have taken careful account of the Strasbourg jurisprudence. I hope that in due course the Strasbourg court may also take account of the reasons that have led me not to apply the sole or decisive test in this case.[91]

83 ibid [46] (Lord Phillips).
84 ibid (emphasis added).
85 ibid.
86 *R (D) v Camberwell Green Youth Court* [2005] UKHL 4; [2005] 1 WLR 393 [10]–[11].
87 *Horncastle* (n 5) [59]–[62].
88 ibid [107].
89 ibid.
90 ibid [108].
91 ibid.

On this analysis, the Supreme Court appears to have used the Commonwealth jurisprudence as a springboard for: (a) taking a robust approach to the Strasbourg jurisprudence; and (b) declining to follow the Strasbourg Court. There are, however, a couple of qualifications to note. As Lord Brown stated, the Supreme Court was not faced with a decision of the Grand Chamber in this case. It was for that reason that Lord Brown felt able to reject the appellant's argument that the Court should follow the 'clear and constant' Strasbourg jurisprudence[92] (as the House of Lords had done in *Secretary of State for the Home Department v AF (No 3)* when faced with a judgment of the Grand Chamber (in *A v UK*)).[93] Lord Brown felt that 'the court's ruling in *Al-Khawaja* [was] not as authoritative as a Grand Chamber decision' and also that it was 'altogether less clear than was the decision in *A*'.[94] Indeed, the Grand Chamber went on to reconsider *Al-Khawaja* and accepted that the admission of hearsay evidence would not inevitably lead to a breach of Article 6 where statements of this kind were used.[95] These features make it difficult to conclude with certainty that the Supreme Court in *Horncastle* is using foreign jurisprudence to support departures from clear and constant Strasbourg jurisprudence, but the example at least provides certain clues. As Dickson has written, it now appears possible to predict the situations in which the Supreme Court will feel itself bound to follow Strasbourg and where it will be more comfortable adopting conclusions at odds with the Strasbourg jurisprudence:

> The case law ... appears to suggest that there are two situations in which the Supreme Court will feel itself bound to follow Strasbourg jurisprudence. The first is where there has been a recent decision of the Grand Chamber expressly addressing the very point at issue, as in *AF* ... The second is where there has been a series of recent Chamber decisions, not yet fully endorsed by the Grand Chamber, in which the attitude of the European Court to the very point at issue has been made clear, as in *Pinnock*. If the relevant Strasbourg decisions are in cases taken against the United Kingdom, they will inevitably carry even greater weight. In a case such as *Horncastle*, which falls into neither of the two categories, the Supreme Court can persist in adopting a national approach to the point at issue, arguing the validity of that approach as authoritatively as it can in the hope that if and when the matter later comes before the Grand Chamber the national position will be

[92] ibid [120].

[93] *Secretary of State for the Home Department v AF (No 3)* [2010] 2 AC 269, *A v UK* (2009) 49 EHRR 625; *Horncastle* (n 5) [118]. However, the Supreme Court has been willing not to follow a decision of the Grand Chamber; see, eg, *Posteh v Royal Borough of Kensington and Chelsea* [2017] UKSC 36; [2017] AC 624 [37].

[94] *Horncastle* (n 5) [120].

[95] *Al-Khawaja and Tahery v UK* [2011] ECHR 2127. The Grand Chamber found no violation of Article 6 in Mr Al-Khawaja's case, although the safeguards remained insufficient to prevent a violation in Mr Tahery's case.

> endorsed. This is precisely what occurred in the aftermath of *Horncastle*: when the Grand Chamber re-examined *Al-Khawaja and Tahery* it effectively accepted the Supreme Court's criticism of the Chamber's judgment ... This episode is an excellent example ... of the much-vaunted 'judicial dialogue' which is meant to characterize the relationship between the highest courts in domestic legal systems and the European Court in Strasbourg.[96]

It has been argued here that foreign jurisprudence played an important role in the Supreme Court's mission when 'arguing the validity of that approach as authoritatively as it can'.[97] Moreover, the Grand Chamber responded in kind when it returned to the issue in *Al-Khawaja and Tahery v UK*.[98] Under the heading 'Relevant Comparative Law', 25 paragraphs of the Grand Chamber's judgment are devoted to a review of the position in Scotland, Ireland, Australia, Canada, Hong Kong, New Zealand, South Africa and the US.[99]

B. Supporting Dissenting Judgments

A slightly different but even more obvious example of using foreign jurisprudence to support conclusions is to be found in dissenting judgments. For example, in *HM Treasury v Ahmed*, foreign jurisprudence appears to have been so persuasive that Lord Brown dissented from the majority view.[100] In *Ahmed*, the Supreme Court was required to consider the lawfulness of the Terrorism Order 2006 and Article 3(1)(b) of the Al-Qaida and Taliban (United Nations Measures) Order 2006. The Orders had been made by the

[96] Brice Dickson, *Human Rights and the United Kingdom Supreme Court* (Oxford University Press, 2013) 59. Dickson makes reference to the judgment in *Manchester City Council v Pinnock* [2010] UKSC 45; [2011] 2 AC 104, which is part of a long line of Article 8 cases including *Qazi v Harrow London Borough Council* [2003] UKHL 43; [2004] 1 AC 983; *Kay v Lambeth London Borough Council* [2006] UKHL 10; [2006] 2 AC 465; *Doherty v Birmingham County Council* [2008] UKHL 57; [2009] 1 AC 367; and *Frisby v Birmingham County Council* [2011] UKSC 8; [2011] 2 AC 186. Space precludes extensive analysis of these decisions. After a period of extended dialogue with the Strasbourg Court, *Pinnock* confirmed that the Strasbourg jurisprudence on the Article 8 issue was 'now ... unambiguous and consistent' and that it should be followed. The principle which settled that Strasbourg jurisprudence should be followed was confirmed again by the Court of Appeal in *RB v Secretary of State for Justice* [2011] EWCA Civ 1608; [2012] 1 WLR 2043. For a recent account of judicial reasoning under section 2 of the HRA 1998, see Helen Fenwick and Roger Masterman, 'The Conservative Project to "Break the Link between British Courts and Strasbourg": Rhetoric or Reality' (2017) 80(6) *MLR* 1111.

[97] Dickson (n 96).

[98] *Al-Khawaja and Tahery v UK* (Application Nos 26766/05 and 22228/06) (2012) 54 EHRR 23.

[99] ibid [63]–[87].

[100] *HM Treasury v Mohammed Jabar Ahmed and Others (No 2) (FC)* [2010] UKSC 2; [2010] 2 AC 534.

Treasury under the United Nations Act 1946 to give effect to resolutions of the UN Security Council designed to prevent the financing of acts of terrorism. The effect of the Orders was to deprive designated persons of all resources, save for basic expenses. The Terrorism Order empowered the Treasury to give a direction that an individual was so designated if it had reasonable grounds for suspecting that the individual 'is or may be' a person who committed, attempted to commit, participated in or facilitated the commission of acts of terrorism. The Al-Qaida Order provided that persons on a list compiled by the sanctions committee of the Security Council (the 1267 Committee) were designated persons. The questions common to both Orders were: whether the Orders were ultra vires the 1946 Act; and whether the Orders were incompatible with the Convention rights under the HRA 1998.[101]

While the Supreme Court held, unanimously, that the Terrorism Order should be quashed as ultra vires the 1946 Act, Lord Brown dissented on the conclusion that Article 3(1)(b) of the Al-Qaida Order must also be quashed as ultra vires. A crucial difference between the dissenting and majority judgments on this point related to the principle of legality. Unlike the majority, Lord Brown found it difficult to accept that the Al-Qaida Order achieves anything more than was mandated by the relevant Security Council Regulation. Concluding on this, Lord Brown stated that it was:

> instructive in this regard to see how certain other Commonwealth countries have given effect to these same UNSCRs. Australia, New Zealand and Canada all have legislation akin to our 1946 Act.[102]

Lord Brown added that:

> The way Australia, New Zealand and Canada have dealt with these UNSCRs to my mind tends to support the conclusions I have reached about the impugned Orders.[103]

It is interesting to note that where a judge has been inclined to use foreign jurisprudence in this way, it is more likely that other members of the court will also engage with those sources. Thus, when considering the way in which decisions under the listing system administered by the 1267 Committee are dealt with, Lord Hope appeared to derive assistance from a number of cases from Canada and the US.[104] The approach adopted by Australia and New Zealand was also considered in relation to the

[101] ibid [41].
[102] ibid [199] (Lord Brown).
[103] ibid [200] (Lord Brown).
[104] ibid [69]–[71]. Lord Hope cited *Abdelrazik v Canada (Foreign Affairs)* 2009 FC 580; *KindHearts for Charitable Humanitarian Development Inc v Geithner* (unreported) 18 August 2009, US District Ct, Northern Ohio; *Diggs v Shultz* (1972) 470 F 2d 461 (DC Cir).

principle of legality.[105] However, Lord Hope emphasised the limitations of these sources:

> Caution must ... be exercised in drawing any firm conclusions from these cases. The decision of the courts in Canada and the United States were not made under reference to an international human rights instrument such as the European Convention.[106]

Lord Phillips was equally reluctant to follow their conclusions:

> These decisions fall short of supporting the proposition that the principle of legality raises a general presumption against Parliament delegating to the executive the power to make regulations that call for legislative design.[107]

In these cases, the impulse to give reasons to an audience is arguably at its greatest. *Horncastle* is a clear example. Because the Supreme Court had reached a conclusion at odds with the Strasbourg jurisprudence, there was a greater impulse towards extending the reasons given by way of explanation for such a time as when the case was to come under review in Strasbourg. In other words, the Court was using foreign jurisprudence in part to defend its conclusions to Strasbourg.

This theory draws parallels with those that explain citations of foreign jurisprudence as part of a 'pedagogical impulse'.[108] Slaughter has given the example of 'the court of a fledgling democracy' which 'might look to the opinions of courts in older and more established democracies as a way of binding its country to this existing community of states'.[109] A similar point has been made by Wheatle, writing that the 'invocation of implied principles as a pathway to adopting the reasoning of judges in the United Kingdom is ... in some respects, an acknowledgment of—and a beckoning towards—a historical framework'.[110] In fact, reference to foreign jurisprudence might 'send a signal to internal and external forces that the state has embraced the tradition of democratic constitutionalism'.[111] Alternatively, recourse to

[105] Under the principle of legality, 'the court must, where possible, interpret a statute in such a way as to avoid encroachment on fundamental rights, sometimes described as constitutional rights'. *HM Treasury v Ahmed (No 2)* (n 100) [111]. See also *R v Secretary of State for the Home Department ex parte Pierson* [1998] AC 539 (Lord Browne-Wilkinson); *R v Secretary of State for the Home Department ex parte Simms* [2000] 2 AC 115, 131 (Lord Hoffmann).

[106] *HM Treasury v Ahmed (No 2)* (n 100) [71] (Lord Hope).

[107] ibid [122] (Lord Phillips).

[108] Christopher McCrudden, 'A Common Law of Human Rights?: Transnational Judicial Conversations on Constitutional Rights' (2000) 20(4) *OJLS* 499, 518.

[109] Anne-Marie Slaughter, 'A Typology of Transjudicial Communication' (1994) 29 *University of Richmond Law Review* 99, 134.

[110] Se-shauna Wheatle, *Principled Reasoning in Human Rights Adjudication* (Hart Publishing, 2017) 148.

[111] ibid 149. Recourse to foreign jurisprudence in the South African Constitutional Court is sometimes explained on this basis. See, eg, Christa Rautenbach, 'South Africa: Teaching an

foreign law might 'send a message that the new state will retain the democratic traditions of the former ruling state'.[112] The use of foreign jurisprudence may thus be 'premised on the felt need to instil habits of Western democratic participation in a body politic that on the whole is inexperienced in the ways of democracy'.[113]

This has also been said to feed a reluctance to use foreign jurisprudence, especially where the domestic court suffers from a particular insularity whereby it sees its own jurisdiction as one which enjoys pre-eminence among civilised countries.[114] The reluctance to draw from foreign jurisprudence in the US is often framed in this way. There, it is generally agreed that the nation sees itself as a leader rather than a follower in the world order and this means that resorting to the approach of other courts is unlikely: the US is known for a limited adherence to international law and '[a]n attitude lingers' that it has 'little to learn from countries whose constitutions have not reached the two-century mark'.[115] Duxbury has also suggested that judges in national courts might occasionally withhold references to foreign jurisprudence 'for fear that their explicitly considering and rejecting that reasoning may diminish or undermine a foreign precedent (and possibly the judges responsible for it) in the jurisdiction from which it hails'.[116]

That judges are themselves conscious of treating foreign jurisprudence in this way is less clear. Justice Breyer of the US Supreme Court has suggested that: 'Foreign courts refer to our decisions ... and if we sometimes refer to their decisions, the references may help those struggling institutions.'[117] Justice Sandra Day O'Connor has also explained that recourse to comparative law can 'create an all-important good impression'; in being 'seen to be cognizant of other judicial systems, our ability to act as a rule-of-law model for other nations will be enhanced'.[118] Baroness Hale thought it unlikely that this was in the forefront of the

"Old Dog" New Tricks? An Empirical Study of the Use of Foreign Precedents by the South African Constitutional Court (1995–2010)' in Tania Groppi and Marie-Claire Ponthoreau (eds), *The Use of Foreign Precedents by Constitutional Judges* (Hart Publishing, 2013) 185.

[112] Wheatle (n 110) 149.

[113] Gary J Jacobsohn, *Apple of Gold: Constitutionalism in Israel and the United States* (Princeton University Press, 1995) 225, cited in Christopher McCrudden, 'Human Rights and Judicial Use of Comparative Law' in Örücü (n 19) 10. See, McCrudden (n 108) 499, 518.

[114] Cram (n 1) 124.

[115] Edward A Mearns, 'Emerging Trends in International Constitutionalism: A Comparative Approach' (1996) 28 *Case Western Reserve Journal of International Law* 1, 1.

[116] Neil Duxbury, 'The Law of the Land' (2015) 78(1) *MLR* 26, 40.

[117] Norman Dorsen, 'A Conversation between U.S. Supreme Court Justices' (2005) 3(3) *International Journal of Constitutional Law* 519, 523 (Justice Breyer).

[118] Sandra Day O'Connor, Southern Centre for International Studies, Atlanta, Georgia, 28 October 2003, www.humanrightsfirst.org/wp-content/uploads/pdf/SOUTHERN_CENTER_INTERNATIONAL_STUDIES_Justice_O'Connor.pdf.

minds of UK Supreme Court Justices. However, she continued that 'it may be unconscious'.[119]

> If you are finding against the Government and on a matter about which the Government feels strongly, you obviously hope that your reasoning will be sufficient to convince them. That is particularly because the Government can't go to Strasbourg. If you are finding against the claimant in a human rights case, you are partly trying to convince the claimant, but you are also trying to convince Strasbourg.[120]

C. Interpreting 'British' and Common Law Rights

A final alternative is that reference to certain sources of comparative law might reflect a shift in perceptions of rights ownership. The Supreme Court does not operate in a political vacuum. As Paterson has pointed out, the political dynamics surrounding the 2010 general election, the threats to the HRA 1998 from the political right, the Brighton Declaration and the prisoner voting saga may all have had an impact on the Supreme Court's relationship with the Strasbourg jurisprudence.[121] As Masterman has blogged:

> [T]he Bill of Rights debate ... has arguably had a damaging effect on political perceptions of the HRA and the link the Act creates between domestic law and the Convention jurisprudence. The relationship between domestic courts and the European Court of Human Rights that *Ullah* embodies is out of touch with the widely-held view that the content of our domestic human rights law should not be 'dictated' to us by the European Court.[122]

The Commission on Human Rights reported that the majority of Commissioners favoured a UK Bill of Rights because 'many people feel alienated from a system they regard as "European" rather than British'.[123] The public had no 'ownership' and this was 'the most powerful argument for a new constitutional instrument'.[124] The HRA 1998 and the ECHR came to be seen as an 'alien intrusion',[125] eroding parliamentary sovereignty and transferring power to foreign judges in a foreign court. Concerns around sovereignty

[119] Interview with Baroness Hale (n 5).

[120] ibid.

[121] Helen Fenwick, 'An Appeasement Approach in the European Court of Human Rights?' *UK Constitutional Law Blog* (5 April 2012), www.ukconstitutionallaw.org/2012/04/05/helen-fenwick-an-appeasement-approach-in-the-european-court-of-human-rights; Alan Paterson, *Final Judgment: The Last Law Lords and the Supreme Court* (Hart Publishing, 2013) 232: 'Certainly Strasbourg has shown signs of being aware of the Tories' distaste for Strasbourg (eg over prisoners' voting rights, and the deportation of alleged terrorists).'

[122] Masterman (n 32); Fenwick and Masterman (n 96) 1122–23.

[123] *A UK Bill of Rights? The Choice before Us*, Commission on Human Rights Report, 18 December 2012, http://webarchive.nationalarchives.gov.uk/20130206065653/https://www.justice.gov.uk/downloads/about/cbr/uk-bill-rights-vol-1.pdf.

[124] ibid.

[125] Conor Gearty, *On Fantasy Island: Britain, Europe and Human Rights* (Oxford University Press, 2016) 3.

were voiced in the early days of the ECHR,[126] but were reinvigorated by unpopular judgments against the UK.[127] Meanwhile, a persistent unease about membership of the EU fed a general anti-European sentiment. 'Europe' became a dirty word and the political discourse centred on asserting the primacy of domestic rights and domestic law, 're-emphasising the national'.[128]

In this context, a number of commentators have interpreted the case law on the development of common law rights as a chance to reinforce the UK rights protected prior to the HRA 1998 and independent of the European Convention.[129] Lord Toulson's explanation in *R (Guardian News and Media Ltd)* is worth repeating:[130]

> I base my decision on the common law principle of open justice. In reaching it I am fortified by the common theme of the judgments in other common law countries to which I have referred. Collectively they are strong persuasive authority. The courts are used to citation of Strasbourg decisions in abundance, but citation of decisions of senior courts in other common law jurisdictions is now less common. I regret the imbalance. The development of the common law did not come to an end on the passing of the Human Rights Act. It is in vigorous health and flourishing in many parts of the world which share a common legal tradition. This case provides a good example of the benefit which can be gained from knowledge of the development of the common law elsewhere.[131]

The 'new toy' that was the Convention and its jurisprudence has apparently lost its sheen.[132] In *Al Rawi*, Lord Dyson was careful to point out that the lawfulness of a closed material procedure under Article 6 ECHR and under the common law were 'distinct questions':

> As Lord Bingham said in *R (Ullah)* ... 'It is of course open to member states to provide for rights more generous than those guaranteed by the Convention.' It is, therefore, open to our courts to provide greater protection through the common

[126] Ed Bates, *The Evolution of the European Convention on Human Rights* (Oxford University Press, 2010) 77 ff.

[127] *Hirst v UK (No 2)* (2005) ECHR 681; *Greens and MT v UK* (2011) 53 EHRR 21. See generally Alexander Horne and Hélène Tyrrell, 'Sovereignty, Privilege and the European Convention on Human Rights' in Alexander Horne and Andrew Le Sueur (eds), *Parliament: Legislation and Accountability* (Hart Publishing, 2016).

[128] Roger Masterman and Se-shauna Wheatle, 'A Common Law Resurgence in Rights Protection' (2015) 1 *European Human Rights Law Review* 57, 61.

[129] ibid 57; Mark Elliott, 'Beyond the European Convention: Human Rights and the Common Law' (2015) 68(1) *Current Legal Problems* 85, 92–95. See generally Dickson (n 96) 20–34; Richard Clayton, 'The Empire Strikes Back' [2015] *PL* 3; Phillip Sales, 'Rights and Fundamental Rights in English Law' [2016] *CLJ* 86; Eirik Bjorg, 'Common Law Rights: Balancing Domestic and International Exigencies' (2016) 75(2) *CLJ* 220.

[130] *R (Guardian News and Media Ltd) v City of Westminster Magistrates' Court* [2012] EWCA Civ 420; [2012] All ER 551.

[131] ibid 88.

[132] Lord Neuberger, 'The Role of Judges in Human Rights Jurisprudence: A Comparison of the Australian and UK Experience', Conference at the Supreme Court of Victoria (Melbourne, 8 August 2014), www.supremecourt.uk/docs/speech-140808.pdf [29].

> law than that which is guaranteed by the Convention. As the Court of Appeal said ... 'never say never' is often an appropriate catchphrase to use in the context of the common law.[133]

In *Kennedy*, Lord Mance reiterated that the domestic law should be the 'natural starting point'; the approach should 'certainly not [be] to focus exclusively on the Convention rights, without surveying the wider common law scene'.[134] Lord Toulson was more direct, condemning the 'baleful and unnecessary tendency to overlook the common law'.[135] In *A v BBC*, Lord Reed also emphasised that, in addition to changes in society and the administration of justice, the principle of open justice 'can also develop having regard to the approach adopted in other common law countries'.[136] However, Lord Reed's reference to the common law jurisprudence retained a Convention flavour, being justified on the basis that some of the constitutional texts in those countries would contain 'guarantees comparable to the Convention rights' or would 'reflect the courts' view of the requirements of justice';[137] 'The development of the common law can also of course be influenced by the ECHR'.[138] Other judges have been more reserved. In O *(A Child)*, Lord Neuberger reiterated that the common law 'should be generally consistent with the Convention and it would be arrogant to assume that there may be no assistance to be gained from the Strasbourg jurisprudence'.[139]

Masterman and Wheatle suggest that the judicial development of common law rights should be seen as a 'contribution to generative discourse'.[140] In this respect, it is entirely unsurprising that the Supreme Court (and other courts below it) would be inclined to prefer to be (and be seen to be) persuaded by the courts of familiar common law countries. Alternatively, the focus on common law rights might be seen as a response to the 'fallibility of Strasbourg and the potential for assertiveness on the part of national courts'.[141] In this light, decisions like *Horncastle* form a part of the common law rights story; the opportunity for dialogue with the Strasbourg court fortifies domestic courts in prioritising domestic conceptions of rights. In similar terms, the Supreme Court has considered the possibility that other international obligations might cover the Convention ground.[142]

133 *Al Rawi and Others v The Security Service and Others* [2011] UKSC 34; [2012] 1 AC 531 [68]–[69].

134 *Kennedy v The Charity Commission* [2014] UKSC 20; [2015] AC 455 [46].

135 ibid [133].

136 *A v BBC* [2014] UKSC 25; [2015] AC 588 [40].

137 ibid.

138 ibid.

139 *O (A Child) v Rhodes and Another (English PEN and Others Intervening)* [2015] UKSC 32; [2016] AC 219 [120].

140 ibid.

141 ibid.

142 *Nzolameso v Westminster City Council* [2015] UKSC 22; [2015] 2 All ER 942 [29]: 'Where Convention Rights under the Human Rights Act 1998 are engaged, it is well established

These common law developments also reflect the ongoing unease about the European source of human rights. In a Conservative Party document, published ahead of the 2015 general election, the government complained of the 'mission creep' developed by the Strasbourg Court.[143] The 2015 Conservative Party Manifesto outlined plans to 'scrap' the HRA 1998 and suggested that the new Bill of Rights would 'remain faithful to the basic principles of human rights, which we signed up to in the original European Convention on Human Rights', but would 'break the formal link between British courts and the European Court of Human Rights, and make our own Supreme Court the ultimate arbiter of human rights matters in the UK'.[144]

There has been little movement on this question at the time of writing. Preoccupied with Brexit politics, the 2017 Conservative Party Manifesto promised a period of relative quiet on the HRA 1998 front, admitting of no intention to withdraw from the ECHR for the duration of the new Parliament (whatever that may be).[145] It is therefore difficult to predict the form of any such instrument. It is, however, possible to predict one aspect of the content. Assuming the UK does not withdraw from the ECHR altogether, it is likely that a British Bill of Rights would need to say something about the weight and treatment of the Strasbourg jurisprudence under the new framework. Since a British Bill of Rights reflects a desire to replace the HRA 1998 with an instrument that is 'tailor made for this country',[146] such an instrument is likely to dilute the attention paid to the European jurisprudence. It is possible that conflict with the jurisprudence from other similar national supreme courts could itself justify departure from relevant,

that they have to be interpreted and applied consistently with international human right standards, including the UNCRC ... We have not heard argument on the interesting question of whether, even where no Convention right is involved, section 11 [of the Children Act 2004] should nevertheless be construed consistently with the international obligations of the United Kingdom under Article 3 of the UNCRC [United Nations Convention on the Rights of the Child]. That must be a question for another day.'

143 Conservative Party, 'Protecting Human Rights in the UK: The Conservatives' Proposals for Changing Britain's Human Rights Laws', www.conservatives.com/~/media/files/downloadable%20Files/human_rights.pdf.

144 Conservative Party Manifesto 2015, 'Strong Leadership, a Clear Economic Plan, a Brighter, More Secure Future', www.conservatives.com/manifesto2015, 60. Other parties took a different stance. The Labour Party stated that it would 'stand up for citizens' individual rights, protecting the Human Rights Act and reforming rather than walking away from the European Court of Human Rights': Labour Party Manifesto 2015, 'Britain Can Be Better', https://www.scribd.com/document/261706542/Labour-Manifesto-2015, 67. The Liberal Democrats promised that 'the Human Rights Act will remain': Liberal Democrat Party Manifesto 2015, 'Stronger Economy. Fairer Society. Opportunity for Everyone', https://d3n8a8pro7vhmx.cloudfront.net/libdems/pages/8907/attachments/original/1429028133/Liberal_Democrat_General_Election_Manifesto_2015.pdf?1429028133, 14.

145 Conservative and Unionist Party Manifesto 2017, 'Forward, Together. Our Plan for a Strong Britain and a Prosperous Future', www.conservatives.com/manifesto, 37.

146 Borrowing from Lord Rodger in *Watkins v Secretary of State for the Home Department* [2006] UKHL 17; [2006] 2 AC 395 [64].

clear and constant Strasbourg case law.[147] This would, as Fenwick and Masterman explain, require that conflicting jurisprudence from foreign courts be treated as having greater significance in interpreting the British Bill of Rights than the Strasbourg jurisprudence.[148] Inspiration might be taken from the Human Rights Act 1998 (Repeal and Substitution) Bill, introduced in 2012–13 by Charlie Elphicke MP. Clause 2 of the Bill purported to grant the jurisprudence of courts in common law jurisdictions at least as much weight as the Strasbourg case law:

> A court or tribunal determining a question which has arisen in connection with a UK right may take account of a judgment of—
>
> (a) a court in Australia, Canada, New Zealand, the United States of America or any country having a common law-based judicial system;
> (b) the European Court of Human Rights; or
> (c) a court in any other jurisdiction which may be relevant to the UK right under consideration,
>
> but shall be bound to follow the judgments of higher courts in the United Kingdom, in accordance with the usual rules of precedent (though, for the avoidance of doubt, precedent relating to rights under the Convention shall not be binding when determining a question in connection with a UK right).[149]

Alternatively, Parliament might decline to do more than reiterate the non-binding nature of the Strasbourg jurisprudence. This was the format of the European Union (Withdrawal) Bill (as introduced) in respect of EU case law: 'A court or tribunal need not have regard to anything done on or after exit day by the European Court [of Justice], another EU entity or the EU but may do so if it considers it appropriate to do so'.[150] But this is unlikely to communicate a clear severance of the link between the UK and Strasbourg—if that is the aim. The HRA 1998 never accorded binding status to the Strasbourg jurisprudence. The most that could be said is that it required judicial awareness of it. Suggesting that the courts 'need not have regard to' the Strasbourg jurisprudence would dilute that duty, but would also be difficult in the context of continued ECHR membership. The requirement to 'take into account' the Strasbourg jurisprudence combined with the power to read legislation compatibly or make declarations of incompatibility serves as an

[147] Fenwick and Masterman (n 96) 1123.
[148] ibid.
[149] Clause 2 of the Human Rights Act 1998 (Repeal and Substitution) Bill, introduced in 2012–13, www.publications.parliament.uk/pa/bills/cbill/2012-2013/0031/2013031.i-ii.html. A motion for the Bill's Second Reading was moved on 1 March 2013, but was withdrawn at the end of the debate.
[150] Clause 6(2) of the European Union (Withdrawal) Bill: 'A court of tribunal need not have regard to anything done on or after exit day by the European Court [of Justice], another EU entity or the EU but may do so if it considers it appropriate to do so.'

early warning mechanism for Parliament. Absent the judicial attention to the Strasbourg jurisprudence, Convention violations would be more likely.

IV. CONCLUSIONS

One of the main criticisms made by those who object to the use of foreign jurisprudence in domestic courts (and particularly in the US) is that the practice is essentially opportunistic. In other words, that comparativism is mainly results-driven:[151] judges use that jurisprudence which is likely to support their own predetermined conclusions, or a means of 'judicial fig-leafing', designed to obscure the reality of judicial choice.[152] Thus, some have seen the use of foreign jurisprudence as 'yet another way that judges will be able to support the political choices that judges anyway wish to make'.[153]

In the UK human rights context, it is difficult to disagree that foreign jurisprudence is used in an instrumental way. But it does not follow that the practice is illegitimate. In human rights cases especially, it is important that the Supreme Court is able to determine cases according to their assessment of the legal settlement in the UK. As Feldman put it, 'comparative study should not lead to attempted mimicry of others but should inform the journey towards a national system *which meets our distinctive needs*'.[154] This reflects the optimism shared by many around the passage of the HRA 1998—that it would foster a domestic law of human rights rather than lead domestic courts to copy the corpus of Strasbourg jurisprudence into domestic law.

This much is clear from the disappointment voiced by the architect of the HRA 1998. Lord Irvine, the Lord Chancellor at the time of the passing of the HRA, argued that the courts had misinterpreted section 2 of the Act and

[151] See, eg, Cram (n 1) 139–41; Wicks (n 63) 410. See also Justice Antonin Scalia, 'The Bill of Rights: Confirmation of Extent Freedoms or Invitation to Judicial Creation?' in Grant Huscroft and Paul Rishworth (eds), *Litigating Rights: Perspectives from Domestic and International Law* (Hart Publishing, 2002); James Allan, 'A Defence of the Status Quo' in Tom Campbell et al (eds), *Protecting Human Rights: Instruments and Institutions* (Oxford University Press, 2003). *cf* McCrudden (n 108) 527: 'One possible explanation is that the use of foreign judgments is simply results-driven … [leading to a] suspicion that the selective use of foreign judgments is inevitably associated with a rights-expanding agenda. But this would be mistaken'; Roger Alford, 'Four Mistakes in the Debate on "Outsourcing Authority"' (2006) 69 *Albany Law Review* 653: '[One] mistake in the debate on outsourcing authority is to assume that the outcome of constitutional comparativism will be an expansion of individual liberties.'

[152] Richard Posner, 'No Thanks, We Already Have Our Own Laws' *Legal Affairs* (July/August 2004), www.legalaffairs.org/issues/July-August-2004/feature_posner_julaug04.msp; Sujit Choudhry (ed), *The Migration of Constitutional Ideas* (Cambridge University Press, 2006), 7.

[153] Christopher McCrudden, 'Judicial Comparativism and Human Rights' in Esin Örücü and David Nelken (eds), *Comparative Law: A Handbook* (Hart Publishing, 2007) 371, 387.

[154] Feldman (n 35) 205 (emphasis added).

had taken too deferential an approach to the Strasbourg Court's case law.[155] He continued that the Supreme Court 'should not abstain from deciding the case for themselves simply because it may cause difficulties for the UK on the international law plane'.[156] In fact, Lord Irvine suggested in that speech that it was the 'constitutional duty' of the Supreme Court's judges to reject Strasbourg decisions that are flawed.[157]

The well-recorded mantra to 'follow' or 'keep pace' with the 'clear and constant' Strasbourg jurisprudence is under development. The interesting and novel development is the use of foreign jurisprudence to support departure from the otherwise 'clear and constant' Strasbourg case law. The two cases discussed in the last section, *Horncastle* and *Ahmed*, provide two such examples. It is also worth noting that in both instances, the Supreme Court was determining issues arising under Article 6 ECHR. This is partly because Article 6 remains the most frequently invoked Convention right.[158] It is also, as Dickson has pointed out, because Article 6 is 'one of the Convention's provisions in respect of which the European Court still permits Member States a fairly wide margin of appreciation in many contexts'.[159] As a result, Dickson agrees that 'the UK Supreme Court appears to be conscious of this and is therefore prepared to be more assertive in this field than in others':[160]

> [T]here are signs that the Supreme Court Justices may be more prepared than their predecessors to 'stand up' to the European Court on points of domestic law which they feel the judges in Strasbourg do not fully understand. Having largely won over the Grand Chamber of the European Court during the 'dialogue' surrounding the use of hearsay evidence in criminal cases (the *Horncastle* and *Al-Khawaja* affair), the Supreme Court may have gained some confidence in its ability to trim the sails of the Strasbourg Court.[161]

The more general conclusion is that the relationship with the Strasbourg jurisprudence is changing. Not only are UK courts increasingly willing to reject Strasbourg jurisprudence as determinative of a particular issue, they are willing to reject the position adopted by the Strasbourg Court altogether—even where it is established by 'clear and constant' case law.

Thus while English courts may have a tendency to follow decisions of the Strasbourg Court, they do so as a matter of choice, not obligation.[162] This review of the *Ullah* approach finds support in Strasbourg. Although Sir Nicolas Bratza, the then President of the Strasbourg Court, felt that clear principles from the Grand Chamber (as in the *AF* case) should generally be

[155] Lord Irvine of Lairg (n 67).
[156] ibid.
[157] ibid.
[158] Dickson (n 96) 226.
[159] ibid.
[160] ibid.
[161] ibid 374.
[162] David Feldman (ed), *English Public Law* (Oxford University Press, 2004) 390.

followed, he also considered 'dialogue through judgments' to be 'of equal importance':[163]

> Even if it is not bound to accept the view of the national courts in their interpretation of Convention rights, it is of untold benefit for the Strasbourg Court that we should have those views ... it is right and healthy that national courts should continue to feel free to criticise Strasbourg judgments where those judgments have applied principles which are unclear or inconsistent or where they have misunderstood national law or practices ... But I also believe that it is important that the superior national courts should, as Lord Phillips put it in the *Horncastle* judgment, on the rare occasions when they have concerns as to whether a decision of the Strasbourg Court sufficiently appreciates or accommodates particular aspects of the domestic process, 'decline to follow the Strasbourg decision, giving reasons for adopting this course'. If, as has happened in the case of *Al-Khawaja*, Strasbourg is given the opportunity to reconsider the decision in issue, what takes place may indeed as Lord Phillips put it, 'prove to be a valuable dialogue between this court and the Strasbourg Court'. I firmly believe that such dialogue can only serve to cement a relationship between the two courts.[164]

The prima facie duty of UK domestic courts under the HRA is to act compatibly with the Convention. A duty to 'take into account' the Strasbourg jurisprudence can assist with that, but is not itself the main objective. For example, it is obvious that a lack of relevant Strasbourg jurisprudence would not prevent the courts from resolving a case according to the rights set out in the Convention. As Lord Kerr has pointed out (extra-judicially):

> Where a court of the UK is faced with a claim to a Convention right, it seems to me clear that it cannot refuse to examine its viability, simply because there is no relevant Strasbourg jurisprudence.[165]

Lord Kerr supported this assertion with three reasons, which are worth setting out in full:

> There are three reasons for this: the first practical, the second a matter of principle and the third the requirement of statute. The practical reason is that many claims to Convention rights will have to be determined by courts at every level in the United Kingdom without the benefit of unequivocal jurisprudence from ECtHR. It is simply not a practical option to adopt an attitude of agnosticism just because Strasbourg has not yet spoken. The second reason, the reason of principle, is elementary. The Human Rights Act gives citizens of this country direct access to the rights which the Convention enshrines through their enforcement by our courts. It is therefore the duty of every court not only to ascertain 'where the jurisprudence

[163] Nicolas Bratza, 'The Relationship between the UK Courts and Strasbourg' [2011] *European Human Rights Law Review* 505, 512.

[164] ibid 505, 512.

[165] Lord Kerr, 'The Modest Underworker of Strasbourg?', Clifford Chance Lecture (London 25 January 2012), https://www.supremecourt.uk/docs/speech_120125.pdf, 7.

of the Strasbourg court clearly shows that it currently stands' (which is how Lord Hope characterised it in *Ambrose*); it is also, in my view, the court's duty to resolve the question whether a claim to a Convention right is viable where there is no clear current view from Strasbourg to be seen. The duty to adjudicate on a claim to a Convention right cannot be extinguished or avoided by the fact that the jurisprudence of the ECtHR has so far failed to supply the answer. The final reason, the statutory imperative, is also elementary. Section 6 of the Human Rights Act leaves no alternative to courts when called upon to adjudicate on claims to a Convention right. This section makes it unlawful for a public authority, including a court, to act in a way which is incompatible with a Convention right. That statutory obligation, to be effective, must carry with it the requirement that the court determine if the Convention right has the effect claimed for, whether or not Strasbourg has pronounced upon it.[166]

The Supreme Court has shown increasing willingness to move away from the deferential *Ullah*-type stance and 'stand up' to the Strasbourg Court where there are misgivings about the helpfulness of its jurisprudence. In such circumstances the jurisprudence of foreign domestic courts may provide an important alternative perspective. Cases like *Horncastle* demonstrate that the adoption of a conclusion at odds with the Strasbourg jurisprudence can be supported in this way, providing a layer of reasoning to the Court's judgment, which may assist the Strasbourg Court in its own review. Viewed in this way, the jurisprudence of foreign domestic courts is more valuable than has so far been considered. By taking those sources into account, judges may take a more theorised approach to human rights cases, working with the Strasbourg Court in human rights cases rather than under it.

Finally, the case law of foreign domestic courts might reinforce the domestic human rights regime. The development of common law rights could be seen as an attempt to emphasise the status of UK rights protected prior to the HRA 1998 and that are independent of the ECHR. In these circumstances, the jurisprudence of other common law courts may be considered less 'foreign' than the jurisprudence of the Strasbourg Court.

[166] ibid 7–8.

9

Conclusions

THE RELATIVE LACK of attention given to the influence of foreign jurisprudence at the UK Supreme Court (or in UK domestic courts generally) might give the impression that the use of these sources is limited or of little substantive relevance to judicial reasoning. The research findings, both from the quantitative data analysis of judgments and the qualitative interviews, paint a different picture. Of the 533 cases handed down by the Supreme Court in the first four years, explicit citations of foreign jurisprudence are found in 157, just under 30 per cent of the total. The Court has been slightly more inclined to refer to foreign jurisprudence in human rights cases. Of the total 533 cases decided by the Supreme Court in the time period, 381 do not engage human rights issues and explicit citations of foreign jurisprudence can be found in 100 of those (or 26 per cent); the remaining 152 can be described as human rights cases and explicit citations of foreign jurisprudence can be found in 57 of those (or 38 per cent). These proportions are not insignificant. Yet a close analysis of the cases does not reveal clear explanations as to why these sources are used; judges rarely articulate the reasons for citing foreign jurisprudence in their judgments.[1]

I. AN ABSENCE OF GUIDING PRINCIPLES

The simplest reason for the use of foreign jurisprudence is that the practice is nowhere prohibited. The Justices of the Supreme Court (and other judges generally) use foreign jurisprudence because they can. It is worth repeating Lord Mance's words, quoted in Chapter 3:

> When judges look to comparative and international material, they may do so for information, inspiration, or confirmation, just as they use domestic decisions that are not binding on them.[2]

[1] Also noted in Ian Cram, 'Resort to Foreign Constitutional Norms in Domestic Human Rights Jurisprudence with Reference to Terrorism Cases' [2009] *CLJ* 118, 140.

[2] Lord Mance, 'Foreign Laws and Languages' in Andrew Burrows, David Johnston and Reinhard Zimmermann (eds), *Judge and Jurist: Essays in Memory of Lord Rodger of Earlsferry* (Oxford University Press, 2013) 87–88.

The Supreme Court is therefore free to derive such assistance as it may find from foreign jurisprudence, in much the same way that it could derive assistance from any other non-binding authority. There is no guidance on using foreign jurisprudence at all. The UK has no provision similar to section 39(1) of the South African Constitution, which provides that the Constitutional Court must consider international law and may consider foreign law. While the HRA 1998 provides that domestic courts 'must take into account' the Strasbourg jurisprudence, the Act is silent on the use of jurisprudence from other jurisdictions. But it is the absence of any legislative guidance that legitimises the use of these sources: 'without the constraints of a constitution or code, the legal systems of England and Scotland have a particular freedom to look to other systems'.[3]

This broad discretion comes with its own risks. As Cram has suggested, resort to foreign jurisprudence has the potential to pose 'awkward questions concerning judicial forays into the policy-making realm of the constitution and the erosion of parliamentary sovereignty'.[4] The risk has not so far manifested itself before the UK Supreme Court and it was clear from the interviews that the judges did not themselves consider there to be any serious threat on that level. It was not found that the Supreme Court's use of foreign jurisprudence supported the most prevalent criticisms about the practice. Decorative or ornamental citations, for example, are unlikely. In fact, the impression from the interviews was that such uses (of any source) were liable to obscure the reasoning of a judgment. Moreover, the impression given by some of the judges interviewed was that the Supreme Court's judgments should be as concise as possible.[5]

II. THE INDIVIDUAL APPROACHES OF THE JUSTICES

The early hypothesis was that the tendency to use foreign jurisprudence would very likely be related to the background and inclination of individual judges.[6] It was not surprising to see certain judges, known for their enthusiasm for comparative law, come out as heavier users of foreign jurisprudence. However, the hypotheses about the individual approaches of the different judges were not consistently supported by the quantitative data analysis.

[3] ibid 87.

[4] Cram (n 1) 125.

[5] See, eg, interview with the Rt Hon Lord Walker of Gestingthorpe, former Justice of the UK Supreme Court (Supreme Court, London, 15 May 2012): 'English judgments ... are far too long'. See also Brice Dickson, *Human Rights and the United Kingdom Supreme Court* (Oxford University Press, 2013) 3–4, commenting on the development of working methods at the Supreme Court in order to 'operate in a more modern and accessible way'.

[6] A point recognised by other works: John Bell, 'Comparative Law in the Supreme Court 2010–11' [2012] *Cambridge Journal of International and Comparative Law* 20; Elaine Mak, 'Why Do Dutch and UK Judges Cite Foreign Law?' [2011] *CLJ* 420.

While some results showed either a greater or lesser likelihood that a certain Supreme Court Justice would cite foreign jurisprudence, some Justices who had a reputation for enthusiasm about comparative law did not actually come out as heavy users of foreign jurisprudence. For example, one surprising finding from the data analysis was that there were very few citations of German jurisprudence: just 19 cases—including nine human rights cases—cited German jurisprudence out of the possible 533 handed down between 2009 and 2017. Given the reputation that Lord Mance (in particular) has for his enthusiasm for German law, it was expected that the number would be much greater.[7] In fact, Lord Mance did not seem to cite foreign jurisprudence any more than the average at the Supreme Court. Of the 71 cases heard by Lord Mance in which foreign jurisprudence was cited, explicit citations could be found in 21 of his judgments (or 30 per cent). For the same reason, it was surprising to see that Lord Rodger did not come out as one of the more frequent users of foreign jurisprudence. Lord Rodger's enthusiasm for using comparative law is well documented.[8] The implication of these results was that foreign jurisprudence must be used more extensively than is possible to tell on the face of the judgments. It was for this reason that the interviews were important; if not all uses of foreign jurisprudence are attributed in the judgments, research based only on explicit citations is not likely to reflect an accurate account of the extent to which foreign jurisprudence is used at the Supreme Court, or the reasons for which these sources are used.

The interview evidence confirmed the hypothesis that the judges take individualised approaches to the use of foreign jurisprudence.[9] As a starting point, some judges were known to have a greater interest in comparative law than others. More specifically, some judges were known to have an interest in certain jurisdictions. Aside from Lord Mance's reputation for interest in German law, reference was frequently made to Lord Collins, who was well known for using American authorities. Other judges expressed confidence in other languages or engaged in discussion with the judges from top courts in other countries. The prevalence of citations of foreign jurisprudence from other common law countries was often explained on this basis.

Although many of the judges agreed that linguistic ability would be a factor in the selection of foreign jurisprudence, ability in a foreign language does not necessarily correlate with the likelihood that a particular judge would use foreign jurisprudence in the first place. Some of the judges feel that a more significant barrier to using foreign jurisprudence was a practical one.

[7] See, eg, *R (on the Application of HS2 Action Alliance Ltd) v Secretary of State for Transport and Another* [2014] UKSC 3; [2014] 1 WLR 324.

[8] Lord Mance (n 2); Tetyana Nesterchuk, 'The View from behind the Bench', in Burrows, Johnston and Zimmermann (n 2).

[9] Similar findings were reported by Mak in 2012 (after the interview period for this study): Elaine Mak, 'Reference to Foreign Law in the Supreme Courts of Britain and the Netherlands: Explaining the Development of Judicial Practices' (2012) 8(2) *Utrecht Law Review* 20, 30.

Thus, Lord Kerr expressed the view that the 'wealth of material' that was typically put forward to the Supreme Court would be more likely to prevent references to foreign jurisprudence than a lack of confidence in any given language.[10] Lord Walker, however, felt that the issue was more likely to do with different judgment styles in different jurisdictions,[11] in that shorter judgments from civil law jurisdictions would not always clearly set out the reasoning.[12] Finally, there is a more general problem surrounding the research framework involved in finding relevant foreign jurisprudence: 'the main barrier is not knowing where to start on the research'.[13]

An effective time-saving measure is to refer to the works of leading academics in the relevant field. A good example of academic work being used in this way can be drawn from the *HJ (Iran)* case,[14] considered in Chapter 7. In that case, Lord Dyson did not 'find it necessary to examine the Australian authorities to which [the Supreme Court] were referred'. Instead, it was 'sufficient' to refer to an academic paper exploring the impact of the troublesome Australian and UK jurisprudence. Lord Dyson was satisfied that the paper showed that 'the reasoning of the majority judgments is being generally applied in Australia'.[15] Lord Walker also noted comparative academic work on this point and reproduced a lengthy paragraph from the paper to which Lord Dyson referred in the judgment.[16] The implicit suggestion is that cases which have not been digested by academic work are not as likely to be used as those that have. Again, this is heavily reliant on the enthusiasm that an individual judge has for reading about the law in foreign jurisdictions or how well stocked their bookcases might be.[17] The feeling is that some judges are simply more inclined to use foreign jurisprudence than others and take a view as to the potential obstacles accordingly. This relationship between the individual approach of a judge and the use of foreign jurisprudence also contributes one explanation for the decline in

[10] Interview with the Rt Hon Lord Kerr of Tonaghmore, Justice of the UK Supreme Court (Supreme Court, London, 9 May 2012). Indeed, Lord Kerr pointed out that it was always possible to get a translation of a particular judgment.

[11] Interview with Lord Walker (n 5).

[12] On different legal styles of common and civil law systems, see, eg, Basil Markesinis, 'A Matter of Style' (1994) 110 *LQR* 607.

[13] Interview with the Rt Hon Lord Sumption, Justice of the UK Supreme Court (Supreme Court, London, 28 May 2012).

[14] *HJ (Iran) (FC) v Secretary of State for the Home Department* [2010] UKSC 31; [2011] 1 AC 596.

[15] ibid [112] (Lord Dyson), citing Jenni Millbank, 'From Discretion to Disbelief: Recent Trends in Refugee Determinations on the Basis of Sexual Orientation in Australia and the United Kingdom' (2009) 13 *International Journal of Human Rights* 391.

[16] *HJ (Iran)* (n 13) [92].

[17] Lord Reed explained: 'There is a practical problem about finding foreign jurisprudence ... I've got ... a French textbook on human rights law, which obviously cites French case law. But not many people have got foreign textbooks on their shelves.' Interview with the Rt Hon Lord Reed, Justice of the UK Supreme Court (Supreme Court, London, 8 May 2012).

the use of foreign jurisprudence in certain years. For example, the drop in the percentage of cases citing foreign jurisprudence between 2011 and 2013 correlates with the retirement of Lord Collins, one of the heaviest users of foreign jurisprudence at the Supreme Court. Lord Collins gave just two written judgments in 2011 before retiring.

III. FOREIGN JURISPRUDENCE AS A HEURISTIC TOOL

Another clear finding is that different judges use foreign jurisprudence for different reasons. In the main, foreign jurisprudence was explained as a heuristic device. In other words, foreign jurisprudence provides judges with a fresh perspective—an analytical lens—through which to reflect on their own reasoning about a problem. This is what appeared to be happening in the House of Lords control order cases, *MB* and *AF (No 3)*,[18] and this is what seemed to drive Lord Collins' insistence on the consideration of American decisions in *Jones v Kaney*.[19] In the latter case, the vast American jurisprudence on 'precisely the same arguments of policy which [had] been argued before [the UK Supreme Court]' was, to Lord Collins, of obvious assistance. This was despite the fact that the culture relating to expert evidence was different in the US because 'the underlying principle is the same'.[20] Thus the Commonwealth and US jurisprudence in *Jones v Kaney* was cited 'as a way of checking that no relevant argument had been ignored'.[21]

None of the judges interviewed felt this use of foreign jurisprudence to be problematic, largely because no particular reliance is placed on these materials. As Saunders has suggested, the reality is simply that 'such cases must be determined … with or without the insights offered by comparative law' and 'in at least some such cases, foreign experience can help to elucidate the issues and options for their resolution'.[22] The purpose served by foreign jurisprudence in these circumstances is simply to provide an opportunity for reflection or to form 'part of the process of reaching a more fully theorised … agreement'.[23]

This sort of purpose is important. In the human rights context, it is worth remembering the relative unfamiliarity of UK judges with human rights

[18] *Secretary of State for the Home Department v MB* [2007] UKHL 46; *Secretary of State for the Home Department v AF and Another* [2009] UKHL 28.

[19] *Jones v Kaney* [2011] UKSC 13.

[20] ibid [77].

[21] Bell (n 6) 21.

[22] Cheryl Saunders, 'Comparative Constitutional Law in the Courts: Is There a Problem?' (2006) 59(1) *Current Legal Problems* 91, 114.

[23] Christopher McCrudden, 'Judicial Comparativism and Human Rights' in Esin Örücü and David Nelken (eds), *Comparative Law: A Handbook* (Hart Publishing, 2007) 371, 374.

adjudication and with the duties imposed upon them by the HRA 1998. For example, prior to the HRA, the balancing exercise required by the qualified rights had been the jurisdiction of the supranational court. A positive duty to 'take into account' one particular pool of otherwise persuasive jurisprudence, to read domestic law compatibly with an international convention and to declare any incompatibilities that could not be so remedied, have all led domestic courts to grapple with greater depth and detail on questions previously unfamiliar to the role of the judge. One of the major justifications for comparativism is therefore that it can encourage the domestic court to adopt a more theorised approach to human rights. As McCrudden recognised: 'Even where the *result* of the foreign judicial approach has not been adopted, it has often been influential in sharpening the understanding of the court's view of domestic law'.[24] 'Foreign law may perform a cognitive function ... the confrontation of both legal systems may force some consideration and better understanding of the nature of domestic law'.[25]

However, heuristic uses of foreign jurisprudence are likely to be the more obscure in the judgment. Where foreign jurisprudence is used as part of an information-gathering exercise, as an analytical lens, yardstick or benchmark against which to measure thinking, it is easy to understand the lack of explicit citations. This finding also goes some way towards explaining the anomalies in the dataset discussed above, particularly where the data on explicit citation did not show some Supreme Court Justices—known for their enthusiasm for comparative law—as heavy users of foreign jurisprudence. This finding also addresses one of the main criticisms about the use of foreign jurisprudence: that these sources mainly perform a legitimation function. If judges are not always citing the foreign jurisprudence used, it is difficult to conclude that these sources are used opportunistically to bolster predetermined conclusions. If that were always the case, references to foreign jurisprudence would always be explicit and detectable on the face of the judgments.

A. Foreign Jurisprudence Used for Consistency

The heuristic uses described above are distinct from the 'gap-filling' thesis offered by much of the literature; that is, that foreign jurisprudence may offer a useful perspective where the indigenous jurisprudence is lacking

[24] Christopher McCrudden, 'Human Rights and Judicial Use of Comparative Law' in Esin Örücü (ed), *Judicial Comparativism in Human Rights Cases* (United Kingdom National Committee of Comparative Law 2003) 17; repeated in Christopher McCrudden, 'A Common Law of Human Rights?: Transnational Judicial Conversations on Constitutional Rights' (2000) 20(4) *Oxford Journal of Legal Studies* 499, 512.

[25] Luc Heuschling, 'Comparative Law in French Human Rights Cases' in Örücü (n 24) 44; see also Rabinder Singh, 'Interpreting Bills of Rights' [2008] *Statute Law Review* 82.

or unsettled. While it is fairly clear that counsel tend to approach foreign jurisprudence in this way, it was not possible to find clear evidence that judges do so. The only evidence might be the tendency to review foreign jurisprudence in human rights cases where the Strasbourg jurisprudence was unhelpful or non-existent. However, even in those instances, other explanations were more realistic. Thus, the use of American and Canadian jurisprudence in *Ambrose v Harris* was more likely to bolster the majority's reluctance to decide the case in a way that was perceived to be advancing on the Strasbourg jurisprudence.[26] Indeed, it is a common feature of judicial reasoning under the HRA 1998 that the ECHR must be understood and applied uniformly amongst all contracting states. Since the Supreme Court also relies on the Strasbourg jurisprudence to set out the position of the various contracting states, it is not surprising that foreign jurisprudence is used less often in cases of this kind. Even where it would be of interest to the Supreme Court to review the position of the other states that are signatories to the Convention, it is clear that the Court prefers to accept the results of the Strasbourg Court's research on the point.

The approach is surprising, given some of the problems that have been associated with the quality and consistency of the Strasbourg Court's decisions. As Amos has written, the Strasbourg case law 'can be unclear, confusing, and admitting of many possible interpretations'.[27] If consistency and uniformity are the aim, the Court may find it necessary to draw assistance from the jurisprudence of foreign domestic states as a means of establishing the common position where the Strasbourg jurisprudence is lacking or unclear. There is some evidence that the Supreme Court has approached foreign jurisprudence in this way—the *Cadder* case discussed in Chapter 7 provides a good example.[28] Although the scope for using foreign jurisprudence is likely to be more limited in Convention cases (where the case law of the supranational court is prioritised), the Supreme Court is willing to make use of those sources where they can provide assistance in confirming the conclusions of the Strasbourg Court and/or confirming the consensus on a position. The feeling lingers, however, that the very existence of the Strasbourg jurisprudence prevents research into foreign jurisprudence in the terms that the Court might otherwise have sought to undertake.

The influence of the Strasbourg Court's jurisprudence is evident when one contrasts the approach in those cases with the approach where there

[26] *Ambrose v Harris (Procurator Fiscal, Oban)* [2011] UKSC 53; [2011] WLR 2435; Lord Kerr, 'The Modest Underworker of Strasbourg?', Clifford Chance Lecture (London 25 January 2012), https://www.supremecourt.uk/docs/speech_120125.pdf, 17.

[27] Merris Amos, 'The Principle of Comity' [2009] *Yearbook of European Law* 503, 525. See also Lord Hoffmann, 'Human Rights and the House of Lords' (1999) 62 *MLR* 159, 162–64, expressing 'doubts ... about the suitability, at least for this country, of having questions of human rights determined by an international tribunal made up of judges from many countries'.

[28] *Cadder v Her Majesty's Advocate (Scotland)* [2010] UKSC 43; [2010] 1 WLR 2601.

is no supranational court jurisprudence to refer to. In these cases, foreign jurisprudence is important precisely because there is no authoritative guidance on the interpretation of the relevant instrument. It is therefore up to the contracting states to work in harmony, balancing the interpretation of the instrument according to common developments with a measure of self-regulation, so that the courts do not attach a meaning to the instrument that was not envisaged by all contracting parties. Far from resorting to foreign jurisprudence where there is a dearth of domestic jurisprudence, in these cases foreign jurisprudence may appropriately be of equal or greater importance than the domestic case law, irrespective of the nature or absence of domestic jurisprudence. The 1951 Convention Relating to the Status of Refugees provides a useful example.[29] As there is no supranational body acting as the final arbiter on the interpretation of the Refugee Convention, it is not surprising to see citations of foreign cases in these judgments. Various examples of this approach were readily discoverable in the jurisprudence of the Supreme Court as well as the earlier case law from the House of Lords. Many of the Supreme Court Justices interviewed highlighted the importance of consensus in such cases. At times, it was suggested that the 'imperative' extends so far that judges will be prepared to suppress certain hesitations in order to achieve uniformity.

Complications may arise where there are many signatories to a Convention, since it is likely to be more difficult to establish an interpretation based on state practice in those circumstances. A shared agreement or a common membership of a legal system does not necessarily require homogeneity. It is important to distinguish between what countries are doing under the Convention and what they are doing as a matter of discretion over and above Convention obligations, in order to avoid the well-articulated risks of rewriting the instrument.[30] As Lord Brown put it in a Refugee Convention case before the House of Lords:

> It is one thing to invite this House to construe the Convention as a living instrument generously and in the light of its underlying humanitarian purposes; quite another to urge your Lordships effectively to rewrite it.[31]

Given the Court's ability to maintain this awareness in these cases, it is not obvious (other than for purely practical reasons) why there is such reluctance to engage in research of this kind into the jurisprudence of the European Member States. Taking a more proactive approach to the ECHR could, for example, provide the Court with an opportunity to conduct its own review

[29] Convention Relating to the Status of Refugees, Geneva, 28 July 1951, 189 UNTS (entered into force on 4 October 1967).
[30] *R (Hoxha) v Special Adjudicator* [2005] 1 WLR 1063.
[31] ibid 1088.

of any evolving consensus about the interpretation of Convention rights, providing the findings as support for its reasoning where required. After all, one of the clearest explanations for references to foreign jurisprudence was that these sources could support or illustrate the reason(s) for a decision.

B. Instrumental Uses: Standing up to Strasbourg

In keeping with the finding that foreign jurisprudence is most likely to be used to support reasons for a decision, there is evidence that some judges are inclined to use foreign jurisprudence to support conclusions that are at odds with the relevant authority. In other words, judges may use foreign jurisprudence instrumentally, as a tool to legitimate a particular result. It is these types of uses that have attracted the most criticism.[32] For example, it is often suggested that judges use that jurisprudence which is likely to support their own predetermined conclusions or, worse, as a means of 'fig-leafing', designed to obscure the reality of judicial choice.[33]

The claims in this book are not as expansive. While it is argued that the UK Supreme Court does use foreign jurisprudence instrumentally, it is not suggested that this instrumentalism is driven by political choice. Rather, the Supreme Court's instrumentalism is driven by a general desire to give reasons for conclusions, especially those that may be unpopular or controversial. This is especially important in human rights cases where, for example, the Supreme Court has reached a conclusion that is at odds with the relevant jurisprudence of the Strasbourg Court. In this way, foreign jurisprudence may provide a useful tool in increasing the confidence of the Supreme Court and may encourage it to develop the domestic law of human rights, which meets the distinctive needs of the UK.

This is in keeping with the evidence that the Supreme Court is willing to reject the Strasbourg jurisprudence where it is unhelpful or at odds with the constitutional arrangements in the UK. This is most obvious in cases where the Strasbourg jurisprudence has been thought to be outdated; implicit in

[32] See, eg, Cram (n 1) 139–41; Elizabeth Wicks, 'Taking Account of Strasbourg? The British Judiciary's Approach to Interpreting Convention Rights' [2005] *European Public Law* 405, 410. See also Antonin Scalia, 'The Bill of Rights: Confirmation of Extent Freedoms or Invitation to Judicial Creation?' in Grant Huscroft and Paul Rishworth (eds), *Litigating Rights: Perspectives from Domestic and International Law* (Hart Publishing, 2002); James Allan, 'A Defence of the Status Quo' in Tom Campbell et al (eds), *Protecting Human Rights: Instruments and Institutions* (Oxford University Press, 2003). *cf* McCrudden, 'A Common Law of Human Rights? (n 24) 527.

[33] Richard Posner, 'No Thanks, We Already Have Our Own Laws' *Legal Affairs* (July/August 2004), www.legalaffairs.org/issues/July-August-2004/feature_posner_julaug04.msp; Sujit Choudhry (ed), *The Migration of Constitutional Ideas* (Cambridge University Press, 2006) 7.

the construction of the ECHR as a 'living instrument'[34] is the presumption that domestic courts may properly conclude that Convention jurisprudence has lost its relevance with age. The decision in *Re P* is a good example of the willingness to construct conclusions on the basis of the way the Strasbourg jurisprudence was thought to be developing.[35]

Another obvious excuse for divergence (also relevant in *Re P*) is created by the operation of the 'margin of appreciation' doctrine, which signifies that there are issues on which there is no relevant Strasbourg authority at all.[36] A connected possibility is related to the nature of the Strasbourg authority itself. Although some commentators have argued that Strasbourg's decisions are so important as to be considered as authority even in instances in which they did not 'argue the point through in a coherent and thorough manner',[37] the prevailing attitude among the judiciary has been that there is 'room for dialogue' where an English court 'considers that the Strasbourg Court has misunderstood or been misinformed about some aspect of English law' and 'it may wish to give a judgment which invites the [Court] to reconsider the question'.[38]

It was argued in Chapter 8 that this evaluative approach to the Strasbourg jurisprudence has developed a step further. The Supreme Court has shown a willingness to reject the Strasbourg jurisprudence as determinative of a particular issue, even in cases where that jurisprudence is clear and constant. This represents a departure from the deferential start to the relationship with the Strasbourg Court and the sense that the UK courts appeared to be acting as 'merely agents or delegates of the ECHR and Council of Europe' of Strasbourg.[39] *Horncastle* is the best example of this approach.[40] The case is illustrative of both the strength attached to the (clear and constant) Strasbourg jurisprudence and of the willingness to depart from it. There is nothing in the judgment given by Lord Phillips (giving the judgment

[34] *Tyrer v UK* (1978) 2 EHRR 1 [31].

[35] *In Re P (A Child) (Adoption: Unmarried Couples)* [2008] UKHL 38; [2009] 1 AC 173.

[36] See, eg, Francesca Klug 'A Bill of Rights: Do We Need One or Do We Already Have One?' [2007] *PL* 701, 708.

[37] Ian Loveland, 'Making it up as They Go Along? The Court of Appeal on Same Sex Spouses and Succession Rights to Tenancies' [2003] *PL* 222, 233.

[38] *R v Lyons (No 3)* [2003] 1 AC 976 [46]. A number of judges have given lectures that have been critical of the Strasbourg Court and its approach to its jurisprudence: Lord Sumption, 'The Limits of Law', 27th Sultan Azlan Shah Lecture (Kuala Lumpur, 20 November 2013); Lord Judge, 'Constitutional Change: Unfinished Business' (University College London, 4 December 2013); Lord Justice Laws, 'The Common Law Constitution', Hamlyn Lectures 2013 (Lecture 3: 'The Common Law and Europe', London, 27 November 2013); Jack Straw, 'Aspects of Law Reform: An Insider's Perspective', Hamlyn Lectures 2012 (Lecture 2: 'The Human Rights Act and Europe'); Baroness Hale, '*Argentoratum Locutum*: Is the Supreme Court Supreme?', Nottingham Human Rights Lecture 2011 (Nottingham, 1 December 2011); Lord Irvine, 'A British Interpretation of Convention Rights' [2012] *PL* 237.

[39] Lord Irvine of Lairg (n 38).

[40] *R v Horncastle and Another* [2009] UKSC 14; [2010] 2 AC 373.

of the Court) to suggest that the Supreme Court felt that the Strasbourg jurisprudence was not 'clear and constant'. Instead, Lord Phillips acknowledged the argument that the Supreme Court 'should treat the judgment of the Chamber in *Al-Khawaja* as determinative of the success of these appeals' and responded by providing reasons for declining to do so.[41] The Supreme Court would 'decline to follow' the relevant Strasbourg jurisprudence on the basis that the Strasbourg Court had not 'sufficiently appreciate[d] or accommodate[d] particular aspects of our domestic process'.[42] The reasons for that conclusion relied heavily on foreign jurisprudence from the established common law courts. *HM Treasury v Ahmed* provided another alternative example from the perspective of dissenting judgments.[43]

It is important that the Supreme Court is able to determine cases according to their assessment of the legal settlement in the UK. As Feldman has put it, 'comparative study should not lead to attempted mimicry of others but should inform the journey towards a national system which meets our distinctive needs'.[44] In the Convention context, this reflects the optimism shared by many that the HRA 1998 would foster a domestic law of human rights rather than copy the corpus of Strasbourg jurisprudence into domestic law. Lord Irvine later confirmed this to have been the intention at the time of the HRA's passage through Parliament: the Supreme Court 'should not abstain from deciding the case for themselves simply because it may cause difficulties for the UK on the international law plane'.[45] In fact, Lord Irvine suggested in that speech that it was the 'constitutional duty' of judges to reject Strasbourg decisions that are flawed.[46] Lord Kerr lent support to this sentiment in a 2011 lecture:

> [I]f we have been the modest underworker [of Strasbourg], we should stop it at once. We should kick the habit. We should stiffen our sinews and stride forward confidently ... even if a case can be made that in the past we were excessively deferential to Strasbourg, there are recently clear and vigorous signals that we are no longer.[47]

IV. PROVIDING A GIVEN AUDIENCE WITH REASONS

The underlying theme running through the different approaches to foreign jurisprudence is that judges are, in part, using those sources to

[41] ibid [10].

[42] ibid [11].

[43] *HM Treasury v Mohammed Jabar Ahmed and Others (No 2) (FC)* [2010] UKSC 2.

[44] David Feldman, 'The Human Rights Act 1998 and Constitutional Principles' [1999] 19(2) *Legal Studies* 165, 205.

[45] Lord Irvine of Lairg (n 38).

[46] ibid.

[47] Lord Kerr (n 26) 1.

communicate with an audience. For the most part, this manifests as the giving of reasons. For example, judges who appear to cite foreign jurisprudence out of courtesy to counsel are also extending reasons for their conclusions; if heavy reliance has been placed on foreign jurisprudence by counsel, it is natural that a judge might address it when explaining his own conclusions in judgment. An extension of that possibility is that judges are simply addressing the cited material as part of their explanation to the parties in the decided case.

Similar theories can be applied to the use of foreign jurisprudence in Convention cases, where the audience is the Strasbourg Court. This is especially clear where the Supreme Court had reached a conclusion that is at odds with the Strasbourg jurisprudence. In such cases, there is a greater impulse towards the giving of reasons in anticipation of such a time as when the case may come before the Strasbourg Court for review. In other words, the Court is using foreign jurisprudence in part to defend its conclusions to Strasbourg. This communication forms part of what is commonly considered to be a growing 'dialogue' with the Strasbourg Court.[48] Cases like *Horncastle* demonstrate that the adoption of a conclusion that is at odds with the Strasbourg jurisprudence can be supported in this way,[49] providing a layer of reasoning to the Court's judgment, which may assist the Strasbourg Court in its own review. The then President of the Strasbourg Court recognised the value of such dialogue, considering that it could 'only serve to cement a relationship between the two courts'.[50] Viewed in this way, the jurisprudence of foreign domestic courts is more valuable than has so far been considered. By taking those sources into account, judges may begin to take a more theorised approach to human rights cases, working with the Strasbourg Court in human rights cases rather than under it.

However, this 'dialogue' is strictly between the Supreme Court and supranational courts, such as the Strasbourg. When interviewed, the Justices of the UK Supreme Court were dismissive about the idea that they would be affected in the way in which they write judgments by the thought of an international audience. When citing foreign jurisprudence, the Justices of the Supreme Court do not consider themselves to be in conversation with

[48] See, eg, Nicolas Bratza, 'The Relationship between the UK Courts and Strasbourg' [2011] *European Human Rights Law Review* 505; Merris Amos, 'The Dialogue between United Kingdom Courts and the European Court of Human Rights' [2012] 61(3) *ICLQ* 557; John Spencer, 'Squaring up to Strasbourg: *Horncastle* in the Supreme Court' [2010] *Archbold Review* 6; Lady Justice Arden, 'Peaceful or Problematic? The Relationship between National Supreme Courts and Supranational Courts in Europe' (2010) 29(1) *Yearbook of European Law* 3; Alan Paterson, *Final Judgment: The Last Law Lords and the Supreme Court* (Hart Publishing, 2013) 222–33.

[49] *Horncastle* (n 40).

[50] Bratza (n 48) 512.

the Justices of other domestic courts. Foreign jurisprudence is cited only when helpful to the instant case. The only obvious exception is where the Court is tasked with the interpretation of an international convention or instrument for which there is no supervisory court. In those circumstances the Supreme Court is likely to review the foreign jurisprudence not only to learn of any common consensus as to the interpretation of the instrument, but also to ensure that it does not leap ahead of any international consensus. In doing so, it necessarily contributes to the body of jurisprudence that the courts of another contracting state will review in a similar case from that jurisdiction.

The influence of transjudicial dialogue (in the sense of international conferences and symposiums, which facilitate a direct exchange of ideas between judges and practitioners from all over the world) are difficult to substantiate in the UK context. Any jurisprudence prompted by international meetings or conferences is likely to be drawn from a small family of courts, since the Justices tend to engage with a small number of jurisdictions, usually in the common law tradition. Moreover, the significance of these events is limited. It is only in very rare cases that such dialogue substantially feeds into judicial reasoning. When it does, it is probably better explained as part of a prior willingness to draw from foreign jurisprudence than as a product of judicial exchanges per se. During the interviews with the Justices of the Supreme Court, only two of the Justices attributed any real weight to these meetings. Rarely was an example given where they could recall an instance of discussion with other judges having a significant effect on judgments.[51]

V. THE EFFECT OF CHANGING WORKING METHODS

Finally, the research findings have also brought into focus certain developments in the working methods of the UK's top court. Most obviously, the decline in the use of foreign jurisprudence during the later years of the research period could be explained as a product of the change in judgment styles. One of the most interesting research findings was that the Supreme Court is increasingly handing down single judgments, which in turn may yield fewer citations to foreign jurisprudence. Of the total 550 cases *reported* by the Supreme Court between 2009 and 2017,[52] the Court was unanimous as to the outcome in 433. There were 43 judgments of the Court, 223 single judgments with which other members of the Court agreed and 25 single

[51] *cf* Penny Darbyshire, *Sitting in Judgment: The Working Lives of the Judges* (Hart Publishing, 2013) 400: 'There is a far more intense international interchange of senior judges, in ideas, visits, exchanges, conferences and publications than outsiders appreciate.'

[52] An explanation of this figure is given in ch 2, text from n 14.

majority judgments, making 291 overall 'single judgments'. This proportion represents a significant increase in the proportion of single judgments in the House of Lords.[53] The proportion of single judgments was highest in 2015–16 and 2016–17 (both 63 per cent), which corresponds with the years showing the lowest proportion of cases citing foreign jurisprudence (22 per cent and 18 per cent respectively).

This is not altogether surprising, given the greater sense of collegiality at the new Supreme Court. For example, Paterson has described the establishment of 'team-working' practices under Lord Phillips and Lord Neuberger as far greater than there had been at the House of Lords.[54] This sense of collaborative work has most obviously manifested itself through changes to the Supreme Court's working methods. As Mak has explained:

> Since October 2009, the judges have been experimenting with a system in which one judge writes the lead opinion and the other judges on the panel may choose to concur with this judge, to write a separate opinion, or to write a dissenting opinion.[55]

Lord Neuberger is well known to support single judgments, so it is no surprise that this change was made most apparent under Lord Neuberger's leadership of the Court.[56] The data showed that, with the exception of 2013–14, concurring majority judgments fell to their lowest point during Lord Neuberger's presidency (2013–17). There has been a corresponding increase in the proportion of single judgments (including judgments of the court and single majority judgments). By changing its working methods in this way, 'the Court aims to create more transparency'.[57] The reasoning is that 'working with majority opinions leads to more consistency and gives clearer guidance to the lower courts on how to operate in the future'.[58] Mak's own interview evidence 'indicated that the use of foreign legal materials need not be hampered by the increased use of majority opinions' because 'an individual judge might still choose to write a separate opinion about foreign law if this judge is not satisfied with the majority opinion'.[59] However, the analysis of the data for this research indicates otherwise: the effect of

[53] Poole and Shah had actually predicted the continuation of 'noise' at the Supreme Court: Thomas Poole and Sangeeta Shah, 'The Law Lords and Human Rights' (2011) 74(1) *MLR* 79, 105.

[54] Paterson (n 48) 141.

[55] Mak (n 6) 430; Elaine Mak, *Judicial Decision-Making in a Globalised World: A Comparative Analysis of the Changing Practices of Western Highest Courts* (Hart Publishing, 2013) 130.

[56] Lord Neuberger, 'Some Thoughts on Judicial Reasoning across Jurisdictions', 2016 Mitchell Lecture (Edinburgh, 11 November 2016) [39], www.supremecourt.uk/docs/speech-161111.pdf.

[57] Mak (n 6) 430; Mak, *Judicial Decision-Making* (n 55) 130.

[58] Mak, *Judicial Decision-Making* (n 55) 130.

[59] ibid.

single judgments on the use of foreign jurisprudence appears to be fairly significant. As explained above, the proportion of citations to foreign jurisprudence is smallest in the years showing the higher percentage of single judgments. Yet, despite the general trend towards single judgments and (it might be thought) more collective approaches to judgment writing, the different Justices continue to take individualised approaches to judicial reasoning. This is because, as Paterson points out, the Supreme Court 'team' is a rather unusual one.[60] Lord Reed explained:

> It is a curious team because the value of the team depends on everybody using their own individual intelligence and their own experience and so forth and bringing all that to the party.[61]

VI. REFLECTIONS ON JUDICIAL REASONING AT THE SUPREME COURT

When writing in memory of Lord Rodger, Lord Mance opened his chapter entitled 'Foreign Laws and Foreign Languages' with the following caption from Thomas Mann's *Josef und seine Brüder*:

> *Denn nur durch Vergleichung unterscheidet man sich und erfährt, was man ist, un ganz zu weden, der man sein soll* ('For only by comparing yourself with others do you learn what you are, in order to realise your full potential').[62]

The quote captures some of the most important research findings presented in this book. The first is the most obvious: since there are no rules governing the use of foreign jurisprudence in the UK, the Supreme Court has been willing to use comparative sources where it is thought to shed light on an issue or provide a useful benchmark (or 'yardstick') against which to measure domestic law. The discretionary nature of these sources means that individual judicial attitudes and approaches play a large part in their use.

These findings also shed light on judicial reasoning in human rights cases more broadly and judicial reasoning at the UK Supreme Court more generally. The willingness to use foreign jurisprudence heuristically, as an analytical lens or yardstick against which to measure a judge's own reasoning, hints at the attempt to ensure that the Court is not looking at matters in 'too parochial a way'.[63] In this regard, the Supreme Court is not very different from other top courts around the world, increasingly ready to accept the protection of human rights and the balance of constitutional powers

[60] Paterson (n 48) 141.

[61] Interview with the Rt Hon Lord Reed, conducted by Alan Paterson (n 48).

[62] Lord Mance (n 2) 85.

[63] Interview with Lord Reed (n 17). This approach to foreign jurisprudence is likely to reflect the Court's use of other persuasive sources more generally, although a fuller study would be required for confirmation.

as part of their role. Similar themes of cooperation with other top courts permeate the explanations about using foreign jurisprudence to identify and maintain consistency with the evolving international consensus. Finally, the support to be derived from foreign jurisprudence where the Supreme Court is seeking to adopt a conclusion that is at odds with the otherwise relevant Strasbourg jurisprudence demonstrates a greater confidence on the part of the UK's top court than was previously evident at the House of Lords.

This is not a claim that the Supreme Court is evolving into a quasi-constitutional court; the Court continues to lack any power to find statutes incompatible with the (uncodified) constitution.[64] Early on in the life of the Supreme Court, Malleson accepted that it may never be a full constitutional court, but argued that the Supreme Court did nevertheless have an 'expanding role' which was 'rooted in continuity rather than radical change'.[65] Moreover, it was the continuity that would 'facilitate rather than inhibit its development into a more powerful judicial body'.[66] The research findings set out in this book support that conclusion.

The use of foreign jurisprudence is not a new phenomenon. When referring to these non-binding sources, the Justices of the UK Supreme Court are simply continuing a long-established tradition from the development of the common law. For example, it is not difficult to understand the tendency to make reference to foreign jurisprudence for the purpose of identifying international consensus as being closely connected to the impulse to compare with past precedents, rationalised on a 'like for like' type of reasoning. Nor did the HRA 1998 effect any change to the legitimacy of references to foreign jurisprudence. The initial tendency to defer to the Strasbourg jurisprudence was in part derived from the duty in section 2 of the Act to 'take into account' those decisions, but the use of foreign jurisprudence is nowhere prohibited.[67] Indeed, it is the continued use of foreign jurisprudence that has provided the opportunity for the Supreme Court to reconsider the scope of the section 2 duty. It is not insignificant that the willingness on the part of the Supreme Court to depart from the clear and constant Strasbourg jurisprudence, as in *Horncastle*, was heavily supported by references to relevant foreign jurisprudence.[68]

These findings also speak to the characteristics of the new Supreme Court. While the Court might be described as more collegiate than the House of Lords, and single judgments are more common, it does not follow that the

64 Andrew Harding and Peter Leyland (eds), *Constitutional Courts: A Comparative Study* (Simmonds & Hill, 2009) 3; Kate Malleson, 'The Evolving Role of the Supreme Court' [2011] *PL* 754, 757.

65 Malleson (n 64) 764.

66 ibid.

67 Jane Wright, 'Interpreting Section 2 of the Human Rights Act 1998: Towards an Indigenous Jurisprudence of Human Rights' [2009] *PL* 595, 614–15.

68 *Horncastle* (n 40).

Justices are becoming homogeneous. One of the clearest conclusions to be drawn from the varied explanations about the value of foreign jurisprudence and the methods through which they are used is that the Justices continue to take individualised approaches to judicial reasoning.[69] The result is that the value to be drawn from foreign jurisprudence is heavily reliant on the individual skills and interests of the Justices. This much is clear from the practical barriers to these sources, leading the Court to rely on the introduction of foreign jurisprudence by counsel or academic texts.[70] As Bobek explains:

> On the whole ... the judicial as well as extra-judicial pronouncements of the senior English judiciary on the use and the utility of comparative law for the decision-making of an English judge are rather positive. The occasional moderate sceptical voices are concerned with 'how can we do it' in terms of (linguistic) competence, time, costs, and resources, pointing out the difficulty an English judge faces when trying to understand the particularities of a foreign system of law. There are, however, no rejections, certainly not outright, of comparative inspiration qua persuasive authority in courts.[71]

If, as has been argued here, foreign jurisprudence can provide useful and significant contributions to judicial reasoning at the UK Supreme Court, it will be important that consideration is given to improving access to these sources. Recognising the value that Lord Rodger had added in this respect, Lord Mance wrote:

> Too often in the highest court, issues arise which one feels must have been considered in other major legal systems. Too often, difficulties of obtaining appropriate information or an appropriate interlocutor to explore or explain a foreign system stand in the way of cross-fertilization of this sort. Lord Rodger's knowledge and experience straddled different legal systems and was, in that respect, unique. His departure invites the thought that the Supreme Court should itself aim to acquire a comparative legal and linguistic expertise.[72]

Foreign jurisprudence remains a non-binding source of law, but it represents an aid to judicial reasoning that would be unfairly characterised as merely 'persuasive'. These sources can be viewed as logical, empirical tools, which serve a wide range of functions. It is also entirely legitimate for UK courts to treat these sources as such. Unlike the US Supreme Court, where the debates about the legitimacy of citations to foreign jurisprudence are most polarised, the UK Supreme Court is not a constitutional court. Rather than

[69] See also Mak (n 9) 30.

[70] Similarly, Bobek has concluded that the limits on (persuasive) authority and citation in English courts are of 'functional, not political origin': 'An open system, such as the English one, might gradually become overburdened ... with the amount of available materials, internal as well as external. Anything might be cited—too much becomes cited, if the technology permits.' Michael Bobek, *Comparative Reasoning in European Supreme Courts* (Oxford University Press, 2013) 79.

[71] ibid 83.

[72] Lord Mance (n 2) 96–97.

searching for compatibility with a domestic constitutional text, the task of a UK court in human rights cases is to ensure compatibility with international instruments (the ECHR in particular) or to develop common law rights. In terms of the Convention rights, the novel duties provided by the HRA 1998 initially led UK courts to adopt a deferential stance towards the Strasbourg jurisprudence. But it is also for this reason that the jurisprudence of other foreign domestic courts remains important. It is worth remembering that the prevailing fear about judicial comparitivism in other jurisdictions has been that it provides an opportunity for judges to obscure the reality of judicial choice. The chief risk is that comparitivism might import foreign standards that were not intended or anticipated by the domestic legislature. In the UK, the situation is reversed. The prevailing fear is that the provisions of a domestic statute—the HRA—are responsible for an overly deferential attitude to the European standards. In Convention cases, the Supreme Court has the peculiar task of achieving compatibility with an international instrument without compromising the domestic character of human rights. In this context, the jurisprudence of foreign domestic courts provides the Supreme Court with the opportunity to measure the Strasbourg case law and support departures from it where necessary. The more recent willingness to prioritise common law rights (and references to the jurisprudence of other common law courts) only proves the point. Paradoxically, it is the jurisprudence of foreign domestic courts that may enable the Supreme Court to realise its full potential: to develop the domestic law of human rights that many hoped the HRA would foster.

Appendix 1

UK Supreme Court Appointments 2009–17[1]

Justice of the Supreme Court	Appointed	Date demitting office
Lord Phillips of Worth Matravers (President)	1 October 2009	Retired 30 September 2012
Lord Hope of Craighead (Deputy President)	1 October 2009	Retired 26 June 2013
Lord Saville of Newdigate	1 October 2009	Retired 30 September 2010
Lord Rodger of Earlsferry	1 October 2009	Died 26 June 2011
Lord Walker of Gestingthorpe	1 October 2009	Retired 17 March 2013
Baroness Hale of Richmond (Deputy President June 2013; President September 2017)	1 October 2009	Retirement by 31 January 2020
Lord Brown of Eaton-under-Heywood	1 October 2009	Retired 9 April 2012
Lord Mance (Deputy President September 2017)	1 October 2009	Retired 6 June 2018
Lord Collins of Mapesbury	1 October 2009	Retired 7 May 2011
Lord Kerr of Tonaghmore	1 October 2009	Retirement by 22 February 2023
Lord Clarke of Stone-cum-Ebony	1 October 2009	Retired 30 September 2017
Lord Dyson	16 April 2010	Resigned 30 September 2012
Lord Wilson of Culworth	26 May 2011	Retirement by 9 May 2020

(*continued*)

[1] This table is inspired by and updates the information given in Brice Dickson, *Human Rights and the United Kingdom Supreme Court* (Oxford University Press, 2013) 381.

(Continued)

Justice of the Supreme Court	Appointed	Date demitting office
Lord Sumption	11 January 2012	Retirement by 9 December 2018
Lord Reed	6 February 2012	Retirement by 7 September 2026
Lord Carnwath of Notting Hill	17 April 2012	Retirement by 15 March 2020
Lord Neuberger of Abbotsbury (President)	1 October 2012	Retired 4 September 2017
Lord Toulson	9 April 2013	Retired 22 September 2016
Lord Hughes of Ombersley	9 April 2013	Retirement by 11 August 2018
Lord Hodge	1 October 2013	Retirement by 19 May 2023
Lady Black of Derwent	2 October 2017	Retirement by 1 June 2024
Lord Lloyd-Jones	2 October 2017	Retirement by 31 January 2022
Lord Briggs of Westbourne	2 October 2017	Retirement by 23 December 2024
Lady Arden[2]	1 October 2018	Retirement by 23 January 2022
Lord Kitchin	1 October 2018	Retirement by 30 April 2025
Lord Sales	11 January 2019	Retirement by 11 February 2032

[2] Lady Justice (Mary) Arden, as she then was, agreed to be interviewed for this book while in post at the Court of Appeal. Her appointment to the Supreme Court was announced on 27 June 2018, three days before this book went to press. At such a late stage in the publishing process, it was not possible to make amendments to the main text. As such, Lady Arden remains 'Lady Justice Arden', reflecting her judicial post at the time of interview.

Appendix 2

Interview Design

The interviews followed a 'semi-standardised' or 'guided semi-structured' method. What follows is an outline of interview questions commonly put to the interviewees, but does not account for deviation or elaboration.

ATTITUDE TO THE USE OF FOREIGN JURISPRUDENCE

— How relevant do you think that foreign domestic case law is to your work as a judge in the Supreme Court?
— What is useful about comparative material?
— From your impressions, would you say that foreign jurisprudence is more or less useful in human rights cases?
— How has the Human Rights Act altered the relevancy or use of foreign jurisprudence?
— Are you able to approximate a proportion of cases in which foreign jurisprudence is used (whether or not explicitly cited)?

THE PURPOSE OF FOREIGN JURISPRUDENCE

— Why is foreign jurisprudence used?
— The literature discusses the possibility that judges use comparative material to fill 'gaps' in the domestic law. Would you agree?
— Is it ever in your mind that other (foreign) courts will be using your judgments and does that alter your use of foreign jurisprudence at all?
— Some claim that foreign jurisprudence is most likely to be used as part of a legitimation exercise; to bolster a conclusion that the court seeks to reach; to reassure the judge; to engage in a 'transjudicial dialogue' per se. How do these explanations relate to your experience?
— Is there a preference for citations from some jurisdictions above others?
— What is the influence of the judicial community (regular meetings with judges from foreign courts, exchanges)? There has been some discussion about a 'transnational dialogue' evolving between judges from various jurisdictions. Do you feel that this is an accurate analysis?

— What are the content and consequences of this dialogue, if it exists? Do these interactions furnish judges with knowledge that they would otherwise not have?
— To what extent does interaction between judges pique curiosity about foreign jurisprudence or encourage greater use of foreign jurisprudence? If you were unable to meet with judges in foreign courts, would the citation of foreign jurisprudence be less likely?
— What is the importance of these judicial dialogues relative to institutional variables, such as judge's own legal training and backgrounds or the support personnel (JAs) who have interest in/experience of foreign jurisprudence?
— Is it appropriate to consider decisions of other European (domestic) courts in human rights cases?
— How much of a problem is the linguistic barrier? Is this a significant hurdle to comparison with countries that do not operate or publish their judgments in English? If this did occur with greater frequency, would you be tempted to draw from foreign jurisprudence more often?
— What weight is attached to comparative material where the court is considering a question that does not fall within the jurisdiction of a supranational court? For example, the Refugee Convention (now widely regarded as a human rights instrument although it wasn't necessarily designed as such) has no supranational body. Similar instruments would be the Hague Convention, the Warsaw Convention and so on.
— In some cases, comparative material appears to be distinguished even though it is not binding. Why do you suppose that is?

WORKING METHODS

— To what extent do you expect counsel to consider relevant comparative material?
— How much of your own research do you conduct beyond the material given to you by counsel?
— To what extent do you ask your judicial assistant to conduct research? If so, would your judicial assistants bring comparative law to your attention or would you be likely to ask them to do a search for any relevant foreign jurisprudence?
— How often would you say that foreign jurisprudence is considered without explicit citation in the judgment? Or, to put it another way, do the law reports accurately reflect the extent to which foreign jurisprudence is used?

Bibliography

Books

Allan, TRS, *Constitutional Justice: A Liberal Theory of the Rule of Law* (Oxford University Press, 2001)
Amos, M, *Human Rights Law* (Hart Publishing, 2006)
——. *Human Rights Law*, 2nd edn (Hart Publishing, 2014)
Andenas, M and Fairgrieve, D, *Courts and Comparative Law* (Oxford University Press, 2015)
Bates, E, *The Evolution of the European Convention on Human Rights* (Oxford University Press, 2010)
Bean, D (ed), *Law Reform for All* (Blackstone, 1996)
Berg, BL, *Qualitative Research Methods for the Social Sciences* (Pearson, 2007)
Bingham, T, *The Business of Judging: Selected Essays and Speeches* (Oxford University Press, 2000)
——. *Widening Horizons: The Influence of Comparative Law and International Law on Domestic Law* (Cambridge University Press, 2010)
——. *The Rule of Law* (Penguin, 2011)
Blom-Cooper, L and Drewry, G, *Final Appeal* (Clarendon Press, 1972)
Bobek, M, *Comparative Reasoning in European Supreme Courts* (Oxford University Press, 2013)
Bryman, A, *Social Research Methods*, 2nd edn (Oxford University Press, 2004)
Burrows, A, Johnston, D and Zimmermann, R (eds), *Judge and Jurist: Essays in Memory of Lord Rodger of Earlsferry* (Oxford University Press, 2013)
Cardozo, BN, *The Nature of the Judicial Process* (Yale University Press, 1921)
Choudhry, S (ed), *The Migration of Constitutional Ideas* (Cambridge University Press, 2006)
Cohler, A, Miller, B and Stone, H (trans and eds), *The Spirit of the Laws* (Cambridge University Press, 1989)
Cross, R and Harris, J W, *Precedent in English Law*, 4th edn (Clarendon Press, 2004)
Darbyshire, P, *Sitting in Judgment: The Working Lives of Judges* (Hart Publishing, 2011)
Denzin, NK, *The Research Act in Sociology* (Aldine, 1970)
Denzin, NK and Lincoln, YS, *The Sage Handbook of Qualitative Research*, 5th edn (Sage, 2018)
Dickson, B (ed), *Judicial Activism in Common Law Supreme Courts* (Oxford University Press, 2007)
——. *Human Rights and the United Kingdom Supreme Court* (Oxford University Press, 2013)
Dworkin, R, *Law's Empire* (Hart Publishing, 1986)
Lord Dyson, *Justice: Continuity and Change* (Hart Publishing, 2018)
Epstein, L and Martin, A, *An Introduction to Empirical Legal Research* (Oxford University Press, 2014)

Fatima, S, *Using International Law in Domestic Courts* (Hart Publishing, 2005)

Feldman, D (ed), *English Public Law* (Oxford University Press, 2004)

Fentiman, R, *Foreign Law in English Courts* (Oxford University Press, 1998)

Fenwick, H, *Civil Liberties and Human Rights* (Cavendish Publishing, 2007)

Gearty, C, *On Fantasy Island: Britain, Europe and Human Rights* (Oxford University Press, 2016)

Glaser, B and Strauss, A, *The Discovery of Grounded Theory: Strategies for Qualitative Research* (Cambridge University Press, 1987)

Groppi, T and Ponthoreau, M-C (eds), *The Use of Foreign Precedents by Constitutional Judges* (Hart Publishing, 2013)

Grosz, S, Beatson, J and Duffy, P, *Human Rights: The 1998 Act and the European Convention* (Sweet & Maxwell, 2000)

Gutteridge, HC, Comparative Law: *An Introduction to the Comparative Method of Legal Study and Research*, 2nd edn (Cambridge University Press, 1949)

Hagan, FE, *Research Methods in Criminal Justice and Criminology* (Allyn & Bacon, 2006)

Harding, Y and Leyland, P (eds), *Constitutional Courts: A Comparative Study* (Simmonds & Hill, 2009)

Horne, A and Le Sueur, A (eds), *Parliament: Legislation and Accountability* (Hart Publishing, 2016)

Hunt, M, *Using Human Rights Law in English Courts* (Hart Publishing, 1998)

Jacobsohn, GJ, *Apple of Gold: Constitutionalism in Israel and the United States* (Princeton University Press, 1995)

Krueger, RA, *Focus Groups: A Practical Guide for Applied Research*, 4th edn (Sage, 2009)

Lee, J (ed), *From House of Lords to Supreme Court: Judges, Jurists and the Process of Judging* (Hart Publishing, 2011)

Legrand, P and Munday, R (eds), *Comparative Legal Studies: Traditions and Transitions* (Cambridge University Press, 2003)

Lucas, J, *The Principles of Politics* (Oxford University Press, 1966)

Mak, E, *Judicial Decision-Making in a Globalised World: A Comparative Analysis of the Changing Practices of Western Highest Courts* (Hart Publishing, 2013)

Markesinis, B, *The Gradual Convergence: Foreign Ideas, Foreign Influences and English Law on the Eve of the 21st Century* (Clarendon Press, 1994)

——. (ed), *Foreign Law & Comparative Methodology: A Subject and a Thesis* (Hart Publishing, 1997)

Markesinis, B and Fedtke, J (eds), *Judicial Recourse to Foreign Law: A New Source of Inspiration?* (University College London Press, 2006)

Merryman, JH and Clark, DS, *Comparative Law: Western European and Latin American Legal Systems. Cases and Materials* (Bobbs-Merrill, 1978)

Mischler, EG, *Research Interviewing: Context and Narrative* (Harvard University Press, 1986)

Muller, S and Richards, S (eds), *Highest Courts and Globalisation* (Hague Academic Press, 2010)

Nachimas, CF and Nachimas, D, *Research Methods for the Social Sciences: Practice and Applications*, 4th edn (St Martin's Press, 1992)

Nelken, D (ed), *Comparing Legal Cultures* (Dartmouth, 1997)

Orücü, E (ed), *Judicial Comparativism in Human Rights Cases* (United Kingdom National Committee of Comparative Law, 2003)
Orücü, E and Nelken, D (eds), *Comparative Law: A Handbook* (Hart Publishing, 2007)
Paterson, A, *The Law Lords* (Macmillan Press, 1982)
——. *Final Judgment: The Last Law Lords and the Supreme Court* (Hart Publishing, 2013)
Popper, KR, *Conjectures and Refutations: The Growth of Scientific Knowledge* (Harper and Row, 1968)
Posner, R, *How Judges Think* (Harvard University Press, 2008)
Raz, J, *The Authority of Law: Essays on Law and Morality* (Oxford University Press, 1979)
Roach Anleu, S and Mack, K, *Performing Judicial Authority in the Lower Courts* (Palgrave Macmillan, 2017)
Robertson, D, *Judicial Discretion in the House of Lords* (Oxford University Press, 1998)
Rosenfeld, M and Sajo, A (eds), *The Oxford Handbook of Comparative Constitutional Law* (Oxford University Press, 2012)
Sedley, S, *Ashes and Sparks: Essays on Law and Justice* (Cambridge University Press, 2011)
——. *Lions under the Throne* (Cambridge University Press, 2015)
Slapper, G, *How the Law Works* (Routledge, 2011)
Slaughter, A-M, *A New World Order* (Princeton University Press, 2004)
Starmer, K, *European Human Rights Law: The Human Rights Act 1998 and the European Convention on Human Rights* (Legal Action Group, 1999)
Straw, J, *Aspects of Law Reform: An Insider's Perspective, Hamlyn Lectures 2012* (Cambridge University Press, 2013)
Sunstein, CR, *Legal Reasoning and Political Conflict* (Oxford University Press, 1996)
——. *A Constitution of Many Minds* (Princeton University Press, 2009)
Twining, W and Miers, D, *How to Do Things with Rules*, 3rd edn (Butterworths, 1991)
Waldron, J, *Law and Disagreement* (Clarendon Press, 1999)
——. *'Partly Laws Common to All Mankind': Foreign Law in American Courts* (Yale University Press, 2012)
Ward, R, Wragg, A and Akhtar, A, *Walker & Walker's English Legal System* (Oxford University Press, 2011)
Warren, CAB and Karner, TX, *Discovering Qualitative Methods* (Roxbury, 2005)
Watson, A, *Legal Transplants: An Approach to Comparative Law*, 2nd edn (University of Georgia Press, 1993)
Webb, EJ et al, *Unobtrusive Measures: Nonreactive Measures in the Social Sciences* (Rand McNally, 1966)
Wheatle, S, *Principled Reasoning in Human Rights Adjudication* (Hart Publishing, 2017)
Zweigert, K and Kötz, H, *An Introduction to Comparative Law*, Tony Weir trans, 3rd edn (Oxford University Press, 1998)

Book Chapters

Allan, J, 'A Defence of the Status Quo' in T Campbell, J Godlsworthy and A Stone (eds), *Protecting Human Rights: Instruments and Institutions* (Oxford University Press, 2003)

Barak, A, 'Comparison in Public Law' in B Markesinis and J Fedtke (eds), *Judicial Recourse to Foreign Law: A New Source of Inspiration?* (University College London Press, 2006)

Bradney, A, 'The Place of Empirical Research in the Law School Curriculum' in P Crane and H Kritzer (eds), *The Oxford Handbook of Empirical Legal Research* (Oxford University Press, 2010)

Burrows, A, 'The Influence of Comparative Law on the English Law of Obligations' in Robertson A and M Tilbury, *The Common Law of Obligations: Divergence and Unity* (Hart Publishing, 2016)

Burton, M, 'Doing Empirical Research' in D Watkins and M Burton, *Research Methods in Law* (Routledge, 2013)

Chang, W-C and Yeh, J-R, 'Internationalization of Constitutional Law' in M Rosenfeld and A Sajo (eds), *The Oxford Handbook of Comparative Constitutional Law* (Oxford University Press, 2012)

——. 'Judges as Discursive Agent: The Use of Foreign Precedents by the Constitutional Court of Taiwan' in T Groppi and M-C Ponthoreau (eds), *The Use of Foreign Precedents by Constitutional Judges* (Hart Publishing, 2013)

Craig, PP, 'Report on the United Kingdom' in A-M Slaughter, AS Sweet and JHH Weiler (eds), *The European Courts and National Courts: Doctrine and Jurisprudence* (Hart Publishing, 1998)

Dickson, B, 'Close Calls in the House of Lords' in J Lee (ed), *From House of Lords to Supreme Court: Judges, Jurists and the Process of Judging* (Hart Publishing, 2011)

Fasone, C, 'The Supreme Court of Ireland and the Use of Foreign Precedents: The Value of Constitutional History' in T Groppi and M-C Ponthoreau (eds), *The Use of Foreign Precedents by Constitutional Judges* (Hart Publishing, 2013)

Feeley, M, 'Comparative Criminal Law for Criminologists: Comparing for What Purpose?' in D Nelken (ed), *Comparing Legal Cultures* (Dartmouth, 1997)

Gentili, G, 'Canada: Protecting Rights in a 'Worldwide Rights Culture. An Empirical Study of the Use of Foreign Precedents by the Supreme Court of Canada (1982–2010)' in T Groppi and M-C Ponthoreau (eds), *The Use of Foreign Precedents by Constitutional Judges* (Hart Publishing, 2013)

Hart, HLA, 'Commands and Authoritative Legal Reasons' in *Essays on Bentham: Studies in Jurisprudence and Political Theory* (Clarendon Press, 1982)

Heuschling, L, 'Comparative Law in French Human Rights Cases' in E Orücü (ed), *Judicial Comparativism in Human Rights Cases* (United Kingdom National Committee of Comparative Law, Birmingham, 2003)

Horne, A and Tyrrell, H, 'Sovereignty, Privilege and the European Convention on Human Rights' in A Horne and A Le Sueur (eds), *Parliament: Legislation and Accountability* (Hart Publishing, 2016)

Lord Irvine, 'The Legal System and Law Reform under Labour' in D Bean (ed), *Law Reform for All* (Blackstone, 1996)

Kearns, P, 'United Kingdom Judges in Human Rights Cases' in E Orücü (ed), *Judicial Comparativism in Human Rights Cases* (United Kingdom National Committee of Comparative Law, Birmingham, 2003)

Legrand, P, 'What 'Legal Transplants' in D Nelken and J Feest (eds), *Adapting Legal Cultures* (Hart Publishing, 2001)

Lester, A and Clapinska, L, 'Human Rights and the British Constitution' in J Jowell and D Oliver (eds), *The Changing Constitution*, 5th edn (Oxford University Press, 2004)

Mahoney, P and Kondak, R, 'Common Ground: A Starting Point or Destination for Comparative-Law Analysis by the European Court of Human Rights?' in M Andenas and D Fairgrieve (eds), *Courts and Comparative Law* (Oxford University Press, 2015)

Lord Mance, 'Foreign Laws and Languages' in A Burrows, D Johnston and R Zimmermann (eds), *Judge and Jurist: Essays in Memory of Lord Rodger of Earlsferry* (Oxford University Press, 2013)

McCrudden, C, 'Human Rights and Judicial Use of Comparative Law' in E Orücü (ed), *Judicial Comparativism in Human Rights Cases* (United Kingdom National Committee of Comparative Law, 2003)

——. 'Judicial Comparativism and Human Rights' in E Orücü and Nelken D (eds), *Comparative Law: A Handbook* (Hart Publishing, 2007)

Murdoch, J, 'Comparative Law and the Scottish Judges' in E Orücü (ed), *Judicial Comparativism in Human Rights Cases* (United Kingdom National Committee of Comparative Law, 2003)

Nesterchuk, T, 'The View from Behind the Bench' in A Burrows, D Johnston and R Zimmermann (eds), *Judge and Jurist: Essays in Memory of Lord Rodger of Earlsferry* (Oxford University Press, 2013)

Orücü, E, 'Comparative Law in British Courts' in U Drobnig and S van Erp (eds), *The Use of Comparative Law by Courts* (Kluwer, 1999)

Platt, J, 'The History of the Interview' in JD Gubrium and JA Holstein (eds), *Handbook of Interview Research* (Sage, 2002)

Rautenbach, C, 'South Africa: Teaching an "Old Dog" New Tricks? An Empirical Study of the Use of Foreign Precedents by the South African Constitutional Court (1995–2010)' in T Groppi and M-C Ponthoreau (eds), *The Use of Foreign Precedents by Constitutional Judges* (Hart Publishing, 2013)

Saunders, C and Stone, A, 'Refrence to Foreign Precedents by the Australian High Court: A Matter of Method' in T Groppi and M-C Ponthoreau (eds), *The Use of Foreign Precedents by Constitutional Judges* (Hart Publishing, 2013)

Scalia, A, 'The Bill of Rights: Confirmation of Extent Freedoms or Invitation to Judicial Creation?' in G Huscroft and P Rishworth (eds), *Litigating Rights: Perspectives from Domestic and International Law* (Hart Publishing, 2002)

Scotti, VR, 'India: A "Critical" Use of Foreign Precedents in Constitutional Adjudication' in T Groppi and M-C Ponthoreau (eds), *The Use of Foreign Precedents by Constitutional Judges* (Hart Publishing, 2013)

Sperti, A, 'United States of America: First Cautious Attempts of Judicial Use of Foreign Precedents in the Supreme Court's Jurisprudence' in T Groppi and M-C Ponthoreau (eds), *The Use of Foreign Precedents by Constitutional Judges* (Hart Publishing, 2013)

Szente, Z, 'Hungary: Unsystematic and Incoherent Borrowing of Law. The Use of Judicial Precedents in the Jurisprudence of the Constitutional Court, 1999–2010' in T Groppi and M-C Ponthoreau (eds), *The Use of Foreign Precedents by Constitutional Judges* (Hart Publishing, 2013)

Twining, W, 'Globalisations and Comparative Law' in E Orücü and D Nelken (eds), *Comparative Law: A Handbook* (Hart Publishing, 2007)

Warbrick, C, 'The View from the Outside' in H Fenwick, R Masterman and G Phillipson (eds), *Judicial Reasoning under the UK Human Rights Act* (Cambridge University Press, 2007)

Weiss, N, 'The Impact of the European Convention on Human Rights on German Jurisprudence' in E Orücü (ed), *Judicial Comparativism in Human Rights Cases* (United Kingdom National Committee of Comparative Law, 2003)

Whitman, Q, 'The Neo-Romantic Turn' in P Legrand and R Munday (eds), *Comparative Legal Studies: Traditions and Transitions* (Cambridge University Press, 2003)

Zoltán, S, 'Hungary: Unsystematic and Incoherent Borrowing of Law: The Use of Foreign Judicial Precedents in the Jurisprudence of the Constitutional Court, 1999–2010' in T Groppi and M-C Ponthoreau (eds), *The Use of Foreign Precedents by Constitutional Courts* (Hart Publishing, 2013)

Journal Articles

Ackermann, LH, 'Constitutional Comparativism in South Africa: A Response to Sir Basil Markesinis and Jörg Fedtke' (2005) 80 *Tulane Law Review* 169

Alder, J, 'Dissents in Courts of Last Resort: Tragic Choices' (2000) 20 *OJLS* 221

Alford, R, 'Misusing International Sources to Interpret the Constitution' (2004) 98 *American Journal of International Law* 57

——. 'In Search of a Theory for Constitutional Comparativism' (2005) 52 *ULC Law Review* 639

——. 'Four Mistakes in the Debate on "Outsourcing Authority"' (2006) 69 *Albany Law Review* 653

Allan, J, Huscroft, G and Lynch, N, 'The Citation of Overseas Authority in Rights Litigation in New Zealand: How Much Bark? How Much Bite?' (2007) 11 *Otago Law Review* 433

Amann, DM, '"Raise the Flag and Let it Talk": On the Use of External Norms in Constitutional Decision Making' (2004) 2(4) *International Journal of Constitutional Law* 597

Amos, M, 'The Principle of Comity' [2009] *Yearbook of European Law* 503

——. 'The Dialogue between United Kingdom Courts and the European Court of Human Rights' (2012) 61(3) *ICLQ* 557

Arden, M, 'The Changing Judicial Role: Human Rights, Community Law and the Intention of Parliament' (2008) 67(3) *CLJ* 490

Arvind, TT, 'The "Transplant Effect" in Harmonization' (2010) 59(1) *ICLQ* 65

Arvind, TT and Stirton, L, 'Legal Ideology, Legal Doctrine and the UK's Top Judges' [2016] *PL* 418

Barak, A, 'Constitutional Human Rights and Private Law' (1996) 3 *Review of Constitutional Studies* 218

——. 'Foreword: A Judge on Judging: The Role of a Supreme Court in a Democracy' (2002) 116 *Harvard Law Review* 169
Barak-Erez, D, 'The International Law of Human Rights and Constitutional Law: A Case Study of an Expanding Dialogue' (2004) 2(4) *International Journal of Constitutional Law* 611
Bell, J, 'Comparative Law in the Supreme Court 2010–11' (2012) 1(2) *Cambridge Journal of International and Comparative Law* 20
Bentele, U, 'Mining for Gold: The Constitutional Court of South Africa's Experience with Comparative Constitutional Law' (2009) 37(2) *Georgia Journal of International and Comparative Law* 219
Bingham, TH, 'There is a World Elsewhere: The Changing Perspectives of English Law' (1992) 41 *ICLQ* 513
Lord Bingham, 'The Rule of Law' [2007] *CLJ* 67
——. 'The Human Rights Act' (2010) 6 *European Human Rights Law Review* 568
Bjorg, E, 'Common Law Rights: Balancing Domestic and International Exigencies' (2016) 75(2) *CLJ* 220
Bratza, N, 'The Relationship between the UK Courts and Strasbourg' [2011] *European Human Rights Law Review* 505
Clayton, R, 'Judicial Deference and "Democratic Dialogue": The Legitimacy of Judicial Intervention under the Human Rights Act 1998' [2004] *PL* 33
——. 'The Empire Strikes Back' [2015] *PL* 3
Lord Cooke, 'The Road Ahead for the Common Law' (2004) 53 *ICLQ* 273
Cram, I, 'Resort to Foreign Constitutional Norms in Domestic Human Rights Jurisprudence with Reference to Terrorism Cases' [2009] *CLJ* 118
Donnelly, S, 'No Consensus on Consensus? The Practice of the European Court of Human Rights' (2013) 31 *Human Rights Law Journal* 257
Dorsen, N, 'The Relevance of Foreign Legal Materials in U.S. Constitutional Cases: A Conversation between U.S. Supreme Court Justices' (2005) 3(3) *International Journal of Constitutional Law* 519
Duxbury, N, 'The Law of the Land' (2015) 78(1) *MLR* 26
Elliott, M, 'Beyond the European Convention: Human Rights and the Common Law' (2015) 68(1) *Current Legal Problems* 85
Epstein, L and King, G, 'The Rules of Inference' (2002) 69 *University of Chicago Law Review* 1
Feldman, D, 'The Human Rights Act 1998 and Constitutional Principles' (1999) 19(2) *Legal Studies* 165
Fenwick, H and Masterman, R, 'The Conservative Project to "Break the Link between British Courts and Strasbourg": Rhetoric or Reality' (2017) 80(6) *MLR* 1111
Flanagan, B and Ahern, S, 'Judicial Decision-Making and Transnational Law: A Survey of Common Law Supreme Court Judges' (2011) 60 *ICLQ* 1
Flanders, C, 'Towards a Theory of Persuasive Authority' (2009) 62 *Oklahoma Law Review* 55
Frowein, JA, 'European Integration through Fundamental Rights' (1984) 18 *Michigan Journal of Law Reform* 5
Gelter, M and Siems, M, 'Networks, Dialogue or One-Way Traffic? An Empirical Analysis of Cross-Citations between Ten of Europe's Highest Courts' (2012) 8 *Utrecht Law Review* 88

——. 'Citations to Foreign Courts: Illegitimate and Superfluous or Unavoidable? Evidence from Europe' (2014) 62(1) *American Journal of Comparative Law* 35
Ghai, Y, 'Sentinels of Liberty or Sheep in Woolf's Clothing? Judicial Politics and the Hong Kong Bill of Rights' (1997) 60 *MLR* 459
Glenn, PH, 'Persuasive Authority' (1987) 32(2) *McGill Law Journal* 261
Goodman, R and Jinks, D, 'How to Influence States: Socialization and International Human Rights Law' (2004) 54 *Duke Law Journal* 621
Baroness Hale, 'Who Defines Convention Rights?' (2010) 5(2) *JUSTICE Journal* 10
——. '*Argentoratum Locutum*: Is Strasbourg or the Supreme Court Supreme?' (2012) 12(1) *Human Rights Law Review* 65
Harvey, WS, 'Strategies for Conducting Elite Interviews' (2011) 11(4) *Qualitative Research* 431
Lord Hoffmann, 'Human Rights and the House of Lords' (1999) 62 *MLR* 159
Hol, A et al, 'Special Issue on Highest Courts and Transnational Interaction' (2012) 8(2) *Utrecht Law Review* 1
Lord Hope of Craighead, 'Scots Law Seen from South of the Border' [2012] *Edinburgh Law Review* 58
Lord Irvine, 'A British Interpretation of Convention Rights' [2012] *PL* 237
Jackson, VC, 'Comparative Constitutional Federalism and Transnational Judicial Discourse' (2004) 2(1) *International Journal of Constitutional Law* 91
Johnson, J, 'Human Rights Law' (2016) 7 *UK Supreme Court Yearbook* 459
Kahn-Freund, O, 'On Uses and Misuses of Comparative Law' (1974) 37 *MLR* 1
Kiralfy, A, 'The Persuasive Authority of American Rulings in England' (1948–49) XXIII *Tulane Law Review* 209
Klug, F, 'The Human Rights Act—A "Third Way" or "Third Wave" Bill of Rights' [2001] *European Human Rights Law Review* 361
——. 'A Bill of Rights: Do We Need One or Do We Already Have One?' [2007] *PL* 701
Klug, F and Wildbore, H, 'Follow or Lead? The Human Rights Act and the European Court of Human Rights' (2010) 6 *European Human Rights Law Review* 621
Krisch, N, 'The Open Architecture of European Human Rights Law' (2008) 71 *MLR* 183
Law, DS and Chang, W-C, 'The Limits of Global Judicial Dialogue' [2011] *Washington Law Review* 523
Lee, J, 'A Defence of Concurring Speeches' [2009] *PL* 305
——. 'The Judicial Individuality of Lord Sumption' (2017) 40(2) *University of New South Wales Law Journal* 862
Leigh, I and Lustgarten, L, 'Making Rights Real: The Courts Remedies and the Human Rights Act' (1999) 58 *CLJ* 509
Letsas, G, 'Two Concepts of the Margin of Appreciation' (2006) 26 *OJLS* 705
Lewis, J, 'The European Ceiling on Human Rights' [2007] *PL* 720
——. '*In Re P and Others*: An Exception to the "No More, Certainly No Less" Rule' [2009] *PL* 43
L'Hereux-Dubé, G, 'The Importance of Dialogue: Globalization and the International Impact of the Rehnquist Court' (1998) 34 *Tulsa Law Journal* 15
Loveland, I, 'Making it up as They Go Along? The Court of Appeal on Same Sex Spouses and Succession Rights to Tenancies' [2003] *PL* 222

——. 'The Shifting Sands of Article 8 Jurisprudence in English Housing Law' (2011) 2 *European Human Rights Law Review* 151

Mak, E, 'Why Do Dutch and UK Judges Cite Foreign Law?' [2011] *CLJ* 420

——. 'Reference to Foreign Law in the Supreme Courts of Britain and the Netherlands: Explaining the Development of Judicial Practices' (2012) 8(2) *Utrecht Law Review* 20

Malleson, K, 'The Evolving Role of the Supreme Court' [2011] *PL* 754

Markesinis, B, 'A Matter of Style' (1994) 110 *LQR* 607

——. 'National Self-Sufficiency or Intellectual Arrogance? The Current Attitude of American Courts towards Foreign Law' [2006] *CLJ* 301

Markesinis, B and Fedtke, J, 'The Judge as a Comparatist' (2005) 80 *Tulane Law Review* 11

Masterman, R, 'Section 2(1) of the Human Rights Act: Binding Domestic Courts to Strasbourg' [2004] *PL* 725

——. 'Taking the Strasbourg Jurisprudence into Account, Developing a "Municipal Law of Human Rights" under the Human Rights Act' (2005) 54(4) *ICLQ* 907

Masterman, R and Wheatle, S, 'A Common Law Resurgence in Rights Protection' (2015) 1 *European Human Rights Law Review* 57

McCrudden, C, 'A Common Law of Human Rights? Transnational Judicial Conversations on Constitutional Rights' (2000) 20(4) *OJLS* 499

McDonald, L, 'New Directions in the Australian Bill of Rights Debate' [2004] *PL* 22

Murray, JL, 'Judicial Cosmopolitanism' (2008) 8(2) *Judicial Studies Institute Journal* 1

Perju, VF, 'The Puzzling Parameters of the Foreign Law Debate' (2007) 1 *Utah Law Review* 167

Phillipson, G, 'Transforming Breach of Confidence? Towards a Common Law Right of Privacy under the Human Rights Act' (2003) 65 *MLR* 726

Poole, T and Shah, S, 'The Law Lords and Human Rights' (2011) 74(1) *MLR* 79

Reed, R, 'Foreign Precedents and Judicial Reasoning: The American Debate and British Practice' (2008), 124 *LQR* 253

Richards, D, 'Comparative Revolutionary Constitutionalism: A Research Agenda for Comparative Law' (1993) 26 *New York University Journal of International Law and Politics* 1

Rudden, B, 'Courts and Codes in England, France and Soviet Russia' (1974) 48 *Tulane Law Review* 1010

Sales, P, 'Rights and Fundamental Rights in English Law' [2016] *CLJ* 86

Sargeant, C, 'Human Rights Law' (2016) 6 *UK Supreme Court Yearbook* 392

Saunders, C, 'Comparative Constitutional Law in the Courts: Is There a Problem?' (2006) 59(1) *Current Legal Problems* 91

——. 'The Use and Misuse of Comparative Constitutional Law' (2006) 13 *Indiana Journal of Global Legal Studies* 37

Schauer, F, 'The Questions of Authority' (1992) 81 *Georgetown Law Journal* 95

——. 'Authority and Authorities' (2008) 94 *Virginia Law Review* 1931

Schauer, F and Wise, VJ, 'Legal Positivism as Legal Information' (1997) 82 *Cornell Law Review* 1080

Schwartz, T, 'Cases Time Forgot: Why Judges Can Sometimes Ignore Controlling Precedent' (2007) 56 *Emory Law Journal* 1475

Sedley, S, 'Constitutional Court Judge' in 'Comparative Constitutionalism in Practice: Constitutional Court Judges' Roundtable' (2005) 3 *International Journal of Constitutional Law* 543

Sheldon, N, 'The Effect of the Human Rights Act on Domestic Precedent' [2001] *Judicial Review* 208

Siems, MM, 'Citation Patterns of the German Federal Supreme Court and the Court of Appeal of England and Wales' (2010) 21 *King's Law Journal* 152

Singh, R, 'Interpreting Bills of Rights' [2008] *Statute Law Review* 82

Slaughter, A-M, 'A Typology of Transjudicial Communication' (1994) 39 *University of Richmond Law Review* 99

Smyth, R, 'Trends in the Citation Practice of the Supreme Court of Queensland Over the Course of the Twentieth Century' (2009) 28(1) *University of Queensland Law Journal* 39

Spencer, J, 'Squaring up to Strasbourg: *Horncastle* in the Supreme Court' [2010] *Archbold Review* 6

Stanton, K, 'Comparative Law in the House of Lords and Supreme Court' (2013) 42 *Common Law World Review* 269

Van Hoek, M and Warrington, M, 'Legal Cultures, Legal Paradigms and Legal Doctrine: Towards a New Model for Comparative Law' (1998) 47(3) *ICLQ* 495

Waldron, J, 'Foreign Law and the Modern *Ius Gentium*' (2005) 119 *Harvard Law Review* 129

Watson, A, 'Comparative Law and Legal Change' (1978) 37(2) *CLJ* 31

Wicks, E, 'Taking Account of Strasbourg? The British Judiciary's Approach to Interpreting Convention Rights' (2005) 11(3) *European Public Law* 405

Wright, J, 'Interpreting Section 2 of the Human Rights Act 1998: Towards an Indigenous Jurisprudence of Human Rights' [2009] *PL* 595

Young, EA, 'Foreign Law and the Denominator Problem' (2005) 119 *Harvard Law Review* 148

Electronic Resources

Commission on Human Rights, *A UK Bill of Rights? The Choice before Us* (18 December, 2012), http://webarchive.nationalarchives.gov.uk/20130206065653/https://www.justice.gov.uk/downloads/about/cbr/uk-bill-rights-vol-1.pdf

Conservative Party, 'Protecting Human Rights in the UK: The Conservatives' Proposals for Changing Britain's Human Rights Laws', www.conservatives.com/~/media/files/downloadable%20Files/human_rights.pdf

Conservative Party Manifesto 2015, 'Strong Leadership, a Clear Economic Plan, a Brighter, More Secure Future', www.conservatives.com/manifesto2015

Conservative and Unionist Party Manifesto 2017, 'Forward, Together. Our Plan for a Strong Britain and a Prosperous Future', www.conservatives.com/manifesto

Lord Dyson, 'The Globalisation of Law', Pilgrim Fathers Lecture 2015 (Plymouth University, 6 November, 2015), www.judiciary.gov.uk/wp-content/uploads/2015/11/pilgrim-fathers-lecture.pdf

Fenwick, H, 'An Appeasement Approach in the European Court of Human Rights?' *UK Constitutional Law Blog* (5 April 2012), www.ukconstitutionallaw.org/2012/04/05/helen-fenwick-an-appeasement-approach-in-the-european-court-of-human-rights

Foster, N, 'The Journal of Comparative Law: A New Comparative Resource', www.thejcl.com/pdfs/foster.pdf

Baroness Hale, 'Judgment Writing in the Supreme Court' (First Anniversary Seminar, 30 September, 2010), www.supremecourt.uk/docs/speech_100930.pdf

——. '*Argentoratum Locutum*: Is the Supreme Court Supreme?', Nottingham Human Rights Lecture, 2011 (Nottingham, 1 December 2011), www.supremecourt.gov.uk/docs/speech_111201.pdf

Lady Hale, 'What's the Point of Human Rights?', Warwick Law Lecture 2013 (Warwick, 28 November 2013), www.supremecourt.uk/docs/speech-131128.pdf

Jackson, V, 'Yes Please, I'd Love to Talk with You' *Legal Affairs* (July/August 2004), www.legalaffairs.org/issues/July-August-2004/feature_jackson_julaug04.msp

Labour Party Manifesto 2015, 'Britain Can Be Better', https://www.scribd.com/document/261706542/Labour-Manifesto-2015

Lee, J, 'The Doctrine of Precedent and the Supreme Court', Inner Temple Academic Fellow's Lecture (Inner Temple, London, April 2012), https://d17g388r7gqnd8.cloudfront.net/2017/08/lecture_james_lee.pdf

Liberal Democrat Party Manifesto, 2015 'Stronger Economy. Fairer Society. Opportunity for Everyone', https://d3n8a8pro7vhmx.cloudfront.net/libdems/pages/8907/attachments/original/1429028133/Liberal_Democrat_General_Election_Manifesto_2015.pdf?1429028133

Lord Judge, 'Constitutional Change: Unfinished Business' (University College London, 4 December, 2013), https://www.nottingham.ac.uk/hrlc/documents/specialevents/lordjudgelecture041213.pdf

Lord Kerr, 'The Modest Underworker of Strasbourg?', Clifford Chance Lecture (London, 25 January, 2012), https://www.supremecourt.uk/docs/speech_120125.pdf

——. 'Dissenting Judgments—Self-Indulgence or Self-Sacrifice?', Birkenhead Lecture (London 8 October, 2012), www.supremecourt.uk/docs/speech-121008.pdf

Lord Justice Laws, 'The Common Law Constitution' Hamlyn Lectures 2013 (Lecture 3: 'The Common Law and Europe' (London, 27 November 2013), https://www.globalgovernancewatch.org/docLib/20140213_laws-lj-speech-hamlyn-lecture-2013.pdf

Masterman, R, 'The Mirror Crack'd' *UK Constitutional Law Blog* (13 February 2013), https://ukconstitutionallaw.org/2013/02/13/roger-masterman-the-mirror-crackd

Murkens, JEK, 'Comparative Constitutional Law in the Courts: Reflections' (2008) *LSE Law, Society and Economy Working Papers*, 15/2008, http://www.lse.ac.uk/law/working-paper-series/2007-08/WPS2008-15-Murkens.pdf

Lord Neuberger, 'Who are the Masters Now?', Second Lord Alexander of Weedon Lecture (6 April 2011), http://webarchive.nationalarchives.gov.uk/20131203081513/http://www.judiciary.gov.uk/Resources/JCO/Documents/Speeches/mr-speech-weedon-lecture-110406.pdf

——. 'No Judgment—No Justice', First Annual BAILII Lecture (London, 20 November, 2012), https://www.supremecourt.uk/docs/speech-121120.pdf

——. 'The Role of Judges in Human Rights Jurisprudence: A Comparison of the Australian and UK Experience', Conference at the Supreme Court of Victoria (Melbourne, 8 August, 2014), www.supremecourt.uk/docs/speech-140808.pdf

——. 'The Role of Judges in a Post-Referendum World', opening address to the Public Law Project Annual Judicial Review Trends and Forecasts Conference, (2 November 2017), http://www.publiclawproject.org.uk/resources/265/the-role-of-the-judges-in-a-post-referendum-world

O'Connor, SD, Southern Centre for International Studies (Atlanta, 28 October 2003), http://www.humanrightsfirst.org/wp-content/uploads/pdf/SOUTHERN_CENTER_INTERNATIONAL_STUDIES_Justice_O%27Connor.pdf

Paterson, J, 'The Institutional Relations and Relationships of the United Kingdom Final Court of Appeal: An Empirical Analysis of the UK's Top Courts 2007–2011' (DPhil thesis, Durham University, 2016), http://etheses.dur.ac.uk/11719/1/PhDlibrarysubmissionversion.pdf?DDD19+

Posner, R, 'No Thanks, We Already Have Our Own Laws' *Legal Affairs* (July/August 2004), www.legalaffairs.org/issues/July-August-2004/feature_posner_julaug04.msp

Lord Reed, 'Comparative Law in the Supreme Court of the United Kingdom', Lecture at the Centre for Private Law (University of Edinburgh, 13 October 2017), www.supremecourt.uk/docs/speech-171013.pdf

Select Committee on the European Union Justice Sub-committee, corrected oral evidence, 'Brexit: The Jurisdiction of the CJEU' (21 Novmber 2017), http://data.parliament.uk/writtenevidence/committeeevidence.svc/evidencedocument/eu-justice-subcommittee/brexit-the-jurisdiction-of-the-cjeu/oral/74225.html

Lord Sumption, 'The Limits of Law', 27th Sultan Azlan Shah Lecture (Kuala Lumpur, 20 November 2013), https://www.supremecourt.uk/docs/speech-131120.pdf

Tranch, D and Coogan, L, 'Baroness Brenda Hale: "I Often Ask Myself 'Why am I Here?'" *The Guardian* (London, 16 September 2010), www.theguardian.com/law/2010/sep/16/uk-supreme-court-judiciary

Vermeule, A, 'Many-Minds Arguments in Legal Theory' (2008) *Harvard Public Law Working Paper* No 08-02, https://papers.ssrn.com/sol3/papers.cfm?abstract_id=1087017

Wilson, J and Horne, A, 'Judgment Matters' (2010) 160 *New Law Journal* 7446, www.newlawjournal.co.uk/nlj/content/judgment-matters

Index